IVAN OF THE]

How the Trials and Denials
of Nazi Collaborator John Demjanjuk
Added to Our Understanding of the Holocaust

By Tom Teicholz

Ivan of the Extermination Camp

How the Trials and Denials of
Nazi Collaborator John Demjanjuk
Added to Our Understanding of the Holocaust

Praise for THE TRIAL OF IVAN THE TERRIBLE (St. Martin's Press, 1990):

"The media mangling of the trial of John- Demjanjuk has made Tom Teicholz's painstakingly thorough and accurate chronicle of that case a most necessary and important book."

—Philip Roth

"A playwright who is now the head of a European state has declared that a moral position maintained over a long period of time can become a cliché. Yet in Tom Teicholz's account of the Demjanjuk case—a meticulously fair trial in one of the most meticulous systems of due process anywhere on earth—every possibility of cliché is dismantled and annulled. The Trial of Ivan the Terrible— journalism with the impact of a documentary film—renews and restores moral consciousness by means of a psychological truthfulness and a living immediacy that are as compelling as justice itself." —Cynthia Ozick

"Terror permeates every page of this book.... In the Bible it is said that man was made in the image of G-d; men like Demjanjuk make a mockery of this statement."

—Simon Wiesenthal

ABOUT THE AUTHOR

Tom Teicholz is an award-winning journalist and author, most recently of "9/12: The Epic Battle of Ground Zero Responders" by William Groner and Tom Teicholz (Potomac Books, 2019), His work has appeared in the New York Times Magazine, Forbes.com, Los Angeles Magazine, the Los Angeles Review of Books, and The New Yorker's 'Talk of the Town." His first book, "The Trial of Ivan the Terrible, State of Israel vs. John Demjanjuk" (St. Martin's Press, 1990) was favorably reviewed in the New York Times Sunday Book Review, Time Magazine and The Chicago Tribune among others. He was extensively interviewed for "The Devil Next Door," the Netflix multi-part documentary series on the Demjanjuk case.

Justice, justice shall ye pursue. -
DEUTERONOMY 16:20

Justice must not only be done; it must be seen to be done.
-JUSTICE DOV LEVIN, QUOTING A
TALMUDIC SAYING.

Outside: Jerusalem and the moaning of the Lord's trees, cut down
by her enemies in every generation; clouds heavy with thunders
that, for me, on this night of rain, are tidings from the mouth of
the God of Might to endless generations.
-URI ZVI GREENBERG

Parts of this book originally appeared in an earlier account of the Israeli District Court trial of John Demjanjuk as "The Trial of Ivan the Terrible: State of Israel vs. John Demjanjuk," published by St. Martin's Press in 1990. Thanks to Los Angeles Times where my Op-Ed, "The Pariah Loophole," urging Germany to try Demjanjuk originally appeared (on 6/13/08), as well as the Huffington Post where my "Demjanjuk's Just Epitaph," also appeared (on 3/27/12).

Pondwood Press / Amazon.

Table of Contents

About the Author 4

Foreword 11

Chapter One: That Other Planet Treblinka 15

1. Who Cares? 15

2. Three Extermination Camps 25

3. The Daily Routine of Treblinka 29

4. The Biggest Cemetery 33

5. The Revolt. 38

6. The Veil of Secrecy 43

Chapter Two: The Witnesses 46

1. The Only Family He Had 46

2. Holocaust Trials 50

3. Nazis In America? 54

4. Ivan Of Treblinka 61

5. Dos Iz Ivan 66

6. The Charges Against Demjanjuk 73

7. Federenko's Route 78

8. The Paper Trail 80

9. Punishment Will Come 92

10. They Treated Us Like We Were on Trial 96

11. Message from Moscow 101

12. Conversation by Documents 108

13. That's America? 111

Chapter Three: Israeli Justice.......................... **120**

1.The Right Case 120

2. Enter O'Connor 125

3.Operation Justice 130

4. My Dear Armand. 143

5. Beit HaMisphpat 152

6. Whoever Enters Treblinka 155

7. The Sixth Man 169

8. Those Eyes, Those Murderous Eyes 172

9. The Trial Phenomenon 186

10. Simple Men..187

11. The Investigator..................................196

12. Aging Memories...................................201

13. The Superdemon Of Treblinka 209

14. One of The Surprises of His Life 220

Chapter Four: The Trawniki Card.............. **222**

1.The Rosetta Stone.................................222

2. Putting the Card to The Test..................227

3. Seeing A Nazi In Jerusalem.....................233

4.Demjanjuk Has A Question 235

Chapter Five: The German Role **240**

1. Something Remarkable 240

2. German Witnesses...................................245

Ivan of the Extermination Camp

3. A Hearing in Berlin 250

Chapter Six: Demolishing Demjanjuk's Alibi 255

1. Demjanjuk's History 255

2. O'Connor's Mistake 258

Chapter Seven: Demjanjuk's Testimony 262

1. Utterly Unfounded 262

2. I Am John Demjanjuk......................................266

3. A Mechanic Is A Mechanic 274

4. A Skilled Driver...286

Chapter Eight: Expert Opinions 307

1. Document Examiner..307

2. Notable Experts 315

3. Memory Tests...321

4. Sheftel's Strategy 330

Chapter Nine: Closing In 332

1. Revisiting Treblinka..332

2. Dry River Beds..336

3. What About Sobibor? 338

4. The Prosecutor's Defense and Rebuttal...................343

5. Danylchenko's Statements................................345

6. The Human Face of Evil...................................350

7. Crime and Punishment 369

Chapter Ten: The Appeal and Its Aftermath................. 375

1. Tragedy Strikes the Defense Team 375

2. New Questions 378

3. Hearing the Appeal 383

4. How Terrible Is Ivan? 384

5. The Special Master's Opinion 389

6. Ivan Marshenko Of the Gas Chambers at Treblinka 392

7. More Evidence Emerges 395

8. The Israel Supreme Court's Decision 397

9. Supreme Court Aftermath 401

10. Back to Cleveland 403

11. Denaturalization Redux 405

Chapter Eleven: Hello Munich! 411

1. Who Will Take Demjanjuk? 411

2. Goodbye Cleveland 416

3. A Historic Prison 424

4. Preparing for The German Trial. 426

5. The Victims' Place in The Trial Process 430

6. Demjanjuk's Munich Trial Begins 434

7. The Love of His Life 439

8. Demjanjuk's Roommate 442

9. Something No One imagined Happening in Germany ... 446

Chapter Twelve: Der Deutsche Prozess 449

1. Revisited and Re-Examined 449

2. Demjanjuk's Statement 451

3. Final Words 453

4. The Verdict of The Munich Court 455

5. After the Verdict 462

6. Demjanjuk's Just Epitaph 466

Epilogue: My Verdict **469**

10

FOREWORD

In August 1943, after a failed revolt at the Nazi Extermination Camp at Treblinka, in Nazi-occupied Poland, the remaining Jewish inmates were either shot or transferred to the Sobibor Death Camp. The buildings were demolished. A farmhouse was built from the bricks of the gas chamber and the ground was seeded with lupine grass and pine trees. A farmer was installed there.

At the Sobibor death camp, some 130 miles west of Treblinka, a similar occurrence had taken place. There, too, a revolt had taken place on October 14, 1943 -- after which, there too, the ground was bulldozed, and the earth planted over with pine trees to conceal its murderous history.

The Nazis intended that there be no evidence of the crimes committed at Treblinka, where in little more than a year, more than 870, 000 Jewish men, women and children were murdered in a brutal factory of death where on many days more than 15,000 persons were killed in gas chambers, their possessions collected, their hair shorn, the gold from their teeth extracted from their mouths post-mortem, their bodies incinerated, and their remains dumped in large pits. Nor any trace left at Sobibor where, according to historians, as many as 350,000 innocent Jewish men, women and children were murdered.

There were so few Jewish survivors of Treblinka and Sobibor, perhaps fifty or more at each. Even fewer survived who had worked in the gas chamber and incineration area where the murders took place. It seemed unlikely that the world would ever know what took place in that nightmare world. If survivors lived to tell the tale, it was not evident that they would be believed, or even that the world would care.

Nonetheless, as early as 1945 survivors of the Treblinka death camp gave their testimonies and in 1947, a Polish commission arrived to investigate the Treblinka site. The ground had been looted by locals looking for valuables of the murdered buried in the earth. Bone parts were strewn about the field. There was little to no physical evidence to be gathered from Treblinka, no photos or film, almost no military or official records found there of who served at Treblinka and carried out its genocidal program.

Sobibor kept many of its secrets until September 2014, when the area was excavated by archaeologists who unearthed remains of the gas chamber. In the blood-soaked earth of Sobibor, they found wedding rings, jewelry and personal items of the Jews murdered there.

However, in the more than 75 years since Treblinka and Sobibor were dismantled, our knowledge of those hells has steadily accrued.

Today, we know so much more about Treblinka, Sobibor and the other related extermination camps. We know more about other concentration camps such as Flossenburg where some 30,000 persons were murdered; and so much more about the German officers who served there, some of whom were tried in the 1960s in Germany; so much more about the auxiliary guards, the Wachmann, who were the enthusiastic foot-soldiers in the murderous program to exterminate the Jewish race – how and where they were recruited, how they were trained at the Trawniki Training Camp, where they were posted and what their duties were at those camps – as well as more about who was murdered there and when.

The extensive and detailed record of these crimes, and of these criminals, has become greater known to the world, I would argue, because of Ivan Demjanjuk.

Demjanjuk, that same Cleveland autoworker who, as John Demjanjuk, was first accused in 1975 of being a Nazi death camp guard, and who over the years was tried in the United States, in Israel, and in Germany. In 2011, Germany convicted

Demjanjuk of the murder of 29,000 Jewish men, women and children at Sobibor. Ten months later, he died at age 91 in a nursing home in Germany, while awaiting his appeal.

We don't know all this because Demjanjuk told us so, To the contrary, throughout his long and twisted legal odyssey, he repeatedly denied each and every accusation with fabrications, evasions and lies. His denials and lies continued even when he was proved irrefutably to have been an experienced and accomplished helper in the Nazi's murderous machine and at its death factories whose goal was nothing less than genocide – the final solution, as it was called – the attempted extermination of the Jewish people.

Strangely enough, it is because Demjanjuk would not admit what he had done, and because he denied any involvement whatsoever, that decades of research, and the testimony of expert witnesses had to prove otherwise. And because Demjanjuk's series of trials, appeals, and re-trials in the United States, Israel and Germany were spread out over almost forty years, archives once inaccessible (such as in the former Soviet Union), yielded more evidence; and a new generation of prosecutors arose in Germany that set out to re-interpret German law so as to apply it to Nazi collaborators such as Demjanjuk.

It is fair to say then, that the lasting legacy of the trials of John Demjanjuk is all that we've come to know about the Holocaust – about Treblinka, Sobibor, Trawniki, Flossenburg, and Majdanek. Because of Demjanjuk's lies and denials, prosecutors, judges, historians and the expertise of various professionals was called upon to tell the world the truth of the murderous actions of the Nazis and their collaborators such as Demjanjuk.

That which the Nazis sought to hide and conceal, that which the Nazis and their collaborators believed the world would never know; and if known, would never believe, or wouldn't care about—That is the truth the world has come to know because of the denials and trials of John Demjanjuk.

CHAPTER ONE:

THAT OTHER PLANET TREBLINKA

1. Who Cares?

On Sunday, February 15, 1987, the night before the trial of John Demjanjuk was to begin in Jerusalem, a casual canvassing of local taxi drivers found they had no opinion about the trial.

This was striking because in Israel, everyone has an opinion, about everything. But in the year since Demjanjuk had arrived in custody in Israel from the United States, ambivalence about his trial had permeated the country.

Who could say if he was truly guilty?

Who cared? Not to say that no one cared but to ask who exactly did care.

More questions abounded: Could Israel mount a successful case concerning crimes forty-five years past? Could the memories of Treblinka survivors be trusted? Didn't Israel have more pressing current problems? Why return to Treblinka?

In the United States, public reaction was as curiously low-key, even indifferent-as it was in Israel. The Klaus Barbie trial set for that summer in Lyons, held far greater attention and was of greater interest to serious journalists. That was the important trial. Who was Demjanjuk? A small cog, not a planner; a collaborator, not a German Nazi.

Demjanjuk had been brought to stand trial in Israel because

15

he was alleged to be "Ivan Grozny," or "Ivan the Terrible," the Ukrainian gas-chamber operator at Treblinka who had, with his own hands, murdered hundreds of thousands of men, women, and children, cruelly, zealously, and with a sadism beyond any bounds.

But John Demjanjuk had spent more than thirty years living the successful immigrant's life in the United States, among family, his three children, friends, workers, and fellow congregants who believed in his innocence as fervently as his prosecutors did in his guilt.

On the morning of Monday, February 16, 1987, the opening of Demjanjuk's trial in Israel attracted as many reporters as spectators.

To accommodate security arrangements for Demjanjuk, as well as the public and press, the smaller hall of Jerusalem's convention center, the *Binyanei Haooma* or "The Hall of the People," had been transformed into a courtroom. It had been used often as a movie theater.

As you walked into the building, you had to pass a sign, "Box Office for the Performances," that seemed a cynical portent, given the occasion, and the equally resonant, "Deposit Weapons Here." After clearing a metal detector at the door, you registered your passport number with the guards seated inside the hall.

In the foyer was a small snack bar; off to the left was a counter where reporters and spectators could pick up, at no charge, Walkman-like gear to listen to the simultaneous translation of the testimony from Hebrew into English. To the far right was the press area, with a separate entrance, pay phones, and long-distance operators.

Israel's ambivalence about the trial was evident in the makeshift quality of some of its arrangements: The judges' dais had been hauled over from Jerusalem District Court; the

16

attorneys' desks had been taken from storerooms. Only Demjanjuk's witness booth was newly constructed. Outside the courtroom, a simple sign had been taped to the wall informing visitors of the do's and don'ts of courtroom etiquette.

A former dressing room, off stage left, had been transmuted into a temporary cell for Demjanjuk. As a safety and security precaution, workers had changed all 220-volt outlets in the room to non-dangerous 24 volts. A bed and table were bolted to the floor, and now a closed-circuit camera enabled police to monitor the room from a separate office in the building. The small hall was being rented from its owner, the Jewish Agency, for $17,000 a month.

Arrangements had been made for a three-month lease.

The trapezoid-shaped hall was paneled with blond wood that stretched to a high ceiling of large acoustical tiles. Seating for three hundred was provided; benches would be added later. The balcony was reserved for the press. The trial itself would take place onstage, which had been set as follows:

At the back, center-stage was the raised dais of the three-judge panel that would hear the case. Below the judges would sit their clerk and the official Hebrew translator. On the left was one long table for the defense, angled like a giant eyebrow, where American attorneys Mark O'Connor, John Gill and their Israeli co-counsel Yoram Sheftel would sit. Directly behind them was the dock in which Demjanjuk would sit with a Ukrainian translator at his side, flanked by two police officers.

There had been talk that Demjanjuk would sit in Adolf Eichmann's bulletproof glass booth, but security officials decided against that precaution.

Behind Demjanjuk's two guards, another police officer sat against the left wall, and, on the first day, John Demjanjuk Jr.

During the course of the trial, the police officers and security guards would be rotated regularly. John Demjanjuk

Jr.'s table would be moved back against the wall, and ultimately he would be asked to sit among the spectators.

On the right was the matching eyebrow, the two prosecution tables each seating four. At the front table sat Yonah Blatman, the state attorney; Michael Shaked, in effect the team's lead attorney; Michael Horovitz and Dennis Gouldman. The assistant attorneys sat at the second table.

Behind the prosecution tables was a wall bearing a photographic blowup of a model of the Treblinka extermination camp which a survivor of Treblinka has made after arriving in Israel. And next to the prosecution table was the witness box, from which the witness could face the accused and be scrutinized by the judges.

An Israeli flag stood on each side of the judge's bench; the seal of the State of Israel was affixed to the center of the back wall as if to say: This was no international tribunal. The proceedings were to be conducted in Hebrew, according to Israeli law and procedure.

Dispersed throughout the room were security guards in white shirts, police in blue uniforms, and military personnel in tan or green uniforms.

Shortly before 8:30 A.M., the prosecutors and defense attorneys, all in black robes, took their places, and began to shuffle the masses of documents piled high on their desks. The press had filled several rows downstairs, with television and radio reporters in the balcony. Their cameras, still and video, stood poised on tripods like longnecked cranes peering over the edge.

Demjanjuk entered, surrounded by four policemen. Wearing a brown suit, he had adopted Israeli custom and wore no tie, just an open shirt. He looked ruddy, overweight.

Camera lights went on, as the whirring and clicking of press equipment began, Demjanjuk raised his arm in what some feared would be a salute but turned out to be a gentle wave of his hand. He shouted in his deep voice, "Boker tov"-Hebrew for "good morning"-and then, "Hello Cleveland," to the TV cameras. He shook attorney Mark O'Connor's hand, embraced his other American attorney, John Gill; and then hugged his son. Israeli co-defense counsel Yoram Sheftel entered, sitting down between O'Connor and John Gill.

The court clerk announced "Beit Hamishpat!" sharply. The room came to attention. All rose in anticipation, as the three judges entered from the right in black robes: Judge Zvi Tal, bearded and wearing a kippah, a skullcap, occupied the left chair. In the center was Presiding Justice Dov Levin and on his right judge Dalia Dorner, who like her colleagues was wearing a black tie and white shirt.

"Good morning," Justice Levin said to the assembled crowd. "Please be seated."

The setting was dramatic: the stage, the call to attention, the public, the press. The fact that this trial took place in a public auditorium, was conducted on a stage, and was broadcast live on radio and TV in Israel and had press attending, would lead some to declare this a show trial.

However, there is an important difference between making the trials as accessible to the public as possible -- and how the trial itself was conducted. And Justice Dov Levin was determined to conduct this trial as he did all his trials, in the most professional way possible under the rigors of the Israeli legal system.

This was the first trial of a Nazi war criminal in Israel since Adolf Eichmann's in 1961. In every aspect, it showed how much Israel and the world had changed in twenty-five years.

Eichmann had had to be kidnapped from Argentina to be brought to trial. This time Israel had applied for Demjanjuk's extradition from the United States, which upheld its treaty obligations and delivered him to Israeli authorities.

The trial of Eichmann was very much a trial conducted by the generation that had survived the Holocaust. Although a majority of Israel's population in 1961 was composed of survivors and their families, before the Eichmann trial survivors had rarely spoken out in public. In many ways, the Eichmann trial was proof to the world that the Holocaust did occur and that a Jewish nation had risen from its ashes to sit in judgment.

The trial of Demjanjuk, beginning as it did in the late 1980s, was to be the trial by the generation born since the Holocaust. The population of Israel was by that time made up in majority by Sephardic Jews who had had no direct contact with the Holocaust and of a generation born since 1945. The presiding judge was Israel-born, and the other judges had been in Palestine during the Holocaust. The prosecutors and defense attorneys were almost all born after 1945.

For a generation removed from the crimes of the Holocaust, this was a more graphic trial than Eichmann's. Eichmann was tried as the master planner of the Jews' extermination, Demjanjuk was accused as their murderer.

Inside the courtroom, by the very nature of the legal process, facts emerged slowly; proof and evidence had to be found valid. Inside the courtroom, the process inched forward with great deliberation slowly over time towards a final judgment.

Outside the courtroom, reporters followed a daily story. A story needed headlines, scoops, news-making quotes. The judges and prosecutors, following the prohibition against discussing cases not finally adjudicated, were rarely available for comment. But defense supporters were more than available to speak and volunteered information freely to columnists and reporters.

This was decades before "alternative facts" were a recognized phenomenon. However, the Demjanjuk case had long had a disconnect between the evidence and court decisions and what Demjanjuk, his defense attorneys and supporters said to the Press. The net effect to this day has been confusion in the public mind, and a vagueness outside the courtroom as to what occurred in Court.

Inside the courtroom, prosecutors were compelled by the criminal process to prove beyond any doubt the horrific allegations. This was no simple task, for the prosecution would have to break the conspiracy of silence the Nazis had wished to achieve by razing Treblinka in November 1943.

The first five rows of the courtroom had been cordoned off for dignitaries. Attending that first day were Knesset members Dov Shilansky and Sheva Weiss, as well as official observers from the Polish Nazi War Crimes Commission, the Ukrainian Church Metropolitan from New York, and the children and grandchildren of the Holocaust survivors who were to testify.

The windowless hall could barely contain the tension.

On that first morning of trial, Justice Levin turned to Demjanjuk's attorney, saying: "Mr. O'Connor, please make preliminary arguments."

Mark O'Connor, Demjanjuk's lead defense attorney, then in his early forties, with close-cropped reddish hair and deep blue eyes, presented a certain intensity. Before formally addressing the court, he fiddled with his translation radio and adjusted his headphones. Levin suggested that rather than trouble with translation, he might try to learn Hebrew before the end of the trial. Everyone laughed; it was the last light moment that day.

O'Connor spent two-and-a-half hours arguing that even though Israel had the right to try Demjanjuk by virtue of universal jurisdiction, it should nonetheless return him to the United States because his identification was based on suspect Soviet-supplied evidence.

O'Connor was a theatrical performer. His black robe flowed as he strode across the stage, he waved his hands for emphasis or clasped them in front of himself like a country preacher. His face would tighten like a fist raised in anger; a moment later, his brows would smooth and widen to show his good cheer. His rhetoric was flavored with imaginative phrases-some more colorful than relevant:

"If this is only the second time in history, with regard to the State of Israel, the young State of Israel, that the sword of St. Michael has been taken out in the use of long-arm jurisdiction to bring back into the House of Zion an international criminal, a criminal whose crimes offend all mankind," O'Connor said. "If, in fact, the second time around we have a situation where there is not the proper rationale... what then does the world do with the precedent that's been set down by this tribunal, by this legal Sanhedrin?"

Demjanjuk, O'Connor said, had been caught up in a whirlwind of three great powers-the United States, the USSR, and Israel, each proceeding in this case with different political objectives.

"John Demjanjuk has never been in any death camp in any capacity," O'Connor said.

Israeli defense attorney Yoram Sheftel said the defense was willing to admit all facts stated in the indictment up until Demjanjuk becoming a prisoner of war, and even admit there was a monster Ivan Grozny at Treblinka. But the defense categorically denied that this monster's surname was said to be Demjanjuk. No survivor had ever mentioned his name as being Demjanjuk. And some survivors said Ivan had died in the revolt.

Sheftel asked that the prosecution, in its opening remarks, speak only of Demjanjuk and not of the Holocaust or Treblinka. "After forty years of research and study of the Holocaust, every person with a reasonable amount of education anywhere in the world, unless he declares himself to be anti-Semitic, knows full well the main facts," he said.

But Judge Levin disagreed: "A great many people in the world and in Israel, too, and even in this hall, do not know all the facts in full detail." Levin said it was possible that the evidence should be narrowed, but one just couldn't take it for granted that every person in Israel, or even in the courtroom, knew all the facts of the "Final Solution."

Ivan of the Extermination Camp

"Does this court feel," Judge Levin said, "that all the facts referring to what happened in the camps, which the indictment refers to, are or have been brought to our knowledge? They have not. And it is as simple as that."

On that first day of trial, the Judges halted the proceedings at 1:00 P.M for a break. The judges left; Demjanjuk was led out. Suddenly an elderly Holocaust survivor, Mordechai Fuchs started shouting about Demjanjuk. The police led him out.

Then another survivor, Yisrael Yehezkeli, broke into tears. "They're lying," he said, motioning to the empty defense area. "All my family was killed. .. why did the judges let this man speak and they don't let me speak? I have to get it off my chest ... why do they let them tell such lies? I knew the Red Army." After a few moments, he was led outside.

When the trial resumed, Yonah Blatman, the State Attorney rose to present his case. Wearing a long black robe, Blatman stood, his gray hair a mop, his salt-and-pepper mustache adding a professorial air to his remarks.

"Before us stands an accused by the name of John Demjanjuk," Blatman said. "He is the Demjanjuk who has been known as 'Ivan the Terrible' and he stands before you accused of the most terrible crimes ever committed in the course of history...."

Blatman's opening statement traced the historical, and even philosophical context in which the crimes were committed, from the Nazis coming to power in Germany, through their racial discrimination laws, property confiscation, ghettoization, and the Nazis' murderous policies, begun with deportations and euthanasia, and followed by killing squads and murder vans, the promulgation and adoption of "The Final Solution" for the extermination of European Jewry at the Wansee Conference, the occupation of Poland by the Nazis as the General Gouvernment chosen to be the location of the dedicated extermination camps Belzec, Sobibor and Treblinka.

Blatman stood slightly hunched, his glasses sliding low on his nose, as he read from his notes. He seemed to list to his right,

As he spoke, Demjanjuk and his son listened impassively.

Blatman had outlined the facts of the Treblinka extermination camp but it fell to historian Dr. Yitzhak Arad, the prosecution's first witness, to detail the history and operation of the death camp.

Sheftel objected saying, "If the prosecution insists on calling Dr. Arad, we submit that this is not for the sake of this hearing but for the sake of the sixteen television cameras in the hall. to turn this into a show trial for the sake of the mass media. The most outstanding example in history of this are the Moscow trials...."

Levin fumed with anger: "This remark should not have been sounded in an Israeli courtroom. The court is interested in factual and historical background.... [Dr. Arad's] testimony seems to us to be of importance." Dr. Arad continued with his testimony.

2. Three Extermination Camps

Dr. Arad sat in the witness box looking much like a university professor. Short and sprightly, with glasses framing a broad, cheerful face topped by curly dark hair, Arad spoke in a clear, strong voice. Born in Lithuania in 1926, he was in Warsaw when the war broke out. He managed to return to his Soviet hometown, many of his family died during the Holocaust, some in Treblinka. Since 1972 he had been chairman of Yad Vashem, Israel's Holocaust Memorial Authority. He was the author of a book about the Operation Reinhard camps: "Belzec, Sobibor, and Treblinka," published in 1987 in the United States.

Treblinka, he said, was the culmination of the Nazis long history of anti-Semitism, beginning in the early 1930s with Hitler's speeches, followed by sanctioned persecution of Jews. "Ghetto-ization" was merely the next phase in the overall plan for the annihilation of the Jews.

Arad described at length the work of T4, the institute at 4 Tiergardenstrasse near Berlin, that promoted euthanasia for the mentally deficient and handicapped. Arad told how the T4 personnel trained in the techniques of death later became involved in the death camps.

After the German army invaded the Soviet Union in June 1941, orders were given to four SS Einsatzgruppen to annihilate Jews rounded up in conquered Soviet regions. Pogroms against Jews were encouraged by the local populations, Dr. Arad testified, and Jewish POW camps were selected for "special treatment" --death.

Documents were introduced to show that on July 31, 1941, Reichmarshall Goering wrote of going ahead with the necessary preparation for the *Gesamtlosung*-the "comprehensive solution" of the Jewish problem. Official acts by Hitler,

25

Himmler, and Heydrich led to the "Final Solution" at the Wansee Conference on January 21, 1942.

Blatman had quoted Dr. Josef Buehler, the State Secretary of the Nazi-Occupied territory, who stated in the Wansee conference protocol that "they will be happy if the final solution of this problem has its inception in the Gouvernment General...." The solution was to build concentration camps where mass killings could occur without "arousing disquiet among the population."

After the Wansee Conference in 1942, Reinhard Heydrich was named to head the extermination program and began planning the liquidation of the Jews of Eastern Europe. But Heydrich was killed by Czech underground fighters in May 1942, outside Prague. The extermination of Polish Jewry was then dubbed, in his honor, "Operation Reinhard." Odilo Globochnik, the former Gauletier of Vienna and Heinrich Himmler's personal friend, was put in charge, and a staff was formed to continue Heydrich's planning.

Arad described how the T4 program begat the mobile killing vans of Chelmno (essentially trucks that were loaded with victims who were then gassed with the truck's exhaust) and how Globochnik received the order from Himmler to establish the three extermination camps of Operation Reinhard where Jews were to be murdered in gas chambers at Belzec, Sobibor, and Treblinka, in Nazi-occupied Eastern Poland. Jews from the districts of Lwow and Cracow were to be sent to Belzec; the Lublin district Jews, for the great part, to Sobibor; and Jews from the Warsaw and Radom districts to Treblinka.

To find appropriate staff for the extermination camps, Operation Reinhard needed only to look to its recent past: the T4 workers were unusually well prepared for such a task and were placed in key positions at the camps.

Christian Wirth was made chief extermination specialist,

having proved himself at Chelmno in the operation of the killing vans. He was the first commander of the Belzec camp.

It was Wirth who decided that the camps would use carbon monoxide. And it was Wirth who, after experimenting with carbon monoxide containers sent from Germany, decided that diesel engines should be installed adjacent to the gas chambers to produce the necessary poisonous fumes.

Dr. Irmfried Eberl, who had directed Operation Euthanasia, was Treblinka's first commander. He was replaced by Franz Stangl, who previously was commander at Sobibor. Stangl's deputy commander at Treblinka was Kurt Franz, who had been an SS officer at Belzec. In the last days of Treblinka, Franz would be its third and final commander.

Arad testified that possessions taken from the Jews at Treblinka were valued at 178 million Reichmarks-$445 million dollars.

Arad explained that only about thirty-five German SS men were assigned to each camp, but that they were assisted by some one hundred and ten auxiliaries, most of whom were Soviet citizens recruited from German POW camps. They were trained at the Trawniki camp, not far from Treblinka and Sobibor.

The auxiliaries were given military drilling and dressed in dark brown or black uniforms. They were organized into units, and sent either to the Jewish ghettos, where they were involved in roundups, acts of brutality, and liquidations of the ghetto, or to the extermination camps.

Arad turned to the large photographs mounted on the wall behind him. He explained that they were photographs of a model of Treblinka constructed by Yankel Viernik, a survivor of the camp. The model was inexact in some respects, but accurately represented the landmarks of the camp.

27

As Arad described the model, Demjanjuk peered to get a better look.

The commander of the SS training camp Trawniki, Karl Streibl, personally toured the Soviet prisoner-of-war camps to find suitable volunteers, Arad said. The conditions in POW camps were inhumane. People were dying of starvation, malnutrition, and exposure. Though Streibl's orders were to recruit "Aryan"-looking soldiers, he selected the healthy, and those who had a skill, such as drivers.

Trawniki itself was staffed mostly with Volksdeutsche-ethnic Germans. Approximately five thousand guards were trained at Trawniki during its two-and-a-half years of operation. They were trained in weapons and assigned to liquidate ghettos or guard extermination camps.

Guard units of ninety to one-hundred-twenty men were posted to each camp. They were called Wachmanner but were also known as auxiliaries or Hiwis; they finally became known by Germans and inmates alike simply as the "Ukrainians," for almost all had been born in the Ukraine. They had volunteered for SS service while prisoners of war, captured or surrendered Red Army soldiers.

By the summer of 1942, Treblinka was set up at Malkinia, near the Bug River. Belzec and Sobibor were already in operation, but it was Treblinka that would become the "perfected" death camp. Its location, only forty miles from Warsaw, had been chosen carefully: an elongated wooded elevation, hidden from the surrounding highway and railroad line. In the forest, leafy trees made a shaded glade. One could hear birds singing.

3. The Daily Routine of Treblinka

Arad told of life at Treblinka, speaking matter-of-factly, yet in fast, sometimes indignant bursts. He detailed the daily routines, the discipline of the camp, the division of labor, the different assignments. As he talked, he seemed to be staring Demjanjuk in the eye.

There was a gravel quarry nearby. The SS brought some one thousand Polish and Jewish prisoners there to build what would be known as Treblinka AG, or the Treblinka labor camp. It would be used as a concentration camp for smugglers, but also as a camp to show others, should questions arise. The forced laborers as well as Jews from neighboring villages were part of the site-construction crew for the death camp. The laborers were eventually murdered.

The death camp was laid out as a rectangle, approximately six-hundred-sixty yards by four-hundred-forty yards (fewer than sixty acres), surrounded by a barbed-wire fence about twelve feet high, which was camouflaged by leaves and branches, and surrounded by tree saplings. Immediately behind this fence was a ditch about ten feet wide, behind which lay a bare strip of land some forty-five yards wide. This strip was marked off from the surrounding area by barbed wire and antitank obstacles (also called "Spanish horses"). At all four corners of the camp were watchtowers, some with searchlights, all manned night and day by Ukrainian guards.

Inside the camp, there were three areas of equal dimension: the living quarters of the German and Ukrainian staff; the arrival area for the transports; and the actual extermination area. The living and reception camp was known by the Germans as the "Lower Camp" and by the inmates as "Camp One"; the extermination area as the "Upper Camp" or "Camp Two."

29

The staff living area had two long barracks for bedrooms, the kitchen, and mess hall. Facing the barracks was the commandant's house and the food warehouse (there was no shortage of delicacies confiscated from the Jews). There were also administration buildings, offices, workshops, stores, and an infirmary. A quarter-acre of this area was wired off: here were the Jewish laborers' living quarters, workshop, and square for holding roll call.

Behind the food warehouse was an area for the Jews from neighboring towns who had helped to build the camp. In recognition of their service they wore yellow stars and were allowed to live somewhat longer as the waiters of the Germans and Ukrainians, although in time these workers were murdered as well. Several women worked in the kitchens and laundry and were among the only females allowed to live in Treblinka.

The camp was ready July 11, 1942. Eleven days later, the first transport from Warsaw left for Treblinka. The train would leave daily with no fewer than five-thousand Jews aboard. The transports would continue for the next thirteen months: eight-hundred-seventy thousand Jewish men, women, and children would pass through its gates. More, perhaps. Only fifty would survive.

The trains arrived at the reception area in the southwest section of the camp. Here was the Jews' first sight of Treblinka. They entered through a gate to a square. There they separated, men to the right, women and children to the left, never to see each other again. They were commanded to undress. Two barracks flanked the square: in one, the women and children undressed; in the other, the personal effects of the murdered were sorted and accumulated for shipment out of the camp.

The naked victims were then commanded to run up a fenced-in path. Past the gate, showers awaited them in the bath house. This path, called the Schlauch, the "tube," led to, the death camp. The Germans also called it the Himmel fahrtstrasse, or "road to heaven." The Jews were set upon by dogs and blows from the guards. They ran toward a gate and were forced into a building. Less than two hours after arrival, this was their end.

Except for minor industrial activity, the camp's only contribution to the German war effort was the confiscated property of the inmates. In a little more than a year, the camp shipped out about 25carloads of hair packed in bales; 248 carloads of men's suits; 22 carloads of ready-made textile goods; carloads of medicines, medical equipment, and dentist's metal; 12 carloads of artisans' tools; 260 carloads of bedding, feathers, down quilts; 400 carloads of miscellaneous items. One inmate recalled spending six months sorting out fountain pens; another packing more than fourteen thousand carats in diamonds.

The Jews who survived the initial arrival did so because the Germans selected them to be forced laborers in Camp One.

Jews were forced laborers in the death camp as well. A small work group was selected occasionally from the lower sorting crew to walk the path to the death camp. The gate to the death camp and the fence surrounding it were camouflaged. Germans wanted to keep its activity secret not only to the outside world but also to each new transport of Jews.

Jewish workers who entered the death camp found a human mountain of corpses, among them the men and women of their own transports, of their communities, of their relatives. Under a hail of beatings, they were put to work immediately.

They were assigned various tasks: emptying the gas chambers, cleaning them before the next arrivals, carrying corpses to the pits, examining the corpses' mouths for fillings. In the ditches they found row upon row of dead bodies. Those who didn't work fast enough were shot and buried with the corpses.

31

Most of the buildings were made of wood, but the buildings in the death camp were made of brick. The gas-chamber building itself was hidden from the Lower Camp by a row of trees. The roof of the gas chamber was camouflaged with a green wire net whose edges extended slightly beyond the building's walls. Under the roof was a tangle of pipes. The walls were covered with concrete.

Within, the chambers looked like a regular shower room with all the accouterments of a public bathhouse. Its walls were covered with small white tiles. The floor was covered with terra-cotta tiles. Nickel-plated faucets were set into the ceiling. The work was finely detailed.

Standing next to the bathhouse was a large chest.

A "dentist" would examine the mouth of each corpse as it was dragged out of the chamber and extract any gold, silver, or platinum caps he might find. More than one chest full of precious metal was accumulated each day.

Under a tree about forty meters from the bathhouse, a band of Jewish musicians performed for the Germans and Ukrainians. Concerts were held when new transports arrived, to cover the screams of the dying.

The inmates were marched up to the barracks, unaware of what awaited them. They went stony-faced, naked, pressed together. Fleeing the blows of the guards and the brutal cold of Polish winter, they rushed faster yet toward the chamber.

4. The Biggest Cemetery

Blatman, Shaked and Arad, had each spoken about the death camp area at Treblinka with its gas chambers, the work that those few Jews who worked there did as *Sonderkommando*, and the Germans and the Wachmann who worked there, goading the Jews into the gas chambers, turning on the engines of death, supervising the Jews in their unbearable tasks, as imminent death surrounded them all.

The machinery of the gas chamber was supervised by the Germans Arthur Matthes and Fritz Schmidt; but it was operated most often by two Ukrainians, Ivan and Nikolai.

According to various accounts, at a given signal they would admit the victims. Ivan and Nikolai, holding a heavy lead pipe or a bayonet, would force the Jews inside, beating them savagely as they moved into the chamber. To hurry them along, Ivan often jabbed at them with what was variously described as a knife, a sword or a bayonet; amusing himself by slicing a breast or cutting an ear.

The survivors who lived to record the tale, were haunted by the screams of the women, the weeping of the children, the pleas for mercy, for God's deliverance, that filled the air like the howling of wild animals.

Between four-hundred-fifty and five-hundred people were crowded into a chamber measuring twenty-five square meters. The bedlam lasted only a short while, they said, for soon the doors were slammed shut.

Ivan went then to the engine room at the side of the building and turned on the motor. It was a Russian diesel tank-engine, connected to the chamber's inflow pipes. The exhaust filled the chamber. Within a half hour, the victims lay dead, or were left standing dead, as there was often not an inch of space.

When the gassing was over, Ivan and Nikolai inspected the results. Occasionally the supervising German would put his ear to the door to comment *Alles shlaft* ("all asleep"). Ivan and Nikolai then moved to the other side of the building, where they heaved sliding doors that opened onto a ramp. When the doors opened, bluish smoke escaped.

The Jewish laborers waited there, forced to carry corpses. At first the Jews carried the corpses to the ditches with their hands. Then a narrow-gauge track was built to drive the corpses to the ditches on a rolling platform. Finally, they used wooden stretchers.

The corpse-carriers worked two to a stretcher, they recalled. Each stretcher held one adult, or two children. The workers ran and were allowed to pause only while the "dentists" fulfilled their task of pulling gold or silver from the mouths of the murdered.

The corpses were tossed into deeply carved pits. Once aligned in the ditch, a layer of sand was poured over them; then another layer of corpses; then sand, until the pit was filled. Occasionally the entire mound would heave and resettle. The pits would then be filled more and topped off. The corpse--carriers returned, running, forced at times to gallop like horses, to await the next gassing.

Soon it became clear that the capacity of the structure housing the gas chambers was not sufficient. Ten new chambers were built by the inmates in five weeks' time. Each chamber was twice the size of the old one. As many as twelve hundred persons could be gassed now at one time. Between ten and twelve thousand people were gassed each day, some days as many as fifteen thousand. The entrance to the new chamber bore a Star of David as well as a legend in Hebrew script: "This is the gate through which the righteous shall enter."

When the construction was finished, the Hauptsturmfuhrer, the captain, said to his subordinates, "The Jew-town has been completed at last."

About two to three hundred Jewish forced laborers lived and worked in the death camp. All men. Many knew each other by sight. They were brothers. They had to work in tandem, carrying corpses on stretchers. The "dentist" could give them a moment to breathe. One could save a piece of bread for the other. One slept in the bunk above. One needed help to hang himself.

The Germans in charge, had at their command whatever they wished for, all for their amusement. In Treblinka the cruelty was so pervasive that fear had its gradations, sadism its own hierarchy. Survival was dependent on such knowledge.

Kurt Franz, the assistant commander of the camp, was known as Die Lalke, "The Doll," due to his good looks. He held the roll calls. One survivor recalled that "the earth shook" when he approached. Franz would call to his attack dog, Barry, "Man bite the dog." To Lalke, Barry was the man, the Jews the dog.

According to testimonies, written histories and historians, about fourteen Germans worked in Camp Two; two Ukrainians were permanently posted there. The work-Jews did not know the full names of their tormentors. They heard the names that the Germans and Ukrainians addressed each other by, and they had their own nicknames for them as well.

In Camp One, the Jewish workers had little contact with the guards; but in the death camp they worked in close proximity to the Germans and Ukrainians there.

Arad had found the names of Treblinka gas chamber operators Ivan and Nikolai mentioned in the deposition of Stangl at the first Dusseldorf trial, as well as in the trials of the Treblinka men in Dusseldorf, Germany, in 1964 and 1970

Ivan, according to trial testimonies, was a Ukrainian, and the Ukrainians and Germans alike called him Ivan. Survivors who recalled his sadism called him Ivan Grozny, "Ivan the Terrible."

The whole of the death camp area was 200 by 275 yards, so the actual space the Jewish inmates worked in, between the gas chambers and the pits, was small indeed. Here, they would see Ivan, often day in and day out, at close proximity, over a period of many months. It was as if, one survivor recalled, "they rubbed shoulders" with him. They watched him, they feared him, they knew him. How could they forget him?

During breaks or after gassings, Ivan could be found sitting with Nikolai, or roaming about other parts of the camp. He was free to do so. During the days of the heavy transports in the fall and winter of 1942, he would rush to greet arrivals at the train platform and then rush to greet them at the gas chambers. He was, on occasion, ordered to accompany details to cut trees for camouflage. He ate at the Ukrainian mess in the Lower Camp and slept in the Ukrainian barracks.

Something else distinguished Ivan: he had a talent with engines, and not only the gas-chamber engine. Ivan had been a mechanic. He knew how to drive, which was unusual for a Ukrainian guard. He liked to visit the camp's repair shop, and often tinkered in the garage.

Ivan was well liked by the Germans, it was said, and held the other guards in disdain. On occasion, he was sent out of the camp; he was among the few permitted to leave regularly and venture into neighboring towns.

At the end of his testimony, Dr. Arad asked if he could make a short statement. Judge Levin said no. But after Dr. Arad left the courtroom, he told the reporters that he had wanted to stress that not all Ukrainians were like Ivan the Terrible. "This is important," he said. "Hundreds of thousands of Ukrainians fought loyally in the Red Army to defeat Nazism and many gave their lives. Even in the camps there were other sorts of Ukrainians."

Beginning in January 1943, the pace of transports slackened. Early in the new year, Himmler visited the camp, and the corpses were ordered cremated rather than burned. No remains should exist. Jews were assigned to this task as well. They built a crematoria by placing railroad rails on concrete slabs to form a grill.

The corpses that had been buried in mass graves were exhumed by mechanical excavators. Some of the pits contained seventy thousand corpses. Up to three thousand gassed bodies could be incinerated at a time. After cremation, the ashes were checked for bone particles. The pits were then refilled, with layers of human ash, upon layers of sand, and finally topped off with soil. Seedlings were planted to conceal the evidence of mass killings.

Treblinka was, Dr. Arad said, "the biggest cemetery of Polish Jewry." In little more than a year, more than 843,000 Jewish men, women and children were murdered there.

5. The Revolt.

As the gassings were fewer, the death camp became calmer. "And," recalled a worker, "Ivan became calmer, too." He was seen less, and the workers did not seek him out. The Jews of the death camp, no longer living in a state of perpetual fear, began to think of revolt.

There had been moments of resistance from the first days of Treblinka, but they were small instances, all unsuccessful, with huge consequences: one guard was murdered, and thirty inmates killed; a group escaped, but was caught and then hung and flayed to death; a tunnel was discovered, and workers were selected at random for death.

But now the time had come to act. The workers realized that as long as the Nazis needed them to carry and incinerate corpses they would be kept alive; but when their work was done, the Nazis would have no need for witnesses to their crimes.

During the months of June and July, the summer heat became increasingly unbearable. The leadership for the revolt was in Camp One. They tried to find a way to get arms. Time was running out. They devised a plan. After another postponement, the revolt was set for August 2. The Jews could not sleep beforehand. "The day of Judgment" was at hand.

August 2, 1943 was a sizzling-hot day. The inmates had a lucky break. Assistant Camp Commander Kurt Franz decided to take a group of Ukrainian guard units to go swimming in the nearby Bug River.

Inmates in both Camp One and Two were given preassigned tasks. The revolt was to start in Camp One; in Camp Two they were to cut the fences and ready the escape path. The excitement and tension were high all day. Each moment in the hot sun was an eternity.

The time for the revolt had been set at 5:00 P.M. A group from the nearby Treblinka labor camp was known to pass by the camp then. The plan was to liberate them to join in the revolt. But the nervousness among the inmates was so great, it was agreed they could not wait that long. Later in the day the time was changed to 4:30 P.M. The go-ahead was passed between Camp One and Two by a construction crew.

The prisoners in Camp One had managed to steal some weapons. One young man whose job was to spread disinfectant around the camp filled his canister instead with gasoline. Another young man, at the garage, sabotaged an SS armored car. Axes and wire cutters were stolen.

In Camp Two, because of the heat, the inmates worked at the incinerator from 4:00 A.M. until noon. But on that day, they needed a way to stay outside, near the camp's fences. That morning they worked at excavating corpses with special ardor. By noon there were still many exhumed corpses lying near the grills. The foreman of the Jewish incineration crew offered to keep the men working that afternoon in exchange for an extra bread ration. The SS man agreed.

The Jews prepared themselves for their escape. They would carry blankets to throw over the barbed-wire fences. They thought about the world outside: They would put on clothes under their coveralls. They collected gold and money from hiding places.

The signal was supposed to be an explosion, a grenade in Camp One. But a half hour earlier than expected, a shot rang out in the lower camp, and the revolt began. An SS man had stopped a young boy. Finding money on him, he arrested him and started to take him away. Afraid that the boy would confess to the revolt, another decided then and there to shoot the SS man, Kurt Kuttner, who was left on the ground bleeding.

Pandemonium broke out. The uprising plans were never put into effect. In the Upper Camp, one young man screamed out "Revolution in Berlin" to frighten the guards. The barracks of the Jewish workers were next to the camp's southernmost perimeter fence, where many now ran.

Flames shot up in the Lower Camp. Jews ran for the woods and swamps. The guards followed, shooting. The Jews armed with pickaxes and a few guns defended themselves as best they could and kept moving. Smoke and flame rose around the gas chambers.

The Germans called for reinforcements from the labor camp; Franz and the guards returned to camp. SS men in armored cars with machine guns and guards on horseback took to the woods to chase down the escaped inmates.

Arad estimated there were seven hundred Jews in the entire camp that day; one hundred and fifty were able to escape. Of those, Arad said, "only fifty or sixty actually lived to the day of liberation."

Levin asked, as if he had heard wrong, "Do we take it that from all those who went through the Treblinka camp, only some fifty or sixty survived?"

"Yes, only fifty."

Arad further testified that one German was wounded and two or three Ukrainians were killed in the uprising.

There were rumors of Ivan's death, he said, but no one actually saw him dead. Arad had interviewed Avraham Goldfarb, one of the survivors who had recounted Ivan's death. "I asked him whether he had actually seen Ivan the Terrible being killed. His answer was, `No, I did not see it.' He had merely heard of it."

Dr. Arad had scoured all available research and had never found anyone who admitted to killing Ivan or to seeing him dead. Because there were no transports on that day or the preceding ones, Arad believed that Ivan and Nikolai had nothing to do in the death camp at the time of the revolt. And SS officer Gustav Munzberger had testified at his trial at Dusseldorf that Ivan had fought with him among the partisans in Italy after the closing of the camp.

At Treblinka, the brick gas chambers had been set on fire but did not burn down. Though shots had been fired at many of the Germans and Ukrainians, there were few casualties.

After the revolt the camp was not rebuilt in its original form, but the gassings continued. During the month of August, several additional transports of Jews from Bialystok were killed in the gas chambers.

Treblinka Commander Franz Stangl was afraid he would be punished for the revolt at Treblinka. But because more than eight-hundred-seventy-thousand Jews had been killed there, the SS still considered the camp a success. Now the Russian front was advancing, and the camps needed to be dismantled, their "success" hidden. Stangl's talents were needed elsewhere. By the end of August, he had been reassigned to a combat position, leading an anti-partisan force in Trieste. Several other Treblinka men would join him.

Kurt Franz became the camp's commander. By November 1943, every trace of the death camp was to be eliminated. One hundred Jewish prisoners remained to aid in this task.

The buildings were demolished. The Jewish workers were housed in railway cars. Thirty to fifty of them were sent to Sobibor for the dismantling work there. The rest were taken in groups of five to be shot. But before their death, they were given a final task: to cremate the group that had gone before them. The last group was burned by the Ukrainians. Then Franz and the remaining Ukrainian guards drove to Sobibor.

The landscape was leveled. All that remained as testament

to what had occurred were sections of barbed wire, heaps of sand. A farmhouse was built with bricks from the gas chambers. A former Ukrainian guard brought his family and began farming the area. The fields were plowed and sown with lupine grass. Pine woods were planted. Treblinka was no more.

Toward the end of 1943, after Sobibor was dismantled, the guards of Treblinka were reassigned from Sobibor, some south to Trieste to help fight the Yugoslav partisans. Others were sent north to guard other small concentration camps.

6. The Veil of Secrecy

The prosecution had compiled a painstakingly comprehensive record of train transports from Jewish communities to Treblinka that Blatman wished to submit as corroboration of the more than eight-hundred-seventy-thousand murders. Prosecutors felt the impact of the statistics would remain vivid in the judges' memory long after Arad had left the stand. It had taken months to assemble this information. But Levin would not allow its admission because the train transports records, he said, were not facts in dispute

In his opening remarks, the State's Prosecutor Blatman told the court that the extermination camps were shrouded in a veil of secrecy. German documents referred to them only in euphemisms. Secrecy oaths were taken, and relevant documents destroyed. Even today, a visitor to Treblinka finds no trace of the actual camp; it was all hidden, he said, destroyed so the world would never know, never believe.

It would seem, Blatman suggested, that the murderers who took their lives had also sought to deprive them of their deaths. "The more Jews they slaughtered, the fewer witnesses remained to testify to the atrocities." But the Nazis didn't succeed, he said, in eradicating the facts from the annals of history: "The survivors who lived through the most horrendous deeds in the history of mankind have not forgotten the Nazis and cannot forget what the Nazis perpetrated against them."

Blatman now set the individual acts back into the larger context: "How could it happen that precisely when human culture arrived at such a pinnacle of success, the concept of mass annihilation was invented? ... How is it possible that a people that gave rights to some of the finest minds, philosophies, and ethics also conceived of the concept of genocide? ... How can it be [that] precisely the same people who were considered to be the inferior races were willing to cooperate in perpetrating this horrendous deed?"

As Germany extended beyond its own borders, so did its policies of hatred toward Jews. "The German occupiers saw fit in all cases to find those who would collaborate with them in the countries occupied.... We will prove that Ivan Demjanjuk is one of those taken prisoner who collaborated with Germans."

Fault lay not with the Ukrainian nation or all of its people, said Blatman. Though the testimonies of survivors are rife with tales of persecution by Ukrainian nationals in the ghettos and in the camps, this was not the case with all Ukrainians: "Everywhere there were some who did not agree with what was going on. That was their moment of glory. There were some individuals who risked their own lives to save Jews. . . ." "But," Blatman continued, "this was but a drop in the sea of hatred toward Jews."

In part because his face had been partially paralyzed (the result of a stroke), in part because of his professorial manner, there were no dramatics in Blatman's presentation. His comments were delivered straightforwardly. There was no art to his oratory. Yet the courtroom spectators strained to hear every word.

Blatman read from a presentation Heinrich Himmler made to SS officers on October 4, 1943:

"I want, in all sincerity, to present to you a very difficult chapter, and we must discuss this most frankly. Nonetheless, we will never talk about it in public. I am now referring to the evacuation of the Jews, to the annihilation of the Jewish people. This belongs to those matters that can be uttered easily. The Jewish people will be destroyed, says every party member. It says clearly in our platform that the Jewish people must be destroyed, and we are carrying this out. But how can one stand up to all this? There is a certain amount of frailty involved sometimes.... We have been forced to carry out this most difficult task. It is a glorious page in our history, but it is one that has never been recorded, and never will be. We have taken their wealth.... All in all, we are entitled to say that at this point, that out of a love of our people, we have fulfilled this difficult task, and this has not caused any damage to our soul, to our spirit, and to our character."

Today, Treblinka is but a field of commemorative stones, unable to speak the truth of its history. And in Jerusalem sat a man who denied any role in the murders that had taken place there.

To accept that there even was an Ivan the Terrible, first the horrendous crimes recounted in court had to become real again. To believe the witnesses and their identifications, what transpired at Treblinka would need to be understood more deeply and in more intimate detail.

In many ways, the Demjanjuk case was about the extraordinary becoming everyday and the mundane becoming extraordinary. The crimes of that "other planet," Treblinka, were tried in an Israeli court of law; and the accused "master sadist" of Treblinka sat in the dock in Jerusalem, very much a simple creature.

The prosecutors were, for the most part, young, unknown, and untested. The defense was more heard from, than heard of. The judges were respected jurists, but of no international renown. Yet by the everyday process of law, the most extraordinary crimes in history were to be revealed.

CHAPTER TWO:

THE WITNESSES

1. The Only Family He Had

Among those deathcamp survivors who escaped Treblinka was Eliahu Rosenberg. After surviving the uprising, he escaped to the forest where he joined a partisan fighting unit and later the Polish Army from which he was discharged in November 1946. He did not remain in Poland but instead went to Vienna where he served in the Bricha, the underground organization that fostered illegal Jewish immigration to Palestine, before arriving himself in Israel in 1948.

It was a few years later, in the early 1950s, while Rosenberg walked along a street in Tel Aviv, that he first saw someone from the other world, Yankel Viernik.

Originally from Warsaw, Viernik had been trained as a carpenter. At Treblinka, he headed the crew that built the larger gas chambers. As one of the few inmates allowed to go between Camp One and Camp Two, Viernik played a major role in the uprising. He had published his memoirs of Treblinka and then moved to Israel.

Viernik, along with survivors of the Warsaw Ghetto, had founded their own kibbutz, Lohamei Haghetaot ("the ghetto fighter's house"). Years later, he built from memory a model of Treblinka that sits today in the kibbutz's museum. Photographs of it would be used at the Demjanjuk trial as an approximate, if

46

not exact, representation of Treblinka.

Now Rosenberg excitedly asked if Viernik knew of other Treblinka survivors in Israel. Viernik mentioned some names, inmates of Camp One whom Rosenberg did not know.

What about the death camp? asked Rosenberg.

Viernik mentioned that he knew one survivor, Sonia Lewkowicz, worked somewhere in Tel Aviv. Rosenberg remembered her: She had worked in the death camp's laundry. He couldn't believe she had survived. Where did she live? he asked. Viernik knew only that the store she worked in was on Dizengoff, the city's main street.

Rosenberg spent all his free time trying to find Sonia. He was obsessed with the fact that she was still alive; it was as if his own sister had survived Treblinka. He walked Dizengoff from beginning to end, from eight in the morning until night he searched for her. He went in one store after another.

Finally, he found Sonia, at work in a hardware store. They wept in each other's arms.

Sonia told him about another woman, Bronka Sukno, whom they knew from the camp and who was also in Israel. She lived in a settlement, but Sonia did not know the exact address. Rosenberg searched from house to house until he found her.

Rosenberg had an Army friend named Yossef who told him that he, too, knew someone from Treblinka, a man called Pinhas Epstein who lived in Petah Tikvah. Rosenberg didn't know the name, so he decided against making the trip to see him. But years later when they finally met, Rosenberg recognized him as Pavel, whom he indeed had known at Treblinka. They hadn't been good friends there, but in Israel their friendship grew.

Rosenberg continued the pursuit for his lost brothers and

47

sisters. One day in the street in Tel Aviv, he ran into another death-camp survivor, Chaim Staier, who said he had seen Shlomo Hellman, also of the death camp. Rosenberg knew no Hellman, but he went to find him, and Rosenberg found the man he knew as Shlomo Becker.

Hellman, in turn, had found another survivor, Avraham Lindvasser, with whom Rosenberg had worked at Treblinka. They now renewed their close friendship.

Eliahu Rosenberg had married and had two daughters. His wife knew he had been in a camp; she never asked about it and he rarely spoke about it. That was understood. On those few occasions when, with others, he did speak about Treblinka, she saw the effect it had on him: he couldn't sleep or would have terrible nightmares. The sound of his cries during the night, the look on his face in the morning —she wanted to protect him from those harsh emotions. She came to realize that his friends from the death camp were really the only family he had.

Rosenberg later heard that the man who had slept in the bunk above him at Treblinka, a slightly older fellow, Yehiel Reichman, was alive and had emigrated to Montevideo, Uruguay. After Treblinka, Reichman, like Viernik, had made his way back to Warsaw only to participate in the Warsaw Ghetto uprising.

In 1945, Reichman was part of a Polish fact-finding commission that revisited Treblinka. Reichman arrived at Treblinka to find nothing but fields of black earth. A gang of Gentile youths had taken over the area and were combing the earth for valuables: The Soviet bombings had first revealed the earth's true contents. The gang continued to plow for gold or jewelry. The youths left lying about those items that held no interest for them: whole collections of braided Sabbath candlesticks, women's marriage wigs. Bones, skulls, and piles of white ash heaped with soil stood where the incineration had taken place. It was the valley of bones.

"We stood and we cried," Reichman recalled. "What can you say? Each remembered who they had left there."

2.Holocaust Trials

Israel did not rush to commemorate the Holocaust. It was only in 1952 that the nation established a Holocaust Day. It would be seven more years before some form of public observance was set. Even then what was emphasized was not those who died but those who fought. As the Israeli daily Davar wrote on the first Holocaust Day, "The one suitable monument to the memory of European Jewry ... is the State of Israel."

When the day was created to memorialize Holocaust victims, it was called "memorial for the Holocaust and Ghetto revolts." When Yad Vashem, Israel's Holocaust Memorial Museum, was formed in 1953, it was subtitled: "Memorial Authority for the Holocaust and Bravery."

In 1950, the Knesset passed the Nazi and Nazi Collaborators Law, whose language came from United Nations declarations that granted universal jurisdiction to try war crimes and crimes against humanity. The UN declarations had been the basis for the Nuremberg trials. In passing the Nazi and Nazi Collaborators Law, the Knesset affirmed both Israel's commitment to the prosecution of the perpetrators of the Holocaust and its moral authority to stand in judgment of them. But as there were no Nazi war criminals residing in Israel (nor were there likely to be any found), they first turned to trying their own.

Between 1951 and 1954, Israel tried a number of Jewish Kapos and ghetto policemen who had entered the country with the wave of mass immigration. In 1954, capital punishment was abolished for the crime of murder under the penal law, but it remained enforceable for those tried under the Nazi and Nazi Collaborators Law.

In 1959, *Yom Hashoah,* Holocaust Remembrance Day, was 50

officially set in the Israeli calendar the week before Independence Day, and on a day when the Warsaw Ghetto revolt was still in progress. The timing was meant to put the survivors forward as heroes rather than victims. And what better show of strength to those who survived and their nation, than what followed the next year: the kidnapping and trial of Adolf Eichmann.

Eichmann's trial ran for more than four months, from April to August 1961. The Jerusalem District Court issued its verdict on December 12, 1961. The Israel Supreme Court heard the appeal soon thereafter and issued its verdict on May 29, 1962, upholding both the verdict of the District Court and the sentence of death. After an unsuccessful appeal for mercy to the President of Israel, Eichmann was hanged in Ramla Prison on May 31, 1962.

Eliahu Rosenberg was a witness at the Eichmann trial. It was not something he discussed with his family. He did not ask them to attend. His eldest daughter recalled that all he told her was that he was going to Jerusalem for the weekend.

In his testimony, he spoke of Treblinka and of Ivan and Nikolai. Watching his testimony, on film, I was struck by his boyish features. At Treblinka, he must have looked so incredibly young. How unmarked was this man who still looked like a child! One expected to see some visual evidence of his suffering. But that would follow. For to compare Rosenberg in 1961 to how Rosenberg looked in 1987 at the trial in Jerusalem, was to see how his features had hardened. One could only assume that the lines finally etched in his face were pain not only from the telling, but from the retelling.

The Eichmann trial gave dignity to the survivors living in Israel; and allowed the Holocaust to find its place in Israeli history. The trial showcased Israel as a country living by the rule of law, and the Holocaust as a chapter of heroes, in which Israel could provide a heroic finale.

51

Soon after the Eichmann trial many Treblinka survivors were contacted about planned West German trials of former camp officers.

The German investigations had been organized not by specific perpetrators but by the site of the crimes: Auschwitz, Majdanek, Treblinka.

A trial of former Treblinka SS men was held in Dusseldorf, West Germany, between October 1964 and August 1965. Ten men were tried. Among them was Kurt Franz, the infamous "Lalka"; Arthur Matthes, chief officer of Camp Two who supervised the gas chambers; as well as Gustav Munzberger, Franz Suchomel, and Kurt Kuttner, the chief officer of Camp One.

Though none of the Wachmanner were on trial, mention was made of the gas-chamber operators, Ukrainians named Ivan and Nikolai. Munzberger said that after the dismantling of Treblinka he had served in Trieste with Ivan. He had no idea what had become of him. There was a rumor he had been killed by the partisans.

West German law confined the trials to strictly personal guilt and individual excessive actions, above and beyond the Nazi framework. There was no guilt for complicity and conspiracy or for "following orders" at Treblinka. Kurt Franz, who recalled Treblinka as "the best years of my life," was sentenced to life imprisonment with three other defendants. Five others were given lesser sentences of three to twelve years. One, Otto Horn, was acquitted.

Horn, a former male nurse in the euthanasia operation, had been assigned to the death camp at Treblinka where he supervised the incinerations. Charged as an accessory to murder, there was no proof of "excessive actions" on his part such as voluntary stabbing or killing. Holocaust survivors spoke in his defense. But as one of them later recalled, "Let's just say that from among all of them, he was less evil."

Franz Stangl, the commander of Treblinka, was tried in Dusseldorf in 1970 and sentenced to life imprisonment. He died in prison, of a heart attack, a few months after the end of the trial.

Shortly before his death, Stangl was interviewed at length by British journalist Gitta Sereny who would write one of the most authoritative books about Treblinka, "Into that Darkness" one of the few works of investigative journalism to focus on one of the mass- murdering perpetrators of the Holocaust.

Survivors were shocked at the Dusseldorf trials to learn that Germans whom they believed were killed in the revolt, such as Matthes and Kuttner, were in fact alive. The revolt had started when one of the inmates shot Kuttner, and there he was sitting in the dock. "When I saw him there in court," one witness said, "I had such a shock that they had to stop the court proceedings for a half-an-hour until I could regain my composure."

It was difficult for those who attended the trial in Dusseldorf to believe such creatures had been allowed to continue to walk the earth; that it had taken nearly two, almost three, decades to find them and bring them to justice. Kurtz Franz had lived undisturbed in his native city for fourteen years before he was arrested; Franz Stangl, though officially registered at the Austrian Consulate in Sao Paulo, Brazil, couldn't be "located" until 1967, twenty-two years after the end of World War II. How could that be?

3. Nazis in America?

Following World War II, many Holocaust survivors, determined to leave the past behind, emigrated to the United States. The few who spoke of their private hell did not find many who wanted to listen, and fewer still who believed them. The crimes of the Nazis were past. Hitler couldn't happen in America.

But others could not leave the past behind. It followed them everywhere, in their waking hours and in their sleep. When they read the newspapers, they clipped articles. They sought the few others who could understand where they had come from and what they had been through. They searched for lost relatives and friends. They hunted for news. They corresponded and met in European-style cafes to gossip. Who had lived? What had become of him or her?

For the past, they had their own shorthand. A glimpse of numbers tattooed on a forearm told the story; others let it be known that they, too, had suffered, or that they had suffered more.

Their primary interest, however, was not what they had been through, but how they were getting along. Who was a success? Who wasn't? Who had kids? Who didn't? The Old World nightmares had been their past; the American Dream was their future.

After the war, the Immigration and Naturalization Service (INS) began to receive allegations of Nazis living in America. Field agents were instructed to investigate each accusation. But there was no policy for prosecuting illegal Nazi aliens. The reports were treated like any case of fraud or misrepresentation, as if Nazis were no different than quislings or prostitutes who had falsely entered the country.

Cases involving Nazis were not easy to document or

prosecute, much less win. Proper investigation required extensive historical background. Budgets were small. Hence the priority was low. Even the Eichmann trial, which attracted international coverage when it was held in Jerusalem in 1962, had virtually no impact on prosecutions in the United States.

By 1970, a poll taken by the Union of Hebrew American Congregations found that Jewish students had little interest in the Holocaust. It seemed ancient history at a time when Vietnam and Cambodia were being bombed daily.

All this would change, however, by the end of 1970s. Major universities would start Jewish history departments with over-subscribed offerings on the Holocaust. Congress would enact national days of remembrance for the Holocaust, and commemorative ceremonies would be held in many major cities. A national Holocaust Memorial and Museum on the Mall in Washington, D.C., would follow and Holocaust archives and memorials would be built across the country.

For the most part, the survivors themselves deserve credit. They realized time was running out. In the late 1970s, anti-Semitic incidents increased worldwide, as documented by the Anti-Defamation League. Simultaneously, revisionist historians claiming that the Holocaust had not occurred began to receive national media attention. Enraged, the survivors spoke up, and now found people ready to listen. They asked the world not to forget. Nazis were living in America. Why didn't the government do anything about it?

No one played a more pivotal role in advancing the prosecution of Nazi war criminals than Congresswoman Elizabeth Holtzman. In April 1974, Holtzman held a press conference and accused the government of failing to investigate and prosecute known Nazi war criminals living in the United States. From that moment on, she relentlessly goaded the government to action.

Before 1975, there was no systematic effort to investigate allegations of Nazi war criminals living in this country. The INS commissioner admitted that the government at the time had a list of fifty-three alleged Nazi war criminals, compiled primarily by the World Jewish Congress.

Holtzman, looked at the files: "It was appalling. It was no serious investigation. The most they ever did is to go interview the suspect or the person against whom the allegation was made and ask about their health. In some cases, there would be leads given to them and they would never follow up."

In response to Holtzman's charges, the State Department agreed to help secure evidence outside the United States, where it was more likely to be found. This meant not only Israel, where many of the survivors lived, but also Germany, the Eastern European countries, and the Soviet Union. This had never been done.

Contacts with the Soviet Union were established in June 1975 when Representative Joshua Eilberg of Pennsylvania, and other members of the House Judiciary Committee, including Holtzman, visited Moscow to discuss Jewish immigration. They met with the Soviet Deputy Procurator General but the talks produced little more than rhetoric. But when asked whether they would cooperate with American requests for information on Nazi war criminals, the Soviet response was unequivocal: Yes.

The Soviets had been interested in the prosecution of Nazi war criminals, or "Hitlerites," as the Soviets called them, since even before the end of World War II. The Soviet officials promised the American delegation that justice Department lawyers would be put in contact with their counterparts in the Soviet Union. Though the Soviets had been aiding the West Germans in their prosecutions of war criminals since the 1960s, this marked the first time since the Nuremberg trials that there was any cooperation with the United States.

In 1973 the INS had set up a one-man office in New York to investigate Nazi war criminals; by 1977 it agreed to establish a special five-attorney litigation task force to prepare cases. Those cases involving U.S. citizens would still be filed and argued by the local U.S. Attorney.

The American public confronted the survivors' plight in another way during the 1978 NBC broadcast of the miniseries, Holocaust, on four consecutive nights. Although reviews were mixed, no one denied that the Holocaust had become a proper discussion subject for all Americans. The survivors found themselves heroes.

Still, not much progress had been made as to Nazi prosecutions; a few cases had been filed, with mixed results. In 1978, Representatives Holtzman and Eilberg ordered the General Accounting Office (GAO), the investigative arm of Congress, to inspect all records of the INS pertaining to alleged Nazi war criminals.

The GAO concluded that from 1946 to 1973 the INS had received allegations of possible former Nazi activity concerning fifty-seven people in the United States; charges were filed in only nine cases. Of these nine, three were lost at trial. Of the six that were won, the INS Board of Appeals reversed three. The GAO further found that in two out of three cases the INS investigators had not done an adequate job. There was, however, no evidence of a conspiracy. Rather, the INS failure was a matter of bureaucratic neglect.

The Holtzman-Eilberg investigations led to a political and public consensus for new action, no matter how late. Eilberg was defeated for reelection in 1978, but Elizabeth Holtzman kept her seat. As the new chair of the House subcommittee on immigration, she wanted the INS to have nothing further to do with the prosecution of Nazis. "It was impossible for a unit to function effectively within the Service because of the bureaucracy and the red tape and the general low morale within that agency." Specifically, she wanted the Justice Department to assume responsibility.

That wish was granted. On March 28, 1979, Representative Elizabeth Holtzman announced Attorney General Griffin Bell's decision to establish within the Criminal Prosecution Division of the Justice Department, the Office of Special Investigations (OSI), a unit specifically charged with investigating and prosecuting alleged Nazi criminals. The OSI annual budget was only 1 percent of the total justice Department budget ($2.3 million); yet it was enough to fund an eclectic and committed staff of historians, researchers, and litigators.

A few years earlier, in 1975, the INS had received a list of possible Ukrainian Nazi collaborators at large in the U.S. Demjanjuk's name was among them, and he was listed as having been a guard at Sobibor. The list was compiled by Michael Hanusiak, an editor of the Ukrainian Daily News, a pro-Soviet newspaper published in New York.

Hanusiak, who was in his seventies when I met with him at his offices in New York's East Village, (he has since died), was raised in the United States, the son of Ukrainian immigrants. In 1969 the Ukrainian American League offered him a trip to revisit his parents' homeland. This proved an emotional experience for Hanusiak, he said.

In the early 1970s, Hanusiak returned several times to the Ukraine. At that time, he was working for the Ukrainian Daily News, a member of the Society for Cultural Exchange, a Soviet organization that promotes contact between the U.S. and the Ukraine, and who, Hanusiak said, got him the access and contacts necessary to conduct research in the Soviet Union into Nazi collaborators at large in the United States. He combed through newspaper archives, met with Soviet journalists, Polish attorneys, and editors of the Soviet News from Ukraine, also a member of the Society. By the mid-1970s Hanusiak had compiled a list of seventy alleged Nazi collaborators living in the United States.

One of them, Ivan Demjanjuk, was described as currently living in Cleveland and as also being known as Demjanjuk, Ivan Nikolayevich (the son of Nikolai), born on April 3, 1920, in the Ukrainian village of Dub Macharenzi. Demjanjuk was sought for having allegedly: "Volunteered for the German SS troops and Security Police. Underwent training in the German training camp in town of Trawniki, Poland. In this camp those trained became masters in the art of hanging and torturing of civilians. From March 1943 served as a Wachmann with the SS unit in the town of Sobibor, Poland and later (from October 1943) served as a guardsman in the concentration camp in the town of Flossenburg, Germany. Personally, participated in the mass executions of the Jewish population in the death camp Sobibor in Poland."

Also on the list was another Ukrainian, Fedor Fedorenko, living in Connecticut. He, too, was accused of being trained at Trawniki and serving as a high-ranking guard at Treblinka.

We will never know how Hanusiak received this information. When I interviewed him, he could not recall, saying it may have come from one of the lawyers he met with in the Soviet Union or from a Soviet publication. Hanusiak was interviewed in 1979 for Cleveland Magazine by Mark Gottlieb where he said he found the allegations against Demjanjuk in the Soviet War Archives in Kiev. Whether the ultimate source of this information was the KGB, as has often been alleged, or an arm of the Soviet Judiciary remains unknown.

Did it serve the Soviet agenda to announce that Nazis remained at liberty, unprosecuted, in the United States? Undoubtably. But that did not mean the information wasn't correct.

Regardless, what we do know with certainty is what

Hanusiak did with the information.

In October 1975, Hanusiak sent his list of alleged Nazi collaborators to Senator Jacob Javits of New York and Senator Abraham Ribicoff of Connecticut. On November 6, 1975 Senator Javits confirmed receipt of the list and noted that he forwarded it to the Immigration Service's newly created task force for the investigation of Nazi war criminals.

By late November 1975, the investigation had begun in earnest. Before the end of the year, the INS set about locating and interviewing survivors of Sobibor. Progress was slow.

Investigators learned Demjanjuk's current address from the Cleveland telephone directory and verified that he lived with his wife and children in nearby Seven Hills. Without giving out any names, the Cleveland INS office began to contact Jewish organizations and survivor groups to locate potential witnesses. The New York office also contacted Jewish organizations they thought might be helpful.

But the INS thought it best not to confine its search for witnesses to the United States alone. Maurice F. Kiley, the New York INS District Director, wrote in mid-March to the Israel Police. The letter enclosed photos and information, asking assistance in the investigation of several alleged Ukrainian Nazi war collaborators, including Demjanjuk and Fedorenko.

4.Ivan of Treblinka

Israel's Special Unit of the Israel Police for the investigation of Nazi crimes assigned the cases sent by the INS to Miriam Radiwker, one of the unit's most adept investigators.

Radiwker, who would testify at length at the Israeli trial had arrived in Israel in 1964. Born in Poland, she had been an attorney in Russia before emigrating. Her legal background as well as her ability to speak Polish, Russian, German, and Hebrew, helped her obtain a position with the unit. More important was her sensibility: as a Polish Jew herself, Radiwker could understand the language of the camps and of the survivors.

Radiwker reviewed the INS files. She had received nine names, seven of whom had been active only in the Ukraine. There was only a slight chance of obtaining information in Israel about their crimes. The other two, Fedorenko and Demjanjuk, had been active in Nazi-Occupied Poland. Perhaps she could find survivors who could identify them.

First she placed a notice in the Jewish press: survivors with information about the activities of either Fedor Fedorenko of Treblinka or an Ivan Demjanjuk of Sobibor, two Ukrainian camp guards, were asked to come forward. She received no response.

She then decided to summon witnesses herself. She began her investigation with Fedorenko. She believed she was more likely to find persons who could identify a high-ranking Treblinka guard accused of mass murders. Demjanjuk was a lesser priority because there were fewer survivors of Sobibor, and Demjanjuk's role in the killings was not clear.

The Nazi war crimes unit maintained photo albums of suspects, called "photospreads," cataloged by nationality. The photospreads were an investigative tool, used like a police book of mugshots to locate witnesses. The photos sent by the INS, including Demjanjuk's 1951 visa photo and Fedorenko's 1949 visa photo, were pasted onto pages and placed in the album, labeled "Ukrainians." The photographs were all passport-type portraits, head-and-shoulders shots of men, more often than not, in coat and tie. Demjanjuk's and Fedorenko's photos were numbers sixteen and seventeen, respectively, and appeared among five others on page three of the album. Potential witnesses would be asked if they could identify anyone.

Radiwker, who had worked with two Treblinka survivors on another case, called them back in.

Eugen Turovsky came to her office on the morning of May 9. Radiwker asked him to recall his experiences at Treblinka. She asked if he recalled any Ukrainians. Then she showed him the photospread. "Please, sir," she said, "look at these, maybe you find anyone you know?"

Turovsky looked over the first page, and then the second, but when he came to the third, he became agitated. "That's Ivan!" He said, "That's Ivan of Treblinka."

Treblinka? Her information put Demjanjuk at Sobibor. Turovsky had made a mistake, surely. But Radiwker said nothing. Turovsky wanted to talk at length about this Ivan. She said he could return tomorrow to do so, but first he must calm down and see if he recognized anyone else. Turovsky then identified Fedorenko.

She summoned Avraham Goldfarb that afternoon. He had built the large gas chamber at Treblinka, and later carried corpses to the pits. He was now in his seventies. He found the photo of Demjanjuk familiar, even though he was in civilian clothes and older. It was, Goldfarb said, the Treblinka death camp guard who had "caused the gas to flow from the diesel engine into the gas chambers." The engine was located near the well at which Goldfarb worked: "I approached the well during the time that the same Ivan was pushing people into the gas chambers. He did this in the most cruel manner. We, the workers, nicknamed him Ivan Grozny, Ivan the Terrible."

Radiwker decided to confront Goldfarb about her information that put Demjanjuk at Trawniki and Sobibor. About Sobibor and Trawniki he could not say, but about Treblinka he was sure: "I can say that during 1942-43 he certainly was at Treblinka. But before the uprising in the summer of 1943, he already was not, as I recall, at Treblinka."

Goldfarb could not forget this man. "I saw clearly how he pushed the victims into the gas chambers with iron sticks and a bayonet. Even with his knife he cut the flesh off living people. I saw with my own eyes how, at the entrance to the gas chambers, he cut with his knife pieces of flesh from living people. I also saw that he cut the ears of those workers who were busy near the gas chambers at the times the bodies were removed." He had witnessed these events, he said, "from a distance of a few meters."

The next morning, Radiwker opened up a separate investigative file on Demjanjuk.

When Turovsky returned, she asked him if he knew the name Demjanjuk. "I am familiar with the name Demjanjuk," he said, "but even more so with the first name Ivan. I can well remember this Ukrainian. I knew him personally because he sometimes came into the shop to repair something."

He was shown the photos again. Again, he pointed to Demjanjuk's photo. "That is Ivan," he declared. "Him, I recognize immediately and with perfect certainty." Turovsky gave a detailed physical description of the Ivan he knew: "Even then his hair looked the way it is here in the photograph, a high forehead starting to bald."

Turovsky had no access to the death camp, so could not, from personal observation, describe Ivan at work. But

Turovsky said he saw Ivan when he passed through the workshop and near his living quarters. He also saw Ivan when he and other guards caught Jews and dragged them from the woods into the camp.

Radiwker decided to call another Treblinka survivor, Eliahu Rosenberg, whose testimony she knew from the Eichmann trial. He told her he couldn't leave his job at the Ashdod Port. She offered to visit him.

The next day, in Rosenberg's office, Miriam Radiwker followed her usual procedure. When she showed the Ukrainian album to Rosenberg, asking him if he "recognized anybody," he singled out Demjanjuk. "That man looks very similar to the Ukrainian Ivan. I see great similarity with Ivan who was active in Camp Two and whom they call Ivan Grozny." Rosenberg was not willing to identify him with certainty-the man in the picture was older and in civilian dress. Ivan, at the time he knew him, was maybe twenty-two to twenty-three years old and always in uniform. But he was struck by the likeness. The distinctive facial construction was the same, the incipient balding at such a young age, the ears sticking out. Rosenberg believed that should he see Ivan, alive, before him now -- he would recognize him.

Radiwker explained that her information placed the man he pointed to not at Treblinka, but at Sobibor. Rosenberg replied that although in the course of 1942 some Ukrainians were known to have been sent to Sobibor, he had seen Ivan until the last day at Treblinka. Radiwker asked if Ivan acted independently or on orders of higher officials.

"I can state with certainty," Rosenberg said, "that such cruelties and such sadistic murders as he perpetrated each and every day, were certainly not done by orders.... I saw from a distance of about four meters [thirteen feet] as he cut up people with his sword, mostly women on their naked bodies. This he certainly did on his own initiative.... [He] directly

64

participated in the gassing. This I saw each and every day in the nearest proximity. I was not farther away than one or two meters from him. It was there I worked. I saw he shot a worker carrying corpses.... I personally received thirty whippings at a roll call [from him] because I had purloined a small piece of bread. There was a time when he ordered me to perform a sexual act with a dead woman who had been pulled out from the gas chambers. He was drunk at the time and I knew that it meant my death, because I was unable to commit such an act. The German Scharfuhrer [staff sergeant] Loeffler saved me from him."

The photo left Rosenberg in shock. To see Ivan alive, healthy, fat, well fed! He could see nothing else before him but Ivan, Ivan, Ivan. He did not identify anyone else at that time. Radiwker wrote up his statement.

As the INS requested, she had been asking each survivor for the names of others who might have knowledge of Nazi collaborators. Rosenberg suggested Pinhas Epstein. Finally, she warned Rosenberg that to talk about an investigation in process would jeopardize it. That presented no problem, as Rosenberg later explained succinctly: "I am good at keeping secrets."

Radiwker wrote up her report of the three interviews and on May 14, her superior, Major Gershon Lengsfelder, forwarded the surprising results to the INS.

The Demjanjuk case was under way.

5.Dos Iz Ivan

John Demjanjuk often said that he knew nothing of the allegations against him until the day the government filed its complaint on August 25, 1977. But they should have come as no surprise.

Early in May 1976, Vera Demjanjuk received a call from a man asking to speak to her husband. John Demjanjuk wasn't at home. The caller refused to reveal the purpose of his call but said he would call again. He called twice more. Again, Demjanjuk wasn't there; again, the caller would not say why he was calling.

Within the week, however, he visited the Demjanjuks at home. As Vera told a reporter, he showed them his identification. He was Dirk Pauls, an official attached to the West German Consulate in Detroit. Repeatedly referring to the German telegram he held before him, Pauls said that John Demjanjuk was needed as a prosecution witness at a war crimes trial in Germany.

The trial, he said, related to wartime activity at two locations in Nazi-occupied Poland: Sobibor and Trawniki.

Vera and her husband were startled, confounded, and somewhat frightened by the German's statement. John Demjanjuk refused to go to Germany. He knew nothing about Sobibor or Trawniki. Surely Pauls had made a mistake. The name on the telegram, "John Nikolaiyevich Demjanjuk," he said, was not his. His name, he explained, was John Mikolayevich Demjanjuk.

Little did it matter that the former was just the Russian language equivalent of the latter Ukrainian patronymic, and that Demjanjuk himself had stated on his visa application that Nikolai was his father's name. The Demjanjuks told Pauls to leave. They insisted that he had found the wrong man. They insisted it was a case of mistaken identity.

By this time, the Cleveland INS office had begun its investigation of Demjanjuk. Agents were already interviewing survivors of Sobibor, but without success.

However, in late May 1976 when the INS received Miriam Radiwker's report on the identifications by Turovsky, Goldfarb, and Rosenberg that identified Demjanjuk as having served at Treblinka, the INS refocused its investigation and began contacting Treblinka survivors.

The INS also contacted the witnesses on Demjanjuk's naturalization application, two friends from the displaced persons (DP) camps. Both lived in the Cleveland area. The INS contacted them in early June 1976, asking if they knew anything about Demjanjuk's wartime activities.

Demjanjuk, they both said, had never spoken to them about the war. One couple said they thought John Demjanjuk was a very good man; that they would cry when they talked about how hard life had been in the Ukraine. Later they wondered to Demjanjuk why they had been questioned. He said he had no idea.

That INS agents were investigating alleged Nazi war criminals in the Cleveland area became the subject of radio programs and articles in the Cleveland Jewish News. Survivors of the camps with knowledge of atrocities were urged to come forward. A few responded, but there were none who personally knew Ivan the Terrible.

The INS also turned to Bessy Pupko, an indefatigable septuagenarian at the World Jewish Congress in New York. She provided a list of more than a dozen Treblinka survivors compiled from her own files. A few had since died; none of the others had been in the death camp. Of the thirteen interviewed, none could identify either Demjanjuk or Fedorenko.

The problem was that few survivors from Camp One knew Ivan, and the majority of those who did from Camp Two saw him only once -- as they entered the gas chambers.

Meanwhile, Miriam Radiwker continued her investigation in Israel. She was baffled by whether Demjanjuk had, in fact, been at Sobibor and she decided to summon some witnesses from that camp to see if they could provide some clue to the mystery.

Dov Freiberg came in May 30. Demjanjuk's 1951 visa photo reminded him of someone, but he wasn't sure. Meir Weiss, another Sobibor survivor, recognized no one.

Undeterred, Radiwker shifted her focus back to Fedorenko, calling survivors from Treblinka's Camp One.

On June 7, Shalom Cohen was shown Demjanjuk's photo and said it seemed familiar, but he couldn't identify him positively. He remembered that there had been a Ukrainian known as Ivan Grozny, but he was active only in Camp Two.

On July 4, she met with Shimon Greenspan, who recognized Fedorenko. But the next survivor, Arye Kudlik, didn't recognize anyone. Neither did Kalman Tideman, on August 17.

Then on September 21, Yossef Czarny came to her office. Czarny had survived Treblinka, and in 1945 ended up in Bergen-Belsen, where he met his future wife Frieda. In 1947 he obtained false documents to travel to Palestine clandestinely aboard the aptly named ship, Providence.

Neither Czarny, an accountant, nor his wife was comfortable talking about the war. It was, as Czarny later recalled, "a closed box."

Yet he had opened that box for the Dusseldorf trial and he was ready to do so again.

Czarny told Radiwker that he was born in Warsaw in 1926 and arrived at Treblinka having just turned sixteen. Czarny had been in Camp One where as a *Hofjuden,* a "Court-Jew," he had free access to the Germans' compound and the Ukrainians' kitchen. *Hofjuden* were Jewish workers used by the Germans to maintain the camp. They lived apart from and in better conditions than the other inmates.

When Radiwker placed the photo album of Ukrainian suspects before him, Czarny immediately, at first glance, pointed to the photo of Demjanjuk "*Dos iz Ivan!*" he blurted out excitedly in Yiddish. "*Ivan Grozny von Treblinka.* My God! He lives!"

Later, he told Radiwker, "Thirty-three years have gone by, but I recognize him at first sight with full certainty. I think I would recognize him even by night.... It is the same facial build, the same nose, the same eyes, the same forehead. There can be no mistake."

Radiwker told him that according to her information this man was not at Treblinka but at Sobibor. Czarny disagreed strongly: "This man is Ivan Grozny. He was in Treblinka until the last minute, until the uprising."

Czarny was confident: at the time he had been only four to five years younger than Ivan. He said Ivan was almost always drunk. And although Ivan worked at the gas chambers in the death camp, Czarny sometimes saw him at the transport reception.

She asked why he knew him with such certainty. Czarny answered: "He stood out and he distinguished himself. His terrible job was known. And his sadism was known. He was one of the most frightening images in the Treblinka camp, and, therefore, he will rest engraved in my memory forever and ever."

When he was over the shock of identifying Ivan, Radiwker asked Czarny if he recognized anyone else. He pointed to Fedorenko, saying that this man worked in Camp One but he did not recall his name. She took one statement regarding Fedorenko, and another about Demjanjuk.

On September 28, Radiwker interviewed Shlomo Hellman, who had been in Treblinka longer than anyone else she interviewed. Hellman, almost seventy, was retired. At Treblinka he had been part of the crew that built the large gas chamber and later carried corpses. He recalled Ivan Grozny as "a monster of a man."

Radiwker asked if he knew the name Demjanjuk. He responded, "It means nothing to me." Asked to describe Ivan he could only say, "He was tall in height, and as far as I recall was about thirty years old. I don't remember that he had any rank or insignias." Radiwker showed him five photos. Among them was the 1951 photo of Demjanjuk. He did not identify him.

The defense would later argue that Hellman, of all people, should have recognized Ivan, if Demjanjuk truly was he. But the prosecution would contend that Hellman's description of someone significantly older than Demjanjuk, reinforced an unfortunate truth: though he had not forgotten what had occurred, he was recalling a different person as Ivan Grozny. Fedorenko's photo struck him as familiar from Camp One, but, he said, "I can't tell you anything about him."

If Hellman's memory was imperfect, Radiwker could have little hope that Gustav Boraks, already in his early seventies, would do much better. Nonetheless, on September 30, she traveled to Haifa to see Boraks, who had arrived in Treblinka on Yom Kippur 1942, with his wife, two sons, and virtually all of his relatives including his brother and sisters. Boraks had been a barber, a skill that saved him upon arrival. The rest of the transport, including his entire family, was sent immediately to the gas chambers. Boraks was put to work cutting the hair of the naked women on their way to the gas chambers.

Questioned by Radiwker, Boraks answered that he was familiar with the Ukrainian known as Ivan Grozny.

When shown eight photographs from the police album, he pointed to the photo of Demjanjuk: "This is the photo of Ivan Grozny. I recognize him with one hundred percent certainty. I recognize him from his facial features. He was younger then, up to twenty-five years old. The face was not as full, but I have no doubt it is he."

Boraks had full opportunity to observe Ivan. "I saw him daily at the gas chambers as he brutally herded people into the gas chambers.... I was an eyewitness," Boraks said, "as Ivan Grozny shot some Jewish workers. It was not long before the uprising in the summer of 1943. There were few transports. We barbers did not have daily work and were taken several times a week to work in the woods. Ivan Grozny, together with a German SS man, went with us. We had to cut down trees. The branches were used for camouflage. The heavy tree trunks had to be carried into the camp. Ivan Grozny ordered us to run with the logs on our shoulders. If someone collapsed under the heavy burden, Ivan shot him on the spot. I saw a number of such cases from close up."

Radiwker's case was growing stronger and stronger. She had one more survivor to interview on October 3, Avraham Lindvasser. He had been a "dentist" in the camp and had worked daily near the gas chambers. Lindvasser, who was born in 1919 in Warsaw, left his hometown on August 28, 1942, on a large train bound for Treblinka. Of the thousands on the transport, Lindvasser told Radiwker, "Only two were separated to work. I, who claimed to be a dentist, and an electronics engineer." The rest were gassed to death.

Did he recall a Ukrainian at the camp by name of Ivan Demjanjuk? "I am not familiar with the name Demjanjuk," he said. "I remember a Ukrainian whose nickname was Ivan Grozny-the Terrible. He was active in Camp Two and I will never forget him." Radiwker showed him the eight photographs and Lindvasser had a strong immediate reaction to Demjanjuk's. "This is Ivan. I identify him with full confidence. That is his nose, his eyes, and his mouth."

Lindvasser said he had constantly worked near him: the dentist cell bordered "Ivan's actual workp l a c e "-the engine room. And he could not forget Ivan's "personal sadism." He told Radiwker, "He was not named Ivan the Terrible for nothing."

The three new identifications of Demjanjuk as Ivan Grozny of Treblinka-by Czarny, Boraks, and Lindvasser-were mailed to the INS. Miriam Radiwker retired soon thereafter.

6.The Charges Against Demjanjuk

The first known public accusation against Demjanjuk by name appeared not in the U.S. or in Israel but in the USSR, in Ukrainian, on August 26, 1976, in an article, "At Different Poles," in the Soviet weekly, *Visti z Ukraini* (News from Ukraine).

The article stated that: "Dem'yanyuk[sic], who lives in the United States of America (3326 New Avenue, Parma, Ohio), does not like to talk about his past. But documents and witnesses talk about it."

Demjanjuk, the article claimed, surrendered to the Germans and ended up himself in a camp. "No, not the one where the Soviet prisoners were held, but where the Fascists trained men for punitive units." The accusations were supported by claims of documentary proof: "Certificate of Service Number 1393 issued by the Trawniki (Poland) training camp in the name of Demjanjuk Ivan Mikolayevych, born in 1920, which bears his photograph, has been preserved among captured German documents."

The document proved, the article contended, that its bearer served from 22 September 1942 at "the Okshu scaffold" and from 27 March 1943 in the Sobibor death camp (Poland)."

Not only was there documentary proof but also the testimony of a colleague, one Danylchenko, who was quoted as saying: "I first met and became acquainted with Demyanyuk [sic] Ivan in March 1943 in the Sobibor death camp (Poland), where he served in the SS secret forces as a Wachmann [guard]...."

Danylchenko goes on to say that Demjanjuk wore an SS uniform, was armed, and participated in the mass murders of Jews at Sobibor, guarding and conveying them to the gas chambers. Danylchenko also stated that in the spring of 1944,

73

he and Demjanjuk were sent to be guards at concentration camps in Flossenburg and Regensburg, Germany.

The article concluded: "Up to the last days of the war the Fascist toady served his masters faithfully; he went abroad after their total defeat.... Today the residents of Parma [a suburb of Cleveland] in the USA know Mr. Demjanjuk as an ordinary automobile inspector. And probably they do not know that in greeting him they are extending their hands to a murderer of innocent people who has escaped just punishment."

The article was puzzling in many respects: Like American-Ukrainian editor Michael Hanusiak's 1975 allegations, it only referred to Demjanjuk's wartime service at Trawniki and Sobibor and did not mention Treblinka. For the first time there was mention of documentary proof: a numbered Trawniki service certificate   in Demjanjuk's name, bearing his photograph; and the   testimony of a former guard, Danylchenko, who testified at an unexplained "preliminary investigation."

Hanusiak said later that Danylchenko was thought to have been tried for war crimes in Kiev in 1955 and that it was from Danylchenko's testimony that Demjanjuk's wartime activities became known to Soviet authorities. Trials of Soviet nationals who had served the Nazis in the death camps had been held in Russia as recently as the early 1960s. There was no information as to whether Danylchenko had, in fact, been put on trial in the Soviet Union, or if he was still alive – if he existed at all.

Although the article was published in August 1976, it would not come to the attention of American authorities until months later. By the fall of 1976, INS investigations in Cleveland had received substantial attention in the local newspapers and on television. Though no names or biographical data had been revealed, it must have been obvious to John Demjanjuk that they were talking about him. Finally, he was asked to appear at his local INS office to discuss allegations about his past with

U.S. attorneys.

The meeting was scheduled for October 19, 1976. Demjanjuk appeared with his attorney, John Martin, a former Cuyahoga County prosecutor who had been recommended to the Demjanjuks by friends from work.

The man who was accused of being the fearsome Ivan the Terrible of Treblinka sat meekly outside the prosecutor's office. His head down, he appeared more like an overgrown child waiting to see the principal than a war criminal.

Martin explained to the U.S. attorneys that Demjanjuk had come to him only that morning and therefore he was not prepared to represent him. A new date, a month later, was set. But the day before, Martin sought another delay.

In January 1977, Jay Bushinsky, the Chicago Daily News's correspondent in Tel Aviv, interviewed several of the survivors who had identified Demjanjuk. He was most impressed by Lindvasser, who died only a few months after Bushinsky interviewed him.

Bushinsky's report was published in the Chicago Daily News in October 1977. Lindvasser was quoted as saying:

"I can still see "Ivan the Cruel" whipping out his sword and swinging at those poor defenseless people, slashing and shoving and screaming at them until all of them were forced inside the chamber. And then he would slam the door shut, check it once to make sure it was closed tight, and then walk calmly down the flight of steel stairs to the basement where the machinery of death was located.

"Once he got there, he would turn on the motors that manufactured the carbon-monoxide gas that went directly into the chambers. Within half an hour, all six hundred or seven hundred people in the three chambers would be dead.

Lindavasser said that the basement below the three gas

75

chambers was known as "Ivan's area. "I saw this beast of a man turn on the motors so often that it pains me now, more than thirty years later, to even think about it," he said. "To do so is almost like killing me."

Lindvasser's work area as a "dentist" looked down upon Ivan's area. "People ask me now, how I could stand it-with all of those horrible things happening so near. With all of the terrible screaming and dying. I will tell you one thing we did. We worked with these little hammers, and every time they would put people in the chambers to die, we would start our hammering, all together, so that we would not be able to hear those terrible sounds of death. So, people went out of this world hearing that strange hammering of ours in the background.... And this man, Ivan, now is living in your country of freedom. It is hard to believe, but it is true."

During 1977, the Demjanjuk matter moved along the legally required step-by-step procedure toward denaturalization. For months the necessary affidavits and approvals shuttled between Cleveland and Washington in Rube Goldberg-like fashion. To all who knew him, Demjanjuk gave no sign that he was even under investigation. Probably, he hoped the inquiries would disappear like the man from the German Consulate.

But on August 25, 1977, the U.S. Attorney for the Northern District of Ohio filed a six-page, six-count complaint that stated that Demjanjuk had not only lied on his immigration papers, but had the truth been known -- that he was Ivan the Terrible of Treblinka -- he surely would have been denied entry to the United States.

In bringing the case to court, the U.S. Attorney would seek to show not only that Demjanjuk lied on his application, but that his lies were incriminating. But first the government would have to show exactly where Demjanjuk had been during the war years.

Lawyers needed to figure out how Demjanjuk had gone from a small village in Ukraine to service in the Treblinka death camp and possibly Sobibor as well. They would also examine the answers Demjanjuk gave on the forms he filled out when applying to enter the United States, he had filled out his forms as he did. In trying to understand why Demjanjuk answered he did, and where he was during the war years, the INS would find information from a surprising source: Fedor Fedorenko.

7. Federenko's Route.

Fedor Fedorenko was living in Waterbury, Connecticut, and was also being investigated by the INS. On May 25, 1976, Fedorenko appeared at the INS Hartford office, at its invitation, to discuss his visa entries for the war years.

Initially, Fedorenko had contended that the INS was investigating the wrong person. Now, he admitted that he had been at Treblinka, but he denied being a high-ranking guard or committing any atrocities. He had written on his immigration papers that he spent the war years in a town named Pelz. That was not entirely true. The clerk who had taken down the information on his application had misheard him. What he meant was Poelitz. And there was more.

Fedorenko said he had been born in Ukraine, had been drafted into the Russian army, and in July 1941, had been captured by the Germans. After being held at POW camp Rovno for two weeks, he was taken to the Chelm camp in Poland, where he stayed for two months. There the Germans picked him and some others as drivers and technicians and took them to Trawniki.

Fedorenko said he spent some eight months at Trawniki and at the end of 1942 was taken with others to Treblinka, where he was trained in weapons and made a camp guard. Although he knew that thousands of Jews had died there, Fedorenko denied any involvement in the killing. He insisted that the Ukrainian guards did not act of their own volition and were not allowed into the death camp area.

However, he said that there were two exceptions: Ivan and Nikolai, who worked alongside the Germans.

Shortly after the uprising, in late 1943, Fedorenko claimed, he left Treblinka and was transferred to Danzig to be a concentration camp guard; and from there to a smaller camp,

78

Poelitz, a concentration camp for criminals. It was at Poelitz, he said, where he remained for a year, that he was a high-ranking guard.

Ultimately, Fedorenko would be shown to be lying about what he did at Treblinka, but not about the route he had taken. As to why he wrote Pelz on his immigration and naturalization forms, Fedorenko said that he wrote Pelz-and meant Poelitz-because Poelitz was not only the name of the camp, but the town nearby. If asked questions, he knew the town well. And that, was better than saying Treblinka.

Poelitz, Fedorenko reasoned, would be less known to investigators as a concentration-camp site; even if it were known, there would be only a slim chance that any survivor could identify him. Finally, even if he was found out to have served at the Poelitz concentration camp, his activities there were less damning than at Treblinka.

This would be of great interest to those trying to resolve why Demjanjuk had written on his application papers that he had spent part of his war years at a town named Sobibor.

8. The Paper Trail

How could Nazis be living in America?

"The overwhelming majority of Nazi war criminals," said former OSI Director Allan Ryan, "came through the front door, with all their papers in order."

After the war, hundreds of thousands of war-torn people from Eastern Europe found themselves with little interest in returning home. If they were Jewish, their homeland held few pleasant memories; if they were non-Jews, their countries had been overrun by Communists. The refugees came to live in displaced persons camps; they were called DPs. The camps, which dotted Europe, were mostly located in Germany and Austria. Responsibility was divided among the Four Powers (the U.S., UK, France, and the USSR), and shared by the United Nations International Refugee Organization (IRO).

The DP camps became small cities of immigrants caught in a holding pattern between their past and their future. For some , such as the victims of the war, the DP camps were a refuge; for others, the perpetrators of those crimes, the camps were a haven where they hoped to assimilate into the masses.

There were few, if any, records of Nazi collaborators. What records existed-such as at the Berlin Documentation Center, and those in the UN archives-were German SS confiscated records. No one was much interested in the collaborators.

At the DP camps, it was easy enough to hide your past; all you needed to claim was that your identity-papers had been destroyed or had disappeared in the war; the IRO would then issue an affidavit of lost papers and a new identity certificate.

Before one could apply for a visa to a foreign country, one had to be certified as a DP by the IRO. Its constitution specifically denied DP status to any war criminal, or person

80

who voluntarily aided enemy forces.

The IRO screenings, however, were at best superficial: the investigators questioned; the applicants answered. Unless the applicant admitted complicity in crimes, or gave obviously false information, he became a DP. In the American zone of Germany, the U.S. Army administered the camps with the IRO. As the camps swelled in the immediate postwar years, it became apparent that the DP problem had to be dealt with.

Though the Soviet Union considered anyone born in a country now under its rule still a citizen, the U.S. would not allow forcible repatriation for anyone who did not wish to live under Communist rule. The United States slowly began to open its doors to an increased number of immigrants.

In 1948, Congress passed the Displaced Persons Act (the DP Act) that allowed hundreds of thousands of immigrants to arrive on American shores. But many felt that the DP act was written to provide relief to everyone but Hitler's victims --the Jews.

The DP Act was administered by three commissioners. Among them was Edward M. O'Connor, a thirty-nine-year-old New Yorker who had been very involved in Catholic relief in the U.S. and in Europe. He had lobbied strongly in favor of increased admission for Ukrainians and Balts.

As commissioner, O'Connor approved the admission of members of the Waffen SS units and was criticized for favoring admission for Hitler's supporters over his victims. The Balts and Ukrainians were strongly anti-Communist --saving them from return to the Soviet Empire seemed a noble task. That some, as Red Army defectors, may have served on the side of the Germans, did not appear sufficient reason to O'Connor to deny them admission.

But Commissioner Harry Rosenfield, who never saw eye-to-eye with O'Connor on this point, later said, "He felt they were given a bum steer; I felt a lot of them were bums."

Edward O'Connor continued to be a vocal supporter of the "captive nations," as he called them, the rest of his life. Forty years later, his son, Mark, would be Demjanjuk's defense attorney.

To apply for a U.S. visa, the applicant was required to undergo a second screening by an American investigator. The DP Act and U.S. immigration law made it clear that citizenship would not be given to Nazis or Nazi collaborators. But the only security check was against counterintelligence (CIC) records and the records of the Berlin Documentation Center. Anyone who passed the IRO screening could tell the same tale without fear of greater scrutiny. The overwhelming majority of applicants were approved. Visas in hand, they set out for their new lives.

In the years following World War II, among the hundreds of thousands who rightfully came to the U.S. were many Nazi collaborators. The exact number will never be known, though estimates range from several hundred to ten thousand. The same disdain for life under Communist rule that had led them to collaborate with the Fascists was their admission ticket to the U.S. And their anti-Communism would serve them in good stead in America in the 1950s; accusations of Nazi service would be brushed off as a "Communist plot," or a "KGB conspiracy." But it was not anti-Communism that made them Nazi war criminals; it was their murderous service and that they had to hide.

There were few documents, if any, that could prove their crimes. And to find those few documents, one had to know where to look. And to find and receive documents held in foreign archives was beyond the competency of most INS agents.

Who else could provide evidence of their wartime

crimes? Their SS superiors? Their fellow collaborators? Not likely. Their victims? So few had lived. Most never even knew their real names. Anyhow, who would believe them? It would just be one person's word against another's. And as the years passed, who would still care?

Nazi war criminals, Allan Ryan would say, "came here not by conniving with lawless government officials, but by the infinite easier method of simply deceiving the honest ones."

We go through life never thinking that we may have to prove we were here, or more to the point, that we were not there. But as we make our way we also unwittingly leave behind a paper trail --filling out forms for the present, with the answers of the moment-- never thinking it will later come back to haunt us.

Investigators turned to what could be ascertained about John Demjanjuk without speaking to him, to the details of his immigration and naturalization forms. Forms for which Demjanjuk himself had supplied the answers.

Shortly after the war's end, in 1945, Demjanjuk entered a displaced persons camp in Landshut, Germany. He was still known as Ivan Demjanjuk.

It was in the DP camp, two years later, that he met his future wife, Vera. She was a Ukrainian DP, five years his junior, who had been sent out of her native Ukraine as a forced laborer. She spent the war years working in Germany as a housecleaner.

Their courtship was brief. At that time, Vera was still married to another DP, Eugene Sakowski. As Sakowski would later relate, he and Vera had been married on May 1, 1947. A few months later, he was sent from the DP camp to work for three weeks in Belgium. Upon his return, he discovered that his wife was living with another man, Ivan Demjanjuk. They were divorced shortly thereafter.

On September 1, 1947, Ivan Demjanjuk was married to Vera Kowlowa. They moved to the Regensburg DP camp. He was about to begin a new life.

A few weeks later he signed up for a driving course, the prerequisite for a license. He passed with no problem. The license has a handsome photo; it bears his signature, no longer in Cyrillic script, but in Latin characters.

License in hand, he found a job driving trucks for the Americans and working in the motor pool. The Americans found him to be a skilled driver; he drove their trucks long distances, crisscrossing Germany; sometimes traveling alone. He drove eight hundred miles in a day, he would brag later.

In early 1948, Demjanjuk began to fill out forms. First he told the camp police he had lost his personal papers. They issued him a certificate attesting to that; then a few days later he received an ID card from the IRO.

Demjanjuk then applied for assistance and certification from the IRO, the first step in the screening procedures that would lead to a visa out of the DP camps. His form is dated March 3, 1948. The four pages listed twenty-one questions. The form was to remain in IRO custody and be periodically updated. It was an important document. Demjanjuk filled it out for himself and his new wife.

Demjanjuk said he was born in Kiev, USSR. The form requested a listing of the towns, provinces, and countries in which he had spent the last twelve years; and how, by whom, and at what wages he had been employed during that time.

Demjanjuk, who had been born in 1920, stated that from 1935 until April 1937, he was a student, earning no wage, and living with his parents in Koziatyn [also known as Kazatin], USSR. But he also noted that his only schooling was attending grammar school in Koziatyn (Kiev) from 1927-30. Next he was a driver for the Firma Auto (an auto company), earning forty zlotys (Polish currency) in "Sobibor-Chelm-Poland"; and in January 1943 was deported to Germany.

From January 1943, until October 1944, Demjanjuk said he lived in Pilau, Germany, and worked at the Port for twenty Deutschmarks; after which he was transferred to Munich, Germany, where he worked at a warehouse and was paid in food only.

From May 1945 until July 1947, he was at Landshut-the DP camp-where he said he worked as a driver for UNWRA-IRO at the wage of one hundred Reichmarks. Since then he had lived at the Regensburg camp, where he was earning the same wage as a driver for truck company 1049 at the American military post.

He told the officer that his first choice was Argentina; Canada, his second. He didn't want to return to the Soviet Union because of "political and religious reasons." Demjanjuk was sure that as a skilled driver he could find work, as he put it, "in his profession."

The inspecting officer saw nothing in Demjanjuk's personal history to give pause. His story seemed straightforward. The IRO officer summarized: "In the year 1937 he fled from Koziatyn USSR to Poland. In Poland he was living till 1943. In the year 1943, deported to Germany. All the time worked in Germany to end of war. He wants to emigrate with his family to Argentina or Canada."

Only in retrospect can the form be scrutinized, and seen as suspicious, even incriminating. Only someone who knew a great deal about Holocaust history, and who knew Demjanjuk's personal history and later alibis in great detail, would be able to discern telling details hidden among his entries.

Consider the dates: Why mark the time with the months and years of April 1937, January 1943, October 1944, and May 1945? Was it a coincidence that April 1937 was when

Demjanjuk first began to work with tractor engines in the Soviet Union-eventually becoming a tractor driver and mechanic; that January 1943 was when the gassings took on a lesser pace at Treblinka so much so that in March 1943, he was transferred to Sobibor; that October 1944, was when he arrived at the Flossenburg concentration camp; and that May 1945 was when the war ended?

Why list places such as Sobibor, Chelm, and Pilau? Sobibor was the site of a death camp; Chelm, the POW transit camp from which Soviet prisoners were recruited for SS service, and which Demjanjuk would later claim as his alibi. And Pilau? Investigators would later learn that Pilau was a town near the Danzig port, where a small concentration camp existed, and where executions took place. Pilau was part of the Stutthoff complex of concentration camps, of which Poelitz (Fedorenko's alibi) had also been part.

Demjanjuk was listed on the form as a "skilled driver." Years later, Demjanjuk would deny he could operate a car until 1947. This, too, could be seen as incriminating. For throughout the form, he lists his employment as a driver --particularly during the time he was accused of being the mechanic for the gas chamber's diesel engine at Treblinka. The form says Demjanjuk worked after the war as a driver for the IRO itself. Why was he afraid to admit to being a "skilled driver"?

To emigrate to the United States, there had to be at least a sponsor or job waiting. The Demjanjuk family had grown with the birth of daughter Lydia in 1950. They waited with the hope that someone would request their help. In December 1951 they received word that a farmer in Decatur, Indiana, Donald Coulter, had applied that he would employ refugee aid on his farm.

Demjanjuk went to the American consulate in Stuttgart, on December 27, 1951, to fill out a visa application to the United States.

On this form he was again asked to give his residence since age fourteen. He changed the dates slightly, listing himself at Sobibor, Poland, from 1934 to 1943; at "Pilau, Danzig" from 1943 to September 1944; from then until the end of the war in Munich. After that he listed with precision all the DP camps he lived in, even if only for a few months-Landshut, Regensburg, Ulm, Ellwagen, Ulm (again), Bad Reichenall, and Feldafing.

He listed his occupation as driver, his nationality as Polish. He stated that he was able to speak, read, and write Ukrainian, German, and Polish. Asked to list his education, the form said, "total: 5 years" (on the IRO form he had put 1927 to 1930). The address of his parents Nikolai and Olga, he said, was not known. He gave his mother's maiden name as Martschenko.

This would later prove of interest, first of all because it was false. His mother's maiden name was Tabachuk. But Marshenko would later be revealed to be a name by which the gas chamber operator at Treblinka was known. And, later still, when Marshenko's own ID was discovered, it would create an even greater mystery as to why of all possible names to fabricate as his mother's maiden name, he chose Marshenko.

When asked if he had any identifying scars, Demjanjuk answered "scar on left hand." Actually, the scar was on the inside of his left arm-halfway between his elbow and his armpit-from where he had removed a blood group tattoo only a few years before. He also had a large scar several inches long, on his lower back near his spine, that he failed to reveal. He had been wounded while serving as a Red Army soldier. Some of the shrapnel was removed in 1941; the rest, in 1948.

A photo was required. Demjanjuk submitted a passport-sized photo of himself in jacket and tie. He looks smug, happy, confident. His face is full. His dark hair is close-cropped but there is a small tuft atop his head; his hairline recedes around it. His ears stick out.

It was this picture-taken eight years after the Treblinka uprising-that the survivors would see in the late 1970s; in which they would recognize the shape of the forehead, the face, recall the eyes, the neck, the shoulders, the build, the hairline of a person they once knew; upon which they would comment that he looked older, fatter. It was this picture that would make them gasp and say, "This is Ivan."

John, Vera, and Lydia Demjanjuk arrived in the United States in February 1952 aboard a troop ship, the W. G. Haan. The weeklong voyage was rough and crowded; they had to share a cabin with another family, a woman and her four children. But in later years Vera Demjanjuk would recall that when the ship entered New York harbor, and she saw the Statue of Liberty, she cried.

The Demjanjuks, speaking no English, carrying all their possessions in two boxes, traveled by train from New York to Decatur, Indiana. At the Coulter farm, home was a small, cold room of the farmhouse. John tended to a few pigs and sheep. There was not enough work on the farm to employ them full time. In letters to friends from the DP camps, living in nearby Cleveland, Vera told of the cold winter, and the odd jobs they did to make ends meet.

"They had a roof over their heads," Anne Lishuk would later recall, "but not much else. They barely survived. I remember Vera hardly had enough milk to feed the baby. When I wrote Vera that winter, I always put in a little money, because I know how bad it was for them."

Through new friends, the Underwoods, John Demjanjuk soon found a job as a mechanic in an auto-repair shop. But by summer, they were desperate to move. Their friends the Lishuks were living on the west side of Cleveland, among many fellow Ukrainians. William Lishuk had found a job at the Ford Motor Company plant on Brookpark Road, and heard it was expanding. The Demjanjuks decided to give Cleveland a try.

The Lishuks invited them to stay in their home until they got settled. William Lishuk even drove them from Decatur to Cleveland.

It was Vera who found work first, as a scrublady with the Federal Reserve Bank in downtown Cleveland. Soon after Lishuk took Demjanjuk to the Ford employment office and within the month, Demjanjuk was working as a mechanic in the engine hot-test department.

Before long, Demjanjuk rose to the position of "motor balancer." As a member of United Auto Workers of America local 1250, he had a steady job with high union pay, full benefits; he was entitled to overtime as well, which he frequently collected.

"He was always so good with his hands," recalled Gerald Kravchuk, another friend from the DP camps who had settled in Cleveland. "He was willing to work hard and there was a need for good mechanics. He got a pretty good job right away."

Vera also worked hard. She found work as a "coiler" in the General Electric plant.

That fall, the Demjanjuks were able to move into a two-room apartment at Seventh and College Avenue, in a Ukrainian neighborhood on the south side of the city. They went regularly to nearby St. Vladimir's Orthodox Church, built in 1924 by Ukrainians who had left Russia after the Communist Revolution. The church was the center of Ukrainian community life.

In August 1958, after having been in the United States for more than six years, Demjanjuk applied to become a naturalized U.S. citizen. He scrupulously entered the addresses of every home they had ever had in Cleveland, their employment history, all the personal details of their lives --even Vera's brief first marriage.

As to visible distinctive marks, the typed words "operation scar on back" had been crossed out, at his request; "scar on left wrist" was written instead. As one of the judges in Israel would remark, a suspicious person might think he had something to hide.

On November 14, Demjanjuk received his naturalization certificate. At that time Ivan Demjanjuk legally changed his name to John Demjanjuk. He was an American citizen. "It was the happiest day of our lives," Vera later told a reporter.

The next twenty years passed quietly, like a good night's sleep. At Demjanjuk's U.S. denaturalization hearing, almost forty people would offer to testify to his good character. They knew him from work, from church; some had known him since his first days in the United States.

A second daughter, Irene, was born in 1960; son, John Jr., in 1965. They were, in many ways, the picture-perfect immigrant family. John could be seen in his light blue Pinto, driving to work, like any other commuter. Often he worked the night shift; in the day he played with the kids. Other parents envied his ability to fix children's bikes. On the weekends, John mowed the lawn or gardened in his Bermuda shorts. On Sunday, the family went to St. Vladmir's Church.

The children grew up. They were good kids. The girls had their first Communion. John Jr. was an altar boy. Their future seemed bright. They grew up surrounded by community and friends. In 1976, Lydia was married at their church; more than two hundred well-wishers celebrated in St. Vladimir's new banquet room.

The Demjanjuks worked hard; they saved their money to live a better life. They moved many times, each time to a better neighborhood. By the mid-1970s, they had settled in the Seven Hills suburb. Like others on the block, their home was a ranch-style house on a half-acre lot. Two tall, leafy pines stood at the edge of the lawn, sheltering the Demjanjuks from the street. They bought another acre behind the house, "for the future." The inside was filled with Ukrainian handicrafts; group pictures of the three children hung above the fireplace.

The allegations shocked Demjanjuk's friends, one of whom described him as "one of the nicest men you'd ever want to meet. He's the kind of guy who would stop to help you fix a flat on the road, even if he didn't know you. Just a real sweet guy."

Father Stephen Hankevich of St. Vladimir's Ukrainian Orthodox Church told a reporter, "They are good, hard-working people."

"They have had a hard life," said Anne Lishuk. "They come to this country same as us, deaf and dumb. But they learn the language, and they work hard, and now their life should be good. It isn't fair.... For as many years as we've known Johnny, he never once said anything about all this. Even when we are sitting around with the vodka and telling stories, he never says anything about the war years. I don't believe it. It isn't fair."

Demjanjuk led a life of few risks, little danger. It begged the question: How could a person commit such acts of sadism and then live for thirty years as the perfect family man and community member? Wouldn't there be some evidence of rage or anger? There was none.

On the surface, John Demjanjuk's life in America offered no clues as to his past. Perhaps that was the point. Perhaps he had a reason to fear his past being found out. Perhaps there was a reason why Demjanjuk did nothing to call attention to himself, and why he sought, above all, not to be noticed.

9.Punishment Will Come

On the morning of August 25, 1977, John Demjanjuk was working at the factory as usual. At home the phones started ringing, and they would continue to ring all day. The children were the first to pick up and were stunned to hear reporters tell them that the U.S. Attorney wanted to strip their father of his citizenship for having been Ivan the Terrible of Treblinka, a Nazi war criminal, a brutal murderer of men, women, and children. Vera kept reporters at bay, but by the time Demjanjuk got home, photographers were waiting in the driveway.

The next day, newspapers published Demjanjuk's name for the first time. The Demjanjuk home was besieged by journalists from radio and TV. The Demjanjuks consented to one interview that afternoon with a reporter from a local television station, Bob Franken of WJKW-TV whose report aired that night on Channel 8. "The family wanted a chance to deny the allegations," Franken later told a reporter.

Demjanjuk sat on the family couch with his wife. He was wearing an open-neck short-sleeve shirt, and had on thick, black-rimmed glasses. Vera Demjanjuk wore a simple checked dress that belied her distraught look. The tension and stress upon both was apparent. They looked, in one reporter's words, "depressed, haggard, and close to hysteria."

From off-camera, Franken asked if the allegations were true. "No, no," answered Mrs. Demjanjuk. John Demjanjuk said in his thick accent, "I don't know nothing about it. I was not anyplace what they are writing now. I was German prisoner. I don't know nothing about it because ... nobody was here, just call me one time."

"Is not true! Is not true! Is not true!" Vera blurted out, then slumped against her husband's right shoulder. In the film frames, one can see that it took a few seconds before

Demjanjuk realized that she had fainted. Only when he lifted his right arm, intending to put it around her, did he realize she was unconscious. He immediately jumped to his feet, clasped his hands together at his chest, as if in pain himself, turned to look directly at the camera and began crying. Franken called an ambulance and Vera was taken to a hospital. Her blood pressure was abnormal. The next day John Demjanjuk removed the adhesive backed letters spelling his name on the mailbox and ordered an unlisted phone number.

Three-and-a-half years passed before the trial began in February 1981. The delay was caused by the fencing match that is the trial discovery process: the prosecution attempting to get information from the accused, to bolster its case with additional evidence; the defense finding out what the prosecution knew and trying to counter it.

The filing of charges received international attention. But perhaps no article was read with as much interest or would come to play as great a role in the case, as the September 1977 English language edition of News from Ukraine. It contained a quarter-page article on page three entitled, "Punishment Will Come."

The article began, "According to American press, the Department of Justice of the United States brought a criminal charge against war criminal Ivan Demyaniuk [sic] who after the war found refuge in the city of Cleveland and avoided just punishment for his murderous services which he obligingly offered to the Nazis" [the charges were actually civil in nature].

Written by the same journalist as the earlier Ukrainian article about Demjanjuk, it used many of the same phrases. But the source of the subsequent shock waves was not the article's contents but rather the illustration that accompanied it. The earlier piece had mentioned a Trawniki certificate number 1393 that had been issued to Ivan Demjanjuk. This time the certificate itself was reproduced.

93

In two separate photographs were the cover and inside leaf of what would come to be known as "the Trawniki card." The card itself was one piece of green cardboard, printed front and back, and folded across the middle to form a pocket-sized identity document. The cover, two inside leaves, and back cover, all carried important information.

Even more damning, the card bore, on its inside right side, the picture of a young soldier with a striking resemblance to John Demjanjuk.

It placed one Ivan Demjanjuk-one with the same nationality, birth date, place of birth, and father's name as John Demjanjuk-in 1942 at an SS camp, Trawniki, where Soviet war prisoners were recruited and trained for service at the extermination camps. The card said Ivan Demjanjuk had an identifying mark -- a scar on his back. And it listed his assignment in March 1943 to death camp Sobibor.

Though the INS had been trying to interview John Demjanjuk since 1976, he had been able to postpone any actual discussion of his war years until April 1978. Accompanied by his attorney, John Martin, Demjanjuk then met with assistant U.S. Attorney Joseph Cippolone in his Cleveland office.

Demjanjuk claimed to be unable to remember anything thirty-five years ago; but his memory was quite sharp on certain things, such as the series of hospitals he went to after he received his back wound before the battle of Kerch. He was a tractor driver before the war, he said, and a truck driver after.

As to his alibi for the time in question, he said that he was in two camps, Rovno, and another whose name he could not remember. He said he spent the time there building barracks.

Cippolone wanted him to acknowledge either that he had been a Communist Party member because he had served in the Red Army; or that he was a Nazi collaborator who had served at Sobibor or Treblinka. Demjanjuk repeatedly answered the charges with a curt "No."

10. They Treated Us Like We Were on Trial

The INS had asked the Israeli authorities to conduct more interviews. Miriam Radiwker had already retired, so the request was turned over to another investigator, Martin Kollar who was well suited to the task.

A native of Czechoslovakia, Kollar had served after the Second World War as part of the Czech legation to the Nuremberg trials. He moved to Israel in 1965 and soon found work with the Israel Police's war crimes unit. By 1978, he was an experienced member of the staff.

The INS wanted two other Treblinka survivors interviewed, Sonia Lewkowicz and Yakov Shmulewitz. Sonia Lewkowicz, who was born in 1922 in Poland and now lived in Tel Aviv, came to the Yaffo Police station on March 15, 1978. Lewkowicz told Kollar she had worked in the death camp's kitchen and its laundry. She recalled the Ukrainian Ivan who operated the gas-chamber engine: "Ivan was about twenty-five years old. I especially remember his stare, which was frightening. His behavior was the behavior of a man in a trance. He shouted very loudly. He never walked with empty hands. Sometimes with a riding whip, sometimes with a stick, another time with a metal pipe. He always beat on the inmates with everything he had in his fist. I saw this several times. I often hung the laundry on lines that were put up near the gas chambers and took it down after it dried...."

The INS had sent eight loose photographs, each numbered, to be shown one by one to the survivors, to see if they could be identified. The photographs were all of men in civilian dress of the same age. Lewkowicz recognized the visa photo of John Demjanjuk as Ivan, based on the curvature of his forehead. Fedorenko she recognized but could not name.

Kollar reread Radiwker's files and noticed that Rosenberg 96 had recommended she talk to Pinhas Epstein, another survivor. Kollar called Epstein to his office two weeks later.

During the interview, Epstein spoke so fast and with such passion that Kollar found he couldn't take verbatim notes, but when Epstein looked at the photos, Kollar took down his remarks word for word. Epstein examined them closely. When he got to Demjanjuk's picture, he stopped to concentrate. He said the picture was not sharp but it reminded him greatly of Ivan. He was struck by the shape of the face, the high arching forehead. Even the short neck on broad shoulders-this was exactly the way Ivan looked, he said. Then he turned to the photo of Fedorenko and identified it as a true likeness.

The Israel Police were also able to locate Georg Rajgrodski, a death-camp survivor living in Germany, and he, too, identified Demjanjuk as Ivan.

Meanwhile, in the U.S., Demjanjuk continued to deny that he was ever at Treblinka, and the prosecution and defense continued to delay his trial. But in Fedorenko's case the INS and the U.S. Attorney were ready to proceed with his denaturalization before the District Court in Ft. Lauderdale, Florida, where Fedorenko had retired.

Fedorenko had admitted to having been at Treblinka, but only as a perimeter guard. He said he was "forced" to serve the Germans and was innocent of the atrocities attributed to him. Fedorenko claimed that although he joined his fellow guards in shooting at inmates during the Treblinka uprising, he merely "shot over their heads."

The witnesses were many of the same who had identified Demjanjuk: Turovsky, Epstein, Czarny, and Lewkowicz. Israel Police investigators Miriam Radiwker and Martin Kollar also testified.

The witnesses, for the most part, did not speak English. The prosecutors did not speak Hebrew, German, or Yiddish, and were not familiar with the historical background of Treblinka or the background of the witnesses. Little was presented on the role of guards at Treblinka. The defense attorney and even the judge doubted much of what the survivors said about Fedorenko's activities at the camp. This questioning of the very facts of their experience at Treblinka carried over to doubts about the Israel Police investigators and the procedures they had undertaken, and the identifications they had conducted.

The net effect made Fedorenko's claims more credible than they should have been. The question of his crimes at Treblinka somehow became, in the view of judge Norman Roettger, the litmus test; and his claim that he acted under coercive orders, his defense. Further the judge was willing to take into account as a mitigating factor, Fedorenko's many years in the United States as a good citizen.

But Fedorenko was on trial for concealing his Nazi service from the U.S. Immigration authorities. The only question of legal importance should have been: Was he at Treblinka as a guard? To that even he admitted.

Judge Roettger, however, decided for Fedor Fedorenko. He rejected the government's evidence that Fedorenko had committed war crimes and found that the lies on his application were not material misrepresentations great enough to strip him of his citizenship. Moreover, even if the misrepresentations were material, equitable considerations-such as his advanced age and good citizenship-served as alternative grounds for finding in his favor.

After the decision, Sonia Lewkowicz told The Jerusalem Post: "They treated us like we were on trial. In Germany [at the Dusseldorf trials], they would never do such a thing. In Germany, they were very correct. But in Florida, they heard our testimony and they laughed at us."

The Fedorenko appeal was argued by Allan A. Ryan, Jr.,

then an Assistant U.S. Solicitor General. In his early thirties, Ryan was a graduate of Dartmouth and the University of Minnesota Law School and had been a law clerk to justice Byron White of the U.S. Supreme Court. He was tall, thin, with a well-trimmed beard. A former Marine, he brought to his cases a look of authority, efficiency, and integrity.

The Fedorenko case had come to him by routine assignment. His first inclination, based on the judge's decision, was not to appeal. But INS attorney Martin Mendelsohn asked to him read the transcript of the trial. He did and became convinced that he could win. After all, Fedorenko had admitted he was at Treblinka.

The United States Court of Appeals, Fifth Circuit, agreed. It reversed Judge Roettger's decision, and Fedorenko was stripped of his citizenship.

To Allan Ryan, the fact that Nazis were living in safety in America was incredible. It was criminal. But what struck Ryan most, after arguing the Fedorenko appeal, was that he could do something about it. He sent a copy of the decision to the Justice Department's criminal division, which oversaw the Nazi prosecution unit, the Office of Special Investigations (OSI). Ryan asked if he might help with similar cases.

The OSI had been formed in the spring of 1979 and was just getting under way. Walter Rockier was its first director and Martin Mendelsohn, originally head of the INS task force, was made deputy director.

Rockler, a former Nuremberg prosecutor and a senior partner at Arnold & Porter in D.C., had agreed to take a six-month leave to set up the office, hire staff, and make some headway on the backlog of cases, accusations, files, and investigations.

The OSI had inherited several hundred cases from the INS, the Demjanjuk case among them. But responsibility for it fell

99

between the two prosecutorial regimes: though investigated by the INS, the case had been filed by the U.S. Attorney in Cleveland two years ago but the case wasn't ready for trial yet. OSI wasn't happy about that; they wanted to take command. But the assistant U.S. Attorney felt his office was handling matters just fine. The question was, who would be in charge? The OSI or the U.S. Attorney?

The OSI felt that many INS cases had been lost without cause by local prosecutors who had not sufficiently prepared their cases and had not been sufficiently informed of the background of the crimes and witnesses. They did not want to repeat the mistakes of the Fedorenko trial.

After Fedorenko, many of the Israeli witnesses were reluctant to testify again in the U.S.; they felt they had abused not only by the defense but by the court and the prosecutors as well. Mendelsohn had to assure the Israel Police that OSI attorneys would be fully involved in any future prosecutions.

11. Message from Moscow

By 1979, John Horrigan was directing the Demjanjuk case from the U.S. Attorney's office. Mendelsohn would have liked to wrest it away from him, but he found Horrigan a tough, able senior prosecutor who wanted the case. They agreed Horrigan would argue it in partnership with the OSI.

Mendelsohn assigned a young attorney from OSI, Norman Moskowitz, to assist Horrigan. Moskowitz, thin, compact, and with a mustache that accentuated his intensity, was born in New York in 1946. He had been a graduate student in Russian studies at Princeton and was a 1977 Harvard Law School graduate. Before joining OSI he had worked at the National Labor Relations Board for two years.

Mendelsohn assigned Moskowitz because he spoke Russian and Hebrew. It was a lucky choice, because although Mendelsohn and Horrigan didn't get along, Moskowitz and Horrigan did and remain friends to this day. They worked well together and quickly understood each other.

While Horrigan prepared the evidence already gathered, Moskowitz coordinated the gathering of foreign evidence. During the summer of 1979, the question before him was how to establish Demjanjuk's wartime whereabouts. Demjanjuk had been born in the Ukraine and claimed to have been a POW in western Poland during the time he was alleged to have been trained as an SS guard and assigned to Treblinka.

Eli Rosenbaum, then a Harvard law student working at OSI as a summer clerk, remembered seeing in the files a photocopy of the News from Ukraine article with the Trawniki ID card. He was dispatched to the Library of Congress to obtain an original issue of the paper. He then took that to the FBI lab to reproduce the card. But when enlarged the card became a fuzzy series of dots.

Moskowitz decided to cable the American Embassy in Moscow: would the Soviets offer information about the original Trawniki card? Would they consider sending it or even a copy? Were there other records of a man named Ivan Demjanjuk?

Moskowitz had reason to hope so. At war's end, as Russian armies pushed the Germans westward across Poland, they seized many war documents, including the administrative files of the German SS in Lublin, the capital of the district responsible for the Trawniki camp.

The Soviets had maintained extensive war records and statistics. Further, more than twenty-six million Soviet citizens had died during World War II, leaving a deep wound in the Russian political consciousness.

The Soviets had participated in the Nuremberg prosecutions and had even held their own trials of "Hitlerites" that the Soviet media covered extensively.

In the pages of Soviet propaganda, they vaunted their assiduous prosecution of Nazi war criminals and often criticized the United States for its inaction. In 1976, the INS had formally requested the Russians' cooperation in American trials of former Soviet citizens who had committed Nazi atrocities on what was now Soviet soil. And in several instances, including the Fedorenko appeal, the Soviets had sent documents or depositions to the INS, most of which had remained in file cabinets throughout the years of INS inaction.

Horrigan and Moskowitz were determined that even without the original card, they would confirm its contents and existence.

In the fall of 1979, Moskowitz and OSI criminal investigator Bernard Dougherty traveled to West Germany. They visited the Berlin Documentation Center   and the Ludwigsberg archives, and met with West German prosecutors to study past

102

prosecutions relating to Treblinka and Trawniki. Accompanying them as translator was OSI's George Garand, who had been a translator at the Nuremberg trials.

On the morning of November 14, OSI investigators went to the home of Otto Horn, a male nurse, who had worked at T4 (the Euthanasia Institute) and had been assigned to Treblinka. Tried and acquitted at the Dusseldorf trials, Horn was later interviewed by Gitta Sereny for her book on Treblinka commander Franz Stangl, Into That Darkness. The OSI had contacted her, and she had informed them Horn was alive and residing in Berlin.

Otto Horn was shown a site plan of Treblinka. He appeared familiar with the camp in general and the death-camp area in particular.

Ivan of the gas chambers, he recalled, was stocky, had black hair, cut short, and a full rounded face with no distinguishing marks. Horn remarked that Ivan had enough technical ability to repair and maintain the gas-chamber engine, and that he, was known to be able to drive an automobile, which, Horn said, was rare among the Ukrainian guards. During the evenings, Ivan and some of the others would travel into nearby Polish towns and become drunk and boisterous. Horn stated that he had never seen Ivan abusing prisoners.

Horn was then shown two sets of eight loose photographs. The first, of men in civilian clothes, had among them Demjanjuk's visa photograph; the other, of young men in uniform, included a photograph of the soldier on the Trawniki card. Horn studied them at length. He picked out the visa photo, then the Trawniki photo. They were, he said, photos of the same person.

They resembled, he said, Ivan of the death camp.

After a few more moments, Horn was willing to positively identify the photos as being of the Ivan he knew. He said he would be willing to do so again in a more formal setting-as long as there was no press or publicity.

Later that same day, Moskowitz and Dougherty visited Dr. Wolfgang Sheffler, an acknowledged expert on Nazi history. They were full of questions concerning the Trawniki card. Sheffler had never seen such a document before. It was a Dienstausweis, a service pass. Sheffler explained that such documents were issued to guards, Wachmanner, who were, at Trawniki, mostly Soviets. The Trawniki trials had been of Germans; most documents he had seen from the camp pertained to Germans. He would check to see if such a document did, in fact, exist; and whether this one was historically accurate.

Were documents from Soviet archives reliable? In twenty-five years of research, Sheffler said, he had never encountered evidence of tampering. If the Soviets were sincere in their desire to see Nazi war criminals prosecuted, fabricating documents was not in their interest. One forged document would destroy their credibility forever.

Moskowitz pointed out that the card had one weak area: there was no indication of Demjanjuk's assignment to Treblinka. The card showed him transferred only to Sobibor. Moskowitz suggested it was possible that Demjanjuk may have been transferred back and forth between the two camps, with no official record. Sheffler agreed to look into it. He was also prepared to testify as an expert witness, but only on certain conditions: he wished to be completely neutral: his name had to be provided to the defense, so it, too, could utilize his expertise.

In late November, Moskowitz called Martin Kollar at the Israel Police. His call was followed by a letter a few weeks later asking him to notify Rosenberg, Epstein, and Lewkowicz that they were to appear as witnesses in the case of U.S. v. Demjanjuk. Moskowitz told Kollar that as the main investigator on the case, he, too, would be called as a witness. Moskowitz predicted that the trial would begin in March 1980. But there was more. Included in the letter were eight loose head shots of young men-all in similar uniforms, all of similar age and ethnic background.

Among them was the man from the Trawniki card, enlarged and cropped to the same size as the others, which the OSI said represented Demjanjuk in the years 1942-43.

The OSI asked that the pack of photographs be shown to the three persons mentioned above. Moskowitz wrote "It is most important that the photospread be shown under conditions that are above any suspicion of suggestiveness."

The Trawniki photo, placed among the loose photographs, was shown to Epstein, Rosenberg, and Lewkowicz in a series of separate interviews. Each immediately recognized the photo as Ivan, and as looking closer in age and weight to Ivan at Treblinka than the visa photo. Rosenberg even remarked: "This very much reminds me of [Ivan], but I think that it is a photograph from a period before Treblinka. I saw him with a fuller face, perhaps by then he managed to eat better."

Rosenberg was right about the time sequence. And it made sense that Demjanjuk would be thinner arriving from the POW camps than at Treblinka.

In late 1979, Rockler and Mendelsohn decided they could not work together. Mendelsohn was allowed to assume another post in the criminal division of the justice Department, but he soon entered private practice in Washington, D.C.

Allan Ryan, who had sent the Fedorenko appeal to OSI with a note saying he would like to help in other such cases, was now asked if he wanted to be its next director. But, he replied, he was no expert. Having won one case, Rockler said, made him more expert than anyone else at OSI.

Rockler explained that he had only taken the position

temporarily and offered that Ryan could come on as his deputy for the next three months if he would assume the directorship afterward. Ryan accepted.

In January 1980, shortly before Ryan assumed the directorship, he and Rockier took a trip to the Soviet Union. They were there from January 26 through 31. They met with General Roman A. Rudenko, the Procurator General of the Soviet Union, and his associates. General Rudenko, who was in his seventies, had been the Soviet Union's prosecutor at the Nuremberg trials. He was of the Stalin era, and was a fearsome and feared personage. Nonetheless, Rockier and Ryan received a pledge of cooperation in trying Nazi war criminals issued by Aleksandr M. Rekunkov, the First Deputy Prosecutor who would replace General Rudenko after his death several months later.

"Soviet prosecutors have expressed willingness to permit Soviet witnesses to testify in American courts against former Nazi collaborators, providing they are healthy enough to travel and are willing to go," Rockier and Ryan told The New York Times, a few days after their meeting. They said the Russians had also agreed to allow lawyers to take testimony and cross-examine witnesses in the Soviet Union and to videotape proceedings for use in denaturalization trials. The Soviets would respond to requests from the prosecution as well as the defense.

In return, the Soviet Union asked whether citizens deported from the U.S. could be sent to the Soviet Union to stand trial. Ryan gave the Soviets no guarantees.

From the Soviet Union, their next stop was Israel. "The general purpose was to introduce ourselves, meet with all the people, to tell them what we were doing and to convey our seriousness," Ryan said later.

Upon his return to the United States, he followed up the

meeting in Moscow with a long diplomatic cable. The pledges of cooperation, Ryan said, "were very vague." The Demjanjuk case had been mentioned in Moscow. As for the card, "My approach was to say to the Soviets that we need the material direct from the source."

Several months down the road, in the spring of 1980, Ryan said, "we received a photostat of the Trawniki card and a general assurance that the original would be made available at trial."

12. Conversation by Documents

Meanwhile, pretrial discovery was still under way. Between the filing of the complaint in 1977 and the actual trial, attorneys for each side conducted a conversation through a series of documents. In "written interrogatories" and "supplemental answers," one side asked, the other told. One side told; the other asked for more information. No one gave away more than was necessary; but each let the other side know enough to conduct its own further inquiries, should it feel so inclined.

In December 1979, Demjanjuk visited his attorney's office in Cleveland to reply to a questionnaire the prosecution had sent. It had been over two years since the initial complaint against him was filed, and over a year-and-half since he'd been deposed at the U.S. attorney's office. Asked, among the questions, to cite the places he had been a POW and the type of work he had done there, he replied, "Russia-laying of railroad tracks. Poland-(Chelm) building huts." This was the first time Chelm was named as part of his alibi. He also said that before the war's end he had been taken to Graz, Heuberg, and Bishophofen. This too, was new.

John Horrigan wanted to ask Demjanjuk a few questions in person. Courts tend not to favor the "redeposition" of witnesses, but Horrigan asked for the right to do so, based on new evidence uncovered since the 1978 deposition such as about the Trawniki card and other new witness statements.

On February 26, 1980, Horrigan questioned Demjanjuk, in the presence of his attorney. Demjanjuk repeated that he had been a POW during the war years. Horrigan confronted Demjanjuk with his own signature in Cyrillic on a copy of the Trawniki card. Demjanjuk would not say it was his.

But could he say, without a doubt, that it wasn't like the way he wrote his name in 1942?

Demjanjuk replied, "It is like I wrote my name."

The prosecution informed the defense of the names and addresses of new witnesses; when they were interviewed and who interviewed them. The documents revealed who among those contacted identified Demjanjuk's visa picture as Ivan, who did not; who recognized

the Trawniki picture as Ivan, who did not. Survivors had been contacted from both Camp One and Camp Two; from Sobibor, and even from Flossenburg.

There was also a notation that the OSI had received protocols from witnesses in the Soviet Union, some of whom identified Demjanjuk at Trawniki, including one from Danylchenko, the original source of the allegations.

On March 14, the government filed a supplemental answer in which they again listed the names of persons contacted. Among those was a new name: Yehiel Reichman of Montevideo, Uruguay.

Reichman, whose family in Lodz, Poland, had been in the textile business for more than three generations, had spent the last thirty years as a leader of the Uruguayan textile industry. But he had not forgotten, for one moment, why he lived in South America rather than his native Lodz. Before the war he had five brothers and sisters. One brother had been sent to the Soviet Union; the others accompanied him to Treblinka and were murdered shortly after arrival. He survived because he volunteered as a barber and later as a dentist.

Reichman had been a witness at the Treblinka trial in Dusseldorf, and this was how U.S. investigators learned of his existence. In 1980 they called him, asking if they could question him about atrocities at Treblinka. He responded that he would travel anywhere, at his own expense, to give his testimony. Reichman occasionally went to New York on business and said he would call before his next trip to arrange a meeting.

On March 12, Yehiel Reichman met with OSI attorneys Moskowitz and George Parker at the New York Statler Hilton. Also present was Helen Meyerowitz to translate for Reichman, who spoke in Yiddish. Reichman was shown a stack of loose photographs and asked if there was among them a person familiar to him from Treblinka. He studied them for a long time, examining each one carefully.

As Reichman later explained, he is not a person to make rash decisions. He examined the pictures over and over, but finally, he singled out Demjanjuk's 1951 visa photograph, saying he believed it was a photograph of Ivan from Treblinka. He was asked to sign the back of the photograph.

Demjanjuk's trial did not begin until February 1981. On January 31, 1981, Kollar received a telegram, asking him to call again upon Gustav Boraks. Kollar asked Boraks, who lived in Haifa, to meet him at the police station there on February 3. Boraks was helped to the station by his son Yoram because of his age and because Boraks was illiterate and spoke only in Yiddish.

Kollar held in his hand Boraks's 1976 deposition. But he need not have worried. Boraks recalled every detail of his experience in Treblinka. Kollar was so impressed that years later he would recall how Boraks, when shown the photos, pointed immediately to the Trawniki photo and slapped down his finger on it, saying, "Ivan."

In December 1979, Norman Moskowitz had predicted that the trial of U.S. v. Demjanjuk would commence in March 1980. He was too optimistic by only a year.

13. That's America?

When Jerome A. Brentar, a Cleveland travel agent, heard in 1980 that Soviet-supplied evidence was being used against Demjanjuk, he took it upon himself to support the defense financially. Brentar was a deeply religious man of Croatian upbringing and anti-Communist sentiment. A former officer of the International Refugee Organization (IRO) in Europe, Brentar saw the Trawniki card as another example of how far the Russians will go to spread fear among Eastern European immigrants in the United States.

"The Soviets are dead afraid of the Ukrainians," Brentar has said. "They want to show that they can use the Justice Department of this country to do their dirty work."

Brentar feared Demjanjuk's extradition would lead to other extraditions based on equally false Soviet-supplied evidence. His belief in Demjanjuk's innocence was absolute: "You get a sense when you talk to someone whether they're telling the truth," Brentar said. "I would put my hand in the fire for him."

But Brentar's background was suspect. He was associated with Holocaust revisionist groups and his own business card listed him as the Ohio representative of the St. Raphael Society, whose motto was "aid for the traveler in need." It was a St. Raphael Society in Italy that aided one "traveler in need," Adolf Eichmann, to escape to Argentina in 1947, as well as other Nazis before and after him.

Others were not as convinced of Demjanjuk's innocence as Brentar. Charles Nicodemus of the Chicago Sun-Times, saw a different side of Demjanjuk, in 1977. Wrote Nicodemus: "He was a muscular, thickset six-footer and his eyes blazed with anger as his moon-shaped face darkened in what seemed like a blush of hate. "Get off of my property," he growled, stepping from behind his power mower and picking up a bamboo rake.

111

"Go. Go. No questions. I answer nothing. Go," he repeated, brandishing the rake like a baseball bat. Coming face-to-face with the man raised a chill along the back of my neck and a sickness in the gut.... When Demjanjuk brandished that rake it was easy to picture "Ivan the Terrible" [wielding his six-foot pipe]...."

United States of America, plaintiff v. John Demjanjuk, defendant, began on February 10, 1981, in Federal District Court in Cleveland before Chief Judge Frank Battisti. Denaturalization cases are civil; there was no jury present for the six-week trial.

A few days before it opened, about four hundred and fifty Ukrainians attended a rally at St. Vladimir's Church to raise funds for Demjanjuk's defense. On the day of the trial, a group of supporters gathered in downtown Cleveland to burn a Soviet flag and picket the courthouse. Protests and counter-protests continued outside the courtroom throughout the trial. Among the placards were many signs questioning the use of Soviet evidence, such as, "Get USSR out of U.S. Courts." Others had different agendas -- "Six Million Lies," one sign read.

Twenty federal marshals stood ready inside the courthouse to keep the peace. Judge Battisti had reserved the largest courtroom in the building, the ceremonial courtroom, the room in which new citizens were sworn in, so that all who wished might be able to attend the trial. Vera and the three Demjanjuk children sat in the front row every day. The empty jury box was reserved for journalists and sketch artists.

The prosecution began by presenting an expert witness, Professor Earl Ziemke of the University of Georgia, to explain the military history behind the capture and recruitment of Red Army soldiers by the Germans. Next, Professor Dr. Wolfgang Sheffler explained the "Final Solution" and the role of the Trawniki camp. Dr. Sheffler testified that although he had never seen a card identical to the Trawniki card, all the information on the card-the issuing authority, the chain of command, the ranks of the signatories, the equipment issued, the oath given, the seals used, the typeface, printing, and type of paper, were all historically accurate. There was no reason to suspect it was a forgery.

The testimony of Dr. Sheffler was corroborated by Heinrich Schaeffer, a former Trawniki paymaster for Ukrainian guards. When showed the ID card, Schaeffer recognized it as the official ID card issued to all persons training at Trawniki, adding that he himself had been issued such a card. Schaeffer said photographs were taken of everyone at Trawniki in the summer of 1942.

The first "eyewitness," Otto Horn, the former Treblinka SS man, did not actually appear in court. He appeared on videotape. Horn spoke dispassionately of the events at Treblinka as though he were a bank clerk talking about a bad check. Horn recalled seeing Ivan at the gas chamber, directing the prisoners inside.

"This is Ivan probably," Horn said, pointing to Demjanjuk's 1951 visa photo; when shown the Trawniki photo, he said, "As far as I can recall, Ivan looked like this."

Horn's testimony was followed by the testimony of five Holocaust survivors. They brought forth the full power of their memories to recreate the unimaginable, the unbelievable. Their words took on heightened intensity amid the formality of the ceremonial courtroom with its high ceiling and gold-leafed frieze.

When the survivors testified, the Court was once again witness to the victims' arrival in cattle cars. Once more they undressed and walked past the barracks and the rag-sorters. They made their way through Camp One, the work camp, and up the path to Camp Two, the Upper Camp, the death camp.

113

In the hushed courtroom, the witnesses seemed once again to hear the engine to the gas chambers, the cries of the murdered. There, once again, they saw Ivan, ablaze with anger, drunk with viciousness. Ivan, in his early twenties, balding, with his ears sticking out ... tall, strong, his thick neck, his broad shoulders, his high forehead ... Ivan the Terrible.

They recalled in detail meeting with Israel Police officers and looking at the 1951 photo. It was Ivan --older, fatter, but the same man. And the Trawniki photo-it looked even more as he was then.

Yehiel Reichman, then sixty-six, testified first because the prosecutors felt he was the most personally impressive of the witnesses. As a "dentist," Reichman had seen Ivan at the gas chambers day in and day out. He had identified the 1951 photograph in New York, the year before. He had no problem doing so again.

But Demjanjuk's attorney, John Martin, asked him, in cross-examination, if he hadn't been shown another folder of several photos in New York, from which he'd failed to identify anyone? Reichman denied this. He recalled only one stack of photos each of which he had examined carefully, one after another, for a long time. Martin asked that Reichman now be given the folder of photos he was speaking of. But before Martin could pose another question, Reichman immediately pointed to one of the photos.

Judge Battisti intervened: What was he pointing to? Reichman answered that among the photos there was one that looked even more like Ivan looked at Treblinka than the visa photo. It was the photo from the Trawniki card. Martin would argue that Reichman had been shown the photo in New York and had had no reaction to it. But Reichman would maintain that he saw only one pack of photos in New York, and that today on the stand he saw the face of Ivan.

Reichman was followed to the stand by Pinhas Epstein. He, too, identified the visa photo of the Cleveland auto worker and the Trawniki photo as the Ivan he knew. Next was Eliahu Rosenberg, whose testimony would place Demjanjuk at the gas chambers.

When Rosenberg had first arrived in Cleveland for the trial, he was in a terrible state of tension. His wife feared the hostility of the local Ukrainian community, but Rosenberg was anxious about seeing Ivan again.

The day of Rosenberg's testimony, Demjanjuk was already seated at the defense table. Cleveland in February is still very cold. Demjanjuk had on an overcoat and a hat and was wearing his glasses. The prosecution and defense tables stood next to each other, so even though Rosenberg tried, he could not look Demjanjuk straight in the face. "He was sitting near me but he didn't look at me," Rosenberg recalled. But at the end of the session, Demjanjuk got up and started to leave. As John Demjanjuk stood before him, Rosenberg reacted: "That's him!" Rosenberg said to his wife.

At first Rosenberg felt relief that his identification from a photo had been confirmed by seeing the man in person. But it soon turned to anger. Ivan arrived unescorted by police and left surrounded by friends and family-a totally free man! It threw Rosenberg into a total outrage.

"That's America?" Rosenberg said to prosecuting attorney Norman Moskowitz. "That a criminal like this can go about completely free?" Moskowitz assured him this was not the end of the story, only the beginning of the process.

Georg Rajgrodski, a seventy-one-year-old architect who lived in Germany, had been assigned at Treblinka to carry corpses from the chambers to the burning pits. Sometimes he had to remove corpses from the gas chambers. From his work at the chambers he knew Ivan well.

Ivan had once given him twenty lashes for being late to a roll call. "I exerted all the effort I could to keep from crying out, and that's why I'm here today." Rajgrodski explained that if someone cried out while Ivan was whipping him, he continued to beat them until they were quiet. "And then he would shoot them in the back of the neck."

In November 1942, Rajgrodski testified, a violin was found among the possessions of the dead. The inmates of the death camp were asked if anyone could play the instrument. Rajgrodski said he could. Afterward, a Kapo (Jewish foreman) named Singer recruited him to work in the kitchen. Singer wanted him to play Viennese songs for him.

Rajgrodski recalled that in the summer of 1943, he played in a trio with a clarinetist and a harmonica player. The guards, Ivan among them, he testified, often came to hear them play. That sweet music played in the death camp seemed shocking; but stranger still, was that the music affected the murderers. Rajgrodski related that one time Ivan "turned around and wiped tears from his eyes."

Rajgrodski had no trouble identifying Ivan from either the visa photograph or the Trawniki card.

Sonia Lewkowicz, then fifty-nine, testified that upon arrival at Treblinka she said she was a laundress. This saved her life. During her testimony, Lewkowicz tried as best she could to look Demjanjuk in the eyes. Horrigan asked her: "What do you remember about this Ivan?"

"Terrible fear," she responded. "He was always busy. He screamed and he ran about. He adopted the style of the Germans. He beat very much and he always threw fear on everybody. We were all terribly afraid of him. He beat the Jewish prisoners." She was asked to describe him. "He was a young man. I don't know his exact age. He was young. He was light; he had light eyes and he had protruding ears."

116

The prosecutors were troubled by Demjanjuk's total complacency during the recitation of his atrocities. "The look in his eyes," Moskowitz told The Miami Review in 1987. "I'll never forget the look or the man: there was no remorse on his part."

The U.S. government had made many requests to the Soviet Embassy, all to no avail, for the original of the Trawniki card. But, in the second week of the trial, the OSI received a phone call from the Soviet Embassy: the Trawniki card was there. The examination could be conducted at the Embassy, but the Soviets would not even be present. Each side could call its own expert, who could use his own instruments in an unhampered fashion. The card could be presented to Judge Battisti for inspection, after which it must be returned to the Soviets.

Gideon Epstein of the INS, a forensic expert on disputed documents, inspected the Trawniki card for the prosecution. He tested the paper and the ink and made photographic blowups of the document so he could check for signs of tampering. The Trawniki card, he concluded, had not been altered. He found the signatures by Trawniki SS officials authentic. He could not verify the signature of Demjanjuk, however, because there were no other examples of Demjanjuk's signature in the Russian alphabet.

The prosecution's final witnesses were immigration officials. Harold Henrikson, the vice-consul who processed Demjanjuk's visa application, testified that if he knew an applicant had served in a camp such as Trawniki, or been an extermination-camp guard, he denied him a visa. The prosecution rested.

If the defense could cast even a shadow of reasonable doubt, Demjanjuk would be acquitted. Demjanjuk offered, in his defense, a written statement from Fedor Fedorenko.

Fedorenko had been shown copies of both the Trawniki card and the visa photograph. He denied ever seeing a card like that or ever having seen either the person on it or the person on the visa photo at Treblinka.

But Judge Battisti did not find Fedorenko's testimony credible. At his own trial, Fedorenko had testified that a Ukrainian named Ivan operated the motors of the gas chambers. But for the Demjanjuk trial, he claimed that he didn't know such an Ivan or remember his appearance.

John Demjanjuk took the stand. In his blue three-piece suit, thick black glasses, he looked fit and rested, more like a member of his legal staff than the accused. He spoke in Ukrainian, his deep voice resonant in the courtroom. Demjanjuk showed no emotion as he answered his attorney's questions. He told the judge that he had never been at Treblinka; he had been a prisoner of the Germans, he insisted, briefly at Rovno and then at another camp, Chelm. His entire testimony took less than a half-hour.

John Martin then asked for and received a five-day recess; he wanted to consult his documents expert. Later, Martin would swear that he never had the opportunity to examine the Trawniki card to his satisfaction; that both experts he contacted could not test the card except in their own laboratories; that the Soviet Embassy had refused to release the card to the United States, nor would it release a paper sample; that the documents expert he ultimately engaged to examine photographs of the card, Joseph Tholl, never rendered an opinion.

When the trial reconvened the next week, Martin announced he would call no expert to challenge the authenticity of the card. He had no further evidence to present.

Three months later, on June 23, 1981, in a forty-four-page decision, United States of America, plaintiff v. John Demjanjuk, Judge Battisti found that Demjanjuk had illegally procured his naturalization by concealing his service as a

118

German SS guard at Trawniki and Treblinka and by his subsequent willful misrepresentations. He was Ivan the Terrible of Treblinka; he should have never been allowed to enter the United States. His citizenship was immediately revoked.

Demjanjuk remained free, pending his appeal. Appeals could, and would, take years. He had received news of the verdict at work. He would continue at the Ford plant. He would continue to worship at St. Vladimir's. He had home, work, church, and friends. All still clung to his attorneys' claims that the case was a trumped-up affair based on false, forged, Soviet-supplied documents. All prayed that on appeal he would be vindicated.

CHAPTER THREE:

ISRAELI JUSTICE

1. The Right Case

After the Eichmann trial, many wondered why no other Nazi war criminals were brought to trial in Israel. Some said that any trial after Eichmann would be anticlimactic, others that the young Israeli State had no desire to set up a perpetual gallows in Jerusalem, trying one Nazi after another.

Demjanjuk's Israeli defense attorney would argue that Israel had renounced prosecuting German Nazis after Eichmann because of the reparations agreement with West Germany.

The answer was far simpler. Eichmann had been kidnapped and this was not a precedent that the Israel Police sought to follow. They were interested in upholding the law, not breaking it. That meant extraditions for which Israel had few treaty agreements with other countries.

To investigate Eichmann's crimes in preparation for his trial, the Israel Police created the "06 Bureau" in 1960 (so named because there were five Israeli police departments already in existence). After the trial, the department came to be known as the Unit for the Investigation of Nazi War Crimes.

The unit did not initiate cases. True, there were no war criminals in Israel, but there were witnesses --the Holocaust survivors. After the Eichmann trial, Nazi war crimes prosecutions increased dramatically worldwide and the 06 Unit aided other countries in gathering evidence for their cases.

According to Israel Police statistics, by the end of 1984, investigations had been undertaken against 4,500 suspects. Eight-hundred files, grouped by ghettos, towns, and concentration camps had been opened. Forty thousand depositions had been taken. The great majority of these trials had taken place in Germany. Of the verdicts received, there had been 105 life sentences, and 200 lesser prison terms. Fifty-two committed suicide. The secretary of the unit estimated that as of April 1988, there were 900 files, and there had been 10 percent more verdicts in each category.

In the 1970s, the unit began to hear from the United States, which was commencing several denaturalization proceedings. The Israelis were still focused on police assistance, rather than on war crimes prosecutions taking place in Israel.

"Extradition ... was not something that the Israelis were interested in," said Martin Mendelsohn. "Quite the contrary. The Israelis resented the notion that they should, in effect, become the dust bin again and sweep up all of the world's debris, and have to put them on trial in Israel. The Minister of justice was against extradition. He wanted prosecutions. But he wanted prosecutions in France, in Germany and Austria. He felt that Israel should not be burdened with putting these cases on. The crimes were committed in Nazi-occupied Poland, Germany, and France; that's where the trials should be."

Marvin Henkin and Dennis Gouldman were the two attorneys for the Justice Ministry's International Division. They extradited criminals who had committed fraud, robbery, murder, or who were involved in drug dealing or embezzlement. They had never made a request for a Nazi war criminal.

Yet by 1979, Nazis were being uncovered across the world. The Ministry of Justice began to question: How should it react?

And for the first time, its lawyers wondered if they could, or even should, use extradition for Nazis. They decided to try.

In 1979, Franz Wagner, the deputy commander of Sobibor, was found in Brazil, and Peter Menten, who was accused of murder as well as the looting of Jewish art treasures, was uncovered in Holland. In both cases, Israel filed for extradition. In both instances, the application was denied.

In June 1981, Allan Ryan, then OSI director, visited Jerusalem for the first World Gathering of Jewish Holocaust Survivors. Ryan held a press conference. "I went over there to locate witnesses," he later recalled, "to let the survivors know who we were and what we were doing."

During his trip he met with attorneys from the Ministry of Justice and Foreign Ministry and suggested they take a more aggressive stance toward extradition. The Israelis agreed only to consider such action. "It was a conservative response," Ryan said. "They [Gouldman and Henkin] are careful, analytic attorneys. They proceeded cautiously."

But they did proceed. Some attribute the seeming change of philosophy to the newly elected Begin government. But Gouldman later said it was more a question of evolution: "The question started to arise, well, suppose you complete your denaturalization cases and you get somebody deported. What happens then? We began to ask ourselves: Is it sufficient just for somebody to be deported, or leave to another country? Is there no way they can be tried for what they did?"

Most people in Israel, as well as in the United States, believed that the U.S. forced Israel to accept the Demjanjuk case.

The truth is different.

The wheels of Demjanjuk's Israeli prosecution were set in motion during an hour-long informal meeting between Israeli and U.S. Justice officials at the Justice Ministry offices in

Jerusalem on Sunday morning, January 24, 1982.

Attending were OSI attorneys Neal Sher, Rodney Smith, and Eli Rosenbaum, who were in Israel on other matters; and Israelis Dennis Gouldman, Marvin Henkin, and Colonel Menachem Russek, who had commanded the Nazi war-crimes unit since 1977.

Gouldman was concerned about what would happen to those proven to be Nazis and denaturalized as U.S. citizens. Sher explained the procedures for deportation. From the Israeli point of view, Gouldman said, deportation to a country that would prosecute them would be "satisfactory." He did not want Nazis sent to countries that refused to put them on trial.

Under U.S. law, Sher said, deportees usually can choose the country to which they will be deported. But the Attorney General can set aside that first choice, if doing so is in the "national interest."

Israel would consider making an extradition request itself, Gouldman said, but two considerations were paramount: 1) possible legal obstacles to extradition and 2) selection of the "right case" for the first extradition attempt. Sher believed that strong legal arguments could be made for an Israeli extradition request, but he could not guarantee success. He agreed that finding the right case was important.

The first case must be a murder case, said the Israelis, emphatically. Sher told them that several of the U.S. cases involved murderers, but proof of the crimes was not always the basis for denaturalization. For example, in Fedorenko's case, it was enough that he admitted being a former Treblinka guard.

But Gouldman pressed Sher: Was he prepared to suggest a candidate for Israel's first extradition request?

Sher said he wasn't in a position to do so, nor did he think it appropriate for him to volunteer a name.

Gouldman turned to Colonel Russek, head of the Israeli Nazi war crimes unit. Russek had been listening to the careful conversation and did not want the meeting to end so abstractly. A Polish Holocaust survivor himself, Russek was a small but forceful man of military bearing. White-haired, his gaze was direct; his manner, courteous. He was not so much intense as intent.

Gouldman asked if Russek could suggest a suitable subject for an Israeli extradition request.

Russek didn't hesitate. He had a name in mind. "John Demjanjuk," he said.

Demjanjuk was a "proper" first case. He was a mass murderer who had killed with his own hands; his crimes at Treblinka were well known, his American citizenship had already been revoked, based on the testimony of Israeli witnesses. To let him go unpunished was unthinkable to Russek.

And Russek wanted a trial in Israel. It was he who had to deal with the Americans before there even was an OSI; he had watched them approach each case as new. He had stood by the sidelines while the U.S. had lost certain cases or withdrawn in others or won still others only to see the deported criminal spend his remaining days residing comfortably in a Mediterranean beach town. He had listened to the survivors complain about the way the foreign courts had treated them. He, too, was a survivor. He, too, was an Israeli. He felt their anger. He, too, wanted justice. And he wanted it in a courtroom in Jerusalem.

124

2. Enter O'Connor

When John Demjanjuk's citizenship was revoked, it never occurred to him, his family, or his supporters that Israel would request his extradition. They were worried that he would be deported to the Soviet Union, like Federenko.

The denaturalization decision was appealed, to no avail. As a first step to deportation, Demjanjuk received an order to appear in court in July 1982. When, on his lawyer's advice, he didn't show up, he was arrested. A special set of handcuffs had to be used; the normal ones didn't fit his strong wrists.

To protest, he went on a hunger strike. On July 21, the three Demjanjuk children and a friend did the same, sleeping outside the Cleveland Justice Center. Their hunger strike lasted eleven days, until Demjanjuk was released; he later said he didn't appear in court because he was still appealing the denaturalization decision.

It was after that incident that the Demjanjuk family decided to find a new attorney. They turned to their supporter Jerome Brentar for advice.

Brentar turned to his friend Edward M. O'Connor, whom he'd first met in Germany in the early 1950s. One of the three original DP commissioners, O'Connor had long been a friend of the ethnic communities. He had even, at Brentar's suggestion, testified as a defense witness at Demjanjuk's denaturalization trial.

O'Connor's recommendation? His son, Mark. Though Mark O'Connor had no immigration expertise, limited appellate background, and not much major trial experience, Ed O'Connor told Brentar not to worry. He promised he'd stay involved.

Edward O'Connor died in 1985, at age seventy-five. Brentar

125

would later comment that the Demjanjuk defense thought they were hiring the father but got the son instead. "And Mark turned out not to be the man his father was," Brentar said.

Later Mark O'Connor would tell a radio audience that he'd agreed to take the case after Demjanjuk's daughter Lydia called him up in tears.

"Whenever I get a lady on the phone who's crying and begging me to help her father, who was about to be deported to the Soviet Union, I at least take a look at it. Too emotional. That's one of my main problems in my practice. I get too involved with my clients. And as a result of this phone call I went to Cleveland. I stand talked with this lady-Lydia-and after talking to her and talking to the man himself and looking at his other children and his animals and his garden and so forth and the evidence for about three or four months, I got involved."

Following several delays, Demjanjuk's deportation hearing opened on April 11, 1983. During the course of the case, O'Connor brought in Cleveland attorney John Gill as his documents expert.

On October 31, 1983, the State of Israel requested the extradition of John Demjanjuk and asked that a warrant for his arrest be issued on the charge of murder. Demjanjuk, however, remained free after posting a $50,000 bond, secured by the deed to his home.

The extradition proceeding did not begin immediately. First the U.S. had to finish the deportation hearing begun the previous April.

Mark O'Connor became a familiar figure to the Cleveland press. In his mid-thirties then, with red hair, bright blue eyes, and a square jaw, he was a handsome, charismatic figure. He spoke at rallies for Demjanjuk's defense. He gave interviews, he wrote letters to the papers. He was dramatic. He was verbose and argumentative. He was fervent.

O'Connor told the press, for example, that only a Nuremberg-style military tribunal could have jurisdiction over alleged Nazi war criminals.

During the course of the hearing, Demjanjuk would not address the substance of the allegations. Demjanjuk was given the opportunity to choose the country to which, if unsuccessful in his case, he would be deported. He would not name a country. The Soviet Union, being his country of birth, was selected by the court. Demjanjuk requested political asylum: to be deported to the USSR, O'Connor argued, was cruel and inhuman punishment.

During the course of the hearing, the government resubmitted, in effect, the evidence of the denaturalization hearing. Demjanjuk testified again in his defense. He continued to say that he had lied on his immigration papers to avoid repatriation to the Soviet Union. Demjanjuk now added that he'd had to hide not only that he had been a POW but also his service in the Vlassov army (an anti-Soviet fighting unit under the German aegis that Demjanjuk claimed to have been recruited into after his POW service).

"Do you think," OSI attorney Bruce Einhorn asked, "Ukrainians who operated gas chambers in death camps should be citizens of the United States?"

"It depends on the conditions," Demjanjuk answered. "If they were forced to do so or did this voluntarily."

Demjanjuk was uninvolved during most of the case. It was hard for observers to imagine this man holding the fate of so many in his hands. He seemed awkward, far too simple to be "Ivan the Terrible."

Demjanjuk "is a very passive personality," O'Connor would later say. "I observed him in his home in Seven Hills, Ohio. His wife would tell him when to mow the lawn. His wife would tell him when to take out the dog."

But his composure broke when his son took the stand. John Jr. stated that if his father were deported to the Soviet Union, he would have no choice but to go with him, which would be a terrible hardship for him, being an anti-Communist. As soon as John Jr. began to testify, Demjanjuk started to cry. Vera, seated in the front row, also wept hysterically.

As part of Demjanjuk's defense, O'Connor chose some unlikely experts. He called Jerome Brentar to testify about IRO screening procedures. Brentar had not been a screening officer at Demjanjuk's DP camp. He testified that IRO screenings were scrupulously conducted. But if Brentar was right, it made no sense that Demjanjuk would write Sobibor and Pilau if, as he claimed, he'd never been there.

O'Connor also called Rudolf Reiss, a former Nazi who'd been at Trawniki. He claimed to be a documents expert but was found to be no such thing. The defense also called Nicholas Nazarenko, who appeared in full Cossack military dress with saber and bandoliers.

These three would be found by the court to have no information pertinent to the proceeding. But later, all three would be found to have ties to Holocaust revisionists (Both Brentar and Nazarenko would be asked in 1988 to resign from the Ethnic Nationalities Committee of George H. W. Bush's presidential campaign. Brentar, it was reported, had spoken of "alleged gassings" and was described by a Revisionist newsletter as an "energetic Cleveland revisionist").

One day, in April 1984, O'Connor appeared unannounced at the Soviet Embassy in Washington. Shown to a Soviet consul familiar with the Demjanjuk case, O'Connor brought up the Trawniki card. The card bears a Russian translation from 1948, in purple ink. In the photostat of the card that the Soviets first provided, the translator's name had been blocked out. The consul explained this had been done to protect the translator. But the name was clearly to be found on the original. In the United States, the original had been photographed in its entirety, without restriction, and the photos had been submitted in court.

But the "blocking" on the photostat was, to O'Connor, an "alteration." The "altered" evidence was proof of "fraud," and evidence of forgery in the case. He would, even in Jerusalem, still cite this as the central evidence of fraud. It may have sounded good to reporters but it didn't carry much legal weight. Basing his entire defense on the theory that the Trawniki Card was a KGB forgery had failed before, yet O'Connor clung to it.

On May 23, 1984, judge Adolph F. Angelilli found Demjanjuk deportable on all seven counts. The court denied defense motions to terminate deportation, to grant asylum, or to suspend deportation. But the judge did grant Demjanjuk the opportunity to leave voluntarily within thirty days to the country of his choice. If he didn't leave, the deportation order would take immediate effect, and Demjanjuk would be deported to the USSR.

During those thirty days, Demjanjuk might have gone to any country where there was little chance of his being prosecuted such Canada, which was only an hour's drive from Cleveland.

Demjanjuk appealed and chose not to leave the U.S. However, on February 14, 1985, the INS Board of Appeals not only denied his appeal but held he should not have been given the privilege of voluntary departure which was unavailable as a matter of law to someone who had participated in Nazi persecution.

Demjanjuk was placed in the Cleveland County Jail in April 1985. Shortly thereafter, he was transferred to the federal prison in Missouri. During the end of 1985, Demjanjuk was found extraditable. An appeal was made to the Supreme Court, which declined to hear the case. All legal remedies had been exhausted, but O'Connor nevertheless insisted to the Demjanjuk family that it was unimaginable that Demjanjuk would be extradited based on "Soviet evidence."

Senators and other politicians were called, the media was alerted. Nonetheless, in February 1986, Demjanjuk was moved to the Metropolitan Correctional Center on Park Row in New York City and prepared for departure.

A last-minute appeal was made to the Attorney General on February 27, 1986. It was rejected. On that same day, Demjanjuk's extradition was authorized by U.S. Secretary of State George Schultz.

That same evening, Demjanjuk was led aboard a regularly scheduled El Al 747 and seated in the business-class section. He was handcuffed and accompanied by two U.S. marshals. The flight left John F. Kennedy International Airport around six in the evening.

Next stop: Tel Aviv.

3.Operation Justice

In 1985, as Demjanjuk appealed his order of extradition in the United States, Dennis Gouldman, in Israel, pressed the Israeli Ministry of justice to assemble a prosecution staff. But the ministry was cautious. It waited. When the U.S. Court of Appeals for the Sixth Circuit affirmed the order of extradition on October 31, 1985, only then did the whole matter, suddenly, become real.

Usually in a criminal case, a crime is discovered, the police department conducts an investigation, an arrest is made, an indictment is drawn up by the state attorney. But here, the first three stages were compressed into one. The Ministry of justice decided that the investigation had to be coordinated by both the State Attorney and the Israel Police. The joint team was dubbed "Operation Justice."

On the police side, Assistant Commander Alexander Ish Shalom was put in charge. Dog-faced, with a permanent five-o'clock shadow, Ish Shalom had a certain notoriety for extracting testimony from suspects in the "Jewish Underground", a group of extremist Jewish terrorists).

For his staff, Ish Shalom recruited Colonel Menachem Russek, police officers Chief Superintendent Zvi Ariel (who spoke German fluently and had worked on other international criminal matters), Sergeant-Major Zvi Shalom Tamari, Superintendent Arye Kaplan (who spoke Russian), Inspector Izia Sobelman (who spoke Ukrainian), and investigator Etty Hai.

State Attorney Yonah Blatman assembled his staff. Dennis Gouldman was assigned to prepare the legal issues relating to Demjanjuk's detention during investigation, and to research answers to any possible legal challenges to Israel's right to try him.

Michael Horovitz, an attorney in the Tel Aviv prosecutor's office, applied to be part of the prosecution team. Fluent in English, German, and Dutch, Horovitz had been born in New York, raised in Holland, and was a child of Holocaust survivors. A tall, thin, nervous man with a quick mind and a dark sense of humor, Horovitz once said "you could say I was raised in the lap of the Holocaust." He had come to Israel as a volunteer during the Yom Kippur War, and a year later settled in Tel Aviv. A former police fraud investigator, he had worked on large criminal conspiracy and drug cases as an attorney in Tel Aviv's State Attorney's office.

Blatman also recruited three lawyers in their early twenties and thirties, Eli Gabai, Eli Avraham, and Gabriel Finder, who would work long hours to provide a backbone of research. They would track down obscure articles, contact foreign experts, work out every possible cross-examination question. All were familiar with the American legal system, (two of the three, in fact, were graduates of American law schools). And among them they were familiar with German, Hebrew, Yiddish, and Russian, languages that would be necessary in their research. As children of Holocaust survivors, Finder and Avraham were committed to the case not only professionally, but emotionally as well. Dafna Bainvol, a senior litigator in the Jerusalem District Attorney's office, would later join the team.

Blatman quickly realized that preparing the Demjanjuk case was a full-time job. But as State Attorney he had other responsibilities. He needed to find someone whom he could trust to lead the team, to coordinate with the police, to delegate and oversee the prosecution. He turned to a young man in the Jerusalem District Attorney's office, Michael Shaked.

Shaked was born in Jerusalem in 1945 to a Polish father and German mother, both of whom had left Europe before the war. German was spoken in the home. A graduate of Hebrew University's law school, at the District Attorney's office he had worked on a series of complex criminal litigation, some political in nature. His success in these cases had earned him the respect of the Jerusalem District Attorney and brought him to Blatman's attention.

Shaked was a serious man with a polite, forthright manner. He was modest, and it was with some difficulty that one learned that he had been decorated in the Yom Kippur War, or that he had served his country in intelligence and diplomatic posts. But Shaked was not without ambition, although his aspirations were more personal than material. He had spent most of his legal career in the Jerusalem District Attorney's office and did not seek out the Demjanjuk case. He was aware, however, of its importance.

Gideon Hausner, Israel's Attorney General, had argued the Eichmann case. Shaked was only a senior attorney in the State Attorney's office. He was aware that in the eyes of the Israeli public and the legal community, there were other, more likely, candidates for the job. But offered the task, he readily accepted.

Many in Israel had assumed the U.S. had delivered to Israel an open-and-shut case. Yet Shaked found a far more difficult case than he or anyone had imagined. Of the survivors who had positively identified Demjanjuk over the years, four had died since the original investigation began (Turovsky, Goldfarb, and Lindvasser in the late 1970s; Rajgrodski, just weeks after testifying at Demjanjuk's denaturalization trial).

There was also the problem of the Trawniki card. The Americans had received the card from the Soviet Embassy during the trial. But the Soviet Union had broken off diplomatic relations with Israel after the 1967 Six Day War. There was no reason to believe that the Soviets would cooperate with Israeli prosecutors. They asked whether the U.S. might approach the USSR about acting as custodian for the card during the trial, but there was little hope that the Soviets would agree.

The prosecutors had their work cut out for them.

On the morning of February 28, 1986, El Al Flight 004 cut through the bright winter sky, landing at Tel Aviv's Ben-Gurion Airport. The plane taxied to an out-of-the-way runway and came to a halt. A staircase was rushed to the plane's front door.

Within moments, Demjanjuk appeared. He was in a brown suit, shirt open at the neck, no tie; his hands were cuffed in front. Standing between two burly U.S. marshals, he looked pale, pudgy, overweight. As they descended the steps, a trio of

133

Israeli Police officials, with Alex Ish Shalom in the lead, walked up. They met halfway.

The marshals uncuffed Demjanjuk, and Ish Shalom instructed Israel Police officers to place their set of cuffs on him.

Ish Shalom, his comments translated into Ukrainian, identified himself as a police officer, then told Demjanjuk he was being arrested under an Israeli statute for bringing Nazis to justice; that he had the right to remain silent; and that anything he said would be used against him. The marshals then handed over his U.S. prison medical files.

Walking between the Israel Police officers, Demjanjuk proceeded down the stairs. With only a few steps to go, he stopped and turned, and pointed emphatically to the ground, despite his handcuffs. Demjanjuk asked if he could "kiss the ground of the Holy Land."

Officer Izia Sobelman conveyed the request to Ish Shalom. No, he said, dismissing the idea with a flip of his hands, keep moving. A gaggle of reporters was waiting on the tarmac, shouting questions at Demjanjuk as he was led straight into a police van and taken to nearby Ayalon Prison.

Israel's ambivalence about the upcoming trial was evident in that day's editorial in The Jerusalem Post:

"Truth to tell, there can be little satisfaction for Israelis in the coming trial here of Ivan Demjanjuk.... The trial will not be much of an educational experience: since Eichmann, awareness of the Holocaust by the Israeli post-Holocaust generation needs no such boost, while people abroad who still deny the Holocaust will keep denying it even after the verdict is rendered. Thus, the verdict will have no deterrent effect. What, then, is the point of the coming trial? The point, very simply, is that Israel had no other choice."

At Ayalon Prison, where Eichmann had also been held,

Demjanjuk was housed in a newly built wing. Officials originally had said Eichmann's same cell would be used, but it was not suitable for modern security and surveillance.

Demjanjuk's cell was installed in a large yellow room divided into two parts: one, the cell itself; the other, for warders who would watch Demjanjuk twenty-four hours a day. The windowless cell contained a single bed, closet, table, and chair. Lying on the bed was his new wardrobe: two orange jumpsuits, a pair of blue pajamas, socks, rubber slippers, and underwear.

For his court appearances, Demjanjuk would be allowed to dress in his own clothes.

The cell was examined to ensure that Demjanjuk could not harm either himself or his guards. Wooden boxes were placed over pipes and protruding edges; all eating utensils were made of plastic. The wing had its own cement exercise yard where Demjanjuk would have a one-hour exercise period twice a day.

The marshals had reported to Ish Shalom that during the flight from New York, Demjanjuk had looked out at the window and said, "They don't understand. It was wartime...." Ish Shalom asked Demjanjuk about this. Demjanjuk answered, "If I had been at Treblinka, and there was a war on, then I would merely be fulfilling orders."

On Monday, after a weekend in prison, Demjanjuk traveled under heavy guard from Ayalon Prison to the Jerusalem police headquarters for his first detention hearing, held to determine whether a suspect against whom charges have not yet been filed should continue to be held in prison.

The officer's lounge had been converted into a courtroom for the hearing. Demjanjuk's handcuffs were removed. Judge Aaron Simcha, a Jerusalem magistrate court judge, reviewed a file the police had prepared. Its aim was to show that Demjanjuk should be kept in prison because there was sufficient evidence to show he was Ivan the Terrible of

Treblinka. Testimony was given by Ish Shalom. As he spoke, Demjanjuk looked down and shook his head, "No, no, no."

Judge Simcha asked Demjanjuk if he had anything to say to the court. Demjanjuk stood up and, ignoring his interpreter, spoke directly to the judge in English. "I was never in the place you call Treblinka, and I never served the Nazis. I was myself a prisoner of war. How you can transform a prisoner of war into a gas-chamber operator is beyond me."

"It seems to me," Demjanjuk said, "that you've already determined my guilt and that my punishment is certain to be death."

Simcha assured him that he would be tried fairly under the Nazi and Nazi Collaborators Law but if proven guilty, he was likely to be punished by death.

Back at Ayalon, Demjanjuk underwent his first interrogation. As with the many others that would follow, Demjanjuk began by saying he refused to cooperate. The police officers questioned him anyhow. And Demjanjuk would always answer the questions posed.

Usually, three investigators sat a table, asking questions in English. When Demjanjuk insisted on having words translated into Ukrainian, Officer Sobelman did so. At the end of each session, a report of the interrogation was drawn up. Demjanjuk refused to sign it.

Izia Sobelman told The Jerusalem Post that Demjanjuk appeared calm, "but I feel that, behind his civilized facade, he's actually quite afraid of what lies ahead of him."

Ish Shalom would later recount that his questioning followed the pattern of: "You say you were there. Convince me. Where were you? You say you were in a POW camp. Who was there with you? You say you slept in bunk beds. Who was in the upper bunk? It stands to reason that you would know these people."

136

"He was not able," Ish Shalom would say later, "to give so much as one name. He couldn't. He didn't remember or he didn't want to."

The police team found Demjanjuk's answer, when cornered, was always the same: "We couldn't act differently, there were pressures. We were prisoners of war." He would immediately insist, "I wasn't in Treblinka; but even the Ukrainians who were in Treblinka, they really had absolutely no choice at all."

Demjanjuk claimed that the investigators had no right to question him, that they shouted at him. But Demjanjuk did not, could not, keep his mouth shut. He had a need to explain himself.

Asked how he had spent the war years, Demjanjuk would invariably add new inconsistencies and incongruous facts to his previous accounts.

For example, he continued to deny that he had been recruited to the Trawniki training camp from a POW camp and from there to Treblinka; or seen others recruited. He insisted that he couldn't have been taken to Treblinka from Chelm (the POW camp he claimed he remained at), because he was "skin and bones." But this implied that he knew that the healthy were recruited, as the prosecution would argue later. Why, if he was so weak, would he have been recruited as a soldier for the Vlassov Russian Liberation Army?

If he was a POW at Chelm, for so many months, why didn't the Germans ever take down his name? For the first time, Demjanjuk said they had. Asked how old he was when the German ID card was issued, he said: "I was twenty-one or twenty-one-and-a-half. I don't know what they wrote on the card." That was about the age on the Trawniki card. Demjanjuk must have realized this, for after a moment's reflection, he changed his mind and said, "I've never seen such a thing."

137

Demjanjuk also mentioned that his group at the POW camp -- he used the German word *Gruppe*-- had a Jewish *Kapo*. Prosecutors and historians would show that Jews were not allowed to remain alive as German POWs at Chelm. *Kapo* was a term, they insisted, Demjanjuk had learned elsewhere.

As to what he did at Chelm, Demjanjuk now said, for the first time, that he dug peat. That he had put Sobibor on his visa applications, and had admitted to lying on the forms, was, to Demjanjuk, of little consequence. "Everyone lied and Jews lied, too," he said.

Demjanjuk did not feel that his case was worth so much trouble. He asked investigators: "Why are you making a big deal out of me? Eichmann was big and Ivan was small. Besides, I'm not Ivan. There's a mistaken identification."

One of the most important and damning exchanges occurred on April 4, 1986.

Russek asked a seemingly casual question: Had Demjanjuk ever visited the Polish villages of Kosow or Miedzyrec Podlaski? It was not an innocent question. The first town is near Treblinka; the second is a larger city almost halfway on the road between Treblinka and Sobibor.

Demjanjuk's reaction was strange. He said nothing and looked away. Russek repeated the question and asked for an answer. Demjanjuk said, "No comment."

Ish Shalom expressed surprise and asked, "Why no comment?"

Said Demjanjuk: "You are pushing me to Treblinka."

But as Russek would later observe, they had not mentioned Treblinka.

Despite his denials, Demjanjuk still felt some need to explain. At a subsequent interrogation in April, he said, "Can you imagine ... the Germans come up to you and tell you, you

138

must come with us. Who can refuse? This, they don't understand. So, what trials? To try, for what? ... When the Germans would offer to collaborate, who could have refused? Isn't that clear? There was a war. Germans who were in the SS. Why aren't they asking them? Why aren't they tried? [Why] only the Ukrainians?"

Though Demjanjuk would claim he was being persecuted and harassed, he did not complain about prison life. He spent much of his time reading The Jerusalem Post, writing letters, and compiling a Ukrainian-Hebrew phrase book. He decorated his cell with letters from well-wishers and pictures from his family. He sang Ukrainian songs. He exercised regularly.

Demjanjuk had taken to doing push-ups in his cell. He could do sixty at a time. Once he reportedly challenged his guards to a contest. But young and healthy as they were, they were no match for Demjanjuk.

He was friendly with his warders. He practiced his Hebrew. With one guard, who spoke Russian, he often conversed at length, telling about life in the Ukraine, and wondering why he was being held in prison. But Demjanjuk was not always so calm and easygoing. One day, a few weeks before the trial was to begin, Ish Shalom went to Demjanjuk's cell. Demjanjuk demanded that he leave and started to push him, his large hands grabbing the policeman. Ish Shalom knocked Demjanjuk's hands off him and shouted: "This is Israel and you should not push me. This is not your private cell. This is not Treblinka."

He explained that they had come to show him some pictures. Then he noticed that Demjanjuk's cell was decorated with letters and he saw hanging there a picture of his wife, Vera, holding a photo of the two of them from the time of their wedding. Ish Shalom said "Look, I have the same picture." He had a photostat that he gave to Demjanjuk. He kissed the photo, then returned it, refusing to keep it.

During his incarceration, Demjanjuk was visited by a group from the Israeli parliament, the Knesset, that inquired about his treatment. He had no complaints. But one day, when former Soviet dissident Natan Sharansky was touring the prison, he was shown Demjanjuk's quarters. Demjanjuk started shouting at Sharansky that he was innocent.

Sharansky, who was born in the Ukraine, told him in their native tongue: "I don't know. But I met people like you in prison. And all I can say is that here [in Israel] you will have a fair trial, and there [in the Soviet Union], you know you would not. So, you are better off here than there."

Demjanjuk's first detention hearing had occurred in Jerusalem. The second took place at Ayalon Prison. Because of security precautions, it was easier to transport the judge to the prisoner than the prisoner to the judge. A makeshift courtroom was set up in the warder's lounge.

In mid-March, Mark O'Connor arrived in Israel. The next day he met with Demjanjuk for an hour. The day after, he met with ministry officials, who outlined the trial procedure.

Demjanjuk had the right to appoint his own counsel; if he could find no suitable attorney, one would be appointed for him. Generally speaking, Demjanjuk's attorney would have to be admitted to the Israel Bar. But in 1961 an amendment was passed to permit Eichmann's attorney, Dr. Robert Servatius, to appear with permission from the President of the Israel Supreme Court and the Justice Minister.

The Chamber of Advocates recommended that O'Connor be accepted as Demjanjuk's attorney but criticized him for talking to the press so often. In his last official act as Justice Minister, Moshe Nissim approved O'Connor's request for permission to represent Demjanjuk.

O'Connor asked the State to pay his fees, claiming that Dr. Servatius had been paid 10,000 German Marks ($5,000) per month while representing Eichmann. This was not true. A sum equal to approximately $30,000 was set aside for translation services. The same arrangement was made for the defense in the Demjanjuk case.

O'Connor did not attend the April 15 detention hearing. He was out of the country searching for witnesses. But over the next few months, O'Connor began to outline his defense, scattershot, in the pages of the Israeli dailies. That Ivan of Treblinka was dead, he said, was confirmed by statements given by Eliahu Rosenberg in 1947 and Avraham Goldfarb in 1961.

About the Trawniki card, he said: "Valery Kubanov of the Soviet Embassy and Judge Frank Battisti told me they knew of the forgeries yet proceeded with Demjanjuk's deportation in light of OSI and KGB pressure." There were mistakes in the angle of the photo on the card; the uniform was the wrong one.

O'Connor promised that for each witness who identified Demjanjuk, he would present another who would swear this was a case of mistaken identity. Two of the witnesses in the denaturalization case had already recanted, he said. Three of the eyewitnesses had been declared unfit and were suspected of having coordinated their evidence at the Fedorenko trial. Finally, O'Connor claimed to have uncovered three witnesses in Poland who knew the real Ivan the Terrible and would verify that Demjanjuk was not the man who manned the gas chambers.

In early July, the Demjanjuk family, Vera, Irene, her husband, Ed Nishnic, and their baby, Eddie Jr., flew to Israel. They went directly from the airport to Ayalon Prison. Appearing unannounced, they asked to be let in and were refused. Vera burst into tears, "We've come all this way. Why won't they let us see him?" she asked.

141

They were informed that prison has visiting days and hours. They would be allowed inside two days later, on Friday, and although prison regulations allowed only for a thirty-minute visit once a week, they would be allowed two-hour visits twice a week.

The family's reunion took place with O'Connor and James McDonald, a fellow traveler of Brentar's, who appeared as O'Connor's assistant. They were escorted to Demjanjuk's cell and they found a suntanned, robust, and trimmer John Demjanjuk waiting to greet his family. He rushed to his wife and showered her with kisses, then turned to his grandson, whom he had seen only once previously. The family was surprised to find him so fit and in such good spirits. The conditions were better than they had been in the U.S., and Demjanjuk reportedly offered this critique of prison fare: "They put too much vinegar in the salad but the outstanding bread makes up for this inconvenience."

There was no talk of the upcoming trial. Demjanjuk asked about family finances and about his son. He was concerned that they watch over their own lives.

4. My Dear Armand

Meanwhile, the prosecution staff began to visit the survivors´and their families. Rosenberg recalled one evening when he talked late into the night with Michael "Mickey" Shaked. They ended up in tears; in each other's arms. Shaked also visited Boraks in Haifa and was struck by the sharpness of the memory of this man in his eighties.

Meanwhile, Israel Police received a phone call from Yehiel Reichman, who was visiting Israel with his grandchildren. Reichman said he would travel there at any time to testify at his own expense. Horovitz ultimately spent many hours with him on the telephone in Montevideo and they would form a kinship, a friendship.

There was still the problem of the Trawniki card. Prosecutors made a formal request for it, and an informal one, too, through the special interest section of the Netherlands Embassy in Moscow. The Soviet Union did not reply. Appeals also were made by private individuals, such as Allan Ryan, and by organizations, such as the World Jewish Congress. Still, no answer.

There was, however, one more trump card to play. In August 1986, the Prime Minister of Israel, Shimon Peres, wrote to "My Dear Armand" -- Dr. Armand Hammer -- and asked that in his upcoming conversations with Soviet leaders, he request the Trawniki card and other documents that might be relevant. As a P.S., Peres suggested that it would help if the Soviets would allow Israeli prosecutors to come to the Soviet Union to work with their Soviet counterparts.

Peres attached a brief "Note concerning Ivan Demjanjuk" written expressly for the Soviets. Demjanjuk was described as having "betrayed his homeland by volunteering to serve with the German SS forces," which sounded like Soviet agitprop.

Even more telling was that in all the description of Demjanjuk's activities at Treblinka and the atrocities committed there, the word "Jew" did not appear; instead the word "victims" was used.

Horovitz was dispatched now to Germany, where he spent long hours in the archives, searching for documents and depositions to buttress their case. Gabriel Finder traveled to the United States to review materials and meet with experts. The pieces were falling into place.

But all the while concern was growing among the Israeli public that no indictment had been filed. Demjanjuk himself addressed this at his hearing on August 23, reading a prepared statement in Ukrainian: "Nine years ago, the Americans started to investigate suspicions against me. In Israel they knew this. What have they done so far? On what grounds have they brought me here and on what basis did they ask for my extradition? They brought me here-they had nothing against me and now they have only started to search. Six months is a long time and yet they have not pressed charges. Looking for false witnesses would take them many years, because I did not do anything they accuse me of."

On September 16, 1986, Barbara Amouyal wrote in an editorial for The Jerusalem Post, "John Demjanjuk is no Adolf Eichmann, nor will his sentencing arouse feelings of sweet revenge and pride in Israeli law so widely felt by the community at large and the world's Holocaust survivors during the Eichmann trial.... The Demjanjuk trial has also become a trial for the Israeli justice system."

On September 29, Attorney General Yosef Harish released the indictment. The prosecution staff sent one of their youngest members, Eli Gabai, to deliver the indictment to the clerk of the Jerusalem District Court sending a message-that as far as the State Attorney was concerned, the Demjanjuk case was a routine criminal prosecution.

The suspect was charged under the Nazi and Nazi Collaborators Law with crimes against humanity, war crimes, and crimes against the Jewish people, and with murder under the penal code of the State of Israel. The indictment ran seventeen pages in Hebrew, twenty-six in English.

Ernie Meyer wrote in The Jerusalem Post, "The indictment makes hair-raising reading even to those well acquainted with the facts of the Holocaust."

On October 1, Chief Justice Meir Shamgar appointed the panel to hear the Demjanjuk case. Justice Dov Levin would preside; District Court Judges Zvi Tal and Dalia Dorner would also serve.

As a judge, Dov Levin was thought to be easygoing during the proceedings and stern in the verdict and sentencing. Eschewing neither a purely liberal nor conservative stance, Levin's decisions could be characterized only as a "case-by-case" approach. His clerks said he was able to dictate quickly a cogent opinion that was elegantly phrased. He was said to have been chosen for the case because of his reputation for "managing" a trial and because, being a recent appointment to the Supreme Court, trial experience was not so distant in his memory.

Judge Tal, an orthodox Jew, was known as a strong supporter of defendants' rights; Judge Dorner, a former military judge, was thought to be tough on prosecutors and defense counsels alike. All in all, the three judges, one religious, one a woman, none a Holocaust survivor, was deemed a good team by the Israeli legal community.

Under Israeli law, the defense has sixty days after the indictment to prepare its case. O'Connor began by taking the offensive. He described the detention hearings at the prison as a "star chamber process."

"We will prove on an almost day-to-day basis the

145

whereabouts of John Demjanjuk," O'Connor told the Associated Press (AP). O'Connor lamented frequently that he could not find local counsel. The Israeli Bar Association provided a list of attorneys.

On October 15 The Jerusalem Post published a report about defense efforts in Poland. Jacek Wilczur, chief specialist at the Central Commission for the Investigation of Nazi War Crimes in Poland, said that several U.S. citizens and their Polish assistants had been trying for years to find "false witnesses" to help prove John Demjanjuk was not Ivan the Terrible.

Jerome Brentar had reportedly visited Poland in 1984 and received from one Tadeus Bernarczyk a false description of Ivan the Terrible. James McDonald visited Poland at the end of September 1986. Residents near Treblinka reported McDonald's visits to authorities, saying he had told them exactly what evidence he sought. The Polish "witnesses" were promised trips to the U.S. and financial rewards that would be considered generous by Polish standards. Such promises had been made in the past, Wilczur said, and the central commission, which is part of the Polish judicial system, knew that McDonald, too, had employed this technique.

McDonald would appear at the Jerusalem courtroom during the trial. He was very much a 'hail-fellow-well-met," gregarious and personable. He told me that he didn't deny the Holocaust, but he just questioned some of the facts. "I'm just a truth seeker," he told me (but McDonald's links to Holocaust revisionists would later be confirmed).

Frank Walus also made several trips to Poland on behalf of the defense, at Brentar's expense, to locate evidence. But there was no evidence that linked him to the effort to locate "false" witnesses.

The prosecution also had their doubts about the value of

Bernarczyk as a witness but they placed him on the list of potential witnesses, as a sign to the defense that, as one young prosecutor said, paraphrasing Shakespeare's Hamlet, "Something's rotten in Poland."

O'Connor's response, that "Wilczur's wild, unsupported claims smack of a typical KGB-style smear campaign, using Communist Party organs to discredit potential defense witnesses," failed to address the substance of the charges.

On November 18, O'Connor asked the court for a six-month delay, saying that he had not yet found an Israeli lawyer to his liking. He was given a list of six available attorneys. The three-judge panel instead scheduled the trial for January19, 1987

In the following weeks, former Justice Chaim Cohn said he was willing to join the defense and Tel Aviv attorney Gershon Orion said he had accepted a Bar Association proposal to assist O'Connor. But O'Connor engaged neither.

Under Israeli law, a trial must begin sixty days after the indictment is issued; a postponement may be granted, but only if the defense agrees to it. O'Connor refused to make any agreement with the prosecution-even if it would grant him the delay he requested. Therefore, the trial had to begin by the end of November. The judges decided to open the trial officially on November 26. At that time, they could recess until January.

John Demjanjuk was brought by police convoy to the Jerusalem District Court in East Jerusalem. The small courtroom was filled with justice Ministry officials and the media. During the forty-minute hearing, Judge Levin asked whether Demjanjuk understood the charges against him. O'Connor replied that the defendant would waive further explanations. But Judge Levin insisted on hearing from the accused himself. Demjanjuk shouted in Ukrainian, "I am not Ivan the Terrible! I am innocent! They want to hang me!" The judge asked him to respond instead to the question, as posed. Demjanjuk said he understood the indictment; but was not the person to whom it referred.

Levin then asked O'Connor to respond to the indictment. O'Connor said he was not yet prepared to do so. But he did say: "The accused is not the man to whom the [indictment] refers." He complained that he had been able to review only 5 or 6 percent of the case documents. O'Connor asked, "to reserve my plea till the beginning of the full trial." Levin replied that at this stage, that amounted to a plea of not guilty. The judge announced that the trial's next session would be in January. He hoped that by that time O'Connor would be more familiar with the prosecution material and would have an Israeli attorney to assist him.

The delay proved fortunate for the prosecution as well. In mid-December, Prime Minister Shimon Peres received a surprise phone call from Armand Hammer. The Soviets had granted him temporary custody of the Trawniki card. If the Prime Minister might dispatch someone to London ... Peres did so immediately.

The envoy returned with a letter from Hammer. Enclosed was a small green cardboard document, the original of the Trawniki card. The Israelis could examine it as they liked. The Soviets requested only that the document be returned by Hammer when the Israelis were done with it. The card was taken directly to the Israel Police.

On December 30, Yoram Sheftel, a thirty-eight-year-old Israeli attorney, appeared in court for O'Connor. He announced that he was acting as O'Connor's assistant, and had come to seek a further delay in the case.

Sheftel, or "Sheffie" as he liked to be called, was not an unknown in Israel. He had more than ten years' experience in criminal law. He was flamboyant had several past cases that

148

had attracted tabloid attention.

Sheftel told the court that O'Connor, who had just returned to Israel on December 22, had to leave again suddenly. O'Connor had hastily summoned him to a 5:00 A.M. meeting at Ben-Gurion Airport to ask him to substitute for him at the hearing.

"We are very unhappy about the way in which Mr. O'Connor conducts himself," said judge Levin. "We have granted him several delays: we, too, have schedules and we're treating him with kid gloves." But the court agreed to a one-month postponement until February 16, at the suggestion of the prosecution (which welcomed the additional month to prepare its case).

Sheftel later revealed he first met O'Connor in late November at Ayalon Prison. O'Connor had seen him there, meeting with clients, and watched as he was deferred to by guards and prisoners. It was clear he knew his way around. Sheftel said he knew immediately who O'Connor was and who his client was. They met, they talked, they came to terms: O'Connor was to be "lead counsel," Sheftel was to be defense adviser on Israeli criminal law and procedure. His expertise would be in Israeli police and identification procedures. At his own insistence, Sheftel would not cross-examine Holocaust survivors about their memory or Treblinka, only about police procedures and photo identifications.

This was, Sheftel would say, the sort of case a lawyer dreams about, that comes once in a lifetime. It appealed to Sheftel's politics, which can best be described as anti-establishment and Nationalist. He leans to the right in matters of Israeli politics, and to the left on personal freedoms. Sheftel was strongly anti-Communist and suspicious of the Soviet Union, believing the KGB was capable of any sort of treachery.

More importantly, Sheftel was a militant Zionist and

Nationalist. He resented the Israeli establishment for accepting the case: he believed the U.S. had forced this case upon them. He was angered that Israel wanted to use Demjanjuk, a "common Ukrainian peasant," as a scapegoat for having shirked its duty to prosecute Nazis for the last twenty-five years.

Sheftel's anti-establishment views were also reflected in his lifestyle. Slight in stature and build, he wore a closely trimmed beard and when not in his lawyer's robes, he was often seen in a Japanese T-shirt, love beads, and a key chain with the Playboy "bunny" logo attached to his pants buckle. He drove a white Porsche, one of the few in Israel.

With O'Connor as lead counsel, John Gill the documents expert, and Sheftel, local expert on police procedure and criminal law, the defense team was complete.

What distinguished this trial from routine cases was how well the broad outlines of the case were known to both sides beforehand. Like a symphony that has been performed by many orchestras, the testimonies of the survivors, and the Trawniki card, were not new to the players.

Eichmann's trial in Israel twenty-five years ago marked his first appearance in court. The testimony was unexpected. Here, many of the same witnesses had already testified in the United States.

Demjanjuk and his supporters had more than a decade of depositions, hearings and trials to prove his innocence and invalidate the evidence against him. The Israeli prosecutors, for their part, had spent a year conducting extensive and exhaustive preparations. Now, at this juncture in Jerusalem, the burden of proof was greater for the prosecution than it had ever been, but the stakes were much, much higher for the defense: Demjanjuk's life hung in the balance. Now, in Jerusalem, the symphony was to be given what the prosecution hoped was its final performance.

All that preceded it was rehearsal.

5. Beit HaMisphpat

Demjanjuk's Israeli trial had begun with questions over the Court's right to try Demjanjuk, which the Court ruled they could under Israel's Nazi and Nazi Collaborators Law. State Attorney Yonah Blatman and lead prosecution attorney followed with their opening statements.

"Until the Second World War," Blatman said, "Nobody considered that millions of men, women, and children, naked, could be driven with the help of whips and iron rods into the gas chambers, where they were gassed and were taken out dead."

Blatman had pointed to a map of Nazi-Occupied Poland and showed the remote areas where the three camps were established, Belzec in March 1942, Sobibor in May 1942, Treblinka in July 1942. "They were active for a year-and-a-half and in them one million-eight-hundred-thousand Jews were exterminated." Blatman said.

Shaked had made the point that historian Yitzhak Arad's testimony was critical to set the historical context of the crimes. This was necessary, Shaked said, because the testimonies of survivors "seem to be taken from a different planet."

"However," he said, "we would be escaping reality were we to attribute these deeds to some distant planet...."

"It is true they took place in the very cradle of European civilization and it is, of course, very difficult for us as human beings to comprehend a single moment of what took place at Treblinka. In fact, it is inconceivable for us to either understand or believe that such a phenomenon as the transportation of human beings in cattle cars, six thousand or eight thousand human beings in cattle cars, to a train station, actually took place. To believe that two hours later, this entire human cargo disappeared in the gas chamber as though it had never existed, and the train was to return with the clothing, with the teeth in well-sorted packages for recycling. This is something that, when recounted here, simply cann ot be grasped. Human nature seeks to escape these descriptions. Human nature, I believe, cann ot fully take in, cann ot comprehend the phenomenon of what happened at Treblinka."

Shaked said they would call witnesses to the stand that had worked in close proximity to the accused.

"There can be no doubt," he said, "this may be one of the last trials where it is possible to bring to the stand witnesses who can say, `We were there, we saw what happened with our own eyes. We can testify as to what happened.'"

"The subject sooner or later will have to step down from the witness stand and become a part of history."

Each night after the trial, the prosecuting attorneys would retreat to their offices to continue working. The press would wait. After the public had cleared the hall, Demjanjuk was led through the courtroom and into a police van. On the night that ended the first week of testimony, as he passed by the officers he laughed merrily and said, Leila Tov ("Good evening" in Hebrew). They laughed, too, and shrugged.

Somewhat later the defense attorneys left the convention center. They got into a small white rented Subaru. John Jr. drove O'Connor and Gill to the American Colony Hotel, where they were staying. A few minutes later, Sheftel got into his white Porsche.

The American Colony Hotel in East Jerusalem is a former pasha's residence. The staff is mostly Arab; the food, non-kosher; the decoration, Moorish. The bar is a well-known hangout for foreign journalists. Each night after court, members of the defense team, as well as Demjanjuk family members, were willing to talk to the press about the trial. At first, they spoke with confidence about their performance, the innocence of their client, and their inevitable vindication.

On the Sunday evening after the first week of the trial, the mood at the American Colony was upbeat. The first Holocaust survivor was to testify the next day, and the defense was sure that discrepancies would be brought out to prove that the wrong man had been accused. But none could deny the strain. And John Jr., not yet hardened by the trial, broke down in tears in front of a Cleveland journalist, expressing his frustration that it was his father at whom everyone had been staring. And it was his father whom the first survivor would accuse tomorrow.

6. Whoever Enters Treblinka

"My name is Epstein, Pinhas. Son of Dov and Sara. I was born in Czestochowa in 1925 on the third of March. I lived together with my parents and the other members of our family in Czestochowa until the day we were removed from there and we were taken to the place where we were taken." With these words began the testimony of Pinhas Epstein, the first survivor to take the stand in Jerusalem as a witness.

Today, after more than 75 years of Holocaust accounts, we can say that many of the accounts follow similar trajectories. Whether the account takes place in Warsaw, or Czestochowa; at Treblinka, or another camp, it is one tale, a death-filled narrative of ghettos, roundups, boxcar trains, brutal arrivals. Even the German commandants at these camps seem alike -- imperious, arbitrary, cruel in surprising ways. Stories of dogs trained to bite genitals: even that, is heard more than once.

Yet, each time a survivor speaks, we learn again that his or her individual experiences were unlike another's. Words fail to communicate the humiliations, and degradations. To be at a camp, one survivor has said, was like receiving a hard slap on the face, from which one reeled, surprised, stunned, dazed, hurt. And then another; and then another ...

Because of this, the testimony of the survivors in Jerusalem was never less than compelling. As they took the stand, the entire country seemed to come to a standstill. The trial testimony was broadcast live on television and radio. It was broadcast everywhere: on public buses, in every shop, in people's offices and their homes. Drivers on the way to work would pull their cars over to pay closer attention to the radio.

For a nation that had heard enough of the Holocaust, for a generation that had learned it all in school- -- they knew; but they didn't know. No one had anticipated the pull of the truth, the power of the survivors' tale. No one had realized that while all slaps may feel alike, each hurt is unique.

No survivor had seen everything or had known everything. And in court, no survivor could tell everything they had seen or known of Treblinka. But what they did tell painted a nightmare world.

Dr. Arad had given the context of events, but he could not speak for the survivors. A generation needed to be reminded in a courtroom in Jerusalem that no account of the Holocaust, no testimony of Treblinka, could speak for the survivors themselves.

Epstein, who was sixty-two at the time, had retired from his job as a heavy machinery operator with Solel Boneh, an Israeli construction company. A tall, sturdy man with wavy reddish hair and gold-rimmed glasses, he had the look of a scientist. He wore a brown sports jacket and radiated a certain formality. He spoke with conviction and the entire room fell silent for his testimony.

Pinhas Epstein was fifteen in 1940, when the Czestochowa ghetto was established. For the next two years, he was idle: Jews could neither go to school or work. He recalled that on the evening following Yom Kippur, the doorbell rang at each and every house in the ghetto. Jews were ordered out and taken to the railroad station. There they were forced to board boxcars. He was separated from his family.

Soon after arriving at Treblinka, Epstein was ordered to accompany an old woman to the "lazarette." As far as he knew, a lazarette was an infirmary. But not at Treblinka. When he arrived at the so-called lazarette, he found a pit. In it were two live babies. "And then an SS man told us to go up to this woman and put her into the pit," he testified, "and once she was in the pit, he shot her, and the woman fell out of our hands. In the pit there was a fire not a flame, it was a sort of . . .

how shall I describe it? ... this smoldering fire, and these babies were on top of this fire. The weeping, the crying of these babies, is ringing in my ears to this day."

Epstein tried to describe Treblinka as he saw it then: "The air was impregnated with death.... I was seventeen years old, Your Honor, I had never seen a corpse up till that moment.... I was absolutely paralyzed. And this continued for three days. There was murder, there were beatings, there were stabbings. It was quite indescribable."

They were commanded to sit on the ground. Epstein recalled they saw a bathtub of water. This was a trap. Whoever took a drink had his head whacked by a German rifle butt.

An SS man pointed at Epstein and said, "You! You go this way," motioning him out of the group. "I moved over to the side, then my younger brother, David, spotted me, and he got up and approached me. An SS man saw him doing so. He turned to him and with the butt of his gun, cracked open his skull. I became dizzy for a moment and [when I looked again] this young boy had disappeared. I never saw him again."

Epstein spent three days in the Lower Camp before being chosen to work in the death camp. He would remain there for almost eleven months, until the uprising. He carried corpses.

Epstein testified that while waiting to gather the corpses from the gas chambers, "We heard cries, screams – unbelievable-- I sat down in a place where I could see the entrance of the gas chambers. This was the so-called Machinehaus, the engine house. I saw someone go into this engine room, and later I was told this was Ivan, Ivan the Terrible.

"After the people had been introduced into the gas chambers and after the screams and when all this had died down, the gas engine was activated, the engine that introduced the gas into the chambers. I saw this man-a big, thickset man who activated and operated the engine. He pressed a button and disactivated the engine. And then we would wait about twenty minutes or half-an-hour and then we were told to open the doors -- very wide doors -- and remove the corpses."

Most of the SS men, Epstein testified, seemed indifferent to the atrocities; yet one officer, new to the camp, was horrified by what he saw. To get away from the corpses, he ordered Epstein and another inmate to rake the Schlauch under his supervision. Though no longer standing directly at the chambers, Epstein now witnessed the naked prisoners running toward the chambers.

He recounted how assistant camp commander Kurt Franz, having heard that an escape was being planned, gathered the inmates. Franz got hold of a boy named Kamera, a foreman of the corpse-carriers. He had been a neighbor of Epstein's in Czestochowa. Kamera was asked to point out who was going to escape.

He was beaten savagely. "This young man had no control left at all. You could not recognize any face; his face was just a bloody mess." Kamera pointed indiscriminately to some twenty-odd people. They were told to leave the line and lie down on the ground facedown to await punishment.

"And this is how the massacre began. Ivan, with his iron pipe, Nikolai with his sword, the SS people with their whips. And the massacre began, blood began, blood was flowing freely."

Epstein's face flushed with anger; his revulsion obvious.

On another occasion, he recounted, a group managed to escape the camp's perimeter. But the first snow had just fallen, so the prisoners were tracked down easily and returned to camp. They were beaten for the entire day. Epstein recalled that Ivan was among those tormentors who broke the prisoners' arms, hands, and legs. The escapees were then hanged.

"Your Honor, I remember one other instance, and I have nightmares about this to this very day," he testified. "One day a living little girl managed to get out of the gas chambers. She was alive. She was speaking. A girl of about twelve or fourteen. People who took the corpses out of the gas chambers made her sit down on the side, and this little girl, her words ring in my ears still. She said, `I want my mother.'" Epstein paused, to wipe away tears from his eyes.

"After all of these corpses were taken out and placed on the side, we were commanded to sit down as always. Ivan took one young man from among us, whose name was Jubas. He struck him brutally with his whip, he lashed at him, he ordered him: 'Take off your pants.'

"I am ashamed before this court to repeat the words that Ivan used. If I may ... it would be outright blasphemy for me to repeat this. This is also vulgar language.," Epstein said.

Levin reassured him: "If you feel this is important, then say it. If it's not too disturbing for you . . ."

"He struck Jubas," Epstein said, "and he ordered him-'take off your pants, and davay ye batch....'"

"What does that mean?" Levin asked.

"`Come fuck' . . . And Jubas leaned over this little girl, and this act, as I understand it, did not actually take place. He leaned over this child-it was an act of obscenity against this child...."

Jubas eventually died in the typhus epidemic. As for the little girl: "Later [she] was taken wherever all of the corpses were taken near the pit-and there she was shot. I didn't see who shot her.

" Ivan was one of the.... -- I find it difficult to compare him to anyone -- not even to an animal," Epstein said. "Because I know that animals, when they are satisfied, they do not attack. I

159

once saw on television an animal researcher who studied animals in the jungle, and she explained that when a herd of animals is hungry, they prey upon other animals and they tear the other animal, the prey, to shreds. But once they are satisfied, they lie beneath a tree. Gazelles may pass by, and the predators do not attack them. Even if this is a predatory animal, Ivan was never satisfied. He would prey upon his victims every day, every minute so that I cannot even compare him to an animal, to a beast. He was never satisfied."

Epstein brushed away tears. He testified that he had watched Ivan at work from yet another vantage point. One day, Epstein testified, an SS man named Karol promised to assign him to the kitchen detail: "He said to me ... with eyes like that, with hair like that, with the way I looked then ... I was made to go into a kitchen to work. And there I worked for a brief period, maybe a week. And from that kitchen, when I went to bring water to the kitchen, or when I went to bring firewood, I saw all of the most terrible spectacles of what Ivan would do, day in and day out, each and every hour of the day."

Epstein found it difficult to describe the conditions under which they labored in the death camp. He said, "I should also like to add that there wasn't a single night when there weren't people who took their own lives, people who cracked up, people who broke down spiritually, mentally, physically. People who had found among the corpses a sister, a relative, a neighbor, a friend. These were spectacles that I cannot find words in the human language to describe. And no matter how much I try to explain and to describe this -- it cannot be described. There is no beginning and no end ... you need years to describe it and to try and understand it. I think that the human brain cannot conceive, cannot grasp-I'm not talking about seeing it, but yet you can't grasp it when it's being retold.

"It's inconceivable to understand what took place in this abattoir, in this slaughterhouse, what was done to human beings.... Ivan would be especially bestial toward people whom he discovered to be religious. I can't describe it. I can't explain it. I don't know how to go about explaining things logically." Epstein put his head down on the lectern.

Levin asked him to regain his composure. This was a court of law, he said, and Epstein would have to restrain himself from emotional outbursts.

With Shaked gently leading, Epstein completed his narrative of Treblinka, concluding with, as Shaked put it, the one happy moment, the uprising. From the death camp Epstein had escaped into the forest. "I kept going," he testified, "I went as far as I could. I didn't know really where I was going ... I went wherever my eyes led me. I didn't have a specific place to go to. I didn't know whom to go to. I didn't have a name of anyone, I didn't have an identity. I didn't exist. I hadn't been born. I didn't belong to anyone. No one belonged to me."

Epstein made his way back to his hometown of Czestochowa: "On the first night I slept in the cemetery, the Polish cemetery of the non-Jews.... On the following day I entered the city. I went into a courtyard where I had lived, myself, and I looked around. There was complete chaos. I looked through the windows and I clung to the ground. I couldn't move-- I knew that this is the place where this person lived and where that person lived and all of my neighbors. After all, I had grown up there, and all this no longer exists. All of it has disappeared. And where am I to go? Whom am I to turn to? And the world was going on as if nothing had changed.

"I used to go out and sleep in different ruins of houses that had been demolished by the Germans in the ghettos. I would go out in the morning. I'd see children going to school, people going to work-the world went on with business as usual, as if nothing had changed.... What helped me at the time was to see how the world was going on. This is what drove me on.

"I kept wandering. It was worse than being a dog. Because if you are a dog, at least no one pays any attention to you. But if anyone had caught me, if anyone had noticed me, if anyone had found out that I'd escaped from Treblinka, it's difficult to describe the torture I would have had to endure.

"Finally, with the help of one Pole who was the only ... good-natured, good-hearted woman in this ocean of hatred- there was this one spark of humanity, and there were so very few such sparks-this person helped me, this angel, helped me to forge documents." The papers enabled Epstein to get to Germany, where he spent the rest of the war working with a group of laborers.

Shaked led Epstein to his safe arrival in Israel in 1948, and life thereafter. "I have children," Epstein said. "I have five grandchildren. And I have rehabilitated myself and this nightmare called Treblinka, which is called Ivan, which is called Nikolai, which is called Gustav; and all of those names pursue me to this very day.

"A few days ago," he continued, "We celebrated a holiday in Israel, *Tu B'shvat* [Arbor Day], the day dedicated to the trees, and I was watching the little children of the kindergartens, small children, marching out to plant trees. And I observed them, and I saw these children, these small children, who did not know that after marching a few steps in Treblinka their lives would be severed. Innocent children."

Intently watching this exchange was an aristocratic-looking woman who had been attending the trial for several days with her children. Asked then why she had brought her children, she had answered, "It's so important. They must know." But there was another reason. She was Epstein's eldest daughter.

Levin, clearly uncomfortable, turned to the prosecutor. "Mr. Shaked, any other questions?"

Shaked put the Israel Police's album of Ukrainian

photographs before Epstein; it had been almost nine years since he had identified Demjanjuk. Now he recalled full well his identification and the physical characteristics upon which it was based: "The brow, the round face, the very short neck, the wide, well-set shoulders and slightly protruding ears --this is Ivan as I remembered him.... When I met him in Treblinka, he must have been between twenty-two and twenty-five."

Epstein pointed spontaneously at Demjanjuk, and said, "Yes, he's sitting there. There he is!"

A gasp came from the audience. A few persons applauded.

Judge Levin immediately called the room to order, admonishing the public not to interfere with the proceeding.

Epstein also remembered his identification of the Trawniki card photo in 1979. "I said this is Ivan as I remembered him from Treblinka...."

Michael Shaked had a final question: When he had just then pointed at Demjanjuk and said, "There he is," how could he be sure it was Ivan after so many years?

"If it please the court, when I was brought to Treblinka, I was a boy of seventeen. Ivan was twenty-five. We, `together' were at a certain place for eleven months, together in very close quarters. He carried out deeds so atrocious that no words can describe them, deeds that have become so indelibly imbedded in my memory. A man of that age has not changed to this day to the point where he would become unrecognizable. There are certain features that after so many years are marked in one's memory and cannot be erased."

With increasing agitation, he testified, "I see Ivan every night. My poor wife, I dream about Ivan every night. I envision him every night, he is imprinted in my memory. I cannot free myself of these impressions."

Epstein began to describe how he had recognized Ivan

when he saw him on TV, stepping off the plane in Israel, but Levin said what he had seen on television was not of interest to the court right now.

"Well, then," said Epstein angrily, "I see Ivan the way I remember him, the way he is in my mind's eye. There he is," he pointed at Demjanjuk, "just the way he is!" Epstein, his face taut with frustration, angrily hammered the witness stand,

"There he is! There he is! There he is!"

Judge Levin told Epstein to restrain himself: "I realize that it is difficult to contain your excitement," he said, "but, please, we are in the process of a trial here and things must be conducted in a calmer manner."

"I apologize," Epstein said, "but still ..."

Levin: "Yes, we understood you, sir, but please understand us, too."

"This is the man, the man sitting over there."

"Yes, we heard you," the judge replied.

"Age has, of course, changed matters, but not to the point where he would become unrecognizable. I see him, I see him, I see him. . . ." Epstein sobbed.

Levin again turned to the prosecutor: "Mr. Shaked?" he asked.

"I have finished, no more questions," Shaked said.

Judge Levin explained to Epstein that he would be questioned now by Mr. O'Connor, who had the right to defend his client to the best of his ability. And it was Epstein's duty to answer questions, no matter how difficult, as calmly as possible.

"Mar Epstein, tzohoraim tovim. Shalom [Mr, Epstein, good afternoon]. Baruch Hashem [Praise God].

164

Mark O'Connor began in his American-accented Hebrew. He quickly switched to English. O'Connor started by questioning Epstein's assertion that he had recognized Demjanjuk as Ivan when he saw him on television.

O'Connor's goal was to show that Epstein's identification was prejudiced by media exposure, but the strategy backfired: Epstein explained that Demjanjuk's "way of walking was the one I remember at Treblinka."

O'Connor would ask him later to demonstrate the walk. That, too, proved a miscalculation. Epstein stood, and with small steps and arms swinging, walked a few steps. It was a striking identification: Epstein had accurately portrayed Demjanjuk's distinctive gait. Demjanjuk watched with great interest, and everyone else watched Demjanjuk.

O'Connor, yellow legal pad in hand, heels together, toes pointing out, knees slightly bent, said he wanted to question "the mind of the seventeen-year-old boy from Czestochowa," but for the great part, his questions probed irrelevant details about Treblinka such as whether Treblinka SS officer could have been born on the Volga. Epstein, annoyed, replied, "How could I know?"

At the lunch recess, Epstein's wife, his son, and two daughters and his five grandchildren, rushed to the stage. The policemen did not stop them. The family embraced in one hug, tears flowing. Epstein's son had never heard the particulars of his experience; his daughters knew even less. "You're too young," he used to tell them, even after they were grown with their own children.

When the court reconvened, O'Connor questioned Epstein's contacts with other Treblinka survivors to suggest they had colluded on their identifications.

Epstein confirmed that in the years since the uprising he had met with other Treblinka survivors, and had testified with them at trials in Dusseldorf, Ft. Lauderdale, and Cleveland.

Epstein had attended with other survivors a ceremony at Yad Vashem on the fortieth anniversary of the uprising. Epstein also confirmed that the survivors also used to gather on August 2, at a Tel Aviv cemetery, Nahalat Yitzhak, where a memorial stands to the survivors of Treblinka. "That is a day and an hour when we remember all that we had to go through," Epstein said. As to Eliahu Rosenberg, they met often at weddings, social occasions, and funerals as well.

O'Connor asked if they ever discussed their experiences of Treblinka. "Sir, we are comrades, we are more than comrades, we are brothers, because we were born on the same date, on the second of August 1943. 1 have two birthdates." Epstein said he would recall with others what they had been through "to the end of our days," however, there was no evidence that they had ever discussed the Demjanjuk case, or any other, among them, or had coordinated their identifications or their testimony.

As a concluding question, O'Connor wondered again about Epstein's in-court identification. "I am convinced," Epstein testified, "convinced that opposite me is sitting the man Ivan the Terrible, the Horrible, who was at Treblinka."

Judge Dorner had a question: "Tell me, Mr. Epstein, how often did you see Ivan?"

"Your Honor, I saw Ivan every day, at all hours. I rubbed shoulders with him, if I can so put it...."

"How is that possible?" asked judge Dorner.

"Well, he was passing by me. It was such a very small area. Everything took place in this very limited area. He was active near the gas chambers, and I would come to the gas chambers in order to pick up the corpses, and he was there all the time.

"After the corpses were taken out of the gas chambers, he

166

would stand there and he would look at the results of what he had done to them, this gouging of eyes, the cutting-off of parts of a girl's breast. He was standing there enjoying his handiwork; he would hit the prisoners with his iron rod and enjoy seeing the cracked skull. This was just a few inches away from me.

"It was such a very, very narrow piece of ground on which we were; and he was looking at it with such enjoyment-the cracked skulls, the crushed faces, babies still tied to their mothers by the navel-looking at it as if he had done a tremendously good job; and, of course, he would brutalize the victims, brutalize the prisoners. I cannot find a word in the human language, in a cultured language, what to compare him to. It was a creature not from this planet, Your Honor.

"One says `murderer,' `assassin,' or writes `murder,' but then once he has done the deed and he sees the results, there is usually a feeling of regret, but Ivan never, ever in the eleven months I was in Treblinka, never, ever showed the slightest regret. It is inconceivable, incomprehensible, how a person could act like that. Women who were pregnant with stab wounds in the abdomen. I have no words. I cannot, Your Honor, really, not describe this. A man's healthy brain cannot take in, cannot grasp what went on in Treblinka. It is not on this planet.

"Almost one million people were massacred, assassinated: women, children, old people. Why? I ask. Why? Because they were Jews. It was Ivan.... How this horror who is not from this planet ... I just cannot grasp it ... if I were to tell the tale to the end of my days, every day, and each day.

Then Epstein said something that would stay with everyone who heard until the end of their days:

"Treblinka has no beginning and no end. And whoever was in Treblinka will never get out of it; and whoever was not in

Treblinka will not go into Treblinka. It was the sort of horror that did not take place on this planet."

Defense counsel Yoram Sheftel wanted Epstein to acknowledge that at Treblinka he never heard Ivan called Demjanjuk and that he had no way of knowing Ivan Grozny's real first or last name.

"I knew that Ivan was his first name," Epstein said. "I heard everybody calling him Ivan. Nikolai called him Ivan. The SS men called him Ivan, and from this I know that this was his name ... but no, I did not [hear] mention the name Demjanjuk."

Epstein had one more request: "If the bench permits me to say one sentence to the accused."

Levin was adamant: "No, no, no. No, by no means."

Outside the courtroom, the reporters gathered around Epstein. "What was the comment you wanted to make?" one asked.

"If the judge wouldn't let me make it to him, do you think I'll tell you?" Epstein said gruffly as he headed out to meet his family.

But after the trial had ended, Epstein shared what he had wanted to say to Demjanjuk:

"You, who were so powerful at Treblinka, who held the lives of people in your hands, and you who did with them whatever you wanted; you, who were so brave, be brave now. Tell the court who you are and what you did."

7. The Sixth Man

During his testimony Israel Assistant Police Commander Ish Shalom revealed during his testimony that there had been a sixth-and secret-police member of Operation Justice. One of Demjanjuk's prison guards had been a police "plant," assigned to befriend him and pry information out of him.

His name was Arye Kaplan. Born in Vilna, Lithuania, he had served in the Red Army for two years, he told the court, before coming to Israel in 1973. His recent cover, he said, was not ideal; he'd told Demjanjuk that he was the son of a Lithuanian father and a Jewish mother, and was a private in the Red Army, that he had emigrated to Israel but that he didn't like it there, and hoped to emigrate soon to the United States.

He spoke Russian, so he and Demjanjuk had conversed a great deal. Kaplan was never sure he had Demjanjuk's complete confidence. He offered to help Demjanjuk avoid the prison censor by sending and receiving the mail at his home. Demjanjuk agreed.

When the Demjanjuk family visited, Kaplan was introduced as a friend.

When they talked, Kaplan testified, often Demjanjuk volunteered information. But when Kaplan pressed beyond a certain point, Demjanjuk would end the conversation. A certain leitmotif ran through their conversation: Demjanjuk was not at Treblinka, but Kaplan, as a soldier, could understand that a war was on and one should not try those who were only following orders. Describing his suffering at the POW camp, Demjanjuk said he would have killed for a loaf of bread.

On one occasion, Demjanjuk said, "At Ford plant working with me were Germans who were in the SS. Why didn't anyone question them? They're only after Ukrainians. Isn't that clear?

169

There was at work Germans who were in the SS. Any witness who speaks against me will be from the SS. We had to collaborate." He made it seem as though anyone who had burned a corpse of a Jew was a collaborator. Jews had also been collaborators, according to him, and he mentioned the Judenrat (Jewish council). He was also interested in Kurt Waldheim, about whom he had read.

Demjanjuk was interested and involved in his defense, Kaplan testified. He was cheered when newspapers reported accounts saying Ivan had died in the uprising, and the fact that a man in Spain, Garcia de Ribes, had said he was at Treblinka, that he knew Ivan the Terrible and Demjanjuk was not he. (Garcia de Ribes, who spent only a day in Treblinka's Lower Camp, was visited by the Demjanjuk defense. But they did not find his evidence credible enough to call him as a witness.)

Kaplan reported that Demjanjuk was obsessed about the report of an eighty-five-year-old in Trieste who said he knew the family name of Ivan Grozny. Demjanjuk said, "To this day the family name of Ivan Grozny is not known." (This man was visited by the prosecution. And though the Italian government would later announce that they were investigating Demjanjuk's activities in Trieste in 1943-44, the prosecution did not think the evidence strong enough to stand up in court.)

Kaplan asked Demjanjuk about how Ukrainian Church members and other Ukrainians in the United States viewed his case. Demjanjuk said they well understood that a person who became a German prisoner of war had to carry out orders, as the Germans would otherwise have punished him. But, he said, it was unjustifiable if the person, performing his duty, exceeded orders and acted on his own initiative. Such a person should be punished. Demjanjuk agreed that Eichmann should have been punished because he gave orders, "but those who didn't give orders, the smaller ones, performed them as they were told, and the question is whether they added on [acts] on their own."

A few weeks later, Demjanjuk told Kaplan that "the conditions in the prisoner-of-war camps were inhuman, that when a German would appear, a Kapo would immediately order [the prisoners] to remove hats and the people stood and were afraid to move. If the German didn't like something about someone, he would shoot him on the spot." Demjanjuk again made it clear that he wasn't talking about himself. But, he said, "if we assume that we are speaking of himself, although this isn't so, then it is also clear that there is nothing to try [him] for." The prosecution found this incriminating: There were no Kapos in POW camps; Kapo was a term used in the concentration camps.

Demjanjuk insisted that he could not operate an engine before the end of the war. He would have had to have been a driver; to be a driver in the Soviet Union, he said, you need seven years of education-and he had only four.

Demjanjuk blamed the Ukrainian famine, Kaplan testified, on a Soviet official named Kaganovich, who was, Demjanjuk said, a zhid --the derogatory term for Jew.

On cross-examination O'Connor argued that zhid is the normal term for Jew in Western Poland. "Ask your client," said Kaplan, "but to me it's derogatory." In fact, there was a period in the Soviet Union when it was a criminal offense to use this term.

At the day's end, Demjanjuk rose from his seat, heaved a sigh of dismissal, and made a downward dismissive motion with his hands, to show his disgust and frustration; then he hugged his son.

8. Those Eyes, Those Murderous Eyes

Eliahu Rosenberg gripped the witness stand firmly. Long retired from his job as a warehouse manager at the Ashdod port, Rosenberg worked part-time at a bank. He stood barely five feet tall, yet he was a powerful, intimidating presence. Dark curly hair with silver waves complemented his deeply furrowed face; he wore thick glasses with purplish frames, and his eyes were dark and intense. As he stood in court, barrel-chested, refusing to sit, he seemed like a small bull, ready to charge.

Rosenberg was born in Warsaw and grew up in an orthodox home. He lived with his parents and sisters, attending private school, until the outbreak of the war. His father, who ran a mirror factory, was murdered by Germans one winter night in 1941, while out to buy milk. Rosenberg, nineteen at the time, became the family's breadwinner, scavenging the streets of the Warsaw Ghetto for food.

He last saw his mother on the train to Treblinka. She just had time to hand him something, a ring, and they agreed to contact each other if they escaped, through a certain Christian acquaintance. Rosenberg never saw his mother again. He later traded the ring for a piece of bread.

Now he was asked to identify the camp from the blowup behind him. His memory was sharp. As he pointed, he made some corrections: "This was here ... this was later moved." Where he had been, he could describe; what he had seen was before him again.

Rosenberg stood at the lectern, his fists clenched, his face tensed with rage, as he described the Jews running up the Schlauch and into the gas chambers, to their deaths. His fists shook in the air, as he recalled their last cries. Winter, he said, was worse than summer: "Polish winter is ... very, very cold, twenty or thirty degrees below [centigrade]. You must understand that these children were naked. A hundred or eighty meters away from me, and they came from the direction of Camp One, in that cold winter.... You can't imagine the kind of screams that human beings can emit ... like dogs. The children wailed in a manner that filled the entire space around us. In the beginning, I, too, was very affected by this, but I later became numb. It was so difficult. No one asked me to look at them. I could see them for myself. And then when people ran into the gas chambers, they ran, they just wanted to get out of the cold. They saw something in front of them and they ran."

Rosenberg had worked first as a corpse-carrier. This exhausted him, but to save his own life he had to find ways to conserve his strength: "I managed to make a friend of one of the Dentisten, by name of Lindvasser, who has since died. Now when I came to Lindvasser, this Dentisten, he, too, was scared to death. I said, Avraham, be a little slower in looking for the gold teeth, because that was the one second where I could rest. Somehow I rested the stretcher on my knees, because I was crouching, as it were. For me, this one second made all the difference. It did give me this tiny bit of respite...."

Rosenberg later managed to get assigned to details that lessened his chance of being beaten. He became one of the Bademeisters, the "shower cleaners," who washed the chambers and cleaned the ramp between gassings. Sitting there on the ramp, he saw Ivan and Nikolai perform their tasks and heard death come to those inside the chamber.

Levin asked if he saw Ivan and Nikolai operate the engine.

"Yes," he answered. "I didn't see his finger pressing, I didn't see him moving a handle."

Rosenberg said he always saw them in the engine room, though not always together; sometimes one was inside, one of them was outside.

"And you saw them?" asked Judge Levin.

173

"With my very own eyes," he said. Rosenberg wanted to tell the court what he heard inside the chambers as he sat outside. "It's a very agitating and very shocking thing. I'll try and tell it. slowly," he said. "When the victims were inside, the first ones did not know where they were going, it was so very well decoyed and camouflaged.... But by the time the chambers had filled up, I would start hearing at the other end a most ghastly scream, crying, weeping, `Mame,' 'Tate,' 'Aba,' 'Ima,' the names of children. It was dark inside. No light. Even the openings in the roof did not let any light in ... the screams, the shouts were terrible. 'Mame!' `Tate!'-- Mother!, Father!-'Hear, O God of Israel -- Shema Yisrael.'

"I listened to this for fifteen-twenty minutes. Then these screams died down. And then I heard moaning, groans, and that, too, subsided until it became quiet. Often I saw inside strong young people. It is inconceivable, it is incomprehensible, how they were fighting and trying to get their heads above the others in order to get a tiny bit of air."

Finally, Rosenberg agreed to sit down. He went on to testify that he worked on the incineration crew, which also put him in a position to observe Ivan. Next to Ivan's work area were barrels of fuel, and Rosenberg was given permission to retrieve a bucket of diesel fuel to pour on the corpses.

Shaked now tread lightly: "Mr. Rosenberg ... a general question. You spent eleven months at Treblinka. How did you endure that?"

"To receive beatings was an everyday matter over there," Rosenberg answered, "but I was careful not to be beaten in a murderous fashion, in a brutal fashion. Why do I say murderous? Because if any of us was beaten on an exposed part of our body, he was a candidate, so to speak, to be killed. Again, we weren't afraid of being killed. I wanted to be killed, but with a bullet in the head ... there was no other hope there anyhow. If I tell you that if I had any hope, there was a sort of dream; but hope to get out of there, there was no hope. So, my only hope, my only aspiration, was to get a bullet in the head and to finish with it all.

"How did I survive, however, how was it possible for me to spend eleven months or more in that place? There were two reasons. First, I mentioned earlier that I worked for several months in the gas chambers. The murderers did not enter the gas chambers themselves ... except for one who would count the corpses together with me.... When I was there, I was far from the actual field of bloodshed ... so I had a sort of breathing time, to catch a friend of mine and we told one another that if we want to live at all-however absurd that may seem-we must not work too hard and we must think up something.

"Whenever we would carry a corpse ... or whenever we would walk from the pit to the incinerator, we both had to agree to throw this stretcher down and hide. You couldn't do it by yourself, because if one did it, they would ask where is the other one? So, we always had to act together. And then we would hide, it was a little bit later on, in the time of the incinerators, we would hide under the incinerators.... We hid in the smoke, which is why to this day I have a bad eye and a bad throat. We could hide in the smoke, as long as an hour or two and rest from this hard labor and the beatings. This was one period.

"At a different period, when I took the corpses out of the gas chambers, and there were big piles there, I had to join and help carry. I could not sit down and rest. So, I walked with this friend of mine again. We always walked together. So, we went together to relieve ourselves, and we couldn't go one by one. We would throw the stretcher down. No one would notice a stretcher lying on the side. And thus, I could hide out for an hour or an hour-and-a-half, until a German spotted us or one of the people in black spotted us. And they could not see us more than once, because if they'd seen us even once, I'd wind up being a candidate for death. And thus, I managed. Somehow I was quicker than others, or I don't know what, and I survived. I'm not claiming to be a hero or anything."

Shaked asked, "What did you see Ivan inflict on the victims, things that you saw with your own eyes?"

"In the earlier months, I would stand on the Rampe [the platform and ramp outside the gas chamber's exterior doors-by which the corpses were removed], I would see him holding a sort of sword in his hand ... and sometimes he would cut off a piece of nose, a piece of ear, stab, you just cannot comprehend why, why.... After all, there was no very good reason why he should go up to a person and cut off a part of his ear. He was not a human being. He was not being a rational human being at all, and he was a young man, to boot. He had some sort of education. He came from a certain country ... to get blows, to beat-all right, yes, we'd seen where people beat you. But this sort of torture --this brutalizing-- this torturing people by cutting off parts of their ears? Nobody had ordered him to do so. He did it of his own accord. I never heard a German tell him to do so.... A little later, a German, in fact, told him to keep off doing such things."

Rosenberg told of one incident in which three escapees were apprehended. He saw Ivan coming out of his cabin with a new instrument of torture, a large nail. But a German officer by the name of Loeffler saw what Ivan was about to do and shouted at him: "Los! Los! [Get off, get away!]" and ordered him back to his cabin.

Strangely enough, this one German officer, whom Rosenberg recalled as puny, seemed the only person Ivan feared at Treblinka. But Loeffler was no humanitarian. It was he who ordered Rosenberg and others to escort the captured to the gas chambers and lock them up. Later Lalke held a roll call where the three men were hanged on a tree.

"I understand," Shaked said, "that this Loeffler also saved your life on one occasion."

Rosenberg nodded yes: "This was at an earlier time-- much before the incident that I have just described. It was in late summer. We had cleared the corpses from the gas chambers. As soon as I got to the ramp, Ivan came out of his cabin.... I stood there and he beckoned me. He told me to take off my trousers and lie down on them [to have intercourse with one of the corpses there]. I had no choice. I saw this, and within a minute I understood, this is it. I have had it. [I would be killed] Either [by] his iron pipe or else some other way.

"Loeffler, he was looking there. I ran toward him. I said to him, Herr Scharfuhrer [Sergeant, sir], Ivan tells me to have sexual intercourse with a dead woman. So Loeffler approached Ivan, screamed at him. And Ivan turned to me and said, `You will pay for this.'"

Rosenberg had no way of knowing if Ivan had remembered his threat; but some months later Ivan did punish him. While removing garbage from the kitchen, Rosenberg stole some bread and shared it with others. A young boy was found with the stolen bread and when asked where he had got it, he blamed Rosenberg.

Rosenberg's punishment was thirty lashes of the whip. "Ivan got out from his cabin with his Peicher-a whip. There was another one, Gustav. He did not do it alone. I had to count, Your Honor. In the end, I said "spaciba" ["thank you" in Russian]. I immediately pulled up my trousers and put on my clothes and ran back to the barracks. I couldn't move for a couple of hours, but I got over it."

Rosenberg also recalled that in 1942, he was on the Rampe when he saw Ivan leading an elderly Jew toward the fence. Religious Jews appeared to provide Ivan with a special provocation.

"I saw that he was accompanied by an elderly Jew with sidelocks [who]did not have any hair on his head, a long beard, and Ivan went up to the fence pulled the fence apart and this Jew was pushed by him, either by his feet or his trunk, into this barbed-wire fence, and Ivan started beating him with his iron pipe. This Jew was writhing in pain and screamed until he stopped screaming and crying."

On the day of the uprising, Rosenberg testified, his job was to puta blanket over the barbed-wire fence so others could climb over.

When the revolt broke out, earlier than expected, he ran to the fence with the blanket, but he didn't have to throw it on the fence because others had already broken out, and there was an opening.

He ran and climbed over the antitank obstacles. "I still don't know to this day how I managed to climb over it," he said. "I jumped ...it must have been about three meters."

Shaked now addressed Rosenberg's 1947 statement that Ivan had been killed. Rosenberg explained that he was in Vienna in 1947 for the Bricha (the Underground to Palestine). When people heard that he had survived Treblinka, they urged him to speak to Tadik Friedman, a Polish Jew who worked at the Jewish Agency and tried to track Nazis. Rosenberg agreed. The conversations occurred at two sessions. Rosenberg spoke in Yiddish, and Friedman translated his comments into German as a typist recorded the interview.

Rosenberg's 1947 account is detailed and intimate. The document does, however, give his birthdate as May 10, 1924, (Rosenberg was born in 1921) and the date of his arrival at Treblinka as August 20 (Rosenberg arrived in September). Those discrepancies would be brought out in the cross-examination; but he told Friedman that his first night in Treblinka was the eve of a Jewish Holiday and some religious

Jews prayed in the barracks (In 1942, the Jewish Holidays were, in fact, in September).

As for Ivan, Rosenberg did not describe his physique, but his function at the gas chambers and that he was "feared because of his especial bestial brutality." Rosenberg described instances of his brutality. He also noted that "Ivan was the only Ukrainian who was allowed without any special permit to go to the nearby village, where he got himself whiskey and food." Rosenberg described the revolt and said, "some prisoners stormed the barracks of the Ukrainians, where Ivan slept, and beat them to death with shovels."

Shaked placed the original crumbling, yellowing typescript before the court. Rosenberg explained that he'd found out later that what his friends had told him in the forest was, "a story-fiction-a mere boast ... even those who had told the tale hadn't seen it for themselves." It had been wishful thinking.

If Ivan hadn't been killed, what had become of him? Rosenberg said he first found out in 1976. Shaked asked him to recall Israel Police investigator Miriam Radiwker's 1976 visit. When Rosenberg saw the 1951 visa picture, he said that the man looked familiar from Treblinka. But Mrs. Radiwker said he wasn't at Treblinka. "She said he was at Sobibor. I said, I know this man. Ivan. Ivan Grozny. Madame, I said, he was different, a little younger, a little leaner." Rosenberg recalled that at Treblinka, Ivan was twenty-two to twenty-three years old, tall, with light-colored eyes, a receding hairline, dark, close-cropped hair, a strong man." Later he also told how in 1979 he had identified the Trawniki photo for Inspector Kollar.

Shaked showed Rosenberg the police photo album from which he had identified Demjanjuk, then asked: "You told Mrs. Radiwker if you saw Ivan alive today you would recognize him?"

"*Nahon* [true]," Rosenberg replied.

179

Sheftel realized what was coming and jumped up to object. He insisted that an in-court identification was irrelevant, misleading, and of little probative weight. The court overruled him.

Shaked said "I should ask you to look at the accused."

Rosenberg, looking straight at Demjanjuk, had a request: "Will you ask the accused to take off his glasses." Before the translation, Demjanjuk removed his glasses; but as O'Connor rose, he quickly put them back on. Judge Levin asked, "Mr. O'Connor what is your position?" After some hesitation, O'Connor said, "My client has nothing to hide."

Demjanjuk stood and removed his glasses. He leaned over to O'Connor: "I want that he come close to me-right here." Demjanjuk pointed to the edge of his booth. "Shh," said O'Connor, but honored the request. With a flip of his hand, O'Connor ordered, "Mar Rosenberg, come over."

Rosenberg stared straight at Demjanjuk. He stepped away from the witness stand, their eyes still locked, and took off his glasses. As he walked across the room there was complete silence and time stopped.

Demjanjuk stood, awaiting him, smiling. O'Connor had a demonic grin. Rosenberg walked quickly. He stopped at the edge of the booth, no more than a foot from Demjanjuk. They stared at each other for a second. It seemed like an hour.

"*Posmotree*! [Look at me!]" Rosenberg barked at him angrily in Russian.

Demjanjuk suddenly stuck out his hand, and said, "Shalom" with childish glee.

Rosenberg recoiled in shock and disgust; he stumbled backward. He cried out "Murderer! Bandit! How dare you put out your hand to me!"

Rosenberg never heard the cry that rose from the spectators

as his wife, Adina, sitting in the third row, fainted; their daughter, Rivka, caught her in her arms. The police promptly carried her out of the courtroom.

What had been Demjanjuk's intention? To show that forty years later, they were equals; that bygones were bygones? To show that he was not a monster, but just a man? Or was Demjanjuk mocking him, challenging him now, even as he had then?

Rosenberg returned to the witness stand and rested his head on the lectern. A few moments passed. Judge Levin called the room to order and turned to the witness and said, "You were asked to come close. You stopped and looked. What is your answer?"

Rosenberg stood again. He said, "This is Ivan. I say so unhesitatingly and without the slightest doubt. Ivan from Treblinka from the gas chambers. The man I am looking at now. I saw those eyes, those murderous eyes."

Could O'Connor convince the court otherwise?

"Shalom Mar Rosenberg, Baruch Hashem [Hello Mr. Rosenberg, praise God]," O'Connor began.

"Shalom, to you, too," Rosenberg replied.

O'Connor asked Rosenberg about the differing dates for his arrival at Treblinka. Rosenberg maintained that he had always told investigators he arrived before the Jewish New Year and he had left it to them to supply a date consistent with the Gregorian calendar. O'Connor came back to this several times. Finally, Rosenberg said, "I repeat again and even if he asks me a million times that I arrived in Treblinka before the Jewish New Year."

O'Connor asked Rosenberg if he had ever written down his experiences of Treblinka. To everyone's great surprise, Rosenberg revealed that before the war was over, he had written something in Yiddish. He had given the document to a representative of the Polish government; he had not seen or heard of it since. Sheftel took note of this. Later, the defense would locate this document and Rosenberg would be recalled to be cross-examined about it. In it, as in the 1947 Friedman document, he recounted the death of Ivan.

O'Connor returned to the Friedman document. Rosenberg replied that he had initialed each page without actually reading the German. "Perhaps I was naive," he said. "I never thought it would come to court. We spoke to each other in Yiddish."

But O'Connor had a more provocative line to pursue. Earlier, he had made Rosenberg detail all the tasks he was made to perform while others died. Now he asked him about the Jews from Grodno. O'Connor's strategy was not yet clear. But Rosenberg retold the incident: a transport of Jews from Grodno had dared to try to escape while running up the Schlauch. They had pushed aside the branch-covered wire fence and scattered.

Rosenberg and other death-camp workers were immediately ordered into their barracks enclosure. From there Rosenberg watched the fate of the escapees. The greater part were shot trying to flee. Approximately thirty men were caught alive and were led to the small gas chamber and locked inside.

O'Connor asked whether it was Rosenberg's "option" in the death camp to stay outside or to go into the safety of the barracks.

"I don't understand what you ask about options," Rosenberg responded angrily. "They did whatever they wanted.... They weren't afraid of us, for heaven's sake: It was a slaughterhouse. The Germans weren't afraid of us; because a second later I could have been [murdered] instead of one of the victims."

An especially gruesome death was inflicted upon the

captured who were locked in the gas chamber, Rosenberg recalled. Rather than turning on the diesel engine, the Germans poured chlorine through a window above the chamber. The victims were left overnight to decompose and die.

In the morning, Rosenberg was assigned to pull them out. "They were not even bodies anymore," he testified. "We had to grab them by the heads and pull them out, because their skin was red. They were bloated. And when we touched such a victim, the skin came off."

O'Connor now asked, "Mr. Rosenberg, was it ever in your heart the time you were watching this happen-to try and do something to help those men that were running outside naked?"

Rosenberg was anguished: "How could I have done so? How could I have helped them? I had no contact with living human beings there. If I saw what I saw, all I saw was people who were getting into the gas chambers. I had no contact with them. I could see them in front of me, five meters [sixteen feet] away from me. They didn't even have a chance to look up at me...."

Shaked objected, saying the question had a provocative element and O'Connor could argue what he wished in summation. But Judge Levin told Rosenberg he must answer.

Rosenberg responded, calmly at first: "In what manner could I help these people? How? With what? With screaming?" With increasing anger, he said: "Should I have screamed at them: `Don't get into those gas chambers?' They didn't want to get into the gas chambers. And if, God forbid, any of us would have screamed, shouted toward them-I don't wish you, Mr. O'Connor, to even look at what would have happened to such a person. They would have shoved him straight alive into a pit full of blood.

"So, don't ask me questions of that manner, Mr. O'Connor.

I implore you. You weren't there. I was there- Ask him!"
Rosenberg pointed to Demjanjuk in the dock. "Ask him!" he
began to shout. "Let him tell you. Let him tell you what he
would have done to me." Rosenberg was overwrought.

"Mr. Rosenberg, Mr. Rosenberg ..." Judge Levin told him
that his shouting was out of place.

"I was never asked such a painful question in my life,"
Rosenberg said. "Even the worst anti-Semite never asked me a
question of this type. Whether I could have. helped such an
unfortunate. Who could have helped me then? You want me to
tell you what went on there?"

"Mr. Rosenberg," said Levin sternly, "that completes your
answer to this question."

Judge Levin, though, had a question for O'Connor. During
Rosenberg's reply, Demjanjuk, his face deeply flushed, had
shouted something at Rosenberg, which O'Connor had not
heard because of his translation headset.

O'Connor conferred with Demjanjuk for a second, then
announced that he wished Demjanjuk to repeat his comment. He
asked that the comment be seen "in the proper context of a
man who has been in a jail cell for almost a year in solitary
confinement, sitting, listening patiently-suffering in his own
way; holding it all in, trying to maintain his spirituality-he did
say something, Your Honor. It shows he's human. And he said it
in Hebrew." Sheftel had told him, "Two words he heard were:
'Atah shakran [You are a liar]."

Judge Dorner had a question. She wanted to know from
Rosenberg, as she had from Epstein, why he was certain that
this was Ivan and not someone who looked like him.

When he saw the picture of Ivan for the first time in 1976,
Rosenberg said, he recognized the face, although it was fatter
and older. Still, he was hesitant about making a positive
identification. But at Demjanjuk's denaturalization trial in

Cleveland in 1981, he had sat across from the defendant and been unable to take his eyes off him. Although Ivan kept trying not to look at him, Rosenberg managed nonetheless to get his glance. And when he saw his face, he had no doubt. And finally, now, now that he had walked up to Demjanjuk and looked into his eyes, "I have no shadow of a doubt, Your Honor. This is him."

Sheftel took over the questioning. Rosenberg had been shown the same photospread twice, once in 1976 by Radiwker, and then again by Kollar in 1978. In 1976, he identified Demjanjuk from the spread; in 1978, Fedorenko. Why, Sheftel asked, didn't he mention Ivan again in 1978? Rosenberg insisted he did. But then why didn't he identify Fedorenko in 1976, when he was first shown the photospread? "In 1976, when I found out he [Ivan] was alive," Rosenberg said, "I was in shock."

Wasn't the real reason, Sheftel surmised, that Rosenberg asked to approach Demjanjuk here in court, that he couldn't be sure from the witness stand that he was Ivan? Judge Levin interrupted the defense counsel to remind him that it was O'Connor who had asked Rosenberg to come closer. Levin assured Sheftel he would remember that moment full well until the end of the trial. Sheftel rephrased his question accordingly: did Rosenberg respond to the request to come closer in order to better identify him?

"No, sir," said Rosenberg. "The truth is entirely different.... The intention was for him to look at me and perhaps to remember me.... Every day I was next to him ... I was beaten by him. I saw what he did. Refresh his memory full well, he'll remember me."

9. The Trial Phenomenon

The survivors' testimony received coverage the world over. Britain's tabloids gave great play to the gruesome details. Newspapers in the Netherlands and Germany ran daily accounts. In the United States, only Cleveland's The Plain Dealer carried daily reports. Most major newspapers reported the more dramatic moments of survivor testimony. But the coverage of testimony gave way quickly to coverage of "the trial phenomenon."

During the survivors' testimony, the courtroom was so crowded that an annex had to be built so the trial could be broadcast over closed-circuit video on a large screen.

Buses full of schoolchildren, groups of young soldiers, foreign visitors, foreign journalists and authors, all came to attend the trial. It is important to say that despite its characterization as otherwise, this was no show trial. It was a legal trial, and as such its popularity and the attention it received certainly served Israeli internal and external political agendas — seeing an Israeli trial in process made the case convincingly that Israel was a country that held to the rule of law. That the judiciary were serious professionals as were the prosecutors. As much as Sheftel was an object of scorn to many Israelis — nonetheless they were proud that Demjanjuk entrusted his defense to an Israeli.

10. Simple Men

On the trial's tenth day, a small man, somewhat disheveled, took the stand and identified himself as "Yossef Czarny, son of Abraham, born on the twenty-seventh of July 1926 in Warsaw." If Epstein radiated dignity, and Rosenberg animal instinct, then Czarny was the simple man, a poor soul whose misfortune it was to have been sent to Treblinka.

When war broke out, Czarny had just had his bar mitzvah. His mother, a diabetic, died as the ghetto was starting. "But at least she was buried in an honorable way," he testified.

Food, said Czarny, was scarce. With great emotion, he recalled scavenging in the ghetto to find food. "I humiliated myself. We were begging. We had no choice." Police were posted on every corner. Threats were carried out routinely. Czarny lived with his father, a Hasidic businessman, and his three younger sisters.

"The greatest shock that I remember," Czarny told the court, "was when my father of blessed memory came home before curfew ... I thought I didn't see right. I said, 'Tate, is that you?' The policeman had cut off his beard and his sidelocks. I was brokenhearted. He was brokenhearted."

As conditions in the ghetto worsened, there was less and less food. Czarny's father was so weak with hunger he could no longer speak; his sisters did not have the strength to leave their beds and wait in food lines. His father died and was taken to the gates of the ghetto in a wheelbarrow. Czarny ran after it to cover his father's face with a piece of paper.

In Warsaw, a notice was posted a few days before Rosh Hashanah, promising bread and jam to anyone who went to the train station. "It is difficult to describe," Czarny testified, "what that meant. This word bread. Whoever has not lived through this and felt [what it was like] not to have bread ... the

187

jewel in the British Crown was not as valuable as a piece of bread."

They were told that they were being sent east, to work in the fields of Russia. "But to say we did not know that this was our end --we did know," Czarny said. Remembering the thirst of the people inside the boxcars, Czarny brought his fingers to his lips. "I remember people were going stark raving mad. They began drinking urine. A *bisele pishi.* They actually did that." He began to sob. He apologized. Levin suggested he have a drink of water and calm down before continuing.

But Czarny could not restrain himself. "Excuse me," he said in Yiddish between sobs, "my daughter is listening to me. Why does she have to hear this? Why?" His eyes searched out his daughter from among the spectators, "*Zippele, dos iz vos iz gevorn, fun dayn tatn* [Zippele, this is what became of your father]."

He recalled in such great detail his arrival and first day at Treblinka that he had to remind the judges, "Everything that I am telling the court took not hours, but seconds."

Czarny wanted to explain how it was that he had survived to tell his tale. At the end of the woman's shed, he said, at the very entrance that led to the gas chambers, a Ukrainian guard crooked his finger and motioned to him to step out of the line of newly arrived Jews.

Czarny joined a group who were led into a shed and locked in while the gassings occurred. Inside, he could hear the Jews from the transports meeting their fate. "I could hear the same spectacle ... the same `Sh'ma Yisroel' . . . the same heartrending cries and the shouts of the Germans, too, in German, 'Schneller, schneller,' and the same murderous blows. And the bodies left lying in the courtyard. The same thing happened again. But later we heard, perhaps it was an hour or so later, and by then I could pick up more of what was happening around me, there was pastoral peace, pastoral calm.

"Everyone was already dead. You could hear the birds singing, since the camp was in a forest clearing, surrounded by woods."

In between the gassings of the arriving transports, the Jews in the shed were let out to pick up the victims' clothing from the courtyard and sort it. Czarny estimated there were six transports that day. In the late afternoon, he hid among the clothing. The others in his group were murdered. He was discovered by Jewish forced laborers who gave him clothes. "There was no lack of clothing, "or food and water.

The next morning, he went out with the workers and met the Kapo, named Krakowsky. "He asked me: `How are you doing?'" Czarny said. "`How are things in Warsaw?' ---as though I knew what things were like in Warsaw. He said, `Don't be afraid, you're new here.' But I was afraid to say, to ask, `Why am I new?' I understood that something was strange: He said, `*Yo, Yo mayn kind*-yes, yes, my child. Don't be afraid.'" Czarny was assigned to sort the clothing.

Czarny had arrived there after the High Holidays. "There was already frost," he recalled, "ground frost. This was already autumn in Poland. And I was employed in this sorting job until about May, until after Passover. And then I was transferred to the *Hofjuden* [court-Jews] detail, that was the cleaning of the yard and the square."

Czarny was asked how he came to be transferred to the Hofjuden. "One day, Lalke, Kurt Franz [deputy commander of Treblinka], called me. It is very, very difficult to describe to the court what this meant when Lalke called you. I simply have no words to describe it. I remember he beckoned to me from afar, he said: `Come on, come on-you-little one. Come here.'

"And I said to myself, well, that's it. This is the end.... I stood to attention and he asked me, `How old are you?' And I answered him in Yiddish, `I'm eighteen years old.' So Lalke says to me, `No that's not true.' And I said to him: 'Yavol, Herr Scharfuher, Sturm fuhrer[Yes, Sergeant, Lieutenant]' --I don't quite remember what we called him --and he slapped my face. He had gloves, which had been lined with pieces of metal. And he slapped me on the right ear. I fainted. I fell to the ground.

"Somehow I was lifted from the ground, probably some of the forced-laborers whom he had called lifted me from the ground. And I remember blood trickling down from my ear."

Czarny was told he was to report to Franz's living quarters the next day.

"What should I do? Lalke means death. That's it. I so wanted to live. I so wanted to live. I did not want to die. But I had no choice."

After the morning roll call, Czarny reported to Lalke at his quarters in the German compound. "He was sitting there in an armchair, and I remember it-as if it were today. And he said: `Take off the boots.' Instead of pulling back, instead of letting me do so, he pushed his boot into my face. He must have been-- he was drunk. I don't know how I managed to get the boots off his legs.

"After I had taken his boots off, he said to me: you are going to be a *Hofjuden*. I didn't know what a Hofjuden meant, Your Honor. And once again, he slapped me and he said, `Polish.' He said to me, `If it isn't going to be as bright as a mirror, you know what is in store for you --you know what you will get.' I think for two days, a day-and-a-half, I don't quite remember, I polished his boots. Not all the time, of course."

Czarny was taken to the chicken coop. "Altogether what didn't they have? They had a pigsty. They had stables with horses. They had a chicken coop so that they would have fresh eggs. And then I was employed on jobs in the chicken coop."

"Is there even a historian," Czarny asked, "who can understand that sort of thing, and if there is such a person,

190

where is he?" Now he was sobbing.

"My daughter, Zippele," Czarny asked, "where is she? *Ikh hob kayn breyre nisht* [I have no choice but to tell]."

Judge Levin asked him to regain his composure; Shaked offered him a glass of water. But Czarny could not calm down. With his long, fleshy face and gray hair standing on end, he looked the picture of despair.

"Why should I have come to such a path? I am humiliating myself. . . ." Czarny's face folded in on itself as tears streamed down his cheeks.

"Nobody knew about it. What can I do? They ruled our lives. Then he broke into Yiddish, again begging: "Children, don't forget us, don't forget us." His sobs erupted from deep inside him.

Czarny had been a *Hofjuden* from Passover until the day of the uprising. *Hofjuden* had to wear a yellow cloth triangle on their clothes. He was free to move about the chicken-coop area and also had free access to the German compound where he cleaned stoves in the kitchen. Occasionally, he went to the Ukrainians' kitchen after their meals to gather leftovers for the pigsty and chicken coop.

Czarny testified that when the revolt broke out, he ran from the camp. Once outside its boundaries, he kept running. "There was a force within me that drove me to save myself.... I wanted so desperately to live. I did not want to die. Why? I have no answer. I don't know."

Czarny managed to swim across the river, even though he did not know how to swim. Finally, in the forest Czarny fell to the ground. He cried out to his dead parents to ask why he had been allowed to live.

He broke into sobs. The audience was hushed except for the clicking and whirring of cameras.

"Please calm down," Levin said.

"I am trying, Your Honor, I am trying, but I am reliving Treblinka. Your Honor, I am in Treblinka right now. Right now, I am sitting in Treblinka, and in Jerusalem, too ... we have been praying for Jerusalem. Yes, that's right. I am in Jerusalem."

Later Shaked asked him to recall those occasions when he saw Ivan Grozny. Czarny responded that when the transports arrived, the SS would stand there to issue commands and on several occasions Ivan Grozny was among them, "standing together as a peer, as an equal of the masters with them." Ivan was known to be brutal, and Czarny feared him.

Judge Dorner asked if Czarny knew him and came across him.

"Did I come across him? Yes, madame; yes, Your Honor. Not only once. Ivan Grozny I saw more frequently because I had more opportunities, because I was a Hofjuden."

Czarny said he also saw Ivan Grozny because the chicken run where he worked was on the path leading from the death camp to the German quarters. "Throughout all of these transports, as I said, from time to time I saw him. I saw when a transport would arrive. People were not only beaten; they were sometimes shot. On one of these transports, I saw how Ivan Grozny was pointing his pistol and shooting in the direction of the fence, the fence that is in front of a track, the outer fence.

And I saw a young girl, who apparently had succeeded-- you know, when transports arrived everyone knew what was waiting for them --in spite of everything. So, each person sought some way of saving his life ... and I could see him pointing his pistol in this direction. But since the fence is green, apparently the reflection of a human being was not so obvious on that background. I could see her climbing up the fence, but he pulled out his pistol and shot at her. In those moments I saw him shooting her, and I still had a chance to see, I just had a chance to catch the look of this girl as she fell down."

Czarny said he also saw Ivan as he walked around or went to get food or when he went to the Germans' living quarters. Czarny said he often saw Ivan Grozny coming along the path from the death camp. "Even if I didn't want to, I always wound up seeing him. I wanted to keep away, but I did see him often-often when I was going to pick up food from the Ukrainian kitchen, too." Czarny testified that Ivan was four, five, or six years older than him at the time.

When Miriam Radiwker put the album of photographs before him in 1976, "I opened it up," he now testified, "and saw a number of pictures. I came to one, and I said immediately, Your Honor, immediately, *Dos iz Ivan --Ivan Grozny von Treblinka.* I recognized him from the first look, immediately, without a shadow of a doubt."

Czarny said he had become quite agitated because the picture was of a man older than the one he knew at Treblinka; the man in the photo was in civilian clothes and his face was fuller.

"Well, I saw this, my God, he's alive, he's alive."

"You are saying this with a certain amount of agitation," Levin said, "and forgive the expression, rather dramatically, but how was it at the time?"

"It was the same dramatic expression as I am using here. This dramatic touch will accompany me for whatever is left of my life."

Czarny testified that after he identified Ivan as having been at Treblinka, Radiwker said he had been at Sobibor. "I said, that's impossible, he was in Treblinka, he was not in Sobibor. Ivan Grozny was in Treblinka."

Cross-examination was comparatively short-only three

hours long. Czarny had been in Camp One, not the death camp, and O'Connor wanted to ascertain how Czarny could know Ivan or know what he did. Czarny answered that Ivan's normal place of assignment was in the death camp and his duty was to introduce gas into the gas chambers. Said Czarny, matter-of-factly, "He was a sort of mechanic."

Judge Dorner asked, "How did you know this?"

"It was no secret. Of course, we were living on borrowed time, but we knew what was going on. There was some sort of contact. There were no secrets."

There were moments, when Czarny grew tired and would answer unapologetically, "I just can't remember." Yet his willingness to define those matters he recalled and those he didn't lent his testimony even greater credibility.

Czarny had been afraid that testifying would be too emotionally stressful. He had even asked the prosecution if he might be excused from it. But the prosecutors had said, "If not you, who?" "What could I answer them?" he said later. "So, I agreed."

Testifying in Jerusalem proved both easier and harder than it had been in Dusseldorf or Ft. Lauderdale. A court is a court, he said, wherever it is, but the difference is the public. "I feel at home in Jerusalem"-which made it easier. But to relive the experiences of Treblinka there, was more difficult. Recounting his testimony, Czarny's eyes started to tear: "I never believed that I would stand in Jerusalem and speak in Hebrew and give testimony about what happened to us there.... Even though I was in Jerusalem, I felt that day that I was exactly in Treblinka. I didn't know anything, just that I was in Treblinka.... The hardest part was seeing my children upset. The whole time I was talking and feeling as though I was in Treblinka, I was still thinking, `I don't want to upset my children.'"

Professor Dina Porat, a historian of the Holocaust, had

interviewed Czarny on videotape for Tel Aviv's Beth Hatfutsot (Museum of the Diaspora). She offered Czarny a copy of the tape for his family, but although his wife was also a survivor, he would not accept. Until that day in court, he had never told them of his experiences. He reacted the way he did, Porat said, because of the public disclosure, or exposure, which weighed heavily upon him. She believed he felt humiliated, "because he is among those survivors, who almost apologize for surviving."

After testifying, Czarny said that when his children were young they would ask his wife about the number on her arm. His wife was more open in talking about the Holocaust than he was; but even she became upset when Holocaust programs were broadcast on television. Their children learned to turn the programs off. Once they became older, Czarny said, there was an "agreement of silence." "The children did not want to distress us by asking, and we did not want to distress them by telling." Czarny's wife could not come to court, but the children did. And the children, they were themselves in hell while hearing what happened."

Nevertheless, he said that he felt after the testimony, "as though a huge weight has been lifted from me, even though this weight has accompanied me my whole life, every day. Something has gone from me." He smiled.

"There are two things the Germans could not take away from me, my memory and my spirituality."

11. The Investigator

The identifications by Epstein, Rosenberg and Czarny had all been conducted by Miriam Radiwker, a senior investigator of Israel's Nazi War Crimes Special Police Unit 06, who was called to the stand in Jerusalem.

Radiwker was petite with short, frosted hair. She looked twenty years younger than her actual eighty-one years. In her stylish black-and-white knit dress, she looked more like a fussy Polish wife at a ladies' luncheon than a veteran police officer on the witness stand.

Radiwker's testimony retraced the steps of her investigation. She identified the photos she had shown and described the witnesses interviewed, their reactions, including those who had identified Fedorenko and those who had failed to identify Demjanjuk. All this was told in a forthright and detailed manner, leaving an impression of thorough police work.

Three of the survivors Radiwker interviewed, Turovsky, Goldfarb, and Lindvasser, had since died. Normally their statements would be inadmissible, as the judges couldn't gain an impression of their credibility. But the Nazi and Nazi Collaborators Law had provided for just this situation, allowing evidence to be introduced in Nazi cases that might not otherwise be admitted. This provision, known as Section 15, was used more than a hundred times in the Eichmann trial. As Judge Levin explained, Section 15 does not dictate how the court should regard the evidence, it only allows its consideration.

Shaked argued that some of the identifications -- Lindvasser's, in particular --were unequivocal.

Proving himself a keen observer of human behavior, Levin said, "'Unequivocal' depends on the vocabulary and the nature of a person. A person who never admits to being one hundred percent sure of something, when he is, that is unequivocal, but the person who is only ninety-seven percent sure when they always say one hundred percent, is not so sure. That is why it is important for the court to observe the demeanor of the witnesses." The court said the weight of the statements would be decided, after summation, in the verdict.

On this day, as in the past, O'Connor became, as one of judge Levin's clerks observed, something of a nudnick --a nuisance. Throughout the direct examination, he objected, and often commented in the form of an objection.

In 1976, at the start of the Demjanjuk investigation, Radiwker was seventy. At first, one wondered at the wisdom of having so aged an investigator in charge of a case that would, no doubt, take years to come to judgment. But in the course of O'Connor's cross-examination, Radiwker showed herself to be a formidable personage with a vital and precise memory.

Just before leaving Poland, Radiwker told the court, she took her husband and daughter to Auschwitz. What she saw there moved her to vow that "I would do anything to bring these people to justice." Once in Israel, she learned the police were recruiting. Despite her age, she was hired by the war-crimes unit after impressing its director with her legal background and language abilities.

O'Connor probed as to the source of the original allegations against Demjanjuk. Radiwker said she knew only that they came from the U.S. As far as she knew from the information, he was charged with having been at Sobibor. She didn't have a chance to look into his having been at Flossenburg. As to Trawniki, she did speak to one survivor, a Mrs. Engelman, but she had been there during a completely different period. And as to Sobibor, "I did everything in my power to find out whether he had, in fact, been in Sobibor or not."

Radiwker said she had called witnesses from Sobibor. She

had even asked the witnesses from Treblinka about whether Demjanjuk might not have been in Sobibor instead; but when she did, "I really ended in an argument with them.... Goldfarb's answer, for example was 'no-and yes.' But before the uprising, he was no longer there. Rosenberg said that he was there until the last day. Czarny, I remember ... I said to him, 'Listen, on the basis of the information that we have, he was in Sobibor and not in Treblinka,' so Czarny told me: 'Madame, that is not true. That is not the truth. He was in Treblinka up to the last day, he was there.'

"What else could I do? I really did my very best to carry out the investigation as fairly and as objectively as possible. I asked Czarny, and I did everything in this case beyond the call of duty. I asked Czarny, 'Why Ivan? Why do you remember Ivan more than anyone else? Why not Fedorenko?' So Czarny said in simple words: 'He stood out. He was extremely good in this horrible task. He was the most brutal among them, and that is why I remember him, and I will remember him to the end of my days.' So, what else could I do? If he did not know Fedorenko, well, he did not know Fedorenko. And if there was the tiniest little nuance, any shades of meaning, it was put down in the protocol."

As to the trial in Florida, Radiwker maintained her conduct was above reproach: she came by separate flight, stayed in the same motel but not the same room, ate in the motel dining room but not at the same table as the witnesses. She had no contact with them except at one festive meal given by a woman from Miami for the witnesses and prosecutors. All in all, she complied with arrangements made by the U.S. Justice Department.

She did remark how rudely, poorly, and roughly the judge treated the witnesses in the Fedorenko case. "It was harsh, it was unpleasant, ostensibly every witness was a liar, a deceitful person, I cannot imagine, I cannot describe for you the kind of treatment they received."

O'Connor asked, "Was it not true that there was some indication by this judge that, in fact, the witnesses that you had examined were coached?"

"My witnesses don't need coaching," Radiwker said angrily. "I didn't hear this type of criticism, but I felt the atmosphere."

Sheftel then cross-examined Radiwker, finding much at fault with the identifications she had conducted, pointing out inaccuracies in her testimony at the Fedorenko trial. Radiwker explained that at the trial, she was not allowed to check her notes, so she may have spoken inaccurately.

What was the purpose, Sheftel asked, of showing the survivors the photospread?

Radiwker's answer crystallized the identification issue in the trial: "Well, to test his powers of memory, his impressions, but there is a difference according to my own experience, whether the witness was for a considerable length of time in the proximity of this criminal, and then you accept things in a different way when he identifies a person. It's a different sort of identification from what the judge did in a hall full of the public. Maybe I am wrong, and you need fewer photos. Some people can identify someone from only a few photos, and another person, if you put thirty photos to him, unless he had been in the proximity of the person involved, would not recognize him."

Sheftel wanted to know why she didn't arrange the photos differently, why Demjanjuk was the only almost-bald head on the page.

"I simply put before them what I had received. I am really not responsible for Demjanjuk's bald pate."

People in the audience began to laugh, and Demjanjuk himself doubled over in laughter at this, his whole head turning red as he slapped his knees.

Sheftel probed why she didn't attach any importance to those Treblinka survivors who didn't identify anyone, or why she didn't confront survivors about testimony that Ivan died in the revolt.

Radiwker was aghast: it would have been inappropriate to confront the witnesses. What they said, or didn't say, she took down, as they said it. That was all. Anything else was forbidden and would have been improper.

She was, after all, she said, an investigator.

12. Aging Memories

In contrast to Demjanjuk's ruddy good health, the next witness, Gustav Boraks, was the frailest thus far. His wife helped him to the podium; she was led to a seat in the front row.

Seated, Gustav Boraks could barely see above the podium. He had a full head of white hair and a face as brown as a paper bag. He wore a white turtleneck and tan jacket. Boraks was forty-one years old when he arrived at Treblinka. His wife and two children were killed there. In Israel, Boraks started a new family and was now a grandfather.

Shaked stood close to Boraks who testified in Yiddish. Born in 1901, in Vienun, Poland, a small town near Lodz, he had been a barber and had had his own barbershop. He was married with two children, "Pinhas,"-he gave a pause that must have struck the prosecution with fear for his memory-"and Yossef."

Boraks's barbershop was confiscated. He was taken to a prison and transferred to Cracow. There he was arrested for not wearing an armband. The Gestapo beat him mercilessly and amused themselves by throwing him down four flights of stairs. His wife was able to save him by trading her fur coat for his life. From Cracow, Boraks and his family were transferred to the Czestochowa ghetto.

As Boraks testified, Shaked tried to put him at ease. It was not easy. Four months earlier, when Shaked had visited Boraks in Haifa, his mind was clear and his answers poured forth. Eighty-six years old now, under the glare of the klieg lights, his age had caught up with him. Shaked asked questions to which Boraks offered no answer. So Shaked asked more precise questions to which Boraks needed reply only "yes" or "no."

After testimony by the intense Epstein, the energetic

Rosenberg, and the emotional Czarny, Boraks's very frailty seemed itself a statement about the future of Nazi war-crimes prosecution. The witnesses were a limited precious resource. A matter of a few months could make a great difference in their cognition.

Boraks was like a cranky child. Upon hearing judge Tal's deep Yiddish, he said he preferred Tal as an interpreter to the court's. "Him, I understand," said the witness. Judge Tal agreed to oblige him. Many in the audience smiled.

With Tal as translator, Boraks became more animated. As he focused on Treblinka, his memory seemed to flow again. He told how upon arrival at Treblinka he was thrown from the boxcars to the ground. He didn't know what was happening. They asked for barbers, but Boraks didn't reply, "My wife and children were going to be killed, I wasn't going to raise my hand." Later when they found out he was a barber; he was beaten about the head for not having volunteered.

At first the barbershop was in the Lower Camp in a shed where fifteen benches were arranged for fifteen or sixteen barbers. He was to cut the women's hair. He recalled that "They didn't want to come in, but Ivan would take his bayonet and with his bayonet he would force them into the barbershop.... The women were wounded and pieces of flesh, whole pieces of flesh were hanging behind them, the blood was dripping."

Every time a transport arrived, there was a signal-- a whistle -- and the barbers were to show up to cut hair. When there was no transport, he sorted clothes, putting them into bundles to be loaded back onto the trains and taken away. If a Jew did not do his job well, if he didn't remove the Jewish patch from the clothing, he was shot. He remembered Lalke riding his horse and shooting into the latrines when the Jews were in the toilets.

Boraks also worked on a camouflage detail. Workers would

collect branches. "Two people would carry a tree, and I was walking with a young man of seventeen or eighteen. I was strong enough to carry the tree, but the young boy didn't have the strength, and he fell down. So, Ivan walked over to him, when he fell, and shot him."

Shaked shortened his usual questions and jumped forward to the critical moment-Boraks's meeting with Radiwker. Shaked asked what he had said after looking at the photo album of Ukrainians. "I said to her," Boraks testified, "I know Ivan and the other one what's his name." Never mind, Shaked said. But a few moments later, Boraks said excitedly, "Fedorenko is the other one. I just remembered his name was Fedorenko." This, too, elicited smiles.

Shaked handed him the album. He opened it. Turning over the first page slowly, he immediately pointed to a face on the next leaf. "That is Fedorenko," he said, "and this is Ivan." He pointed with assurance to Demjanjuk's photo.

Shaked asked why he recognized him. "He had a full face, a high forehead, and small eyes."

"Why do you remember Ivan?" Shaked asked again. "Because he was all the time at the place where the hair was being cut," Boraks said. A bit exasperated, Shaked said, "But why did he stick in your memory?" "Why? Because he was tall... ," Boraks said, "he had an elongated face and a peaked cap."

Shaked decided to try a different tact. He showed Boraks his deposition from 1976. Boraks recalled it and said Radiwker's arm was in a sling, so she had brought along someone else. Boraks said that at the time of Treblinka, Ivan must have been twenty-two or twenty-three.

He said Ivan's uniform was green. But the auxiliary uniforms were. usually black, as Boraks had told Radiwker in 1976. Shaked asked if he would like his memory to be refreshed by his earlier deposition. Sheftel objected, and it was sustained. Shaked tried ano ther tact, asking Boraks whether the court should rely on his statement in 1976 or his testimony in court.

The earlier statement, Boraks said sincerely. Shaked left it at that.

Boraks recalled Kollar's visit in 1981. Shaked asked if he had found anything in the photographs. "Fedorenko and Ivan," he testified. Shaked began to follow this up, but Sheftel objected that if the answer Boraks gave did not suit the prosecution, they nonetheless had to accept it.

"I think the witness may remember better than we do," Shaked said. In fact, Kollar had shown Boraks two stacks of photographs that day, one with Ivan and the other with Fedorenko. Shaked set about putting the same photographs before him. They had since been glued to a cardboard sheet.

Boraks pointed at the Trawniki card photo, saying: "Ivan. Ivan Grozny." Boraks repeated that he recalled him because, "He used to roam around the area where we would cut the women's hair."

Levin asked how much hair he cut off. "It wasn't a haircut," Boraks said. "We would grab the hair and cut it all off." Under further questioning, Boraks said the hair was sorted and put in an oven where it was cleaned. He said children were also brought to him, but a few minutes later he said their hair wasn't cut. At first, he couldn't remember whether the women were dressed or naked, but then he recalled they were ordered to undress. He said Fedorenko once shot a woman who refused.

Gustav Boraks looked out at the audience; his small, dark eyes set in a pug face. At the recess, he pulled a small sandwich from his pocket and munched on it peacefully.

"Mar Boraks," O'Connor began the cross-examination, "can you indicate what color my gown is?" Was O'Connor mocking

Borak's reply that Ivan wore a green uniform? His next question also went straight for the jugular: he asked Boraks if he could name his children. Boraks replied, without difficulty, that he had two sons, Pinhas and Yossef, who were killed with his first wife in Treblinka; and one from his second wife, named Yoram.

But Boraks was tired, and the long day now began to wear on him. At moments he became confused. O'Connor asked him about Fedorenko: "Do you remember testifying against Fedorenko in the United States?"

"Yes."

"Do you remember the year?"

"No."

"Do you remember how you traveled from Israel to Florida so that you could speak to the court in that trial?"

"Yes. We went by train." But O'Connor continued, asking where he stayed in Florida. Boraks answered, "In a hotel."

O'Connor discussed the Fedorenko case. Boraks said he had traveled with Sonia Lewkowicz but had not spoken with her in a great many years.

There was the possibility that Boraks would say something damaging to the prosecution case. Yet for all his weaknesses, he yielded nothing. Boraks said that the survivors had sat together in the courtroom and had had dinner together. But when asked, "Did you talk about Treblinka?" The answer was emphatic: "No, we didn't speak about that."

O'Connor asked Boraks if he remembered the number for his barracks. "One hundred," he answered. This was wrong but, on reexamination, Boraks instinctively pointed to his coat lapel, to show that one hundred was his number at Treblinka, not the number of his barracks.

O'Connor asked about an SS man named Suchomel. Boraks surprised the spectators by replying, "Suchomel wasn't a bad man. He was OK." Boraks said Suchomel oversaw the Goldjuden (literally "Gold Jews"-Jewish workers whose job it was to sort the gold, currency, and other valuables which were to be sent to Germany).

O'Connor asked if Suchomel had ever come to his aid before Commander Stangl. Boraks told how, one day, as he was performing his duties as a barber, his sister-in-law and her children came before him. She knew her husband was dead, and that she was about to die.. But she begged him to save her children. She wept and fell all over him. Boraks was powerless.

For this, that his sister-in-law wept in his arms, Lalke ordered Boraks to undress and enter the gas chamber. But Suchomel intervened on his behalf. He said Boraks was a good barber and that he should be saved. Boraks was allowed to live, but his sister-in-law and the children went to the gas chamber.

Suchomel, he testified, would come in and say hello to him every other day or so. Boraks saw him up to the day of the uprising and even on the day itself. Boraks said Suchomel had hidden in a barracks because he was afraid the Jews would kill him.

"Did you kill him?" O'Connor asked.

"No-ohhh," said Boraks. "If not for him I would not be alive."

Levin asked if he knew whether Suchomel was killed in the uprising. He said he didn't. Judge Dorner asked, "Did you kill anyone?" Said Boraks, "Heaven forbid, no, I couldn't so much as kill a fly!"

O'Connor asked why the prisoners called him Ivan Grozny. "Because he was a groyser bandit [a great criminal]-he killed children," said Boraks. He admitted he had seen Ivan only in Camp One.

Boraks had left Haifa at 5:00 A.M. that morning. As the afternoon wore on, it became obvious that Boraks's mind was weakening under the strain. The more tired he became, the less he could remember or wanted to remember. After a short while, the defense rested.

Yet the prosecution forged ahead with its redirect. It seemed heartless to continue, yet it would have been worse to ask Boraks to return the next day. Shaked felt there were a few points that needed clarification. He brought out that Boraks had testified at Dusseldorf against Suchomel. Boraks nonetheless maintained that Suchomel was "the best of all of them." The prosecution rested at 5:55 P.M.

Still Judge Levin had two questions. First, he asked Boraks to repeat the story about Suchomel saving his life. He did, with precision. Levin asked his second question: "You said you went to Florida by train. What train stop did you get on at?"

"I was wrong," Boraks said, "I made a mistake. I flew." Levin smiled. "From where to where did you fly?"

"From Katowice," he replied. This was a city in Poland. Some in the audience giggled in embarrassment.

"From where did you depart?"

"From Poland. From Poland I went to America."

Judge Dorner tried to change the subject and asked, "Have you

heard of Demjanjuk in Treblinka?"

"Yes," Boraks said.

"Who was he?" Dorner asked.

"He's sitting over there," Boraks said, nodding his head in Demjanjuk's direction.

Levin thanked the witness, and said in heartfelt tones, "We

wish you a long life, and we hope you never have to think back to those experiences publicly again."

"Amen," Boraks said.

13. The SuperDemon of Treblinka

When the final survivor was called to the stand, it was easy to be distracted by the dignity of his appearance, the eloquence with which he spoke of the unspeakable, but months later, his account of Treblinka would haunt many as the one that brought them closest to an intimation of hell.

Yehiel Meir Reichman spoke in Yiddish in a tired but lilting voice. As he was the fifth witness to tell his tale, the territory was familiar. Reichman's descriptions, however, were particularly concrete.

He began, "Your Honor, I will tell you everything on behalf of those who can no longer tell the story, my sister and the others." At seventy-two, he was an impressive figure. But as he talked of Treblinka, the weight of the subject bore down on him, dulling the usual sparkle in his eyes.

When Reichman arrived at Treblinka, he knew their journey, as well as their lives, had come to an end. He told his sister to leave their suitcases: "We will not be needing them here." Because Reichman had thought they were embarking on a short trip, he had advised his sister not to eat before. She went to the gas chambers hungry. He would never forgive himself for that.

Shortly after his arrival, Reichman, like the others who had survived, was chosen to sort clothing. As he ran to gather clothes, he saw a naked woman holding her son in her arms. "At that moment," Reichman testified, "one of the blaggards came and tore the child out of his mother's arms, grabbed him by the feet and smashed his skull before his mother's eyes." The whole room gasped.

Reichman spoke directly to the judges, his heavy face turned toward them. He told the court he volunteered to be a barber. "What did I have to lose?" he said. The next morning,

Reichman heard the cry, "Barbers out." He went with a friend who had told him to prepare scissors, and they were led toward the gas chambers. "This was the most horrifying job, even though I spent only three days there. There they brought in running naked women, and we were made to cut off their hair in five cuts, five snips of the scissors."

The barbering took place between the gas chambers. "There was one chamber that was open on both sides, and there they arranged benches where they put the victims-the victims who, a few minutes later, would no longer be alive. There were moments, terrible moments there, and you saw the reaction of the people there.... For example, a woman sat down in front of me and said, `Do me a favor. I'm here with my daughter, but she is still in line behind. Don't cut my hair so quickly. I want to go to my death with her.' But I could not even fulfill this last request because I was being whipped."

Blatman asked if he remembered anything else from that place. Reichman recalled a woman who said: `Tell me the truth, I see that I am about to die. But young people, are they allowed to live? Will my son survive? Will he be allowed to live and take revenge?' A young girl came in, and when she saw everyone crying, she broke into hysterical laughter and cried out: `You should be ashamed of yourselves. Who are you crying for? Let us not show our enemies that we are about to die frightened.'"

The barbers had to pack the hair very painstakingly into bags. There was a rumor, Reichman testified, that the hair was used to reinforce metal for ammunition. The Ukrainian guards and a German supervised the barbers, who were forced to sort clothes when they were not cutting hair. When a transport arrived, they would hear the call for barbers.

Reichman wore a gray three-piece suit. His expressive face grew red under the lights, but remained soft, set off by his silver-white hair and creamy complexion, wrinkled only at the eyes. The memories were like a weight, forcing his chin down on his chest.

"When you were working at the sorting area," Blatman asked, "did you find anything personal?"

"Among the clothes, I found my sister's frock. I tore off the cloth and kept a piece. I had it in my pocket for many months."

Once in the death camp, Reichman became friends with Dr. Zimmerman, a Kapo of the dentists. Zimmerman knew the Germans and the Ukrainians because he held the key to a box near the workshops where valuables, taken from the corpses, were stored. When the Ukrainians and Germans went on leave, they would come to him and pick up valuables for which he would get a loaf of bread. The bread was often wrapped in a newspaper; in this way the prisoners learned what was going on in the outside world.

Reichman asked Zimmerman to give him cyanide because he didn't have the courage to hang himself. Zimmerman didn't have any but told Reichman to hold on-he would try and get him assigned to the dentist's crew. Zimmerman told Matthes, the German in charge of the death camp, that more dentists were needed. So, the order was issued: anyone who was a dentist, step forward.

Reichman, with no true training, marched out of line and thus became one of the dentists.

"The work was as follows," he testified: "Every time a transport arrived with people who within a few minutes would be dead, we were called. We would go down. There were many bowls, one on top of the other. We were arranged in a group of six ... six of us for each lane. The first person would have a bowl in front of him with water in it [the bowls and water were for cleaning the extracted teeth]. He had to check the stretcher-bearers and to see whether the corpse on the stretcher had any teeth, any false teeth.... If it did, he would pull the stretcher-bearer out of line ... and pull out those teeth...." Each dentist carried out a similar function and that way all of the corpses were checked.

"When there were no transports, we were in our shed. There we were supposed to separate the teeth in different types, to separate the natural, the real teeth from the false.

Sometimes inside the crowns, there were valuables like diamonds. In addition, we were supposed to clean thoroughly the gold teeth so that they would be absolutely spotless. Each week we turned over a suitcase of teeth that we estimated at ten kilograms [twenty-two pounds]."

The teeth were washed in a well that was located, in Reichman's estimation, some three to four meters from the gas chambers.

"I would like to tell the court what happened near the well to mein Haver [my friend], Finkelstein. While I was washing teeth there together with Finkelstein, next to this well, this demon Ivan"-Reichman pointed spontaneously at Demjanjuk-"came with a drill ... he turned it into the buttocks of Finkelstein, telling him: `If you yell, I shall shoot you.' Finkelstein was seriously wounded. Blood was streaming from him. He was suffering unutterable pain but he could not yell because he was given this order that if he dared to yell, he would be shot. Ivan threatened him." Finkelstein kept his silence and survived the drilling.

Throughout this account, Demjanjuk was slowly shaking his head "no."

"Ivan was the superdemon of Treblinka," Reichman testified. After Treblinka, while still in a bunker in Warsaw in 1944, Reichman began to think of giving evidence, and he thought of Ivan. "He is engraved in my memory, night and day, and I've never had any peace."

Reichman was asked to describe Ivan's job at Treblinka. He

212

answered, as Czarny had: "He was a mechanic.... It was his job to start the gas in order to kill the people in the gas chambers. In Treblinka, there were two buildings of gas chambers. The first had three chambers. Next to it stood a separate entrance, and there stood a machine rather like a car engine. It was here that Ivan had his seat ... he had the honor of turning on the gas."

"With what loyalty he fulfilled his task." Reichman sighed. His large, expressive hands were held out in front of him, his arms moved like a bellows, in and out, as he exhaled.

"One day, when I was sitting at this bowl to do with the false teeth, Ivan drove past with a horse and cart carrying products to Camp Two. As he passed by, one could hear screams from the gas chambers; when he heard those screams, it meant that people were being shepherded into the gas chambers. He left the horse and cart, and ran to his quarters to take a long iron bar, a round bar, took it on his shoulders, and ran over to the gas chamber so that he would get there in time to beat up the people being shepherded into the Schlauch.... That was his pleasure. That was what he lived for and was his greatest pleasure in life.... The sadism of this demon has no equal anywhere. It was his pleasure to take a knife, to go up to an ordinary worker, to cut off his ears. When [the worker] came back, he would tell him to strip and then shoot him to death....

At that particular moment, he didn't have any obligation to do that. But when he heard the screams and the cries, he was so enthusiastic that he abandoned his horse and cart ... to give his last presents to the victims as they were going to the chamber."

Levin's face clouded. The judge asked where the iron bar was located. Within the building of the small gas chambers, Reichman explained, there was a small room that housed the machine. "He was the mechanic who turned on the gas, and it was there that he kept all his tools, the drill, the knives, and the iron bar that he used to hurt people."

Blatman wanted to stress how much contact Reichman had with Ivan. "He was my neighbor," Reichman testified. "I saw him on every occasion. From the well, it was very close to the engine room." Reichman enumerated the opportunities he had to see Ivan. He saw him outside working hours, from the yard of their barracks. He often saw him sitting with his friend Nikolai on a bench outside the engine room. The two men, Reichman said, would spend "companionable hours together." When Reichman carried corpses, he frequently saw Ivan because the carriers would have to wait the half-hour while victims were gassed.

"And we had to sing for them," he testified. Judge Dorner asked for an explanation. "This was between one group of the dead and the next," Reichman said. "We would have to carry corpses away as quickly as possible, because they shouted at us that `these pieces of shit' had to be disposed of as fast as possible. But while we were waiting for the next set of victims to be gassed, we were told to sit down and then we were told to sing songs that they liked."

When working as a dentist, Reichman saw Ivan several times a day. The dentists, as he had testified earlier, worked in a group of six in a line. When he was among the first in line, closer to the gas chambers, he would almost always see Ivan.

In 1945, when hiding in a bunker in Warsaw, Reichman wrote his memoir of Treblinka, recalling his eleven months there. He remembered a few of the criminals' names, but he remembered Ivan the most.

Judge Dorner asked why.

"This devil I carried within me," Reichman testified. "I saw him every step. I saw him at night, I saw him during the day. I saw his murderous sadism. I saw him everywhere I turned. I saw him in everything I did, with his heinous deeds."

Reichman testified that the American Embassy in Montevideo contacted him in 1980. He was asked if he would take part in trials relating to Treblinka. Reichman said that whenever called, he would "speak in the name of those who can no longer speak for themselves."

He told the court that he made arrangements so that the next time he was in New York, he met with officials from the OSI. Four persons were waiting for him, with a recording machine. Sheftel objected, saying the defense had never received a transcript and didn't know one to exist.

The prosecution said it, too, knew nothing of a recording of the session. Reichman continued, saying, he was shown a stack of photographs. He examined them at length, looking at each picture several times. "I, by nature, do not easily say `yes' or `no' off the cuff, so it took me awhile. I concentrated until I said what I said.... I said, my opinion is that this is Ivan of Treblinka." It was the only photograph he selected.

Afterward, he returned to Montevideo until summoned to Cleveland for Demjanjuk's denaturalization trial. At that trial, he singled out the photo he had identified previously. But he was also shown another set of photos. "There I recognized a picture that was even more similar than the other one, because in court they showed me a picture that was just the right weight, even more similar to the way he looked in Treblinka." It was the Trawniki photo.

Shown the set again, he quickly pointed to the Trawniki photo, saying, "This is Ivan."

Gill led the cross-examination. He stressed that Reichman would not have looked at Ivan because the prisoner worked at a run and feared him so and was afraid of being "gestampelt" (marked). Gill had read Allan Ryan's book, in which Ryan had written, "At Treblinka, eye contact was forbidden." Ryan also had written that at the denaturalization trial, Reichman would not look Demjanjuk in the eye. But Reichman tried to make it clear to Gill that though he did work at a run and under a hail of beatings, there was still great opportunity to look around and observe.

Gill also suggested that the Kapos provided a layer of insulation between forced laborers and Ukrainians, and asked Reichman about his, as if this subject, which Gill seemed to think was taboo, would unnerve him.

Reichman was not ashamed to speak of Kapos. His own Kapo, Zimmerman, had saved his life. Gill asked if Kapos could punish fellow Jews. Reichman said that he was never the subject of such punitive measures, nor did he ever see them carried out. He could only speak of what he knew.

Gill's focus continued to be on the misdeeds of the Jews. He asked questions such as, "People like yourself, sorting clothes, were all of them taking money, or was it just your friend that suggested it to you?"

The Court gave Gill great latitude in his cross-examination but Gill's lengthy questions of what Reichmann recalled today of areas of the camp that didn't concern his identification of Ivan bordered on the trivial.

Gill challenged Reichman's descriptions of landmarks on the diagram of the camp, in. "You indicated earlier that this was the women's section, is that correct?" Gill said, Reichman looked at the diagram. There was one building in the women's area. Reichman recalled two structures there.

"My question, Herr Reichman was: Do you know where the laundry was hung up to dry after it was done by the women that were forced to do this task?"

Judge Levin interrupted: "Mr. Gill, I have a question.... Of everything of the camp at Treblinka, where people-more than eight hundred fifty thousand were murdered and thrown into pits-and you do not deny this-is it important for us to know where they hung the laundry?" Levin continued angrily, unable to restrain himself, "Aren't you exaggerating in these questions? Did he hang up the laundry? Why do we have to waste the time of the court on points that are so marginal... ? Are we going to decide whether a person has committed so terrible an offense or not on the basis of where the laundry was hung to dry?"

Some outside observers took Levin's anger as an indication that the Holocaust was a sacrosanct subject in Israeli society, and of Levin's inherent bias towards believing survivor testimony. To the contrary, Levin was irritated by Gill's questions that seemed more interesting in fanning the flames of Anti-Semitic tropes (Jews stealing money, Kapos being worse than the Germans or their henchmen) than in questions relevant to attacking Reichman's credibility.

Doubting the objectivity of the Judges was one thing (it was a constant refrain of Sheftel's) but doubting that an Israeli Court or an Israeli could be fair, was a calumny or bias all its own. A wire service reporter sitting next to me in the press area commented, "The others said they did. Maybe he's the first one to tell the truth." She felt sorry for Demjanjuk, she said, this was a show trial, she said, "because this is Israel," and the verdict and sentence were foregone conclusions.

Gill continued to ask about money taken by Reichman or other Jews from the dead. Gill asked whether some work groups had easier access to valuables. Reichman answered that, of course, the Dentisten had an easier chance than the others. But what was Gill getting at?

He asked whether Reichman knew of Ukrainians being granted furloughs or being transferred from Treblinka only to return after several months. Reichman said that he could not confirm this, but it was the opinion of Jewish inmates that the Ukrainians were given permission occasionally to leave the camp. Reichman wiped his brow with his blue handkerchief.

Gill was so tall, his robe fell only to his knees, and as he went through his questions he made checks on a legal pad. He was nearing the end of the pad when he asked whether the survivors of Treblinka met on a yearly basis. Reichman testified that he did not meet with them on a yearly basis, only when he came to Israel. Gill asked whether they talked about Treblinka.

"We talk about everything," Reichman answered. He was always especially happy to meet old friends from that tragedy. But his regret, he said, his voice sharp, was meeting so few of them; and that each time, there was one less.

Gill brought out the fact that Reichman's 1944 memoir described Ivan only sketchily, as a "healthy powerful horse." Reichman gave this reason for the memoir's brief description and his more detailed one in court: "I never thought that I would have an opportunity, a moment in my life, when I would have to blame, or cast accusations at, this devil. First, because I was not sure that I would ever be reunited with those who lost everyone they had there. He was a devil like all the other devils, but the more I concentrate, the more I think back on it, the more I recall things vividly. Because when it comes to Treblinka, I cannot free myself of Treblinka. Sometimes I do not sleep, I wake up screaming. Believe me, it is impossible to remember everything. They didn't succeed in breaking us totally. We managed to clutch with our very last shreds of strength. What else do they want from us?"

Sheftel had questions about the photo identification in New York. There were certain discrepancies between his and Reichman's version. Reichman could offer no explanation other than that he did not recall being shown the photo in New York.

O'Connor asked: "The fear of the return to the clutches of Ivan was even greater than the fear of death, sir. Is that true?"

Without the slightest doubt, answered Reichman.

Surely the death of Ivan, O'Connor asked, was in the minds of those who took part in the revolt?

Blatman objected to the question as hypothetical and good only for summing up. But Levin allowed it, gently chiding Blatman: "I think that is very cruel, Mr. Blatman. He is now coming to the punch question, as it were, and you want to stop defense counsel."

Reichman prefaced his comments by saying, "I want to make it clear that in Treblinka there were a great many Ivans. He was not the only one in Treblinka. There were a great many Ivans. There were many murderers." But, as to Ivan the Terrible, he said, had they been able to kill him, they would have done so. On redirect, Reichman reaffirmed that on the day of the uprising, as there were no transports, Ivan was not at work. Reichman didn't remember whether he saw Ivan on that day.

One more survivor, Sonia Lewkowicz, was supposed to testify. She had testified at Dusseldorf, in Ft. Lauderdale against Fedorenko, and against Demjanjuk in Cleveland. But she was never called as a witness in Jerusalem. She could not overcome her anxiety and fear of being on the stand, reliving those experiences for direct examination, then enduring the cross-examination. The prosecutors hoped she would change her mind before they rested their case. But she never did.

14. One of the Surprises of his Life

On the morning of Monday, March 23, 1987, Investigator Martin Kollar was ready to take the stand, but instead Sheftel rose. He was calling upon the court to disqualify itself because of its hostility and bias toward the defense.

The court deliberated for a full two hours before returning a decision. "It is our unequivocal opinion that there is no grounds for Mr. Sheftel's case." The court said it had overruled questions by either side. "In the system of adversary trials, the court need not be passive. As the trial proceeds, it must conduct the proceedings by being on the alert to make certain that the deliberations in the case in no way deviate from proper procedure." The court said it had acted "with unusual leeway," noting that "precisely because of the gravity of the case that looms over the accused, we have been unusually patient in the course of this trial and have gone far beyond the usual proceedings. We have allowed far more than what is relevant and customary and permissible in trials that take place in the Israeli court system, even in the gravest among them."

When Kollar finally took the stand, he began with his personal history: Born in Czechoslovakia in 1920, he was held in forced-labor camps during World War H. His family-and all his relatives-were exterminated. "I swore that if I got out alive, I would bring my family's murderers to justice," he testified. In the course of his nineteen years with the police, Kollar had worked at the behest of the governments of Germany, Austria, Canada, the Netherlands, and the United States.

Kollar testified he met with survivors Epstein, Rosenberg, and Lewkowicz, beginning in 1978. He also met in January 1980 with Boraks and his son at the Haifa police station. Kollar had in his hand the statement Boraks had given Radiwker in 1976. "This was one of the surprises of my life. With what accuracy, and with what clarity, he described his life in Treblinka.... His memory was astounding... !"

At the Fedorenko trial, O'Connor asked, had he testified that when Epstein spoke in his office, he needed to, "direct this witness, or give this witness direction?"

"When Epstein began speaking," Kollar answered, "he spoke freely without interruption. He gave me a vast and very plastic description and a very vivid one. Within a few minutes, I had the feeling I was with him, there." But soon Kollar saw that Epstein could continue at great length on aspects of the camp not relevant to his investigation. "At certain points, I said: `Would you please get back to the subject....'"

Next Sheftel cut straight to the heart of the matter: Did he remember when he interviewed Rosenberg about Fedorenko on April 13, 1978, whether Rosenberg at that time also identified Ivan? "I don't rule this out," Kollar said.

Shaked later introduced transcripts of the Fedorenko trial to make it clear that Rosenberg did talk about Ivan when Kollar summoned him to speak about Fedorenko. The defense had failed to extract any major challenges to the veracity of the survivors' identifications.

CHAPTER FOUR:

THE TRAWNIKI CARD

1. The Rosetta Stone

The small green4 X 6-inch carboard German wartime ID document, referred to as "The Trawniki Card," was the Rosetta Stone, as concerned Demjanjuk's history and what was to be gleaned from his Nazi service.

Before Demjanjuk's Trawniki Card first appeared in the U.S. in press accounts, and later at Demjanjuk's US trials, very little was not known about the training of these German auxiliaries, of the men who were assigned to round-up Jews, liquidate Ghettos, who were assigned to concentration, labor, and death camps, and there roles in the murders there.

It was the Trawniki Card that first revealed Demjanjuk's Nazi past, exposing him in the United States, launching the investigation into his past and tt was the picture of Demjanjuk and the identifying details on the card that, over the course of more than 30 years of trials, gave lie to Demjanjuk's denials in his trials in the United States, Israel and Germany.

It was the Trawniki card that linked Demjanjuk to the Sobibor death camp. It was the photo of Demjanjuk on the Trawniki Card in Nazi military uniform and with an identifying badge number 1393 that would follow him from roster to roster, that would, over time, confirm Demjanjuk's murderous Nazi service at Sobibor, Flossenburg and Majdanek, And, finally, it was the picture on the Trawniki Card of a 22-year-old Demjanjuk that many Holocaust survivors would identify as the Ivan they knew at Treblinka.

During the course of the Demjanjuk's Israeli trial, more than eight thousand pages of trial transcript, one-hundred-ninety-nine hours of trial testimony, and fifty days in court would be expended to confirm that a simple four-by-six-inch green cardboard identification document once belonged.

The card, which was inspected and tested during Demjanjuk's U.S. denaturalization trial, in Israel was subjected to the most rigorous analysis imaginable; its many-colored inks, stamps and seals, its photograph of a young soldier, all scrutinized inch for inch, word for word.

Most forged documents, fake IDs, driver's licenses, passports, transcripts, and false papers are meant to be shown to an official, not a forensic documents examiner. Occasionally, they are looked at by dealers, and/or historians. But it is rare that any document is held up to the scrutiny of officials, historians, scientists and forensic documents examiners.

Even in the most famous cases of "successful forgeries," such as the Hitler diaries or the Hofmann Mormon letters forgeries, the falsifications were uncovered quickly when forensic documents experts conducted systematic analyses.

Most observers assumed it was the Israeli prosecution's job to prove the card authentic. In fact, just the opposite was true. Under Israeli law, a government-issued document more than twenty years old was presumed authentic, unless shown otherwise by the defense. In a sense, the card was "innocent until proven guilty," authentic until shown to be a forgery.

Nevertheless, the prosecution was not one to leave things to chance.

Prosecutors called Helge Grabitz, Hamburg state attorney for the prosecution of Nazi war crimes, who had been the chief prosecutor at the trial of Trawniki commander Karl Streibl. (Streibl had been acquitted under the strict German definition of criminal liability). At that time, Grabitz knew more about Trawniki than anyone else. She was followed by Dr. Wolfgang Sheffler, the West German professor and Operation Reinhard expert who had testified at Demjanjuk's denaturalization trial.

The Trawniki camp, as they explained, played an important role in the Final Solution being under the authority of the SS as well as the German police. Its purpose was "instruction" of auxiliary forces. Soviet prisoners recruited from POW camps were trained to participate in each step in the Jews' extermination: to serve as ghetto policemen, to liquidate ghettos, to round up Jews, to load them onto trains, to accompany the transports, and finally, to serve in the death camps in all capacities there from the Jews' arrival there to their murder and beyond, as well as to direct those few Jews kept alive to work in the factory of death.

"The Trawnikis," said Helge Grabitz, "did the dirty work."

Arriving at Trawniki, she said, the former POWs underwent enlistment procedures: a personnel file sheet was made for each; and a service ID was issued, which also listed the equipment he had been issued.

The Trawniki card, Sheffler said, was a Dienstausweis, a service pass-not a file document. It was meant to be carried by the bearer as an identity card.

In 1987, the Trawniki card was still considered as a one-of-a-kind document. To prove that it was a document issued to all Trawniki me, the prosecution had uncovered German archival documents, including correspondence by camp commander Streibl, complaining about problems with the passes; and several letters about a Wachmann named Susslov who had lost his Trawniki card and needed a replacement.

Grabitz and Sheffler confirmed the signatures of Streibl as well as the signature Trawniki supply master Ernst Teufel.

Nonetheless, Demjanjuk's Trawniki card contained several errors: There was no date of issue; the height was incorrect; and the card, although it listed a posting to a camp named "Oksow" in September 1942 and to the death camp Sobibor in March 1943,there was no posting to Treblinka.

Sheffler and Grabitz both testified that Streibl himself had complained to his superiors about chaos in the Trawniki records. They said the documents were full of errors --the prosecution submitted examples of other Trawniki documents with similar errors. They explained that because they were filled in by Volksdeutsche (ethnic Germans) whose proficiency in spelling and German was not great they were error-filled.

Sheffler told the court that the mistakes added to the document's credibility. "The essential elements of this Dienstausweis tally with historical knowledge as we have it, and the individual building blocks fit into each other," he testified.

Silly as it may sound, one of the card's "suspicious" entries was the equipment listing, where a "2" had been entered over a "1," next to "Unterhosen [underwear]." The prosecution introduced the 1942 German order requiring Trawniki men to be issued two pairs of underpants instead of one. This ended the great Trawniki Underpants Debate regarding the card's authenticity.

Sheffler and Grabitz dated the document has having been issue sometime before July 19,1942. Streibl had received a promotion earlier that year; but Teufel was only promoted on July 19, 1942, when Heinrich Himmler inspected the camp. As the card has Streibl's new rank but not Teufel's, they dated the card's issuance as before July 19, 1942.

Training at Trawniki took three to six weeks. By early September, Demjanjuk would most likely have been posted elsewhere. This scenario, according to the prosecution, fit with the survivors' testimony that Ivan was already in the death camp in September, when they arrived there.

Another discrepancy was that the card listed the bearer's height as 175cm (5'8'"), Demjanjuk was180cm (5'10") tall in 1987 and claimed he was taller still during the war

Grabitz testified that Trawniki had no machine to measure each new recruit's height. It was more likely that recruits were asked their heights upon induction (as is done with Drivers' licenses) and the staff of Volksdeuthsche (ethnic Germans) at the camp, wrote what they were told or heard. Even Demjanjuk's various American documents, which he had acknowledged filling out himself, showed his height to range between 5'11" and 6'1".

The prosecution also introduced two documents belonging to defense witness Rudolf Reiss, one of which listed his height at 1 m 70cm (5'6"), the other as 1m 90cm (6'2")-a greater discrepancy even than that on Demjanjuk's Trawniki card.

"Essentially, the card is correct," Sheffler concluded.

"I cann ot stress this enough," Sheffler said, "In the past twenty or twenty-five years, we have not come across a single document that comes from Nazi sources or Nazi files and that has played a part in the different Nazi trials, or that has come from the East Bloc countries, that would have been forged. Not a single one."

2. Putting the Card to the Test

As to the photo on the card, Israel Police Chief Superintendent Amnon Bezalelli, the head of the police laboratory for criminal identification, traveled to Germany to examine other original documents bearing the same stamps and signatures. He found each element of the Trawniki card consistent with them, even under microscopic analysis. He testified that the document gave no indications in any way of being a forgery. Bezalelli shared a detailed letter-by-letter examination of Demjanjuk's signature in Cyrillic on the card, recording forty-one points on the Trawniki signature and was impressed "by the inner authenticity of the signature."

Bezalelli's concluded that, "On the basis of all the examinations I conducted, the document is authentic. I have no doubt of this.... I can determine this with certainty."

Gideon Epstein, the senior forensic documents analyst of the INS, also testified about the signatures. Epstein, who is certified by the American Board of Forensic Documents Examiners (the only certifying body for forensic documents analysts in the United States), had examined the card and the earlier photostat of it several times in the U.S. He first saw the photostat on December 18, 1980, for the OSI; he photographed and examined the original with his own portable laboratory at the Soviet Embassy in Washington on February 27, 1981.

During Epstein's testimony at Demjanjuk's denaturalization trial, the original was brought to the Court where Epstein was allowed to inspect it there. For the trial in Jerusalem, Epstein traveled to Germany and examined the originals of the Streibl and Teufel signatures. "My conclusion to the overall document is that it is a genuine document that it does not bear any evidence of being in any way fraudulently prepared.... The

227

document is genuine."

This opinion was supported by Dr. Anthony Cantu of the U.S. Treasury Bureau, an expert in the chemical analysis of documents. Cantu used a hypodermic-needle probe to take samples from the Trawniki card and its photo and compared them with samples from known Trawniki documents, tested the inks by "thin layer chromatography" (TLC), and by laser. He found them, in all cases, consistent with the other Trawniki documents, available in 1941, and containing no materials from a later date.(the Hitler diaries forgeries were discovered because of the presence of optical brighteners in the paper).

In the card's photo, there is a white rectangle on the bearer's left breast pocket. The number on it is not completely discernible to the naked eye. But by enlarging the photo and printing it on paper of differing contrasts, Bezalelli revealed the number to be 1393 --the same as the document.

In order to prove the Trawniki photo was of Demjanjuk (something Demjanjuk and his defense would not admit), the prosecution called a West German expert, Reinhardt Altmann, from the Bundeskriminalamt (BKA), the West German police's central criminal-identification department who was qualified to appear in court as an expert witness in the identification of a person based on photographs.

Altmann testified that because of the physical uniqueness of each person, individual characteristics could be used for identification, much as fingerprints are. This included "lip mucosa (the grooves on the lip),"the lines on a forehead, or the shape of the ear. Altmann said that often in burglary cases, where no fingerprints could be found, the police uncovered good ear prints on the door.

In analyzing the Trawniki photo he had found twenty-four different facial characteristics that were identifiable and comparable. Using other acknowledged photos of Demjanjuk, he compared each one to the Trawniki card photo. Altmann displayed each on separate TV screens. Then, using a video-mixer, the photos were halved, and combined, making one image. It was clear to the naked eye that the photos were of the same person.

Altmann concluded that there was "a very high degree of probability" that it was Demjanjuk in the Trawniki photo. "For me, there is not the slightest doubt that these photographs are of one and the same person," Altmann said.

Dr. Patricia Smith was one of the trial's most impressive expert witnesses who appeared at trial. Born in England, Smith held a degree in dentistry as well as a master's and Ph.D. in anthropology from the University of Chicago. Her studies had been in physical anthropology, and all her graduate and later work had been in morphology, the study of facial features.

Professor Smith had stopped practicing dentistry full time in 1963; but continued to do so part-time to support herself after she emigrated to Israel in 1969, as well as during her army service and on an emergency basis in the Yom Kippur War. The author of more than seventy-five publications, she was then a professor in the Department of Anatomy and Embryology at Hebrew University.

Smith testified that scientifically, each individual is unique. Individual facial characteristics --morphological features -- can be identified, measured, and compared. No two persons are identical. However, like fingerprints, there is a point beyond which similar characteristics mean that they can only belong to one and the same person.

The two individuals who genetically are most alike are identical twins. A colleague of Smith at the University of Adelaide in Australia had for years been conducting a study of identical twins, in which, under very controlled circumstances, the twins were photographed. Smith requested and received several sets of twin's photos.

She had identified eleven individual features on the human face that were also easily identifiable landmarks on a photo. Smith then took measurements of the eleven morphological landmarks on the sets of twins' photographs. The measurements were repeated five to seven times over an extended period of time. By correlating the figures for each set, Smith established the degree of variation found between two persons who are the least different, genetically, that two different individuals can be.

She then took two photographs that Demjanjuk had acknowledged and the Trawniki photo and measured these by the same method. She was able to carry out measurements for all eleven landmarks, using exactly the same measuring device. Each photograph was measured five times over a period of two weeks; then summed up and averaged, to obtain both an average measurement and also to estimate the error involved.

Smith determined that Demjanjuk and the man in the Trawniki photo were less different than identical twins. They could not be different persons. Demjanjuk and the man in the Trawniki ID photo were one and the same.

Smith told the Court that when trying to identify skeletons, a photo transparency of a missing person is often superimposed over a photo of the skull, to see if they match. Smith performed this comparison as well.

The photos were enlarged so that the distance between the left eye and the mouth was the same. Smith tested the procedure with a set of twins to show that there was no matchup, even with identical twins. Then the Trawniki photo was printed on a transparent sheet and placed over and acknowledged Demjanjuk photo. There was a complete concordance between the two.

"There can be no shadow of a doubt," Smith said, "that we

are dealing with the same individual."

Smith had done one further experiment: She had videotaped Demjanjuk in prison a few months earlier. She now performed superimpositions between a still frame of present-day Demjanjuk and the Trawniki photo.

O'Connor objected vigorously, citing precedents that were more biblical than legal. "Our position," he said, "quite simply stated is this: every human being has a right to his good name and reputation. In essence, to his face." To impose the photo from the Trawniki Card on John Demjanjuk was to slander him. We might just as well have had the witness put [a] Purim mask on the defendant..."

This was slander, O'Connor said, and the slander was upon the one who made it, the ones who hear it, and the worst punishment was for those who allowed it to be heard. O'Connor was not threatening the Judges, he said. The consequence of their actions was their own (implying that it was God Himself who would punish them).

Judge Zvi Tal, an orthodox Jew who gave a well-attended Talmud class every Sabbath, explained to O'Connor that matters uttered in court are not slanderous or libelous. Levin said that throughout O'Connor's long and detailed argument, the court had not heard a single legal point.

The video was allowed.

It was played on three monitors: one to the court, one to the defense, and one to the spectators. The entire room sat silent, entranced, during the seven-minute film.

Demjanjuk is first seen in his orange prison garb, standing in the Ayalon Prison yard. He is smiling and squinting at the light in his eyes. The camera freezes and the superimposition begins: half his face now, half the Trawniki photo.

Like a magic wand waving away the years, one face slowly

faded into the other as each detail-from the tip of the ear through the crease of the nose, the indent in the chin-matched up.

The screen then performed selective impositions: just the eyes ... just the mouth. The 1942 photo had more hair; Demjanjuk's face was now fatter, and the skin sagged, he had little neck-but still one saw the complete similarity between the two.

"The identity of morphological features," Smith said, "The identity of the distance between the morphological features, is identical.... I was asked what was the statistical probability of two individuals having identical morphological features.... [It is] one in several hundred billion.... [Based on] all the examinations that I have carried out, my conclusion is that the 1942 photograph was, in fact, taken of the individual John Demjanjuk seen in the other photographs and seen in the video today."

The frame, with half of the Trawniki man's face, and half Demjanjuk's face now, was a powerful image. The past joined with the present told in one image what, in great part, the prosecution was attempting to prove.

3. Seeing a Nazi in Jerusalem

In April 1987, as the prosecution began presenting evidence on the Trawniki card, the courtroom days lengthened- and there was no quick end in sight. The court had given great leeway for O'Connor's idiosyncratic notions of courtroom behavior and procedure. Sheftel's abrasive manner, however, angered the judges by continuing to make references to a show trial.

Sheftel apologized, but it did little to shake his bad-boy image. He took great delight in all of the attention, asking journalists to call him "Sheffie." Most reporters found him charming.

Sheftel delighted in making deliberately provocative statements to the media, such as, "Demjanjuk told me that if he'd had a Jewish lawyer from the beginning he wouldn't be in the mess he's in now."

Although Sheftel was catnip to the media, the Israeli public had little love for him. Shefte was called "the most hated man in Israel." His Hebrew was said to be lower-class. He was the sort of lawyer, one attorney said, who represented pimps, prostitutes, and drug dealers. He seemed always to be spitting as he talked, a court regular said. For many, his lack of decorum represented the "bad Israeli"-rude, obnoxious, devious.

However, when Sheftel was heckled in Court, it was Judge Levin who silenced the protesters. "He is carrying out a very important role here," Levin said. And when derogatory posters of Sheftel were displayed outside the courtroom, Levin ordered them taken down, and asked police to investigate the persons behind them for possible prosecution.

Still, as the trial dragged on, the momentum slowed. One day, as the Trawniki card's minutiae was being delved into, Demjanjuk claimed he wasn't feeling well and did not want to

233

attend Court. Prison doctors found nothing wrong with him. He was brought to court but allowed to remain on the cot in his holding cell listening to the day's proceedings on closed-circuit transmission.

To have the dock empty was strange. Attendance dropped immediately. It just made clear what had become obvious: People wanted to stare at Demjanjuk, to see him for themselves. To see if evil might have marked his face.

Philip Roth, who attended a few days of the trial and would write, Operation Shylock, a novel that used the trial as a springboard for his imagination, remarked that for a generation that came of age after the Holocaust and after Eichmann, they had never seen a Nazi murderer. For all that they studied the Holocaust, for all that they visited Yad Vashem, or observed Holocaust Remembrance Day, they had never seen or looked into the face of an actual Nazi Camp Guard – the great majority of those who had, were murdered. That is why watching Demjanjuk was so compelling, Roth said.

For many of the journalists in the room, and the regular trial watchers what made Demjanjuk so compelling was that he was a cipher. a blank screen on which viewers projected their own verdict of Demjanjuk's guilt or innocence, and his capacity for good or evil.

4.Demjanjuk has a Question

Mark O'Connor brought his family to Israel, where they ate each night in the American Colony Hotel dining room, like a tableau vivant from Norman Rockwell. His wife, Joyce, and children came to court, where, Joyce, sat in the first row, furiously taking notes. O'Connor talked to the press of his love of Israel, of the Israeli people, of how he was thinking about enrolling his children in school there and opening a law practice.

The O'Connors wanted the press to know that in taking on this case, they, too, had come to understand the survivors. "I've lived with the Holocaust for the last five years," Joyce O'Connor told one reporter. "I've lived in Treblinka for five years," Mark O'Connor told another.

It was difficult to size up O'Connor. Reporters often left interviews with him shaking their heads in puzzlement. He was always so "on," it was hard to tell when he was being sincere. And though he seemed to treat actual legal procedure cavalierly, he seemed to take personally every nuance of the proceedings --each comment of the judges, each objection of the prosecution

At times, O'Connor seemed in a trance. He would repeat words, mantralike, in cross-examination. His anger would erupt and subside. Asked about this, he explained that his main interest was in psychology. That if he had not become a lawyer, he would have wanted to be a Jungian psychologist.

"What you're doing is projecting results," O'Connor said. "At every stage, you're projecting results as if they had happened. There's alterations of that or there's perturbance involved with that; there appears the reaction that takes place and sometimes appears to be anger-but it's pretty well contained...."

But O'Connor's rambling cross-examinations and theatrical gestures made him seem more like a magician, as if his questions were exercises in misdirection.

That John Demjanjuk was both involved in his defense and concerned by its direction, became apparent in an unusual exchange that took place on the last day of the trial before the April Passover break. Although Thursday sessions customarily ended at two-thirty, Levin was allowing the cross-examination of Sheffler to continue as long as necessary so that that afterwards Sheffler could return to Germany.

It was nearing four-thirty and Demjanjuk's daughters had left the courtroom, on their way back to the United States; John Jr. had gone to take them to the airport.

Sheffler had been on the stand the better part of a week in tedious, grueling sessions, difficult to endure except for the hopelessly addicted. Sheftel's questions were becoming more and more speculative and seemed tired too.

Suddenly, Demjanjuk raised his hand like an eager schoolboy. Without his family there, a feeling rushed through the room, as if anything could happen. Demjanjuk told the court he felt his lawyers had not asked Sheffler some important questions.

O'Connor apologized for Demjanjuk's intrusion, but it was clear the defendant had grasped exactly what was happening: Sheffler was about to leave the stand; the historical authenticity of the Trawniki card had met with no serious challenge.

Though the court said Demjanjuk would be allowed, if he wished, to ask the questions himself, O'Connor said he would be the one asking.

Demjanjuk's question was: Could Sheffler comment on the jacket pocket button on the Trawniki photo? Sheffler answered that he wasn't a photographic expert.

Demjanjuk still was not satisfied. Gill rose to ask the same question. Again, Sheffler couldn't reply. Thereupon, Gill announced that "my friend and client," John Demjanjuk, still wanted to ask a few questions himself.

Shaked objected, but Levin was firm: "This is a most important trial, it is very important to the accused to ask one or two questions. The same questions it appears to the accused that the defense doesn't manage to formulate properly."

A microphone was set up for Demjanjuk: "These questions are very important to me," he said. "I'm a long time in jail now, and I don't know what the future may hold for me.'. .. There are a few questions where I don't agree with the testimony that Professor Sheffler delivered.

"Professor Sheffler," Demjanjuk now asked, "you said these black uniforms were introduced into Trawniki later and that at first there were some sort of yellowish uniforms. That's what I heard. That is not true, and I would like you to clarify this."

"I never mentioned any yellow uniforms," Sheffler said. But he had, in fact, mentioned khaki uniforms.

But was he sure, Demjanjuk asked, that they were first black and then later another color? Sheffler said the whole matter of the color of uniforms was a tricky one. Generally speaking, Trawniki started out with the black ones and then used other colors; but at any one given time, there may have been several different-colored uniforms in the camp. At least, this was what he could answer, based on testimonies given at trials by others.

Then Sheffler added, "Maybe you can tell us what happened in this respect, in terms of the uniforms."

Levin reacted quickly: "This last offer is not accepted."

Demjanjuk now prefaced his remarks by saying that he was not speaking from personal knowledge but solely from things he'd learned from his trials.

He asked Sheffler to look at the jacket breast button: Did it have anything to do with the uniform? Was it a field jacket button or a shirt button? Sheffler could only speculate he assumed it to be a tunic, a field jacket, he said, but it should be compared to other Trawniki jackets.

Demjanjuk asked him to examine the collar button under a magnifying glass. Sheffler scrutinized it, but said, "It's very difficult to see where the button belongs.... I don't see that as a historian, I can give information on this button." The judges also examined the photo. And if that was what was so crucial to Demjanjuk, he at least had brought it to the judges' attention.

"I would like to tell the court," Demjanjuk said with some satisfaction, "that it is eight years now in the U.S. that I've been seeing this photograph. I saw it first eight years ago, and I've seen a great many, many things that apparently would show that this is a forgery. For example, I was also wearing a pullover. Now, everything was done in this way in order not to show the identifying details.

"Now I would like here to say to the court that I am very grateful to them because they have acted justly, and today I have seen all of these details."

Demjanjuk thanked Sheffler, the court, and "everybody who has listened to me, and I would like to express my gratitude for this possibility of asking questions. I would like in this way to thank everybody who has taken part in this." He seemed genuinely happy.

But what did he mean when he said, "For example, I was also wearing a pullover?" That was something Demjanjuk would never explain.

Clearly, Demjanjuk knew or saw something in the Trawniki photo that no one else —no journalist, no attorney, no historian of the Nazi era saw. Perhaps Demjanjuk was still wearing a

Russian Army tunic when his photo was taken for the Trawniki card. Maybe what was on the breast pocket was not a button but a further identifier of some kind.

However, the most damning aspect of the photo was the number in the rectangle, 1393, which would directly link him to service at Sobibor, Flossenburg and Majdanek.

To this, for some reason, Demjanjuk had no objection.

CHAPTER FIVE:

THE GERMAN ROLE

1. Something Remarkable

As the Court delved into every detail of the Trawniki card, the trial in Jerusalem became more academic and technical, and to many, slower and less interesting. Yet something remarkable was occurring in the Court in Jerusalem.

Witnesses Helge Grabitz and Wolfgang Sheffler had been children during the Second World War and belonged to the immediate German postwar generation. Grabitz had devoted twenty-one years of her life to the prosecution of Nazi war crimes in West Germany. She had traveled to Israel more than a dozen times to collect evidence and testimony. She had helped Israel locate documents and witnesses. Her daughter had spent summers in Israel on a kibbutz. Sheffler was, to a general observer, more German, an echt German: Saxon, haughty, arrogant in his expertise. Yet he had devoted the last thirty years of his life to the study of the Holocaust; for the last twenty years, he had testified as an expert at trials of Nazi war crimes. To hear their hocht Deutsch (high German) in the halls of the Binyanei Haooma, as prosecution witnesses, was remarkable in itself.

It was Grabitz and Sheffler who, in answer to the questions of O'Connor and Gill, over and over again, repudiated the Nazi racial theories of Aryan supremacy.

When O'Connor probed the psychological dimension of those who killed day in and day out at T4. Grabitz answered: "I will repeat it once again, those who were immune, looked on day in and day out and helped to gas the children and infants. Those who had to participate against their will, they would have preferred to do something else, nevertheless they participated. And finally, there were those who did not know how to bring this into a balance with their own conscience, but they did not have the courage to refuse.... According to my own knowledge, I would say the greatest group was those who did it as a matter of course. They did it indifferently. Those who did it with enthusiasm, that is the second largest, and the least large is that group that had qualms of conscience." These opinions were based, Grabitz said, upon the testimonies of T4 personnel at the Trawniki trials.

It was Grabitz and Sheffler who testified about the crimes of Operation Reinhard, about the induction of collaborators into the program of death. And it was Grabitz and Sheffler who apologized when language failed them, and they had to resort to euphemisms of the Third Reich, such as "selection," and "sorting." They presented this testimony not as penance for being German, but as historically accepted fact.

In the 40 years since Israel had been founded, and the 25 years since the Eichmann Trial, Israel's relationship with West Germany had evolved. In the Eichmann trial it was a point of honor that no help was sought from the German government.

Now in the court in Jerusalem, it was striking to hear Reinhardt Altmann, a West German police officer, say: "The conclusion with regard to identity is based on the uniqueness of each individual. That is to say, each individual is unique in terms of his or her own characteristics. The uniqueness of each individual is the result of biological laws.... That is the theory of human biologists and human geneticists, and in any good biology textbook that deals with the development of man you will find that theory."

This was light years away from the pseudoscience of Aryan supremacy, racial profiles and eugenics that animated Nazi policy and laws a mere fifty years ago.

As if to mirror what was happening in court, on April 6, 1987, Chaim Herzog became the first President of Israel to travel in an official capacity to Germany.

Immediately upon his arrival, President Herzog went to the site of the Bergen-Belsen concentration camp, where he unveiled a commemorative rock quarried in Jerusalem. It was not his first visit to Bergen-Belsen. Herzog, who had served with the British forces during World War II, had been a soldier among the troops that liberated the camp. "I do not bring forgiveness with me, nor forgetfulness," he said. "The only ones who can forgive are dead. The living have no right to forget."

Prior to the Eichmann trial, Israel's relations with postwar Germany were complicated, at best. In its first days, Israel held to a strong anti-German line. Zionism demanded that Israel be seen as the proper response to the Holocaust.

But the Israeli government of Prime Minister David Ben-Gurion wanted allies in the Western world. Chancellor Konrad Adenauer's Germany was interested in allying itself with Israel, so as to distinguish itself from Hitler's Germany. In the 1950s, West Germany came to be Israel's economic development partner. Though many saw this as a devil's pact, Ben-Gurion's slogan was, "Let the murderers of our people not be their inheritors as well."

The opportunity for Israel and West Germany to confront their past and solidify their alliance came in 1960, when Ben-Gurion announced to a startled Knesset that Adolf Eichmann had been apprehended and was in custody in Israel.

World coverage of the Eichmann trial was great. But

perhaps in no foreign country was the reaction stronger than in Germany.

The Eichmann trial could have been the opening of old wounds, but both sides were conscious of avoiding that. Germany publicly supported the trial of Eichmann. Adenauer hoped Israel would distinguish between Eichmann and current-day Germans.

Ben-Gurion obliged, saying, "My views about present-day Germany are unchanged. There is no Nazi Germany anymore." Afterward, Eichmann's conviction and execution was almost completely undisputed. The three major West German parties were unanimous in their assertion that justice had been done.

Subsequent to the Eichmann trial, West Germany entered into new loan agreements with Israel. And in 1965, both Israel and West Germany exchanged ambassadors.

But more significant was the impact of the trial on the young German generation. Writes historian Howard M. Sachar in A History of Israel:

"For the youth of Germany, particularly, the trial was a horrifying revelation. It supplied answers their parents had never given them. As they followed the court sessions in the press or on television, they sensed the truth at last of what their nation had done. Deeply penitent, thousands of them wrote the Israeli government, imploring them to be allowed to atone by working in Israel. For older Germans, too, it was suddenly much easier to talk about Israel, even to meet Israelis, than to face individual Jewish survivors in Germany with whom they had to live side by side. It became the fashion to admire Israel, to laud its achievements, to urge the rising generation to visit it. And the young people did go, fully twenty thousand of them between 1961 and 1967. Some traveled in youth groups, some on their own. Not a few arrived to work in kibbutzim or in development projects. All of them were eager to witness the spirit that had made this Jewish nation victorious against its numerous enemies, and that had enabled it to capture Eichmann. It was ironic, then, that the Eichmann trial played a major role in fostering a new understanding between Germans and Israelis."

And it was that new understanding that was apparent, twenty-five years later in the Demjanjuk trial: the testimonies of Grabitz, Sheffler, and Altmann were testament to the normalization of the relations between the two countries and the trial would make extensive use of German archives.

2. German Witnesses

For Demjanjuk's Israeli trial, it fell to the prosecution's Michael Horovitz, to spend countless hours in German archives, and meeting with West German prosecutors. Searching out former Trawniki and Treblinka men in Germany was personally repugnant to Horovitz, but he did meet with some success.

Vladas Amanaviczius, who was residing in Belgium, and Helmut Leonhardt, now living in Germany, had both served at Trawniki and had agreed to be called as witnesses. In addition, Heinrich Schaeffer, also at Trawniki, and Otto Horn of Treblinka, had been witnesses at Demjanjuk's denaturalization trial and lived in Germany. Neither was willing to travel to Israel, so hearings were arranged for June in their own countries.

In late May 1987, Horovitz left for Germany once again to make final preparations. As his plane was preparing to take off, someone came out of the pilot's cabin and said, "Is there a Mr. Horovitz aboard?" There was a radio call for him.

Amanaviczius, who was ninety-one, had died in his sleep.

A Lithuanian, he had served at Trawniki before being assigned to the Treblinka's labor camp. Amanaviczius would have testified that not only were Trawniki guards issued service passes, but he had one that he carried at all times. And he might have some knowledge to add about the guards at Treblinka.

Undaunted, Horovitz hurried to Germany to hold Leonhardt's hearing, more conscious than ever that time was running out. But upon arrival, he learned that Leonhardt, 71, was on vacation in the Black Forest and would only testify upon his return.

The hearing was held on May 18-21, 1987, at a closed session of the Magistrate's Court in Koln, Germany, before Judge Becker. The public and press were not allowed because the hearing was not considered a court proceeding (technically, the court proceeding would be when the record of the hearing was presented in court in Israel). Prosecutor Horovitz appeared with Israel police investigator Etty Hai as his assistant; Mark O'Connor appeared for the defense, assisted by Rudolf Strattman of Dusseldorf, who had been Treblinka commander Kurtz Franz's attorney.

Leonhardt, a retired policeman and resident of Koln, was balding, short, and red-faced. At times he became emotional during his testimony, but at the end of the day, Horovitz would recall, he always composed himself enough to ask for his day's travel expenses.

Before arriving at Trawniki in June 1942, Leonhardt had been a German police officer. He remained at Trawniki, working in the administration office until July 1944, when he became a prisoner of war. At Trawniki, he was in charge of the file cards on foreign guards. When he arrived at the camp, he recalled, the files were "in complete disorder."

Leonhardt claimed to have had no knowledge about postings, which he said was handled in a different office. And he was hesitant to say what the guards were being training to do. Although he claimed no personal knowledge, he said that he learned from others that the guards were sent to "clean up" villages of their Jews and that the guards were then sent to the work camps Belzec, Sobibor, and Treblinka. Only later did he find out that the work camps were extermination camps.

Trawniki, Leonhardt confirmed, was an "instruction camp" for Soviet war prisoners. He described the camp's induction procedures. The recording of the equipment was done not by Teufel himself, he revealed, but by a non-German guard. This accounted for the misspellings, the prosecution would contend.

As to other mistakes on the card, he later explained that, "When suddenly the many guards were recruited, one needed documents with which the guards could identify themselves. Such little details [as mistakes] were not considered."

Horovitz handed Leonhardt a photo album of pictures taken at Trawniki. Looking closely at the photographs, sometimes using a magnifying glass, he identified the details of the camp, officials, and the uniforms worn, even the window where he worked.

Horovitz placed before Leonhardt two photocopies of the Trawniki document and asked his opinion.

Leonhardt was certain: "The document is authentic." He recognized Streibl's signature and Teufel's distinctive signature in German Gothic script, which he had seen "countless" times.

Horovitz asked: "How did the Dienstausweis look in the original?"

An amazing thing then happened: Leonhardt took the photocopies and folded them together in such a way that they were back to back, and that the photo appeared behind the first page with the inscription "Dienstausweis." It showed a complete familiarity with the document.

While historians had spoken of the document, here was someone who had seen it in use.

The uniform of the person on the Trawniki card, Leonhardt said, was one of the early guard outfits. It could be clearly seen in the photo of Himmler's review. (This perhaps answered Demjanjuk's questions about different uniforms).

Horovitz asked what the numbers were next to each name. "This is a service number ... that is put before the guard when his picture is taken." In a spontaneous, natural gesture, Leonhardt pointed with his right hand to a spot on the left side of his chest, to indicate the white rectangle that appeared on the photo and whose number had to match the Dienstausweis.

In his cross-examination, O'Connor focused on what Leonhardt knew about the killing of Jews at Trawniki or their murder in the extermination camps such as Treblinka.

Leonhardt said that he had learned of the exterminations at Treblinka from a guard named Arthur Raab, who had accompanied a transfer of guards to the camp. Leonhardt claimed to be in the hospital when the nine thousand Jews of Trawniki's labor camp were shot and then incinerated in pits. At the time, his wife and young child were in a house near the camp. A guard had told her, in his broken German, "SS make bum-bum, all Jews kaput." When she told this to Leonhardt, he secured a leave and took her and his child to his aunt's house. When Leonhardt returned, it was all over. "Only this stench was there, and also the ashes...." Leonhardt started to cry. The deposition was stopped for a few minutes.

Leonhardt said the killings affected him so much that "every day I drank between one and one and-a-half liters of forty percent vodka." Leonhardt began to cry again, and at his request, a ten-minute break was taken.

Leonhardt said the postings of guards to concentrations camps was not secret; "every child in Poland knew about" the work camps, he said, and he learned from colleagues who traveled to the camps that mass murders took place there.

"But you indicated earlier guards fled from Trawniki?" O'Connor asked.

"Yes," replied Leonhardt. "If I had had to do the dirty work, I would have fled myself."

Asked by O'Connor about the Trawniki card not having a date of issue, Leonhardt admitted that "normally every Ausweis [identity card] has a date of issue." However, he said, "One would only look at the sealed photo and whether the man coincided with the picture. Whether the Ausweis had a date of issue or not, nobody paid any attention, because for us they were inmates of the camp and no strangers."

Based on the card itself, Leonhardt said, one would have to conclude that the bearer was not at Treblinka but was last in Sobibor.

Horovitz later recalled that during Leonhardt's testimony, one of the translators, a young German woman in her twenties, broke into tears. She later asked Horovitz: "Is it true?" She had never heard a German speak about the murder and incineration of the Jews.

3. A Hearing in Berlin

A few weeks later, the Israeli judges traveled to Berlin to observe the testimony of Otto Horn at the request of both sides. Judge Zvi Tal, arriving at the airport in Berlin, said he "never believed I would set foot on German soil." Tal went to the old synagogue in Berlin; Kosher food was provided for him throughout his stay.

That Jewish judges from the Jewish state traveled to Germany was heady: Who could have imagined this at war's end? Who could have even imagined it twenty-five years before, at the time of the Eichmann trial?

For Horovitz, meeting with the survivors had been heartrending and personally difficult. But spending time with the former Nazis was chilling. "It is very different meeting such a German; it does something to you," Horovitz would recall later.

Why did Leonhardt and Horn testify? Why would they cooperate with the Israelis? The answer was simple: because governmental authorities-American, German, and Israeli-had asked them to. They did not want to testify. But they were-they had always been law-abiding citizens.

The testimony of Otto Horn began June 9, 1987, at the Teirgarten Court of justice. Judge Hans-Jurgen Muller, in his early thirties, presided. The courtroom was small, more like a judge's chambers than a ceremonial courtroom. The three Israeli judges took seats along the side.

Otto Horn, eighty-three at the time, was retired and living in Berlin. With a full head of white hair, he seemed healthy and alert. Now called to testify, Horn set out, above all, to minimize his own role in the death process.

He coldly described his work at T4 as the ordering of jars --

that the jars were for ashes, remains of the murdered, did not affect him. In his description of Treblinka, he was merely a wanderer, an onlooker of the process, never a participant.

Judge Levin, exasperated, said finally: "What did you do?"

"Saubermachen [cleaning up]" was always Horn's answer. He was cleaning up at T4, cleaning up at Treblinka. He was free to wander in the death camp near the incineration process; sometimes he helped hang laundry; and if something happened at the camp, it was during the time he was on leave.

In Horn's account, the Jews were unloaded from the trains; transported to the Schlauch; at the gas chambers, the Jews had to wait until their turn came. "They were pushed into the entrance."

Levin asked what Horn meant by "pushed"?

"If they didn't want to, they were beaten.... They were beaten by Ukrainians and Germans with whips, there were those who moved them forward."

After being in the gas chambers, the Jews were "taken" out, "placed" on the ramp, and afterward "put" in the pit." This businesslike description of the horrors was given by Horn without the slightest sign of emotion. But one thing was clear: Horn knew Treblinka well, and was familiar with the people who worked there. He knew all the German officers, and he knew Ivan.

"Ivan," he said, "he was friendly with Schmidt. They were always together.... He always worked with Schmidt.... He hurried the prisoners inside, together with Schmidt. He stood at the head of the gas chambers.... The people thought that they would be given a bath, and when they saw, they refused to go in, and began screaming. They would be beaten and while being beaten, were put inside."

Who did this? He was asked. Horn answered: "Germans,

Ukrainians, Schmidt and Ivan."

Asked to describe Ivan, he said: "He was big, and had a black uniform. He was big, tall, about 175-180cm approximately.... He had a powerful build.... He was twenty-three.... [His hair was] I don't know ... dark blond."

"After the chambers were full," he testified, "Ivan and Schmidt would go together to the engines.... He was always together with Schmidt, he repaired cars with him. When the transports arrived, he was with Schmidt.... I stood above the Schlauch and could see everything.

"When no transports arrived, he was in the camp very little, he would get supplies. I was then in the Upper Camp. He would run by me; the distance was very small.... When no transports arrived, Ivan would be in the Lower Camp tinkering with cars.... He knew how to drive a car."

How often did he see Ivan? "I saw him almost constantly when I didn't have night guard duty or when I wasn't on furlough." And Horn testified that he saw Ivan after the uprising, when the gas chambers were operated to liquidate the final transports.

Horovitz showed him the first set of photographs. Horn picked the 1951 visa photograph and said: "Ivan's appearance was similar to that." Asked for further clarification, Horn stated, "He appears similar to him, there is a similarity.... He had a round full face, this is what can be seen here."

Horn also recalled that in 1979, a half-hour after he had selected Demjanjuk's visa photo, the investigators had shown him a second pack of photographs, one that included the Trawniki photo: "I said that possibly it is he. This is what he looks like. He looks similar to this." Now Horn picked out the photo of the young soldier and commented, "There is similarity. I can only say there are similarities.... I am as certain today as I was then."

"The Ivan you knew in Treblinka," Horovitz asked, "and the man whom you pointed out in the photographs at your home in 1980, as well as today, are they the same person?"

"Yes," was Horn's unequivocal answer.

Horn was aggressively cross-examined by O'Connor for seven and-a-half hours. The former Treblinka man stood up remarkably well under the strain, but the young German interpreter asked to be replaced after five hours. Except for being hard of hearing, one observer noted, the wiry old man seemed extremely fit.

In 1983, Horn had signed a document recanting part of his testimony. For years, this recantation was part of O'Connor's "proof" of Demjanjuk's innocence. This was to be O'Connor's triumph. But during questioning by the judges, Horn revealed that he had been visited by three persons claiming to be from the Association for Freedom for Eastern European Prisoners. In fact, they were actually associates of the defense. Horn talked to them. They did not write down anything in his apartment.

However, the next day they took him to the U.S. Consulate, where they asked him to sign a typed document. Horn never read the statement; he assumed it contained what he had said. But it did not. In fact, he went to the German police in 1986 to set the record straight that he stood by his earlier testimony.

O'Connor pressed harder: "Do you have any doubts in seeing this photograph whether it is he?"

Horn, suddenly looking every year of his eighty-three years, answered with conviction, "It resembles him." After forty-three years, he could not be one hundred percent certain, but Horn concluded that he could not deny the resemblance, no matter the consequence.

There were many significant aspects of Horn's testimony – some of which mattered greatly to the Israeli Judges, and others that would only resonate in importance years later.

Horn made clear that many people accompanied the unfortunate Jewish men, women, and children to their deaths. Not just Ivan and Nikolai, as others did, but Schmidt and Ivan, as well as other Ukrainians and Germans. Schmidt and Ivan worked with the engines; and Ivan worked on cars and engines and knew how to drive a car. Those descriptions would later weigh heavily as indications Demjanjuk was in Treblinka.

CHAPTER SIX:

DEMOLISHING DEMJANJUK'S ALIBI

1. Demjanjuk's History

Before resting its case, the prosecution intended to demonstrate that Demjanjuk's alibi was false, not credible and was contradicted by historical documents and by experts.

Professor Matityahu Meisel of Tel Aviv University, an expert on Soviet history testified that in the Soviet Union during the 1930s not just anyone was chosen to drive a tractor -- it was a privilege for which one was required to have technical skills and qualifications and for which one received better payment.

Meisel noted that during the Soviet retreat when Demjanjuk, fighting as part of the Red Army, was wounded, hospital records were not kept. Accordingly, that the Trawniki card indicated that Demjanjuk had a scar on his back, Meisel said, could only have come from Demjanjuk himself.

Based on German war diaries, Meisel noted that on May 8, 1942, the German 11th Army launched a renewed offensive in which the Kerch peninsula was taken. More than 175,000 - thousand Russian prisoners were captured, Demjanjuk, he surmised, among them.

The Nazis were not prepared for their success, Meisel said. The transfer route for the POWs was along railway lines. Beginning the next day, POWs started to arrive at the Rovno camp. Transfers, Meisel said, continued until early June.

Demjanjuk was paying close attention and had questions of his own: Were three Red Army units captured in the Kerch Peninsula? as he recalled. Were there historical accounts of forced marches from Kerch to Perikov? Meisel said that three Soviet armies were known to be fighting in the Crimea; but he had found no accounts of the march.

Dr. Shmuel Krakovsky, the director of archives at Yad Vashem and an expert on German POW camps, disputed Demjanjuk's account that his journey to Rovno took more than a month. German orders were that soldiers taken prisoner at the front were to be taken rapidly to POW camps behind the lines-in weeks, not months.

Krakovsky stated that some 5.75-million Red Army soldiers were taken prisoner by the Germans and were kept, as Demjanjuk testified, in inhumane conditions. 800,000 auxiliaries recruited from the POW camps, Krakovsky said, of whom 60 to 70 percent were Ukrainians.

Chelm, the second camp Demjanjuk mentioned, Krakovsky explained was originally set up as a front-line camp for the German invasion of the Soviet Union. It later became a POW camp where Soviet soldiers were held. Krakovsky introduced the German Army statistical lists of POWs to show Chelm was a transit camp with a high turnover and a place where auxiliaries were recruited.

Although the conditions there were inhuman, Meisel and Krakovsky both made clear, that although hundreds of thousands did collaborate, many more chose not to.

At Chelm, Krakovsky said, Jews and commissars were made to fall out immediately. Any Jews were killed immediately; those suspected of being Jewish were ordered to pull down their pants --if circumcised, they, too, were killed.

Although Demjanjuk claimed that his Jewish foreman at

Chelm was called "Kapo," Krakovsky confirmed that the word "Kapo" was only used in concentration and extermination camps, not in POW camps.

Chelm actually housed two camps, a northern and a southern one. By the summer of 1942 the southern camp was merely a transit camp. By spring 1943, there were no longer any Russian POWs there – Italians had taken their place; and by the end of 1943 there none in the northern camp. Accordingly, they found Demjanjuk's timeline and claim of having been at Chelm for 18 months false.

Meisel said Demjanjuk could not have joined the Vlassov army in the Spring of 1944 because it was only established later that fall, assembling its first unit only in January 1945.General Fedor Truckhin only arrived in March to command a division that had uniforms and arms, who were eventually captured by the Americans and later handed over to the Red Army.

Dr. Shmuel Spektor, who also worked at Yad Vashem and was an expert in Ukrainian military formations, testified that in February 1945 there was an SS Waffengrenadiren division in Graz that a month later became known as the First Ukrainian Division. Lieutenant General Pavlo Shandruk was in charge of the division and became Supreme Commander of the Ukrainian National Army. Demjanjuk might have been recruited for the Ukrainian units, but if so, it was not because he had been a German POW but rather because he was an SS death camp guard. Similarly, his tattoo was no evidence of service in the Russian Liberation Army. To the contrary, it indicated SS service.

Professor Meisel said The Soviet Union issued pardons to Vlassov army men in 1955. However, that pardon did not apply to those who were war criminals, such as Demjanjuk.

2. O'Connor's Mistake

The press never tired of writing about the Demjanjuk family as "human interest" stories. There was a great fascination with the family: Did they or did they not know? Some cast them as the trial's innocent victims. There was no question that Demjanjuk had been a good husband and a good father. And, conversely, regarding his children, it was no crime to love your father. The defense encouraged these articles as supportive of their cause – and as a way to draw attention away from the facts of the trial

In April, Demjanjuk's two daughters, Lydia Maday and Irene Nishnic, and Nishnic's infant son, Eddie Jr., attended the trial. They were upset by the judges who seemed to overrule the defense at each turn. They had their doubts about whether the trial was fair. But they were even more troubled by O'Connor whom they found long-winded and not particularly effective.

John Demjanjuk's trust in O'Connor was great. But his family felt that Demjanjuk was not entirely in touch with his case. His daughters complained that when they visited him, he avoided discussing any important issues, preferring to show them letters he had received from well-wishers or to happily sing Ukrainian songs. The family went home to Cleveland uncertain about Demjanjuk's fate.

Demjanjuk's son-in-law, Ed Nishnic, president and administrator of the John Demjanjuk Defense Fund, in turn, came to Jerusalem to observe the trial and to take the measure of O'Connor.

Just a few years before, Nishnic had worked at an Ohio employment agency, where he met his wife, Irene, then a secretary there. He was familiar with the case before he met Irene, but not active in the Demjanjuk defense. That soon

258

changed.

At first, Lydia, the eldest child, had been the family spokesperson. When she stopped doing so, John Jr. took over; but in no time the Demjanjuk defense became Ed Nishnic's full-time occupation. As chief fundraiser, he toured the U.S., Canada, and Australia.

O'Connor claimed that John Demjanjuk's life was in his hands. Without him, O'Connor said, "John would hang." This frightened Vera and Irene. O'Connor portrayed Sheftel as a Mossad (Israeli Secret Service) plant, Gill as brainwashed by Sheftel.

The press hungered for intrigue and the conflicts among the defense team and the Demjanjuk family proved irresistible.

Ed Nishnic had stayed in Israel in April to observe O'Connor in action. He was not pleased by what he saw. Sheftel seized the opportunity to convince Nishnic that Sheftel should lead the defense. While O'Connor was away in May for the German hearings, the family decided, per Sheftel's suggestion, that the defense should proceed by majority rule.

The trial recessed in June. The defense was to begin its presentation on July 27.

However, during the recess letters were brought to Demjanjuk in prison to sign – one to O'Connor firing him; another to the court to inform them of the change of counsel.

Though Demjanjuk trusted O'Connor, he was not going to go against his family. He signed the letter to the court which stated that another attorney, John Broadley, a Washington lawyer who had been working, pro bono, on a Freedom of Information Act (FOIA) suit against the OSI for the Demjanjuk Defense Fund would be joining the defense team.

Following receipt of the letter, a special Court session was held on July 15, 1987, at the request of both O'Connor and

Sheftel.

Judge Levin addressed Demjanjuk, explaining Mark O'Connor had been granted the power of attorney to represent Demjanjuk. Sheftel and Gill had been appointed part of the defense team, according to court records, by O'Connor, not by Demjanjuk. Nonetheless, Demjanjuk had the right to appoint either of them independently, by doing so in writing or by declaring them to be his attorneys in court. Broadley had not yet been admitted to practice in Israel, Levin informed Demjanjuk, so he could not become his counsel at this time.

Demjanjuk, after consulting with Nishnic, told the court, "Since the beginning of the trial, the attorneys have not acted properly.... My family has decided to dismiss Mr. O'Connor, since this will not be in my interest to have him continue to represent me."

But it was not his family who was on trial, Levin said. What was his decision?

"My decision is to follow the advice of my family. I am in a cage. I am in jail. Therefore, I must follow the advice of my family. Whatever my family decides I must do." But his decision must be a voluntary one, Levin said.

Sheftel explained that Demjanjuk had already signed a power of attorney for Gill, which Judge Levin asked Demjanjuk to read over again, and confirm. Sheftel said Demjanjuk had also signed one for him.

Before formally dismissing O'Connor, Demjanjuk asked to speak with his family. Levin recessed the hearing for a week to allow him to do so.

O'Connor's mistake was that he had assumed that as long as he maintained his personal relationship with John Demjanjuk, he was irreplaceable. But what he failed to understand was that the family had become the client. Because they were paying the bills, they wanted to call the shots; and Demjanjuk's loyalty was to his family, above all.

The day before the July 20 hearing, O'Connor wrote a letter, submitting his resignation.

The court released O'Connor from representing Demjanjuk, but added, "we cann ot but express our appreciation to Mr. O'Connor for the efforts he has invested in the defense of the accused, the cross-examinations of the witnesses for the prosecution up to the present stage."

Shortly thereafter, O'Connor left the country and returned to Buffalo.

CHAPTER SEVEN:

DEMJANJUK'S TESTIMONY

1. Utterly Unfounded

On the morning of Monday, July 27, 1987, Sheftel rose to present the defense's opening remarks. He was quick to distance himself from O'Connor, and to heap blame on him. "Your Honors," he began, "at the inception of my remarks, I see fit to apologize most sincerely to the survivors who testified at this trial, for the fact that they had to withstand cross-examination for days on end on matters that touched upon points the defense declared to be incontrovertible and had to answer questions such as what was the color of the flames in the pit where the corpses were burned, what was the distance-from the gas chambers to the pits, and questions of that nature."

Sheftel also apologized to the court "for the fact that the court was forced to deal with dozens of pointless objections, which had no legal grounds."

Sheftel said he did not contest the prosecution's historical presentation, but they had failed to include the role of Soviet treachery – the extent to which Soviet actions such as the Molotov Ribbentrop Non-Aggression pact enabled the Nazi's final solution for the Jews, and all the fictions, lies and forgeries in which the Soviet Union and the KGB engaged, promising to submit an entire book of KGB-forged documents from the war.

As for the identifications by the Treblinka survivors, Sheftel promised to call experts on eyewitness identification to demonstrate that the survivor testimonies should be given little weight. He would also discuss cases such as the Frank Walus case, in which eleven witnesses, who "with the same good memory, the same self-assurance, identified the so-called Butcher of Pilsen, and turned out to be all wrong."

Sheftel also promised to present evidence that others were alleged to be the Ivan of the Gas Chambers at Treblinka. Material recently made available from a Demjanjuk Defense Fund suit against the OSI showed that twenty-one witnesses from Treblinka, including the barber Abraham Bomba who appeared in the film Shoah, could not identify Demjanjuk as Ivan. That made twenty-nine survivors, he said, who did not identify the defendant as opposed to the five who did. "What is more ponderous, the weight of five witnesses or the weight of twenty-nine witnesses?" Sheftel said.

Sheftel said he would call experts who "will shatter this document and leave nothing of it: neither the signatures of Teufel or Streibl, or the one that purports to be that of the accused, nor the picture, nor the stamps, nor any other element relevant to the document in this case. Nothing will remain of the entire document. We will shatter and pulverize this document. We will leave nothing of it."

"You will leave us the original, please," chided Levin. Everyone laughed, and Sheftel suppressed a boyish grin. "Definitely," he answered, "the original alone will remain intact."

Given that The Trawniki Card does not place Demjanjuk in Treblinka, even if it is found to be authentic, Sheftel argued, it stands in direct contradiction to the survivors and therefore their testimony "cann ot serve as grounds for this identification."

Sheftel promised to call an expert to prove the photo was, in fact, attached to another document, that the seals on the document were not the same as on the photo, and that the breast pocket number was, in fact, different from the number on the document.

Sheftel also said that he had received "some very interesting material" that Altmann, Cantu, and Gideon Epstein had been employed by the OSI to identify the body of Nazi war criminal Josef Mengele, and that their opinions had been found unreliable.

Levin asked why these questions were not asked when the witnesses were on the stand. The defense, he answered, didn't have access to those memos yet. "After all," he said, "we are not prophets."

Sheftel was working himself into an excited state, and his voice grew louder and more shrill. The judges asked him to calm down, lest he go hoarse.

As for the historical experts Sheffler and Grabitz, their testimony explained, Sheftel said, why Germany lost the war, and why Grabitz lost the Trawniki trial. Their contentions about forgery were baseless; as all you needed to forge successfully, Sheftel said, was well-oiled machinery.

"When the accused takes the stand, he will show as part of his testimony, that none of the historical witnesses produced by the prosecution, can in any way disprove and refute his alibi."

"Next year, for what the Germans call `humanitarian reasons.'" Sheftel said, "Kurt Franz will be released from prison. Under German law, he will be set free, but under the terms of the Nazi and Nazi Collaborators Law in Israel, he can still be brought to justice in Israel. But I can say with absolute certainty, that Kurt Franz will never be brought to trial."

The reason? Said Sheftel: Wiedergutmachung, German war

reparations. It was Sheftel's belief that the agreements had put an end to the trials of Nazi war criminals in Israel-at a time when many survivors were still able to testify and that since then, not one criminal had been brought to justice, with the exception of Eichmann. So Sheftel concluded: "I must determine that the statements of the learned state prosecutor and Mr. Shaked are utterly unfounded."

2. I Am John Demjanjuk

Judge Levin addressed the defense: "I gather that the accused will be testifying for the defense? Will the accused please rise."

Demjanjuk stood. Levin asked him to state his name.

"If it please the court," he said in Ukrainian, "I am John Demjanjuk."

Gill asked Demjanjuk to address the charges against him. "The Honorable Bench, I am accused here of being at Treblinka," he said. "This is not true. I was never either at Treblinka or at Sobibor nor at Trawniki nor at any other such place."

Gill led Demjanjuk through his personal history which he had told several times before. But never at such length or in such detail, and never for such high stakes.

Demjanjuk spoke calmly, in even tones. He started school, he said, when he was eight. He couldn't attend earlier because of his household duties. He was enrolled for nine years, but only passed the fourth grade. Until now he had spoken of having only a fourth-grade education; he had never said anything about nine years of schooling.

"In each grade, first, second, and fourth, I spent two years," he said. After two years in the fifth grade, he still had not passed. A third year was not allowed, so he received a disqualification report card.

It was not academic failure that held him back, he testified, but poverty. "The reasons are that my parents were very poor, and they had nothing to wear or no shoes to put on. If my father had any job whatsoever, I had to stay home, rather than going to school." Both his parents were invalids: his father had lost several fingers in World War I; his mother had caught a cold while pregnant with him, after which her right leg would no longer bend and she was bedridden for a year.

Demjanjuk was eager to recount to "all the people everywhere" the famine that befell the Ukraine in 1932 and 1933.

"It was so horrible," he said, "it goes beyond anything that humanity had known up unto then. People ate anything they could lay hands on, including dogs and cats.... We and my relatives ate rats, and even our cat and bird. People were lying dead in their homes, in the yards, on the roads, exposed to the sunlight. Nobody collected them; nobody brought them to burial."

Demjanjuk's family sold their possessions and went to live with a relative on a Kolkhoz (collective farm) near Moscow; there, food was more abundant. But there was no work. The family soon returned to their village, he said, where "there was no longer any control.... People were scattered about, lying outside all around. We had no home of our own, and we went to our father's brother. But they were all dead by then."

When he was about seventeen, Demjanjuk went to work in a Kolkhoz. Starting as a plower, he ended up working with tractors. He was put in charge of the work team and became an assistant to the tractor driver.

In 1938, he joined the Komsomol, the Communist youth organization; membership was not mandatory, but those who didn't join, he explained, risked becoming "an object of ridicule." He was given a small identity card with a photograph, he said, but he buried it in the ground when he was later taken captive.

When Russia declared war on Finland in 1939, tractor drivers were drafted immediately. The assistant tractor drivers took over. Demjanjuk was a driver, he said, until he himself was drafted.

In 1940, he and most of his fellow villagers received notice to report for service in the Red Army. Each man was required to have two pairs of underpants, a spoon, and a plate. As Demjanjuk was too poor to produce the required underpants, he was told to return home. In 1941, he was called for the second time. The clothing requirement had been abolished; he was inducted.

Gill asked whether a photo was taken. Demjanjuk could not remember. But he said his hair was cut. (One of Demjanjuk's objections to the Trawniki photo was that he said his hair was never that length.)

His recollection of his Red Army service was detailed: The recruiting office was in a small town, Samgorodok, where all his hair fell out. He was sent from there to Besserabia, to the town of Bielce, to a unit where other members from his village were sent. They underwent artillery training and were sent to the front; their first position was on the banks of the River Prut.

The Soviet army was in retreat and passed through the rivers Prut and Dnieper, he recalled. Near the Dnieper River, he was wounded. He was taken to four Soviet hospitals, the names of which he recalled with precision: Melitopol, Berd'ansk, Stalino, and Tbilisi.

His wound left a scar on his back, but he said the scar that he still bore today was from surgery he underwent in 1948 to remove the remaining shrapnel.

After his recovery, he was sent to an artillery unit in the town of Kottaissi. Demjanjuk was there "perhaps a month or two." The unit was then sent to Baku to complete the full force and from there it was sent to Kerch, where it remained some two weeks or so, before being dispatched to the nearby front.

There were a great many people at the front, he recalled. He could not say how many were in his unit, but "there was talk of three armies." He arrived in Kerch in January or February 1942, where he received no training, just waited for its next posting.

"Once, and I remember this as if it happened yesterday, there was a very heavy rain, and we were all taken prisoner." Demjanjuk's testimony was now at a critical juncture: his alibi depended on it – and his life.

I can't say and I don't know

Levin asked Demjanjuk to give a more precise date of his capture but Demjanjuk could not be more specific. He knew it was 1942, but said, "I can't tell exactly what month it was, but it was very hot and the grass was growing."

Demjanjuk said he was first taken to a small camp. A few days later, he joined a group of some seventy men who were preparing railroad tracks for German trains. He was engaged in this for six weeks to two months. Demjanjuk said he could not be more precise.

The prisoners pushed along a railroad car as they worked, and it was in the car that they slept. "If the weather permitted, we had to get up and work; if the weather was not or did not make it possible, we stayed in the car." They wore their Red Army uniforms and were served bread and coffee three times a day. Rumanian guards were there as well, he said.

Instead of completing the rail work, they joined other prisoners in a march along the canal. Those who stepped out of line to grab something to eat, or to jump in the water, were shot. Eventually, they came to a small camp near the canal. "We spent about a week, and they fed us once a day." Demjanjuk had never before mentioned this camp.

"Later," he testified, "they put us into cars and took us to Rovno.... The camp at Rovno was a very small one in which we could barely stand, so during the day we were taken outside of the camp into a clearing in the forest, where we could either lie down or sit down. We were fed once a day, a pot of some sort of pottage."

Demjanjuk denied being recruited at Rovno for Trawniki. "The prosecution can say whatever it wants, but I was there, and I am the one who knows that I went from Rovno to Chelm. At Rovno I spent only a week or two." Demjanjuk said he believed he was transferred in the fall.

The prosecution had placed him in Trawniki by July and at Treblinka by autumn. Was he ever recruited, Gill asked, to serve in the SS?

"If it please the court and everyone present, I wish to state one thing and one thing only: that I am not the hangman or henchmen that you are speaking of. I was never at Trawniki or at Sobibor."

Because of a translation problem, Demjanjuk was asked to repeat his answer. "Since the beginning of my trial," he said, "I have been sitting here looking at the shadow of death of the accursed Treblinka. My heart aches, and I grieve deeply for what was done to your people by the Nazis during the Second World War and only because of the fact that you were Jews. I wish to be believed, and please do not put the noose around my neck for things that were perpetrated by others."

Judge Levin reminded him that the question was more specific: Was he recruited and, if so, where was he sent?

But Demjanjuk would not answer directly. He pleaded: "Honorable Judge, I have just said that never in my life was I in Treblinka or Trawniki or in Sobibor. I wish to be believed, and please do not put the noose around my neck for the deeds of others."

But was he ever recruited into the SS auxiliary forces?

"Never," Demjanjuk said.

Gill asked him to describe conditions at Chelm.

"First of all," Demjanjuk said, "after we were taken there, there weren't enough barracks, and we had to sleep on the ground. These circumstances, the conditions, were atrocious. We helped to build the barracks. We carried railway tracks from the camp, and we didn't understand what they were for. Later, we understood that these railway tracks that we had carried were to be used to build trenches in the ground."

Judge Dorner wanted to know the time frame. From the fall of 1942, Demjanjuk replied, throughout the winter of 1943- which was precisely the time he was accused of being at Treblinka and Sobibor.

At Chelm, Demjanjuk said, the POWs gathered wooden railway ties and placed them on carts that were taken to the camp. Even after he was transferred to a barracks, there were no beds, only three-tiered slates or pallets to sleep upon. Some prisoners still had to sleep outside, in the winter. In each barracks, there was someone in charge whom the Germans called a "Kapo." The head of his barracks was said to have been Jewish. Reminded that Dr. Krakovsky had said that it was impossible for the person in charge to be Jewish, Demjanjuk answered that in Vlassov's army there were many Jews.

Levin asked him to reply to the specific question about the POW camp, not Vlassov's army. "I don't know who was in charge in other barracks, but the one in charge in my barracks was said to be Jewish."

Gill asked whether there were Jews in the other camps he had been held.

"In the other camps, there were so many of us and we were so cramped together that it was impossible to know who was who. Second, we never took any interest in the nationality of anyone; we were all prisoners, and all of us were just thinking of when we could get something to eat."

Did he see anyone taken away?

Red Army officers, he said, were taken away immediately and never seen again. Accordingly, officers tried to conceal their rank; some succeeded. Likewise, Jews tried to hide their religion. And, he repeated, in Vlassov's army, there were many Jews.

Demjanjuk now returned to Chelm: "In 1943, we were working at various tasks and in the spring I was added to a group that would leave the camp and conduct diggings of turf outside the camp.... Throughout the summer and autumn and even as snow began to fall we were still digging the turf [peat]...."

"When snow fell and covered everything, we stopped, and we did not go out to any more diggings. But we were put on duty for different jobs, such as, for example, unloading trains of whatever products they might have held, such as turnips, potatoes, and coal.... Whenever it was turnips or even potatoes, we tried to eat them, but, of course, on the condition that nobody was watching us."

Gill asked if he had ever seen POWs being removed from the camp. "I saw that many of them were put on trucks but I don't know where they were taken to.... I cannot say whether those

same trucks returned. The trucks took prisoners away and brought prisoners. I don't know whether they were the same ones. That I couldn't say."

Asked by Gill how many POWs were transferred, Demjanjuk answered, "I can't say. It was none of my business, and, in fact, I didn't take an interest where people were taken to, whether they were taken for other jobs elsewhere or whether they were taken to other camps."

Was he ever taken to another camp? Yes, he replied: "In the spring of 1944, we were told to get out of the barracks and line up in rows, not only from my own barracks, but from other barracks.

A German appeared and pointed with his finger at those who were to fall out and line up in a second row. All Ukrainians were ordered to leave the ranks. We were about three-hundred-and-fifty to four hundred people. The others were told to disperse. We were all registered and were sent to other barracks."

Judge Levin asked, "Could the witness tell us how long, to the best of his knowledge or his estimation, he spent at the Chelm POW camp?"

"All in all, I think it must have been some eighteen months."

And that, in effect, was Demjanjuk's alibi.

4. A Mechanic is a Mechanic

It was difficult to parse the details of Demjanjuk's tale — what was true and what was fiction — and what was fiction colored by truth. So, for example, while the specificity of the details of his Red Army service and capture were impressive, his account of being at Rovno and Chelm was all of a jumble.

Some of the details seemed true but whether he experienced them himself or had seen these things while serving as a camp guard (the three tiered pallets, the Kapos) or whether he had transposed the truth of what had happened to him to other locations (being recruited and taken in trucks to a new camp) was hard to discern.

There was also the vehemence and passion of Demjanjuk's blanket denials that he was ever in Trawniki, Sobibor or Treblinka. He was clearly lying about part of that but was he lying about all of it? And why did he insist so vehemently that this was a case of mistaken identity?

Demjanjuk related that some three or four days passed in the new barracks at Chelm, he said. His Soviet uniform was taken away; he was issued an old but clean Italian one. More days passed before he and others were taken by train to Graz. Demjanjuk said he had no idea where he was being taken.

In Graz, the POWs were housed in stables. They underwent a medical exam, which included a blood test; each man's blood type was then tattooed onto his left arm; Demjanjuk still bore the scar from removing it.

Gill asked when and why he had removed the tattoo. "I began removing it when I was in Heuberg, and I continued doing so when I was in Landshut. I began removing it when I found out that the SS division wore the same tattoo."

Demjanjuk said he was among some three-hundred POW

recruits who were taken from Graz to Heuberg, which he said was in the Austrian part of Germany. Gill asked if and when he understood why the Germans were enlisting him. "In Graz we understood something, and in Heuberg we understood exactly," he answered.

In Heuberg, he recalled, "we were told to line up in three rows, and an officer appeared who chose the men. My own posting was to a unit of guard officers, generals, in fact." This unit, he said, was known as the Russian Liberation Army. General Fedor Truckhin commanded the army; his commander, he said, was one Lieutenant Topkar, and the leader of his guard unit was a man named Dubovitz. Recruits could move freely about the camp, he recalled, but were not allowed out of it.

The next day in court, Demjanjuk had changed his mind as to when it was that he first realized he was no longer a POW: it was, he now said, when he was transferred from Chelm to Graz. He also revised his statement that he had received no military training, now saying that at Heuberg "we were taught how to use ammunition, automatic ammunition, rifles, and grenades.... In the very same room where they have this ammunition we were taught how to use them."

He remained at Heuberg, he insisted, until three weeks before the war ended. "Thereafter, the whole army left. I wouldn't know where. But I, together with ten other people, were taken to a certain station. At that station there were some GHQ equipment and cars for the generals."

After a few days they were given gasoline and commandeered a car and drove to Salzburg. Once in Salzburg, the car was taken away by a General Malishkin. From thereon, Demjanjuk said, he was on his own. With some fellow soldiers he walked to Bishophoffen, arriving on "the day of capitulation." American soldiers had gathered there.

Demjanjuk and the other soldiers were now American POWs. One American guarded them but did not stop those who wished to escape. Later, Demjanjuk was among those POWs taken by train to a farm outside Munich. There they spent two months with German farmers, and no one stood guard over them.

Eventually, Americans arrived with trucks; the POWs were taken to Landshut where they were held captive by one guard. "I and another three people left to work with a German farmer." Later on, a United Nations representative appeared and registered them.

When did he remove his tattoo, Gill asked, and how long did it take? "I can't say how long it took exactly," Demjanjuk said, "because you have to wait a long time for the wound to heal and then you start again. And then you start again, waiting for it to heal."

Gill led Demjanjuk through his postwar life-his years in the DP camps; his job as a truck driver for the U.S. Army; his marriage to Vera; the birth of their daughter, Lydia; his application and arrival in the United States; his residence in Indiana, then in Cleveland, where he found work at the Ford plant.

Demjanjuk was evasive about his work at Ford. He would not say whether he'd needed any special training to work on engines there. Basically, Demjanjuk said, he had learned on the job how to test and repair the four-cylinder engines.

Gill confirmed that the engines at Ford were gasoline-operated (as opposed to the diesel engines of the gas chambers at Treblinka and Sobibor).

When Gill asked him about his promotions, Demjanjuk was dismissive: "There was no such thing as a mechanic being promoted. A mechanic is a mechanic."

Demjanjuk made the statement matter-of-factly, but the

remark was haunting. The survivors and even Otto Horn had described Ivan in the same way, with the same words, in the same tone. "He was a mechanic," they'd all said.

As to the lies on his immigration forms? Demjanjuk had something new to relate: At his first screening by the International Refugee Organization (IRO), he had told the truth. It was only at a second screening that he lied. The deputy director of the United Nations War Relief Agency (UNWRA), who spoke Russian, told him that if he did not wish to return to the Soviet Union, he must hide any details that would reveal him to have been a Soviet national or Soviet soldier.

"We were told," he said, "that you must find yourself a place either in Poland, or in Czechoslovakia, or anywhere else, but don't put it down that you came from the Soviet Union and give these details at the time of questioning, and that is what we did.

"At the time, I did not know any Latin-printed language, but we found an atlas and we found a map and randomly picked a place, and I gave that place to the secretary, and later I tried to find that particular place on the map. Now I find on the map only the name Sombor, and I think that was the place."

"Were you ever in Sobibor?" John Gill asked.

"No."

"Never in Pilau?"

"No."

"Or in Danzig?"

"No."

"During that period of time, 1937 to 1943, were you in any other place, other than you have testified yesterday and today?"

"No."

"Why then did you tell that you were in these various places?"

"I said just now that these places were chosen in order to hide the fact that I was a citizen of the Soviet Union, that I had been a member of Vlassov's army."

Judge Levin wanted to give Demjanjuk every possibility to explain himself. He asked, "Are you rejecting the possibility that you may have been at Sobibor?"

"Your Honor ... these ... places were chosen for me by somebody who could read German and he chose them for me."

"In other words," said judge Levin, "you insist on the fact that you were never at Sobibor at any time at all and that that possibility just does not exist?"

"No, never in my life."

"And the mention of the names is [a coincidence] ?"

"I know that we found this on a map and as I am now looking at the map, I find Sombor only." Demjanjuk added that he was never in Sombor either.

But Judge Dorner said that she did not understand his version. "What did you have to hide?"

Demjanjuk repeated that he wanted to conceal his Soviet citizenship. But, Dorner said, didn't the forms he filled out say he was born in the Soviet Union?

Yes, the forms said he was born there, but they also stated that for a number of years, he had lived in Poland.

But he had written that his wife had been in the Soviet Union throughout the period in question.

Demjanjuk at first claimed that his wife had a separate form, but when shown it was one and the same, he said, "My wife wrote what she thought she should have written on that form."

Demjanjuk said his wife wasn't in the army; she wasn't in any danger. Anyway, he said, he and his wife filled these things in because they knew they could change their statements when they applied for American citizenship.

Gill explained that the police assumed he was in Sobibor because his form said so.

Demjanjuk would not answer directly but offered: "The police or the prosecution say this, but I know where I was; and I was never in Sobibor or in Sombor or in anywhere else, not in Treblinka. Otherwise, I, myself, wouldn't have looked like a skeleton, as if I, myself, had been taken out of Sobibor ... as though I, myself, had been in Sobibor, or in Treblinka or in Trawniki. When I was in the camps, I would have given my life in order to get a loaf of bread and survive."

Judge Levin: "You insist most adamantly that you were never in Sobibor. Is that true?"

"I am speaking the truth, no matter how many times you ask. It is the truth as it was." He waved his right hand for emphasis.

"There is a document," Judge Levin said sternly, "around which this trial, to a great extent, is focusing. This is what we call the Trawniki document or the service card.... On that document, it says that you, sir, were for a certain length of time at Sobibor. I would like to know, in light of your very definite, categorical answers, that this entry can, by no stretch of the imagination, be true? Is that what you are saying?"

"I was never at Sobibor, nor at Treblinka. Why it says it there, I don't know. I kept writing letters to my family, and in those letters, I described where I had been. I explained that I had been injured, but I don't know why that entry appears here."

But Judge Tal wondered: "Isn't it a very strange coincidence that on [the Trawniki card], which you say you have never seen in your life, it says Sobibor? And on the form that you submitted to the immigration authorities of the United States, it also says Sobibor?"

"Maybe it is surprising," Demjanjuk answered, "but I have never been in those places in my entire life."

When asked, Demjanjuk said that in the 1960s when his wife traveled twice to the Soviet Union, he stayed behind. He did not go, he said, because he had to care for the children, and because the Soviets still considered him a traitor. "I think they would have arrested me, judged me, and executed me, because that was the law," he said.

The Demjanjuk family had long claimed that the KGB chose to frame him because for those many years since the war, his mother had collected a pension for her son who was presumed killed during the war. When Demjanjuk's family started to send her packages and the Soviets found out he was still alive, the KGB decided to concoct the charges against him.

Gill submitted no documentary evidence to support this contention; rather, he asked Demjanjuk to confirm it. Surprisingly, Demjanjuk was not helpful. He insisted he did not write to his mother for many years, but that his wife wrote her family. Demjanjuk said that he never expressed his fear of repatriation in letters; that the packages were not sent to his mother but his mother-in-law; that he did know his mother was receiving a pension. It seemed that Demjanjuk would not help his case.

Gill came now to his final question: "In conclusion, the question that only you can answer: Are you that terrible and dreadful man from Treblinka, Ivan Grozny?"

"Please listen, Your Honors," said Demjanjuk. "That I should be the man that you claim I'm supposed to be, and that you claim that I was, at Treblinka and Sobibor, I would never, ever, put down these names."

"I apologize. I said these places, and even if I only had four years of schooling, I'm not all that stupid as to write Sobibor. I said I have never, ever, in my life been to such a place and I would never, ever, put it down anywhere.... I reply I never was, and I am not Ivan the Terrible."

"Have you ever killed any person in your life?"

"Never. I cannot even kill a chicken; my wife invariably did it."

Judge Levin had a question, one that he thought the defense counsel should have asked: Was the signature on the Trawniki card his? "How can it be my signature, if I have never been to Trawniki? I never saw such a document, nor did I ever sign such a document."

Lydia Demjanjuk complained to the press about the mood of the courtroom. During Demjanjuk's testimony, members of the prosecution team were smirking. In her opinion, there was all too much joking around. Her father was not being treated with the same respect accorded the Holocaust survivors.

But Demjanjuk, himself, who had been testifying for a day-and-a-half now, seemed positively ebullient, unconcerned about the cross-examination to follow. On his way out of court, he spotted a little boy, bent down and waved at him saying, "Shalom, shalom. . . ."

"I Forgot"

The Israeli Prosecution's cross-examination of Demjanjuk sought to take apart his story piece by piece until there was nothing left in the court's mind save one word: "liar."

Contrary to his prior claims that there was a Ukrainian Army unit at Graz, Demjanjuk said he had no duties there. All he did was play cards and stay in the stables, except when an officer came to take them for meals. There was no SS division there, no Ukrainian division-no Ukrainians at all, save the person who brought him his meals, and the person who accompanied him to Heuberg.

Having to explain so many inconsistencies was stressful for Demjanjuk. He told the court, "I have a pain in my side and could we perhaps conclude for today because I am very tired."

The next day, he told Blatman that, at Heuberg, in Vlassov's army although he was trained in weapons, he did not carry one. Reminded that he had testified he did guard with a gun.

"Maybe that is so," he reflected. "I didn't remember at the moment ... I just recalled it."

Demjanjuk explained that there was a handful of officers at Heuberg, each of whom commanded a different unit. A man named Dubovitz was in charge of the guard section and was with him every day. Demjanjuk said Dubovitz would testify on his behalf (he never did).

Demjanjuk revealed that he had learned a great deal about the Vlassov army while living in Cleveland. He had seen a video that said Jews served in the Vlassov army.

Judge Levin explained to Demjanjuk that the purpose of the questioning was to tell the truth, and to give truthful explanations for previous inconsistencies.

"I try to tell the truth," Demjanjuk said. "I don't want to mislead anyone...I have nothing to hide," Demjanjuk said. "I was never at Treblinka, and I have no reason to seek refuge behind some figment of imagination."

Demjanjuk's alibi for the years he was accused of being at Treblinka and Sobibor was that he was at Rovno and Chelm. Rovno, he said, "was a very small camp. We spent only the nights there, where we could only stand up. Throughout the day we were permitted to leave and spend time in the clearing of woods, and at night we were taken back to the camp and made to remain standing."

Demjanjuk said escape from there would have been impossible, although he did concede that trucks did come and take people away-- but he knew nothing about POWs being taken to perform duties for the Germans.

Despite his earlier testimony that he left Rovno in railroad cars, he now said he left in a covered truck.

Blatman homed in: "Perhaps the lorries you were talking about brought you to Trawniki?"

"That's not true," Demjanjuk said.

"You continue to maintain that you came to Chelm?" "I am not maintaining; I am speaking the truth."

At Chelm, a month after they arrived, once they had moved into barracks, the POWs were registered, Demjanjuk said: "Name, place of birth, where you came from, everything."

Demjanjuk recalled seeing people being taken away in trucks, but he did not know what became of them. No one in his barracks was removed: "Our entire barracks got out to dig peat. Every day we were taken there, and then they took us back." He worked at this "for a long time," he said, "maybe nine or ten months. That is all we did."

Demjanjuk found himself increasingly confronted with contradictions in his testimony. Demjanjuk said there were Kapos at Chelm. "Kapo" was the Germans' word, he said; not his. The POWs called him "by the name of his father plus his first name."

Blatman asked the name of his Kapo. "I don't remember," he said. "I don't want just to throw out any name. I want to speak the truth. I just can't remember now."

Demjanjuk said he could not forget the terrible conditions

in the Chelm Camp where he was "skin and bones": "It is impossible to forget just as it is impossible to forgive what was done to me over the past ten years. This is why I am fighting.... You want to prove now that I am a liar, and that is not true!"

As for the conditions in the camp: "Yes, those were atrocities that I want to forget, but one can't forget them. You can't forget it, just as one can't forget anyone who survived the Holocaust, cannot forget."

If he could not forget the conditions at Chelm, why three times in his 1978 deposition – when he was first accused by US authorities of having been at Sobibor and Treblinka, he was given a chance to give his alibi, but he could not recall the Chelm camp.

"I didn't think of it because it did not come to mind ... what could I do? ...I can't say why I forgot. I forgot."

Judge Levin tried to explain to Demjanjuk just how serious a matter this was: Chelm, in effect was his alibi. "The very same camp that serves as your alibi," the judge said, "that precise camp, you failed to mention. How is that possible?"

Demjanjuk: "I said that I had been in two camps in Poland. One I forgot."

Demjanjuk asked to see the original deposition. Blatman objected, but Levin allowed it: "This is a very difficult and severe trial. The charges are very grave [and] The witness is in a certain quandary, a predicament, and in order to dispel any doubt, however slight, in order to make it perfectly clear that it is not the case that he was not allowed to give a proper answer, let us give him a chance."

Blatman: "Showing the witness these documents is not what is going to alter the fairness of this questioning."

Judge Levin replied with a Talmudic saying, "Justice must

not only be done, it must be seen to be done."

Demjanjuk reviewed the documents seeing the inconsistent answers he had given regarding Chelm and what he did while there, and that he had never mentioned working on peat bogs before.

"...take into account, please, that I am answering in that manner because no one prepared me the way they prepare witnesses in Israel to give replies."

Levin: "You don't have to be prepared to tell the truth."

6.A Skilled Driver

Shaked wondered why, if he so feared the Soviets, Demjanjuk had written to a niece in the Soviet Union to ask her to request his birth certificate and military record from the local authorities. Why put her at risk?

"I sent her, yes," he admitted. By way of explanation, he said, "Actually, you might say my tragic mistake was that I can't think properly and I don't know how to answer accordingly."

Shaked handed him the original of the Trawniki card. Demjanjuk thanked him; in Cleveland, he said, he had not been allowed to hold it. Asked about the signature, he confirmed it said Demjanjuk in Cyrillic but insisted it was not his signature. Although in 1942 he did sign his name in Cyrillic, and he had said the signature was " like I wrote my name," in a 1980 deposition, he now explained that he meant that it was spelled correctly.

Shaked turned his attention to the photograph on the card. "He resembles me, yes," But Demjanjuk stated that the haircut wasn't right and that he had never worn such a uniform.

Shaked went on to consider Demjanjuk's mechanical skills, his knowledge of engines, and his driving abilities. Shaked brought forth an enlarged copy of his 1948 IRO form and pointed to an entry saying that Demjanjuk had been a driver for UNWRA-IRO in Landshut from May 1945 to July 1947. Demjanjuk denied it was true.

"So what?" Shaked said contemptuously. "Were you lying here?"

Why was he so afraid to admit that he knew how to drive before 1947? He was a tractor driver before the war, wasn't he? Didn't he tell the Israeli investigators that at one point in the Red Army he drove an ammunition truck? They must have misunderstood him, he said.

What was the matter with knowing how to drive a truck? Shake thought he knew: Fedorenko had said that when the Germans came to recruit at Chelm, they asked all drivers to step forward.

Didn't Demjanjuk say that the conditions at Chelm were so terrible he would have given his life for a loaf of bread? So why not tell them he was a mechanic and save his life?

Even if he could operate a tractor, Demjanjuk said, he knew nothing about driving a car.

But his 1948 application, filled out only a few months after he received his German driving license, listed him as a "skilled driver." He had been driving for two years for the IRO.

A few weeks later, a photo of Demjanjuk in an IRO uniform surfaced. Although Sheftel had originally said it was taken in 1946, at the Landshut DP camp. Demjanjuk now claimed that in 1951 he worked for a few weeks as a policeman in the Felderfink DP camp; that he was then diagnosed as having tuberculosis and although no longer officially a policeman, he continued to do the same duties and was paid with a carton of cigarettes, or some small pay.

Shaked suggested that perhaps the photo was taken in 1946. But that he wasn't a police officer then, but a driver for the IRO-as written on his 1948 IRO form. Demjanjuk maintained that he couldn't drive until 1947, no matter what the IRO form said. He knew nothing of the photo until he saw it in the newspaper.

Shaked suggested that Demjanjuk had driven before 1945, Shake said. At Treblinka.

"I was never at Treblinka," Demjanjuk said, "and I never drove a truck."

"Look," Shaked said, "there is somebody who was in the SS

and who was at Treblinka. His name is Otto Horn. He is the one who identified your picture as Ivan the Terrible, the Ivan who operated the gas engines, and he says that you, together with Schmidt, were employed on trucks and engines."

Demjanjuk insisted, again, that he was never at Treblinka, and could not drive before 1947. But Shaked, too, insisted: He drove at Treblinka and along the roads in Poland. Shaked showed him a map of Poland. He pointed out where Treblinka was, and where Sobibor was. And he pointed out the two towns, Kosow and Miedzyrec Podlaski, that Inspector Russek had asked him about. Demjanjuk had replied to Russek, "You are pushing me toward Treblinka."

"I may well have said it, but I can't remember," Demjanjuk now responded.

Why did he say on his IRO form that he was at Sobibor from May 1937 to July 1943, and that while there his occupation was "driver"? Demjanjuk answered that the same person who told him to write "Sobibor" on the form told him to write "driver." He said he was surprised to see it written because he could not drive then.

Shake pointed out that Demjanjuk's education and qualification as a driver were greater than he let on. Despite saying the he had only completed four grades, Demjanjuk's 1948 IRO form read not only "primary school education" but also being a student in Kazatin from 1935 to 1937.

Demjanjuk: "I want to say, as you see when I asked for citizenship in the United States, that I changed all the particulars, and I gave the real facts, I said I was born in Dub Macharenzi ... you simply don't want to understand this."

Levin: "Again, I am sorry you are not answering the question. The questions are fairly simple, and I do not accept that you haven't understood the questions. If I thought the questions were too complicated, and if I thought that you, given your intelligence, couldn't understand them, I would simplify them. But the questions are simple, and for some reason, you are not answering them. Please listen to the question. And give an answer to the question that was put to you."

Shaked suggested there was a reason why he lied on his forms. "It was as though," Shaked said, "you would have to invent an alibi for the period of the war."

"That is what we were told, yes," Demjanjuk replied, saying that to hide his Soviet citizenship, he chose a place in Poland for his forms. But what he wrote was that between 1937 and 1943, he was in Sobibor and Chelm where he worked as a driver for an auto firm for pay of forty zlotys (an amount similar to what Wachmann were paid at Sobibor)

What was written on the form, Demjanjuk said, was the problem of whomever wrote it down. As to why he wrote Chelm, Demjanjuk was evasive. "I was in Chelm, but I wasn't in Sobibor, and I don't know how far they are from one another."

About Pilau, where his form said he was in January 1943, Shaked said Fedorenko went to the Stutthoff camps after Treblinka. Within the Stutthoff complex, there were camps at Danzig, where executions were known to have taken place on the seashore near Pilau. Said Shaked: "Don't you think it's a strange coincidence?"

"What you are telling me here about Fedorenko, that's Fedorenko's affair," Demjanjuk said. "He was at Treblinka, and he's on the list of those that had been at Treblinka; but my name is Demjanjuk, and I am not on the list of any camps. If I were the man who had been at the places that you say I had been, I wouldn't be sitting here, because I wouldn't have got to the United States ... I am here today in order to show the truth, the real truth, and that I am a decent person."

Judge Dorner asked Demjanjuk whether the same person who told him to write down Sobibor suggested that he write down Pilau. No, Demjanjuk said, he wrote down Pilau at the first registration.

Then, as he said he told the truth at his first registration, his being at Pilau was the truth?"

Demjanjuk was adamant: "I was not at Pilau." Demjanjuk explained that he lied because having served in Vlassov's Army, he feared repatriation to the Soviet Union.

Shaked agreed that he had reason to fear the Soviets, but it was not because of repatriation, it was because he was a war criminal.

Shaked said that the survivors who had come to court had described all the terrible things they had seen him do. Yet the only thing he had seen fit to say during all of their testimony, was to shout "liar" in Hebrew at one witness.

"I do not know how to say `liar' in Ukrainian," Shaked said. "But as the situation looks now, after all the testimony was heard here against you, and after all those long days of the cross-examination, there is no way of not concluding that you are, in fact, Ivan the Terrible from Treblinka."

"Prosecutor," Demjanjuk said, angry and tired, "witnesses who gave testimony here, and who have claimed to have seen me there, these witnesses never saw me in their lives. You said that they called me Ivan the Terrible. That, too, is a lie, because nobody in my whole life has called me Ivan the Terrible ... I would ask you that if you say that I am Ivan the Terrible, you show me where it says so.... Where is your information? You are trying to trip me up, because I gave confused answers, but of course I am not an educated person, I don't have a tutored mind."

Judge Levin asked if Demjanjuk had anything to add.

"I think, later on," he said, "you will see who I really am."

a. Greeting Card   b. Red Army   c. Service Pass No. 1393   d. Driver's License

e. Wedding Picture   f. Visa Application   g. Naturalization Certificate

Photographs
of
Iwan Demjanjuk

Demjanjuk over the years. Court exhibit. Courtesy of the author.

Demjanjuk's Trawniki ID. (interior). The 1942 service pass issued to Ivan Demjanjuk at the Trawniki Training Camp for SS guards indicating his service at Sobibor. (the handwritten notations are the 1948 Russian translation). Courtesy of the author.

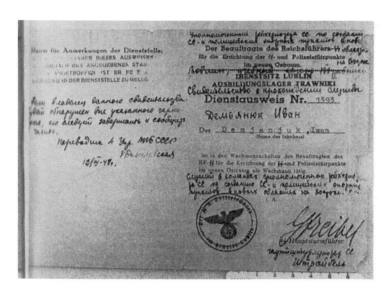

Trawniki Card Exterior. The Card notes that Service Pass Number 1393 has been issued to Iwan Demjanjuk and bears Camp commander Streibl's signature. Courtesy of the author.

Demjanjuk arrives in Israel and is transferred from U.S. custody to Israel Police. Photo Nati Harnik/ Israel

Government Press Office

295

Demjanjuk in his cell at Ayalon Prison in Israel. Photo by
Ya'acov Sa'ar / Israel Government Press Office

Justice Dov Levin. Photo by Ya'acov Sa'ar / Israel
Government Press Office

Justice Dov Levin and Judge Dalia Dorner. Photo by
Ya'acov Sa'ar / Israel Government Press Office.

Judge Zvi Tal. Photo by Ya'acov Sa'ar / Israel Government Press Office

Demjanjuk in court in Jerusalem shouts "Hello Cleveland" as he enters the Jerusalem Courtroom for the first time with his son John, Jr, at his side and attorneys John Gill and Mark O'Connor in front of him. Photo by Ya'acov Sa'ar / Israel Government Press Office.

Israeli Prosecutor Mickey Shaked. Photo by Maggi Ayalon /
Israel Government Press Office.

"Yes, he's sitting there. There he is!" Shouts Treblinka survivor Pinchas Epstein identifying Demjanjuk. Photo by Ya'acov Sa'ar / Israel Government Press Office.

Eliahu Rosenberg is cross-examined by Mark O'Connor as the prosecution team of Mickey Shaked, Michael Horovitz and Yonah Blatman watch with the photo of the model of Treblinka behind them. Photo by Ya'acov Sa'ar / Israel Government Press Office.

Demjanjuk answers during his cross examination. Photo by
Ya'acov Sa'ar / Israel Government Press Office.

Defense attorney Yoram Sheftel (standing) during testimony of Wilhelm Wagenaar. Photo by Maggi Ayalon / Israel Government Press Office

Demjanjuk's Supreme Court Hearing. Photo by Ya'acov Sa'ar / Israel Government Press Office

CHAPTER EIGHT:

EXPERT OPINIONS

1. Document Examiners

The defense was unable to shake the opinions of Sheffler or Grabitz as to the historical authenticity of the Trawniki card, or those of Bezalelli and Epstein as to its signatures. Gill had extracted one concession: Dr. Anthony Cantu, the U.S. chemist and paper and ink expert, did not dispute that his analyses could not uncover a forgery if it had been made from 1941 materials. But this meant that the forgers had preserved the paper and ink since then, and that the forgery was so good it would go undetected. Which was highly unlikely.

The defense then called a series of witnesses to support their contention that the Trawniki card was a forgery.

Edna Robertson, a Florida documents analyst, was president of the World Association of Documents Examiners (WADE). A diminutive, gray-haired woman from Panama City, Florida, with thick glasses, Robertson spoke in a flat, folksy twang. Court observers were ready to cast her as Miss Marple, come to save the day for the defense.

She testified that the card was not as worn as it should be. She was troubled by the rust stain of a paperclip under the Streibl signature. She found that a certain circular stamp did not luminesce as she believed it should. The photo on the card had been removed from somewhere else, she noted, and placed on this card. She was unconvinced about Demjanjuk's Cyrillic signature was authentic.

During cross-examination, Shaked confirmed that Robertson's organization, the World Association of Documents Examiners (WADE), did not require forensic document experience as an admission criterion; that U.S. courts had found their members not qualified to be experts; and that she did not qualify for membership in recognized American professional organizations (which require having worked for a law enforcement agency) like the American Academy of Forensic Documents Examiners, to which Gideon Epstein belonged.

Further, Shaked had Robertson admit that she had no knowledge of chemistry, so she could not speak as an expert about the chemical composition of ink or rust, or stains, glue, and solvents. It was not wear or tear, she had to agree, that defined an identity document. That the photo had been used on a prior document, so what? As for the luminescence Shaked showed that the same effect occurred on Demjanjuk's 1947 Driver's license. Was she saying that was a forgery too?

Shaked then casually asked if she had seen or known of the existence of similar identity documents. At which point, Shaked revealed that just ten days before, the Prime Minister's office had received a call, out of the blue, from Armand Hammer: he would be delivering three other Trawniki service cards from the Soviet Union.

They were striking. The three Trawniki cards were: card no. 847 of Ivan Juchnowski, born in 1913 near Vinnitsa, who was posted to the Lemberg (Lvov) ghetto; card no. 1926 of Nicholas Bondarenko, born in 1922 and posted to the Poniatova concentration camp. Both Juchnowski and Bondarenko had listed their nationality as Ukrainian. Ivan Wollenbach, who was listed as a Russian, had card no. 1211-it listed no posting whatsoever, and the photo from it had fallen off.

To behold them was astounding. The inks, the typewriting, the cardboard, the stamps, were unmistakably the same. They, too, had mistakes. One had the same orange stain on its back. The cards presented a strong visual argument for the Trawniki card not being unique, or as the defense had long claimed, "a one-of-a-kind KGB forgery."

The defense had known of the arrival of these cards but Robertston did not want to examine them outside her laboratory. The Court said the cards could be used for the limited purpose of confronting defense experts and challenging their testimony. Which Shaked did, ending Robertson's time on the stand.

"You must feel relieved that you have concluded your testimony," Judge Levin said.

Anita Pritchard, the next witness told the court she was a member of WADE and described herself as a grapho-analyst-that is, that by looking at someone's face, she could ascertain personality traits. She had been called by the defense to assess whether the photo on the Trawniki card was of Demjanjuk; to counter and critique Altmann's and Smith's photo comparisons; and to testify as to how suggestive photographs may be and how optical illusions can be created in facial montages.

She spoke of how "part of the perception is in the perceiver," and that superimposition is open to misinterpretation. She believed that Altmann had altered the photos by the way he'd mixed them. However, her expertise was not in forensic matters, she said, but in psychology.

Shaked countered by saying that she had no expertise. She had none in either anthropology, anthropomorphy, morphology and no scientific underpinning to her analysis. Pritchard maintained that she was an expert in visual perception.

But Shaked challenged this too: Did she know anything about neurology? Physiognomy? The optics of the human eye? The retina? She did not.

"You're creating the illusion," Shaked said finally, "that you're an expert."

"I was under the impression that I could give my opinion and it was not up to me to decide if I'm the expert."

Sheftel tried on redirect to rehabilitate her, but Judge Levin said, "Why torment the witness further, after she has admitted she is not an expert?"

Avraham Shiffrin was a defense expert in two areas: the forgery abilities of the KGB, and its posture toward the Ukrainian community.

At first, Shiffrin made a good impression: a decorated Red Army soldier, after the war he had worked as a Soviet prosecutorial investigator, working hand in hand with the KGB. In 1953, he was arrested, tried as a Zionist agent, and sentenced to thirty years in prison. He served ten years, and then was exiled to Odessa. He emigrated to Israel in 1973. Since then, he had run an institute devoted to the study of the KGB, staffed by many researchers, and responsible, over the years, for twenty publications. He had testified about the KGB to the U.S. Congress.

Shiffrin was handed the Trawniki card, whose Russian translation in purple ink bore the initials NGB. The NGB, he explained, were the former initials of the KGB.

The KGB, he said, has a special department for forgeries, equipped with materials, inks, papers, and even a special machine to age paper. He personally had seen KGB-warehoused paper and blank German war forms. The examples of KGB forgery of German documents were countless, he said.

Shiffrin said every former Soviet citizen living in the West was considered a defector by the KGB. Someone who had been in Vlassov's army had to be persecuted. He saw a further motive for the KGB in the Demjanjuk case: a provocation between the Ukrainians and Jews, the two most dangerous minorities in the eyes of the KGB. The KGB wished, he said, to sow dissention between them, rather than have them work together against the Soviet Union.

But on cross-examination, Yonah Blatman brought out that Shiffrin's "institute" was, in fact, his apartment. Over the years Shiffrin had been quoted in newspapers claiming that the KGB was using radiation and "psychic" forces to cause heart attacks, control the minds of Western politicians, and cause electrical blackouts. Shiffrin dismissed the articles as ridiculous and his comments in print as misquotes.

Shiffrin did admit that he was involved in parapsychology, which he deemed a serious science. The KGB was interested, he stated, in harnessing paranormal forces, and had recruited sorcerers and witchdoctors throughout the world to study them; while in prison, he testified, he had seen people using parapsychological force to cause trances or fits in others.

So much for Schiffrin's expert testimony.

Next up was "Count" Tolstoy. Born in England in 1935, Nikolai Tolstoy was the author of many books: children's novels, historical novels, and historical nonfiction. He had written several works on Soviet history, including <u>Stalin's Secret War</u>; and two on forced repatriation, <u>Victims of Yalta</u> and <u>The Minister and the Massacres</u>. He held bachelor's and master's degrees in modern history. He had no Ph.D., he said, but understood his research to have been at a postdoctoral level.

Tolstoy was willing to be expert on all things for the Demjanjuk defense: on the forced repatriation, which, he said, never formally ended but went on even in 1950; and the fear of repatriation, which continued even after that. On the Vlassov army, Tolstoy testified that there were hundreds of thousands of Vlassov's soldiers wandering through Western Europe at the time Demjanjuk claimed to have been there; Sheftel then submitted photos of soldiers bearing ROA (Russian Liberation Army) badges from 1943.

Tolstoy also testified about the KGB's history of forging documents. He disputed the findings of Professor Meisel, whose research, he said, he had never come across in his fifteen years of study; and whose statistics he found "in the first instance, easily falsifiable and, in the second, unverifiable." As to Demjanjuk's having lied on his immigration forms, Tolstoy told the court that British officials encouraged Soviet DPs to conceal their Soviet birth and say they were Polish citizens.

He found "nothing inherently implausible" about Demjanjuk's version of being brought to Heuberg and conscripted into a unit of former Soviet POWs who wore ROA badges in the spring of 1944. He knew of no such units before 1945, but it was possible. He confirmed Sheftel's claim that Vlassov's chief propagandist, Zikoff, was thought to be a Jew and that some Jews were known to be concealed in Vlassov's army.

It was possible, he said, that Demjanjuk was assigned in Heuberg to guard generals but was given no weapons because the Vlassov army's function then was, for the great part, propaganda; and all the Russian soldiers there were still prisoners.

Sheftel showed Tolstoy the Trawniki document. It was the regular procedure of the KGB, Tolstoy confirmed, to obtain an authentic document and then doctor it; the correct information on a card is of minimal value. What is crucial, said Tolstoy, is the context of the card. The Trawniki card's provenance was questionable, he felt, not only because of the closed nature of the Soviet archives, and the fact that it was handled by the KGB, but also because of how it came to Israel via Armand Hammer. There was no context to establish the card's authenticity.

Sheftel asked for his overall comment on Demjanjuk's alibi. Tolstoy obliged him: "His account is fully consistent with historical events as they are known to me."

Blatman, on cross-examination, questioned Tolstoy about articles, lectures, pamphlets, and letters to the English papers. At the time of Canada's Deschenes commission deliberations on whether to investigate and try Nazi war criminals, Tolstoy had authored a pamphlet called "Trial and Error." In it he argued that the Soviet Union's crimes were as serious as Nazi war crimes, and the latter should not be prosecuted if justice was not administered to the former. Now Tolstoy distanced himself from the publishers of the pamphlet and the groups that distributed the pamphlet.

But in a letter published in England's Jewish Chronicle, which Blatman produced, Tolstoy had written, "Some Ukrainians persecuted some Jews, some Jews persecuted some Ukrainians, some Ukrainians again persecuted some Jews, and so it went on." This was not the unbiased view of a historian.

Tolstoy conceded that he did not conduct any research in German archives for his book The Long Knives. Tolstoy was revealed to be a popular writer on historical subjects, not a historian. His research technique was acceptable for a writer but not for an academic, as a historical point of view.

Tolstoy complained to the court that his personal views rather than his expert opinion were being attacked. He asked that the proceedings be stopped; he threatened to leave the stand. Without the court's assurance of "fair play in accord with standards of Western justice," Tolstoy declared, he would be "unable to participate further."

313

The court informed Tolstoy that it was not for him to set conditions for his testimony. He had agreed to be a witness. If he did not wish to testify, he could be compelled to do so; or if he left the witness stand, his testimony would be struck as if never given; and if he wished to insult the court, as was the innuendo of his comments, then he could be held in contempt, and tried for slander.

Further, defense counsel had not objected to the questioning, and there was good reason: the questions were legitimate and appropriate. There would be, judge Levin said, no limitations and preconditions placed upon the court. Tolstoy's "subjective feeling," he said, "is not our business." Tolstoy remained on the stand.

Under Blatman's cross-examination, Tolstoy began to make a hasty retreat from his "expert" opinions. Tolstoy admitted that he was not an expert on the Gallician division. As to recruiting in the Graz area, he admitted "to the best of my knowledge there was no such recruiting.... I am not an expert on the German army at that time ... not an expert on German military records.... I do not know to the best of my recollection of forced repatriation after May 1946.... I have a general interest in Vlassov ... what studies I have conducted ... [are] not very far from exhaustive." He conceded there was no evidence of any unit in Heuberg during the summer of 1944. Finally, he conceded that Sheffler's method for determining the historical authenticity of the Trawniki card was valid.

As were the previous witnesses, Tolstoy was more opinion than expert.

2.Notable Experts

In August, the court took a two-week break, which was extended after judge Tal suffered a mild heart attack during another proceeding. During the break, the defense was able to recruit Dr. Julius Grant, one of the world's best-known forensic documents examiners, as well as Arizona documents examiner William Flynn, who had helped uncover the Hofmann Mormon letters forgery.

Grant was born in London in 1901 and received his doctorate in 1926. Between the years 1929 and 1951, he worked in a paper manufacturing plant, first as senior chemist and later as general manager. He developed a method for identifying fingerprints on paper and published many books in his area of expertise. In 1952, he joined with an expert on manuscripts to found an office for forensic investigations with notable success. He'd solved the forgery cases of the Mussolini diaries and the Hitler diaries. In both cases, other experts had adjudged the documents authentic and then Grant discovered them to be forgeries by examining the paper.

Grant examined the Trawniki card in mid-October and again at the beginning of November. At the same time, he also examined the three Trawniki cards that Hammer had delivered. He found them all to be of similar paper composition and printing, and were probably, he wrote in his expert opinion, made in the same mill at the same time. He also found the printed type faces on all three cards to be identical.

Grant was a spry witness. Though eighty-six years old, and seemingly frail, he came alive on the stand. Sitting behind the witness lectern, he drew himself up and spoke in a strong voice, with often cheeky answers to Shaked's cross-examination. He held beside him a green British West Indies Airlines flight bag, which contained his notes and files, as a sort of portable office. Sheftel led him through his direct testimony.

On the Streibl signature, Grant made a determination of "high probability." But the rust line in the shape of a paperclip gave him pause. He had been told that paperclips of this type did not exist at Trawniki. Therefore, he suggested, it may be such a good forgery that it can't be detected. Grant found Teufel's signature very convincing, but because he had examined only photocopies of it, he could rate it only "possible."

As to the Demjanjuk signature on the Trawniki card, Grant did not dispute the prosecution's analysis of its elements. But his doubts of its authenticity arose in comparison to the other signatures he had studied.

Finally, Sheftel asked: "Is this the service pass of the accused or not?"

"The indications [are] that it could not [be]," Grant answered. "I am greatly influenced by the signature-I believe it not to be that of the accused." But he would not base his opinion solely on the basis of the signature. He asked to examine the photo again overnight.

The next day, Grant said that the card was not authentic. The signature was not enough by itself for him to make his conclusion, he was also troubled by the photo. In a decade of trials, Grant was the first reputable examiner to dispute the card's authenticity in court.

Grant's testimony about the card, in effect, formed an equation: doubts about Demjanjuk's signature plus doubts about the photo equaled the card not being authentic. His concerns about either the photo or the card were not by themselves great enough for him to doubt the card's authenticity.

To attack Grant's equation, Shaked first set about examining its components. Grant had testified that he found that the signature was "unlikely" to be Demjanjuk's based on three characteristics: The D, M, and the pen lifts. But Demjanjuk himself, in all his earlier testimony, Shaked pointed out, had never objected to the D or the M (which in Cyrillic looks like a "u"). In fact, Demjanjuk had said in 1980, "It is like I wrote my name [in 1942]."

Did this affect his opinion?

"If what I have been told now is true," Grant said, "then my deduction that the signature was not written by the defendant is not of the same security value, and loses some of the security of its certainty, [it] loses from its certainty."

Shaked now turned to the second half of the equation, the photo. Grant's problems were that in comparing the Trawniki card to the three other supplied, only the Trawniki photo had two holes in it; that purple ink similar to that of the Russian translation on the card was found in the holes; and that the stamp on the photograph did not fit with that part of the stamp on the document.

All this suggested a KGB forgery-purple KGB ink linking the photo to the document.

But Grant had examined only the upper of the photo holes, Shaked revealed, not the lower one; Grant's own examination found that the ink came after the hole, not before. And his examination found the adhesive used was not a strong one. This information, Shaked said, did not necessarily lead to the conclusion that the card was forged by the KGB.

Shaked asked Grant to consider a different scenario: that at Trawniki, Demjanjuk's photo was first affixed to another file document (hence the two holes), then attached to the Trawniki card and stamped, and then at a much later date, fell off (explained by the poor quality adhesive) and was reaffixed (why the stamp doesn't match).

"I admit the possibility," said Grant.

317

Without the photo, could he still conclude that the card was not authentic?

"I cannot," said Grant.

The defense had one more expert on which to pin their hopes for discrediting the Trawniki Card: William Flynn. Flynn had all the proper credentials of a documents examiner; not only that, but he had been a pupil and colleague of Gideon Epstein. He had gained recognition with regard to the Hofmann forgeries case.

Hofmann, a rare documents dealer, had over the years "uncovered" and sold a number of manuscripts about the Mormon Church to dealers, collectors, and even to the church itself. The contents of the documents were often controversial, but their authenticity was unquestioned.

But after a series of bomb-related deaths in Salt Lake City, the police began investigating a possible link with the documents and called in George Throckmorton, a forensic documents examiner.

He, in turn, called in William Flynn from Arizona to help. After examining the questioned documents for a short time, Throckmorton became convinced that they were forgeries; not too long after, Flynn was able to uncover how Hofmann had achieved a certain ink effect.

In September 1986, William Flynn arrived in Israel and conducted three days of tests on the Trawniki card at the forensic laboratories of the Israel Police.

The following month, he convened a meeting of U.S. documents examiners in Palm Springs, on the subject of historical documents.

In the courtroom in Jerusalem, Flynn said it was impossible to give a conclusive opinion about the signatures on a historical document. He was troubled by the holes in the photo, the purple ink in those holes, and the discrepancy in the parts of the stamp.

Flynn had prepared forgeries of the signatures of Streibl and Teufel as well as a photomontage of himself in SS uniform to demonstrate how easily these documents could be forged.

Shaked objected: the issue was not whether Flynn could commit a forgery; the question was whether the Trawniki card was forged.

Sheftel jumped up. If the witness could not present this evidence, then Sheftel asked that he leave the stand and that his testimony be struck from the record. The court refused. Sheftel said the witness had no further testimony.

But Flynn was not yet free to leave. The prosecution insisted on its right to cross-examine. Again, Sheftel asked to withdraw Flynn's testimony. The court again refused.

Flynn was hesitant to go on. His client, he said, the John Demjanjuk Defense Fund, did not wish him to testify. The court explained that he must answer the questions of the prosecution or be held in contempt.

Flynn agreed to continue his testimony.

The prosecution then read from Flynn's comments at a recent convention of document examiners in Palm Springs made after he'd examined the original of the Trawniki Card: "Forensic tests will be conducted, the certificate will be all right, but she [sic] still will not be original." He still agreed with the statement.

But how could the card be, at the same time, a forgery so good it couldn't be detected, yet be found by Flynn to have obvious flaws? Wasn't this a contradiction?

Flynn said that part of the document was orderly, but other things indicated forgery.

The next day, Shaked played the recording of his speech: "I have examined the card firsthand for three days," Flynn could be heard saying. "I have examined the thing microscopically, and there's nothing about the card that I can see that would not have passed muster."

Flynn, clearly uncomfortable, refused to answer any further questions. He told the court that he was in a quandary. He had a "contractual agreement" with the Demjanjuk Defense Fund.

Ed Nishnic, who ran the fund, he said, had ordered him not to reply to questions of the prosecutor; and had threatened to file suit against him in the United States if he did so. Even if he won the suit, it could prove costly.

The court was not familiar with experts who had "contracts"; but they understood that he was in a dilemma. The court would compel him to testify only if the prosecution requested it. It did not and Flynn left the courtroom.

The court asked the Israel Police to question Nishnic to see whether he had intimidated Flynn by threatening litigation, and thereby had attempted an obstruction of justice. Nishnic was visited by the police at the American Colony Hotel for two hours, but no charges were ever filed. Nonetheless, Nishnic left the country soon after, not returning for the rest of the trial.

Once back in the United States, Flynn told the press in Arizona that his testimony had been conclusive, but the "biased" court had disregarded it.

A clue as to why he gave this version of actual events can be found in a comment he made to an Arizona columnist. Asked about the card, Flynn responded, "I've staked my reputation on it."

Clearly it was a reputation better defended in Phoenix, than in Jerusalem.

3. Memory Tests

Sheftel had wanted to attack the eyewitness identifications by calling Dr. Elizabeth Loftus, an experimental psychologist to testify about eyewitness testimony and memory testing, she declined to testify in the Demjanjuk case for personal reasons. Loftus did, however, recommend a colleague with whom she was in frequent email contact, Dr. Willem Wagenaar, a professor of experimental psychology at the University of Leyden in the Netherlands.

Professor Wagenaar took the witness stand in mid-November 1987. A dapper man, with sandy hair and graying mustache, he appeared in a gray suit and bow tie. He submitted a list of eighty-seven publications in which his articles had appeared, and he said he had testified in many cases, more than half concerning memory problems.

To the press, the defense had said that their expert would testify about "memory forty years after," but in court Wagenaar said he would not talk about the reliability of the survivors' memory.

Rather than focus on the survivors and their memories, he would concentrate on the photospread; based on the statements of the survivors, he would critique the identification test, not the survivors.

Wagenaar would also demonstrate how, after forty years, mistakes and slips of memory were common and normal, but he was not talking about the survivors-- he meant Demjanjuk, whose memory gaps made his alibi that much less credible.

Wagenaar's fundamental precept was that a memory problem existed, illustrated by the fact that not all the witnesses were perfectly certain, or perfectly accurate in their police identification statements.

The great majority of scientific studies on such matters involved subjects who'd had limited contact with a person and who were asked to recall him a short time thereafter.

Nonetheless, Wagenaar believed the studies relevant. On the one hand, the Treblinka survivors had had a prolonged and intense contact with Ivan, but Wagenaar felt that this was counterbalanced by the more than thirty-year interval since the survivors had last seen him.

Wagenaar put forward the proposition that, given certain factors, a witness faced with an identification parade (live or photo) may experience a "positive response bias"—that is to say that he or she may feel compelled to point someone out, even if the "target" suspect is not present. And among those who feel such a compulsion, there may be a "specific response bias"-factors by which a person, once having decided to point, will choose one individual over another.

Wagenaar contended that all the survivors had described Ivan as having a round face, short neck, and incipient baldness. He had conducted an experiment at the University of Leyden with students and the very same photographs. Two photospreads were presented, the one used by the Israel Police, and another that placed Demjanjuk's picture among those persons with the same identifying characteristics. Students were asked to pick out the criminal with the round face, short neck, who was balding.

When shown the Israeli photospread, 100 percent of the students chose Demjanjuk; but when using the prepared one, only 8 percent did. The conclusion, Wagenaar said, was that the Israeli photospread would not "for purpose of scientific research ... be considered to constitute valid tests of memory."

Wagenaar surmised that the more severe the crime, the more atrocious the act committed, the higher the probability of such mistaken identifications.. However, he added that "no practical studies had been done to confirm this ... that sort of very much applied literature does not exist."

Wagenaar put forward several theories for Demjanjuk's forgetfulness, omissions and mistakes in recounting his past: Demjanjuk's own experiences might not be so emotionally laden; Demjanjuk may have confused episodes; or perhaps he did not receive the right memory cue for a given episode.

Demjanjuk nodded, paying close attention.

Sheftel then showed Wagenaar a newly uncovered photo of Demjanjuk in a hat and uniform bearing an IRO badge on the arm. For six months in 1946, Sheftel explained, Demjanjuk had been an IRO police officer in the Landshut DP camp but had forgotten the episode until he saw the photo.

To Wagenaar, this was another example of the same phenomenon: if one doesn't receive the right cue, one may not recall a specific episode. He concluded, "There is no scientific basis to interpret these errors as signs of deliberate lying."

During Shaked's cross-examination, Wagenaar begrudgingly agreed that memory of faces was a subject not fully understood, but it was known that the quality of the contact, its duration, and the associations with that face all lent to its being etched in the consciousness of the beholder.

The situation of the survivors remembering Ivan, he had to admit, was vastly different than that of his students who had never known the subject.

So Wagenaar's test was really no test at all.

As to Wagenaar's theories that the photospreads were "biased," Shaked brought out that the scientific basis for both "positive response basis" and "specific response bias" were experimental studies. But there was no scientific basis, whatsoever, for the notion that extrapolating these results to a real-life situation would be valid.

None of the studies used was based on police investigations, or actual police lineups. They had no bearing on the Demjanjuk identifications. Beyond that, there had never been an experimental re-creation of the conditions in a death camp, Wagenaar conceded, nor of the same intense contact, for the same prolonged contact.

Now as to Demjanjuk. How was it, Shaked wanted to know, that Demjanjuk's memory was only selectively defective? That Demjanjuk could recall all the hospitals he was taken to when wounded, and the small towns they were in, but then forgot the details of the many months of his alibi?

Perhaps, Wagenaar suggested, to Demjanjuk they were not so harsh.

But Judge Tal wondered if Wagenaar meant that because a person has had harsh experiences in his past, he was less likely to recall other subsequent harsh experiences? Were there any scientific studies to confirm this? Personality psychology, Wagenaar said, was not really his area.

Wagenaar clung to the explanation that Demjanjuk didn't forget Chelm or his experiences there; he merely skipped over the episode and forgot to bring it up at the right time.

But, as Demjanjuk only first mentioned the name Chelm years after his first questioning, Shaked said, the possibility existed that he'd learned that name only after being questioned.

Wagenaar could not exclude this possibility.

"We have no means of finding this out, do we?" Shaked asked.

"I would say then, you have a problem," Wagenaar said.

"I suggest that you too, Dr. Wagenaar, have a problem," Shaked said.

Demjanjuk never claimed that he didn't know the name

Chelm, just that he didn't say it at first. As for Demjanjuk's IRO photo Wagenaar testified that for a period of at least six months and no more than twelve months in 1946, Demjanjuk was an IRO police officer.

Was he sure? Couldn't it have been from when Demjanjuk was an IRO driver in 1946?

Shaked played a tape for Wagenaar, an interview he had given a Dutch journalist several months before where he spoke of a picture of Demjanjuk when he was an IRO driver. How, Shaked now asked, had he come to the police officer story?

Wagenaar claimed that the mistake was all his: Sheftel had told him that Demjanjuk had been part of the camp's internal order service, but having known Demjanjuk had been a driver, he'd confused the two when talking to the journalist.

Shaked suggested another possibility, that Sheftel had told him that the picture was of Demjanjuk as a driver for the American forces in 1945-46, which is what Demjanjuk had said on his IRO application. Wagenaar said, no, he knew nothing about other forms.

At the break, when asked by the press how the prosecution had got hold of the tape, Wagenaar said, "The journalist was Jewish. He was probably asked to do service to his country."

Finally, Shaked had been critical of Wagenaar's findings because they were based on experimental studies that bore no relation to the case. Now he went a step further. He asked Wagenaar what "expert" opinion could an "experimental" psychologist offer?

Wagenaar said he believed that there was no real controversy on this subject; he felt he did have "expert" testimony to offer to aid the court.

But even that statement was not "expert," Shaked said, it was partisan. Experimental psychology in court was a much debated and much contested subject in the United States; one on which Wagenaar had a clear stand and about which he should have informed the court.

Levin said this, if true, was important: courts must move prudently into new areas of science. Experimental psychologists had never testified in court in Israel and they could only be given weight if they were accepted by the international scientific community. If there was a debate as to this and Wagenaar had taken a partisan stand in the debate, it was his duty not only to inform the court of both sides of the debate, but also of his position.

Shaked also pointed out that although Wagenaar said he had appeared in forty cases, of which twenty dealt with gambling and the remaining twenty with memory. But Shaked interrupted: How many of the memory cases concerned an identity parade, a suspect among photos, or a live lineup?

The answer: "Of such a case, where a suspect was placed among other people and had to be recognized as suspects-I know of only one...."

Shaked revealed that Wagenaar's in-court presentation was not based on his own material but on articles and experiments of others; that Wagenaar had not written a single article concerning identification parades or any aspects thereof.

Shaked also suggested that his testimony was not based on impartial facts. He had given many press interviews before his court appearance. In those, with which he now confronted Wagenaar, he always put forward the defense version of events. Wagenaar said he had presented both possibilities, but he admitted he was ignorant of many of the facts of the case.

Had Wagenaar entertained the "banal possibility," that Demjanjuk's forgetfulness could be lies?

"Of course," Wagenaar said, "that's what this case is all about."

"I can't understand," Shaked said, winding up, "how you can testify about this subject without knowing anything either from the standpoint of experiences, or experiments, or the literature, or any experience in this area."

"My field of experience," said Wagenaar testily, "is how memory is tested in general and whether such a test provides a valid picture of the contents of memory. And the task I've set myself is to evaluate the memory tests that have been set before the witnesses-just the way I would evaluate memory tests in scientific situations, and the question I put myself is, Are the outcomes of such tests acceptable as valid representations of the contents of memory?"

But Shaked asked Wagenaar to recognize the lopsidedness between his experiments, in which he examined the "memory test," and the person whose memory was tested. The essential difference here was that the witnesses knew the suspect. When you are attacked by someone you know, there is no need for a lineup, he said. As Shaked analogized, if his neighbor broke into his apartment and stole his VCR, he would not need a lineup to identify the neighbor.

In all of scientific literature, Shaked said, there was only one study in which memory was tested more than forty years later. This was the Bahrick study, in which persons were confronted up to fifty years later with photographs taken from their high-school yearbooks.

Wagenaar agreed that in more than 90 percent of the cases, they made correct identifications. And that the Bahrick study was scientific evidence for the proposition that a photograph was a good cue to trigger the memory of a person one knew, even forty years later. Just like this case.

So why do you need a lineup? Shaked asked pointedly.

Wagenaar believed you still needed a "test of the accuracy of the memory of the witnesses" to get at information "that can help a court make its determination."

But the court itself was finding that Wagenaar's approach lacked expert underpinnings. "Let me give you an example," said Presiding Judge Levin, "that in a given graduating class of a high school, there were, let us say, ninety students. They spent some time together. A murder was committed by one of the students who disappeared and was not found. The police kept on working on the case. Thirty-five years later, it turned out that the suspect had moved to an enemy country and, therefore, he was inaccessible. Then he is extradited to Israel, and he says I never went to that school. I never spent any time there. I don't know what they want from me. I didn't commit any murder there, either. And then the students from his graduating class are interviewed and they are told, `Look, here you have a picture that we found, and it is-- if he was in high school when he was seventeen years old --this is a picture of him when he was twenty-one,' and when the witness is shown this picture, he says, `Oh, yes, this is the boy who was with me in the graduating class.'" Levin then asked what the witness thought the probability was that a single student would correctly identify the accused.

"There is a ninety-percent chance that indeed this is the person you are looking for, a ten-percent chance that this is not the person," Wagenaar answered.

Following on Levin's question, judge Tal asked what were the average results of accuracy in criminal identifications when the victims were exposed to the accused for even less time?

"There is in general an upper limit of eighty percent correct for one single eyewitness," Wagenaar said.

"I'll let you in on a secret," said judge Tal. "I did not ask this as an idle question, but to the best of my knowledge, and what I have learned so far, the degree of accuracy is, in fact, eighty percent, and your answer, in fact, confirms this. We wanted to be clear in our own minds on this point."

Later in the session, judge Tal had a few more questions. He asked what the odds were of someone by chance picking out an individual from a group of eight photographs?

"One to eight," the professor answered.

"If there are five identifiers," continued judge Tal, "and all of them point to the same photograph, then the chance of their doing this by sheer coincidence, is one to eight to the fifth exponent ... which is a very small chance. Is that correct?

Wagenaar agreed that it was.

Shaked was asked if he had any further questions. He did not.

In that room, on that day, it was clear that the defense attorneys, who were smiling, and Demjanjuk himself, who was smiling at his son-in-law Ed Nishnic in the front row, and the wire-service journalists who were leaving their balcony perch to file their stories, and the hundred or so persons who were scattered through the hall, which was only a third filled- did not realize that Wagenaar had just illuminated the opposite of what he had set out to present.

He had allowed the prosecution to submit the scientific evidence that explained why the identifications by the survivors were credible.

4. Sheftel's Strategy

Sheftel's defense strategy was one of tit for tat. If the prosecution had called two experts; he would call two-and claim his "experts" were more "expert" than theirs.

Before the defense finally rested at the end of December, it called Yitzhak Almagor, an Israeli, to testify that Jews had served in the Vlassov army. Almagor himself had never served in the Vlassov army, but while in a detention camp in 1948, he had met two Jews who had served as army interpreters. So, his evidence was deemed not relevant.

To respond to Patricia Smith's photo and video matchup of the Trawniki photo and Demjanjuk, the defense brought in a Florida anthropologist, Dr. Yascar Iscan. Iscan's expertise was not in morphology, the study of the human face, but in determining the age and sex of skeletons. In cross-examination, Iscan conceded the validity of the scientific basis for Smith's comparison technique. So that ruled his testimony out.

Finally, the defense also called its own German witness, Rudolf Reiss. Reiss, who also testified at Demjanjuk's deportation hearing, had worked at Trawniki. His hearing was held in Germany in October 1987 (as he was not an identifying witness, the judges did not attend).

Reiss had worked in Trawniki's administrative section as a paymaster. He claimed to be a document analyst -- although he was no such thing. When presented with a copy of the Trawniki card, he said he had never seen one at the camp. He then examined it and cited what he claimed was evidence of forgery, all matters previously explained by prosecution experts.

During the course of the hearing, Reiss was difficult and impudent. Several times he refused to answer Horovitz's questions. Reiss called the entire process a "circus." But when

Reiss was asked about identity documents in the camp, his descriptions seemed to support everything the prosecution experts had said about the card, save its actual existence.

Reiss admitted there were two types of camp documents that were not kept in his office but in the office of the battalion command. He recalled that photographs were taken with the rectangle on the left breast and that the photo was first stapled to personal records, then put on a cardboard ID document.

Reiss then described an ID that was similar to the Trawniki card, except that Reiss said it was contained on a metal disk. Finally, Reiss confirmed the existence of paperclips at the Trawniki camp, thereby ending "the great paperclip war" and further diminishing the strength of Grant's opinion.

Horovitz confronted Reiss with a letter he'd written to the American authorities. In it he spoke of: "the singular and unprecedented miscarriage of justice in the history of legal proceedings by the Tribunal at Nuremberg" and "the continued illegal detention of Rudolph Hess, who was acquitted at Nuremberg."

The defense called no more witnesses,

CHAPTER NINE

CLOSING IN

1. Revisiting Treblinka

In cases of a more routine nature, Shaked said in his closing argument, the court is often asked to visit the site of the crime. Shaked proposed to revisit Treblinka through the witnesses' special knowledge. In their accounts, Ivan was the walking weapon upon which they'd focused. No lineup was necessary: his face was etched into their memories.

The Trawniki card, Shaked said, had been shown to be authentic in all its respects. Every question raised by the defense or their experts had been dismissed. Among the defense experts, there who were true experts, such as Grant, Flynn, and Iscan, but their testimony was not beyond reproach; and those who set themselves up to be experts, such as Robertson Pritchard, Shiffrin, Tolstoy, and Wagenaar who were proved to be no such thing.

Demjanjuk's alibi, his jumble of narratives of time spent at Rovno, Chelm, Graz, and Heuberg, in which Demjanjuk had tried to stretch dates and facts to cover up the period when he was a Nazi camp guard, had unraveled completely and were without any historical support.

Fedorenko himself had demonstrated the route taken from the Ukraine through Trawniki to Treblinka. In all this, the Trawniki card was the link. It said Demjanjuk was a

Wachmann, an SS guard.

Blatman argued that Demjanjuk knew his victims were Jews and reflected a deliberate intent to act against the Jewish people. His denials show no remorse and he deserves no mitigation in the penalty for his crimes.

"Even a cog in the machinery, even a driver, can be a party to the crime.... And when it comes to the hierarchy of the Nazi machinery, the accused can indeed be viewed as a small cog in the hell.... However, he was, in fact, an active partner in the very act of carrying out one of the greatest acts of murder ever in history...." Blatman said.

The idea of extermination was the Germans', Blatman said, but they could not provide the manpower to carry out. They needed collaborators and they recruited them from the civilian population of the Soviet Union as well as from the POW camps.

"Here in court, decisive evidence was produced that shows unequivocally that the accused is Ivan the Terrible, who killed scores of thousands of men, women, and children while showing extreme bestiality and torturing his victims and who later found refuge in the United States.... It is our contention that [Demjanjuk's] quiet and peaceful countenance should not be misleading, because behind it lies the face of Ivan the Terrible. We ask that the accused be found guilty of all the charges."

During Eliahu Rosenberg's testimony, almost ten months earlier in March, he had told O'Connor that in 1945 he had given a statement, handwritten in Yiddish to a Polish government representative, that had not been seen or heard of since. The defense had found the statement in the archives of Warsaw's Jewish Historical Society. Now, in the midst of the summations, Rosenberg was recalled to the witness stand to be cross-examined by Paul Chumak, a Canadian attorney of

Ukrainian descent, who had joined the Demjanjuk defense team instead of Broadley after O'Connor was fired.

Chumak, in his mid-forties, was a former prosecutor in Toronto. He had the bearing of a litigator, and he approached Rosenberg with confidence. He showed him the document. Rosenberg confirmed that it was the one he had written in Poland in 1945.

The statement is a far grislier account of Treblinka. But like the 1947 Friedman statement, it also spoke of the death of Ivan.

Chumak, impatient with Rosenberg, asked him to read in Yiddish and translate the passage: "We went out of the barracks and fell on the Ukrainians who were guarding us. Mendel and Chaim, who had pumped water from the well, jumped the Wachmann.... After this we broke into the engine room toward Ivan, he was asleep then. Gustav, [who] was the first, hit him on the head with a spade. Thus, he was left lying there forever...."

"What I said there I didn't see. I heard," Rosenberg said in response to Chumak's questions. "There is a very big difference."

Chumak's voice grew louder: "Did you see that? Mendel and Chaim?"

"No," Rosenberg said. "I didn't have a chance to see. My role, along with five other people, was ... to take blankets and throw them over the fences."

Rosenberg explained that he was too busy escaping to see those other things. "Escape. This was my purpose. The bullets were shrieking all around us," Rosenberg said.

Judge Tal asked, "Why didn't you point out what you did write and what you saw?"

"Perhaps it was a mistake," Rosenberg said contritely. "I

wanted to believe and I did believe. It was a symbol for us. For us, it was a wish come true. It was a success. Can you imagine such a success, where people who were the victims could kill their executioners? I believed it and wish that it were so."

Chumak was frustrated: "How can you come to this court and possibly point the finger?" He was building to a pitch.

"But he's there," Rosenberg pleaded, pointing at Demjanjuk. "He's alive; I'm seeing him there."

But why believe he was dead, Chumak said, and repeat the story?

"It was my fondest wish," Rosenberg answered. "I wanted to believe, to believe that this creature ... Unfortunately, to my great sorrow, he managed to survive. What luck he had!"

Rosenberg said the narrative was not meant as his personal memoir. He'd told what he believed to have happened chronologically, first inside the camp, then outside, regardless of what he personally saw and when he learned it.

Proof that he didn't see it himself, Rosenberg said, was that his 1945 account of Ivan's death was different from his 1947 one; and still different from that he had heard from survivor Chaim Steir. But he'd never corrected any of them, he said, because until 1976, he believed that Ivan was dead. But there he was! – Now! --Sitting across from him, alive!

"Mar Rosenberg," Demjanjuk suddenly shouted, grabbing the microphone, "Atah shakran, shakran, shakran!" Demjanjuk repeated, the words he had said to Rosenberg before: "You are a liar, liar, liar."

Chumak's questioning had taken almost two hours, yet it had failed to prove anything positive for the defense – or that detracted from Rosenberg's testimony and identification. To the contrary, Rosenberg had proved all the more convincing.

2. Dry Riverbeds

The next week, Sheftel led off the defense summation, saying that the prosecution's three streams of evidence --the survivors, the card, and their historians --were upon examination wadis, dry riverbeds.

The first wadi, the testimony of the survivors, he argued, was flawed in a far-reaching manner and should not be given any weight. The same held true for the depositions of the three eyewitnesses who had since died. He contended that the photo spread would not pass muster as a lineup under Israeli law. As there was no single unequivocal identification that was not tainted, Demjanjuk could not be convicted.

The testimony of the survivors was contradictory: some said Ivan had been killed in the uprising, some said he was at Treblinka until the day of uprising. How, then, could he have been posted to Sobibor in March 1943? The survivors had said that when they arrived at Treblinka in September 1942, Ivan was already there-and that they saw him every day thereafter; the Trawniki card said that on September 22, 1942, the bearer was posted to L. G. Okzow.

How could he be in two places at once?

Finally, Sheftel said, the list of Treblinka survivors who did not identify Demjanjuk as Ivan was greater than those who did. Moreover, the witnesses were biased and had obviously colluded. At the Fedorenko trial they were accused of such and had admitted that they had traveled, stayed, and dined together during the trial.

The second stream that failed was the Trawniki card. It was proved to be a forgery through Grant and Flynn. Grant, Sheftel said, was an expert of far higher caliber than Bezalelli. Flynn's testimony, he said, should be treated just like Boraks'-selectively. Sheftel suggested that the judges accept only those

336

areas of Flynn's testimony that he was cross-examined on.

He derided prosecution experts Grabitz and Sheffler: "Grabitz is a lawyer, does that make her an expert? I'm more an expert on Meyer Lansky than she is on Streibl, does that make me an expert on the Mafia? Is a prosecutor of drug cases, an expert on drugs?"

Sheftel derided Sheffler calling him "a German who lives off testifying about the destruction of the Jews." Sheffler was no expert: he had seen only one Dienstausweis ever and had never been in the Soviet archive from which it came. Sheftel believed this was critical, as Tolstoy was of the opinion that custody was the decisive factor in determining its authenticity.

As to the postings, Sheffler and Arad had said that Trawniki was the base camp. For Demjanjuk to have been posted to Treblinka, as the prosecution claimed, and intermittently sent to Okzow and Sobibor, as the card claimed, he would have had to have passed through Trawniki several times, and the card should have listed Treblinka several times.

There were at least three Ivans, according to Sheftel: Ivan of Treblinka, Ivan of Sobibor and the Trawniki card, and Ivan Demjanjuk.

The link between the card and Demjanjuk, Sheftel argued, was the photo. As Demjanjuk himself could not say whether it was his photo or not, Sheftel said, one couldn't accept that it was That's why the prosecution had called experts. And when the court chooses among the expert opinions, he said, the court should prefer the testimony of an anthropologist, Iscan, over that of Smith, a dentist.

3. What about Sobibor?

Justice Levin asked the prosecution to address the fact that Treblinka was not listed on the Trawniki card. What was Demjanjuk's route after Treblinka? Did he, like Fedorenko, travel north to the Stutthoff complex of camps? Or did he travel south to Trieste, as SS man Gustav Munzberger had said? Did one contradict the other? Could he have been at both?

"We don't know," Blatman said. The best he could offer was "What matters for us, is that he survived the uprising.... We are saying," he said, pointing at Demjanjuk, "you were elsewhere. You were at Treblinka."

Demjanjuk shook his head in dispute.

The court also asked the defense to address whether the Trawniki Card posting to L. G. Okzow and Sobibor provide the defendant with an alternative alibi?

"It should not be used as grounds for anything," Shefte argued, as it conflicted with the witnesses' identifications, the court should acquit because there was doubt as to Demjanjuk's exact whereabouts.

The Court did not fully understand Sheftel's position: Were those survivors who identified Demjanjuk biased, while those that did not, were not? If it wasn't Demjanjuk on the Trawniki Card, who was it? And who was it that the survivors were identifying when they saw the Trawniki Card photo: Ivan or Demjanjuk, or neither?

Sheftel said that the position of the defense was that not all the survivors were influenced by positive bias. As for the person on the Trawniki card-- he looks like the accused, Sheftel said, but Demjanjuk could not say it was him, because he never had such an ID, dressed in that uniform. But Sheftel avoided directly addressing the prosecution's contention that Demjanjuk was both in Sobibor and Treblinka.

Chumak now rose to speak. The identifications were flawed, he argued, because Demjanjuk had no identifiable morphological feature- Chumak was arguing, in effect, that all Ukrainians look alike.

Chumak asked the court to consider the political motivations of the USSR and the KGB, the anti-Semitism of the USSR and the anti-Ukrainian unit of the KGB. The KGB, Chumak said, wished to use this case to foster inimical feelings between Ukrainians and Jews. The KGB chose an ordinary person to frame, because famous people have friends. Frank Walus, Chumak said, was lucky that the exonerative evidence he'd needed was in the West and could be obtained. Soviet records could help Demjanjuk but they had no access to those files. Perhaps it would in five or ten years, Chumak said, but without that evidence, the Court should not make a hasty judgment, out of fear.

The court would not be acting out of fear, judge Levin assured him.

"There have been few trials in the history of a nation," Chumak said, concluding, "that are so profoundly affected, where the heart of each and every one is proceeding. The horrors of Treblinka, very few men have stood trial for such enormous crimes. The court must act with great caution. Captain Dreyfus was convicted at the beginning of this century on false charges. This trial has all the earmarks of the Dreyfus trial. . . ."

Levin interrupted, explaining, "in the history of the Jewish people, the Dreyfus trial has a clear meaning." He asked Chumak to reconsider his comments. Chumak and Gill conferred, while Sheftel kept his head down and shrugged.

Chumak started again: "At stake in this trial is not only the name and quality of Israeli justice. . . ." But Levin interrupted again, to explain that Chumak was, by saying that the Court's reputation hung in the balance on this case, in effect, threatening the court. Levin said it might be best for everyone if a recess was called. Perhaps Chumak would consider the matter in a different light tomorrow.

Sheftel turned to Chumak and said: "You have been on your feet all day. You spoke so brilliantly and so well. They use an opportunity to fuck you, to shame you. What you've passed here, now, I've been through since the beginning, every day or two. I told you not to say this. The Dreyfus case has a connotation." Chumak said, "I really don't understand...."

The next day Chumak began: "I innocently referred to the Dreyfus case.... I meant no criticism and disrespect to this honorable court and if there was any such inference I apologize." He said he'd only meant to refer to the Trawniki card and the anti-Ukrainian Unit of the KGB.

But he clearly had not taken the message to heart. He reminded the court that its verdict must stand the test of time, "so that five, ten, or fifty years from now it will be said, justice was done in Jerusalem, Demjanjuk was acquitted according to law. Israeli law will stand as a beacon." He hoped "the three Israeli judges would have the courage to say not guilty."

Gill said, for his part, that the survivors who had made their identifications were not acting out of reason-they were motivated by pure emotion. Gill argued as he had during his cross-examination of the survivors that they could not see Ivan well, and that the Kapos provided a layer of insulation between Ivan and the Jewish workers. Gill read from Ryan's book about Reichman avoiding Ivan's gaze, about their working and running with their heads down.

He reminded the court about the frailty of eyewitness testimony and the danger of a conviction made on that basis against an accused who has an ordinary face with no outstanding morphological features. Mere suspicion, he said, was not enough.

Gill was interrupted by Yisrael Yehezkeli, who had screamed out at various points in the trial and began to do so again. The court ordered him led outside. He continued screaming in the hall: "I can't keep it inside any longer. I'll tell you all about what the Ukrainians did." He had a picture of himself as a boy with his family. "You can still recognize me," he said. The police restrained him, while journalists barraged him with questions.

Gill continued: The Trawniki card could not belong to Demjanjuk. Leonhardt had testified that the bearer of such a card-if found outside a camp-would have been arrested and returned to his last posting, Sobibor. Based on the card, Gill said, Demjanjuk was not posted to Treblinka. And Rudolf Reiss, he said, had also found many errors in the Trawniki card, including the lack of proper postings.

Dorner asked about Reiss's posting to Trawniki.

"I did not find it in his pay book," Gill said.

"I did not find it either," Dorner said.

But proof beyond a reasonable doubt, Gill said, is what separated this society from others that were not democratic. Gill told a parable about a man who held a bird in his hands. The fate of that bird was in the man's hands. So, too, the fate of John Demjanjuk, he said, was in the judges' hands.

Gill concluded with an Irish proverb: "May the sun rise to meet you, may the wind always be at your back, may God hold you in the palm of His hand as you decide the fate of John Demjanjuk

He asked that the defendant be allowed to make a statement. Levin informed him that a statement would not be appropriate at the moment.

4. The Prosecutor's defense and Rebuttal

Shaked now rose. He began, prepared to give a rebuttal to Chumak's earlier charge of an "unfair prosecution" because the defense were not provided with all possible evidence from OSI and the Soviet archives. This is a serious charge and a serious charge at the integrity of the prosecution – a shameful charge taken very seriously by courts.

Levin asked Chumak to reconsider and withdraw the charge, and "strike from the record this dismal event." But Chumak would not.

Shaked then responded to the charge, saying that the prosecution had not only fulfilled its duty to the defense in this case, he said, but had gone beyond that duty by providing documents, summaries of documents, indexes, and translations of documents in German, Yiddish, and Polish.

The prosecution had provided all this, above and beyond the call of duty, even though the defense had its own researchers and investigators, who for years had searched throughout the world for evidence. The prosecution believed that what was important was that there be a good defense, Shaked said. The prosecution had aided the defense's researchers even though some, like Brentar used unsavory methods and were aligned with repugnant organizations that spoke of "the myth of the gas chamber...."

John Demjanjuk Jr. stood up suddenly, brusquely, and walked to the rope at the front of the courtroom to let himself out. His hand was trembling with anger. He walked up the stairs of the proscenium. At the top of the stairs, he stood a few feet from Shaked. They looked at each other. The son of the accused marched offstage.

His sister, Irene, suddenly also stood, and said in a shrill voice, two octaves higher than her normal dulcet tones:

343

"You're lying, that's what it is."

Vera Demjanjuk stood up as well, shouting: "You're liars, you're liars. Shame on you. Shame on you. You have no shame, no heart, no nothing." They made their way to the stairs.

Irene helped Vera up. For a moment it seemed that Vera might faint, but they all exited. The room had fallen silent. Shaked turned back to the court. And then from the wing, the voice of John Demjanjuk Jr. cried out a final salvo: "You lying son-of-a-bitch."

Demjanjuk appeared unfazed throughout this episode. He did not react when his son stood up, or when his daughter and wife walked out. He acted as if nothing had happened.

Shaked finished his argument. Shortly thereafter, Levin ruled that no unfair prosecution had occurred. The judges retired.

The visitors left the room. The hall went silent. Some guards went to take each other's pictures, onstage, before everything-- the judges' bench, the witness dock, all the tables-- was disassembled. It was anticlimactic. On a bus a college student talked about the Demjanjuk family's outburst, "They wanted to leave a bad taste in our mouths."

The trial ended on February 18, 1988, a year and two days after it had begun. Amazingly, at this late date, the public was unsure of the trial's outcome.

How would the court weigh the evidence? Was there a reasonable doubt? No one could say. Court observers were divided. But no one doubted that the judges would address every piece of evidence and every argument raised.

5. Danylchenko's Statements

In mid-March, Sheftel called for an "extraordinary session of the court" to consider new evidence: twelve reports of interviews with Treblinka survivors from Camp One, and the 1979 deposition of a Soviet citizen Ignat Terentyevich Danylchenko --the same Danylchenko whose name appeared in the News from Ukraine articles.

The material had been released in the Demjanjuk Defense Fund's Freedom of Information Act (FOIA) suit against the OSI. Levin decided to accept the evidence under Section 15 and reopened summations for both sides to address what weight it deserved.

Shaked said that the prosecution had chosen its witnesses only from that small circle of survivors who had seen Ivan day in, day out. The persons from the investigatory reports, which Shaked analyzed one by one, were all from Camp One – some had been at Treblinka for only a few hours.

Some of the Camp One survivors had identified the visa or Trawniki card picture, but Shaked said they had not wished to call them as witnesses because their access was so limited. The reports did nothing to advance the case of the defense, Shaked argued, and could serve only to enhance the prosecution's case.

But Sheftel countered that the reports of those who did not identify the photos should carry great weight. Also, the fact that the identifiers described Ivan variously as a watchtower guard, a train driver, a ranking officer, and as being five foot five, all served to confirm the mistaken identification of the survivors. There were at least six Ivans at Treblinka, Sheftel argued, none of whom was John Demjanjuk.

The Danylchenko statement was testimony from a former Wachmann who said he'd served as a guard with an Ivan Demjanjuk in March 1943 at Sobibor and later at the

Flossenburg camp. Given in the presence of Soviet prosecutors in 1979, Danylchenko explained that at Sobibor there were four platoons in the camp, formed according to height, and he said that he belonged to the first platoon-of guards at least 180cm tall.

"Of the guards who served with me in the first platoon," he said, "I remember Ivan Ivchenko, who was our cook, and Ivan Demjanjuk."

"When I arrived at Sobibor [in March 1943]," Danylchenko said, "Demjanjuk already served in the camp as a private in the SS guards. I do not know Demjanjuk's patronymic. From conversations with Demjanjuk I do know that he was from Vinnitsa Oblast. He was roughly two to three years older than I, had light brown hair with noticeable bald spots at that time, was heavyset, had gray eyes, and was slightly taller than I, roughly 186-187cm tall. I remember Demjanjuk's appearance well, and I could possibly identify him. I do not know directly from where and when precisely Demjanjuk arrived at Sobibor. From what Demjanjuk said I know that like all of us [the guards] who served in Sobibor he had been trained at the SS camp in Trawniki....

"Demjanjuk, like all guards in the camp," Danylchenko continued, "participated in the mass killing of Jews. I also participated in this crime and I was convicted and punished for it. While I was at the camp I repeatedly saw Demjanjuk, armed with a rifle, together with other guards and, in many cases, myself, guard prisoners in all areas of the camp, from the unloading platform to the entrance of the gas chambers." Danylchenko said he saw Demjanjuk push Jews with his rifle butt and hit them, but this was a common occurrence during the unloading of the Jews. He did not see Demjanjuk person-ally shoot anyone, although he said this occurred regularly if anyone showed any resistance along the way to the gas chamber.

"Demjanjuk was considered to be an experienced and efficient guard. For example, he was repeatedly assigned by the Germans to get Jews in surrounding ghettos and deliver them in trucks to the camp to be killed. I did not receive any such assignments, since I did not have sufficient experience. Demjanjuk also guarded the outside of the barracks for the special detachment, which serviced the gas chamber. I saw him at this post many times, carrying a rifle. I do not know whether he served guard duty inside the gas-chamber zone. As I remember, Demjanjuk was frequently granted leave because he conscientiously carried out all orders from the Germans."

Danylchenko reported that in March or April of 1944, "Demjanjuk and I were sent from Sobibor to the city of Flossenburg in Germany, where we guarded an aircraft factory and a concentration camp for political prisoners. In case we were wounded, all of the guards at this camp, including Demjanjuk, were given a tattoo on the inside of the left arm, above the elbow designating the blood type.

"In late autumn of 1944 in October or November, Demjanjuk and I [among other guards] were sent to the city of Regensburg, or rather from the concentration camp located in the city of Flossenburg, we escorted two hundred political prisoners to another camp located 18-29 km from Regensburg. Until April 1945 we guarded the prisoners in this camp, who did construction work. In April of 1945, due to the approach of the front, the entire camp was evacuated and marched toward Nuremberg; I escaped along the way but Demjanjuk continued to accompany the prisoners. I suggested that he escape with me, but he refused. I have never seen Demjanjuk since then and his fate is unknown to me."

According to the documents submitted to the court, the day after his deposition Danylchenko returned to the Soviet Procurator's office. There, he was shown three sets of photographs. The first set had three young men in Red Army uniform and caps. Danylchenko selected Demjanjuk's 1941 Red Army photo. The second was of young soldiers without caps-here Danylchenko picked out the Trawniki card photo. And finally, the third set was of men in civilian dress. He selected Demjanjuk's 1951 visa photo as the Ivan he had known. Danylchenko told the Soviet prosecutors that, in each case, he'd singled out Demjanjuk based upon the distinctive facial characteristics he recalled: "oval face, chin, shape of eyes, and protruding ears."

Shaked said the statement "may be a fabrication, it may be that it is not." The prosecution knew nothing about Danylchenko or the circumstances of his questioning. There were also glaring historical problems with the account: Sobibor was dismantled in November 1943, but Danylchenko said he had served there until spring 1944.

The defense need not prove anything, Sheftel argued. The statement only cast further doubt on the prosecution's case, he said, and showed Wagenaar was correct --a memory problem existed.

Judge Dorner suggested that the two could be reconciled: after January 1943, the transports and gassings decreased, and the survivors would have had little contact with Ivan; in March, he could have been at Sobibor.

Sheftel disagreed. There could be no reconciling the two. Even Horn had testified that Ivan was in the camp after the uprising.

It was Shaked's view that Danylchenko had spent more time with Demjanjuk after Sobibor-- at Flossenburg. He found Danylchenko's testimony about Demjanjuk more telling about when they were apart than when they were together: they were posted to different duties, Danylchenko had testified; Demjanjuk was given leaves, and sent out of the camp on various assignments. How long these assignments took, Shaked said, is not clear. Danylchenko recalled Demjanjuk as an experienced Wachmann. As they only met in late March 1943, "[Demjanjuk] must have gained his experience elsewhere," Shaked said. "We say it is at Treblinka."

But as Sheftel pointed out that still contradicted Otto Horn's statements that Ivan had been at Treblinka in late August 1943; and Munzberger's claim that after Treblinka, he had served with Ivan in Trieste.

Judge Tal also wanted to offer an observation, asking Sheftel to forgive him for the analogy he was about to draw. If in another thirty-five years he was asked about the trial, he would say yes, for a whole year, I saw day in and day out the prosecution and the defense. But, of course, there were gaps in the trial. So, too, was it not possible that Danylchenko, in 1979, recalling events almost forty years before, had telescoped several months into one chunk?

Yes, of course that was possible, Sheftel admitted. But with only the statement to go on, Sheftel believed that you couldn't really tie Danylchenko's testimony to the case.

But that was exactly what the court would do.

6. The Human Face of Evil

Demjanjuk was brought out of Ayalon Prison at 5:30 A.M. Camera crews were waiting. "I feel good," Demjanjuk announced. One journalist shouted, "Today's your big day."

"Today is your big day," said Demjanjuk heartily. He got into the police van, and as it made its way through the hills up to Jerusalem, Demjanjuk could be seen in the back in good spirits. The sky was bright blue.

The van was brought to the rear of the courthouse rather than the usual front entrance. But when the doors opened, Demjanjuk would not leave. Sound came out of him in a high-pitched whine. The cry sounded more animal than human. The guards tried to talk to him: "John, come on, John ... John . . ." Then they begged him. Finally, four of them carried Demjanjuk into the building. He was kicking and struggling and continued to cry. He was carried quickly through the courtroom before the spectators entered and put on a cot in the courtroom's holding cell.

The first spectator had arrived at midnight. Most began to gather outside at 6:00 A.M. Teenage students from Jerusalem joined the line a half-hour later. By 8:30 A.M., most had found seats inside.

The court attendant put his cap on, fixed his tie, pulled himself to attention, and then spoke the by-now familiar call to order: "Beit Hamishpat!"

Demjanjuk would not leave his cot; the court agreed to proceed in his absence. Levin then announced that the verdict was more than four hundred pages (in Hebrew; seven hundred in English), so it would not be read it in its entirety. Only main points would be read aloud, but even this would take the entire day. Each judge now opened a black binder.

"We have before us an indictment," Levin read, "a vast and bleak and horrifying one. It is worded in scathing terms. It describes unspeakable acts. It appears that the facts that constitute the basis of this indictment have been depicted with pent-up anguish, with a tearful eye and a quaking hand. For this indictment unfolds ... the most horrifying chapter in the history of the Jewish people, which has suffered such torment throughout its chronicles. It is an unspeakable and indescribable as well as unforgivable chapter in our history of the annihilation of eight-hundred-seventy-thousand men, women, and children, who were led as sheep to the slaughter from throughout Poland and other Jewish communities in Europe and were exterminated with indescribable brutality in the slaughterhouse of the Camp of Treblinka....

"In this indictment, the state attributes to a mortal being the perpetration of brutal and savage acts against hundreds of thousands of human beings until death. These acts as depicted in the indictment were perpetrated, according to the indictment, by the accused zealously and with a thirst for murder....

"It is this bitter and terrifying truth that we are being asked to expose and clarify, so as to determine whether the accused has had any part in these crimes.

"This is a challenging and difficult task that we have been called upon to perform, with a sense of awe, cognizant of the heavy responsibility that rests upon us.

"With a sense of awe, because we are being asked to review the terrible history of the Jewish people in Europe in the most dreadful period of the Holocaust, as our people found itself drenched in blood and shedding tears, and as we remember the eight-hundred-seventy-thousand human beings who were killed, who were slaughtered, who were asphyxiated, burned, and forced to die in the sanctification of the Holy Name by the German murderers and other collaborators from other peoples.

"We are cognizant of the heavy responsibility, because it is incumbent upon us to determine judicially the historical truths with regard to events that beset our people in one of the most difficult periods in the history of mankind and, in particular, in the history of the Jewish nation.

"It is our responsibility to seal a man's fate, a man who, when he was young as a member of the Ukrainian people, suffered famine and persecution by a tyrannical and despotic ruler. Later, he served in the army and fought against the invading German army. He was wounded, hospitalized, then recruited back into duty. He was taken captive. He experienced the horrors of being a prisoner of war. He survived. He emigrated to the United States, built up his home, and lived peacefully with his family, and was a member of his community, until such time as suspicion fell upon him of having perpetrated the terrible crimes attributed to him. It was then that he was extradited to Israel and was put on trial before us.

"Our sense of responsibility makes it necessary for us to examine and weigh these facts, commonly, prudently, and judicially without emotion and in disregard of anything that has been written or said outside of the walls of this courtroom, whether in the media or in the public-at-large....

"Though the events took place over forty-five years ago," Levin said, "the question arises: Can one remember and describe faithfully things that happened so very long ago? Because, seemingly, the passage of time clouds the memory, advancing age dims the senses.... How can an individual, then, recall precisely events to which he was witness or which he experienced? How can a person remember people whom he knew closely, or more superficially, in those horrible and unforgettable days?

"One might ask, is it possible to forget? How can people

who were in that field of carnage, who experienced its atrocities, who lived in the atmosphere of repression and terror of persecution, in the confinement of a death camp-people who witnessed death and humiliation and brutalization day in and day out --who saw the taskmasters and henchmen perform their work at the death camp of Treblinka-- how can they forget all these? People who were forced to perform humiliating and degrading tasks, with the fear of death looming over them day in and day out-could such people possibly repress such heinous events?

"...Is it possible for a person like the accused, and other Ukrainians who had experienced famine and suffering, who themselves were victims of persecution and killings of masses of human beings, is it possible for such people to assist the death units of the SS to serve as their auxiliary forces in putting into effect the plan of annihilating the Jewish people?

"...Is it possible for everything described in the indictment to have happened? Did it, in fact, happen?

"These questions, and the very difficult dilemmas that they raise, obligate us to offer a clear and unequivocal answer beyond a reasonable doubt...."

"We must make reference primarily to the testimony of those survivors who actually experienced the atrocities, who were personally involved, and witnessed firsthand that which took place, people who observed the perpetrators of the crimes in the field of carnage of Treblinka and actually came into contact with them. It is for this reason, naturally, that the testimony of the survivors is so important and powerful. It is they who bear in their minds and hearts the terrible history of these events. But it is precisely because of the great emotion that this involves that we must examine their testimony most prudently and carefully, while at the same time bearing in mind the information that they are capable of sharing with us.

"It is important that we gain an impression of their reliability. We must try to examine whether they may not be swayed, God forbid, by any prior conviction or by hearsay. We must also pay heed to the possibility of a memory that may have betrayed them, a sincere and genuine mistake in identification and other hindrances that are liable to impede a witness as he described such terrible events, etched in their very flesh, albeit fifty years, or forty-five years ago.

"The description of these facts in their entirety, on the historical plain, as well as with regard to the identity of the accused, is, in fact, part of the same entity. These are links in a single chain that is closely interconnected. One matter depends on the other.

"We attribute the utmost importance to the question of the physical proximity, or as this has often been described in the course of the testimony, the actual friction, the actual contact between the survivors and Ivan when, in that period, they lived in close proximity and would come into contact with one another day in and day out, in an atmosphere of continual fear and anguish. . . ."

Judge Levin drew the Final Solution as one bloody trail leading from the speeches of Adolf Hitler as early as 1930, through the racial theories and laws of the Nazi regime, the Wansee Conference, the euthanasia program, the mass killings by shooting, to killing by gassing, and the establishment of the extermination camps, Treblinka among them.

"Treblinka, with the terrible tragedy that it embodies, is, in fact, the very end of a very long, bitter, and tortuous road at the end for millions of Jews, and it was described and it was meant to lead to a single goal, to exterminate the Jewish people and Jewish communities throughout Europe.

"As we hear the survivors unfold before us with emotion, yet fluently, just what happened to them, we feel how deeply these events and experiences are etched in their souls. The atrocities live on with them. The spectacles are part and parcel of their memory. Not everything could be told. Not everything has been told."

The deeds committed at Treblinka could not have been accomplished without the full cooperation of the Ukrainian guards, Levin said, among whom was Ivan, nicknamed Ivan Grozny (Ivan the Terrible). His deeds were known from the testimonies of that handful of survivors who survived the uprising. Levin asked: Could they remember Treblinka and Ivan?

Based on the testimonies before them, he said, the court wished to state: "Yes, one can remember the horrible deeds and the dreadful events that make up the Holocaust and through which the Jewish people passed, even though it is almost fifty years ago.

"We also wish to state that: It is impossible to forget what happened. It is impossible to forget, too, Ivan the Terrible and his misdeeds.

"The witnesses' direct appearance here, their testimony, which was suffused with frankness and honesty, the living eyewitnesses to what went on, and to what is deeply etched in their memories, none of it will they ever forget. And to the person who wonders, even though the mind boggles at what happened, even though it cannot take it in, even though it is inconceivable that this could have happened, it did happen.

"There was the bestiality, there was this horrendous train of events. There was its inception and its perpetration. It is one tiny detail from the overall story of the extermination of the whole of European Jewry, of which the eight-hundred-seventy-thousand Jews in Treblinka was just a tiny part. The memory and the lesson shall be learned, lest it ever be repeated."

To watch the survivors, listen to their own words, as read by

Judge Levin was painful for observers, but more so for the witnesses. Czarny wore aviator glasses, but dabbed at his eyes, brushing away large tears; Epstein sat on the edge of his seat, nervously, his fingertips at his lips; Rosenberg was tightly wound, and his wife held his arm to calm him.

In Levin's accounting, the verdict was no longer a dry legal opinion. It was as if the judges wanted, after fifteen months, to remind not just the listeners, but also the accused of the visceral brutality and the personal, intimate nature of the mass murders committed in the Nazi death camp.

Levin continued to read, without break, for three hours, until 11:45 A.M. Then, after a short break, judge Tal confronted the question, Did Ivan die in the uprising?

None of the accounts of Ivan's death during the uprising, by Rosenberg in 1945 and 1947, by Goldfarb and by Hellman, Judge Tal said--none was an eyewitness account. There were extreme discrepancies within the accounts and among the versions. Rumors heard in camp were later found to be wishful thinking, as when some of the murderers were confronted in Dusseldorf.

Accordingly, the judges found no grounds, he said, whatsoever, to establish that Ivan was killed in the uprising. On the contrary, there was the testimony of Otto Horn, who saw Ivan after the uprising, as well as the deposition of Danylchenko. "The proven truth," Tal said, "is that Ivan Grozny was not killed."

Shortly after this, the Demjanjuk family left the hall. They saw no reason to sit and listen anymore. Turning to the alibi, judge Tal explained that it was critical to Demjanjuk's defense.

"Proof of this contention, even if it were merely to amount to reasonable doubt, would amount to grounds for an acquittal. However," Tal said, "refuting this contention lends support to the positive proof brought by the prosecution."

Demjanjuk's alibi was that during the period he was accused of the horrific acts at Treblinka he was being held captive by the Germans in a POW camp called Chelm. The defense did not cite any evidence to support the alibi, Tal said. Demjanjuk's alibi rested on the credibility his testimony.

Tal said that Demjanjuk gave several reasons for not remembering Chelm when first asked, the camp where he spent the majority of time, or remembering what he did there. Despite the defendant's many reasons and the defense's theories and those of Professor Wagenaar. "Out of respect for Professor Wagenaar," Tal read from the verdict, "we can only say that these explanations do not have a leg to stand on. . . ."

Moreover, Tal said, the judges did not believe that Demjanjuk was at Chelm. "The accused cannot describe the camp or any part," he read. "Neither can he describe those who lived with him in the shed, or anyone else. He cannot name anyone or describe anyone. He cannot describe any of the officeholders in the camp. If anyone spent eighteen months in a given camp, it is inconceivable that he would be unable to give details about the place.

"At the same time, where German records tell us that Chelm was only a transit camp, the accused's version, as if he had spent some eighteen months at Chelm, is totally unacceptable and implausible, in view of the transient nature of the camp."

Not only was Demjanjuk's war-year timetable unbelievable as to time spent in Chelm, but his accounts for what he did in Graz and Heuberg and his service in the Vlassov Army were also not credible. Demjanjuk's claims that he was tattooed while serving at Graz or that there were Rumanians and Jewish Kapos at Chelm were equally unbelievable.

Judge Tal paused. Demjanjuk's alibi, he said, was simply untrue: "It is a lie. The Chelm version is simply unacceptable to us and is not credible. It is very poor. It is not substantiated by anything, and a few details that he brought forth in order to bring it to life have been proved false."

The removal of the tattoo, a long and painful process, Tal said, was incriminating. So, too, were the forms he'd filled out that spoke to Demjanjuk's mechanical abilities. "All the facts known about Demjanjuk," Tal said, "added up to a picture of a young man who, through the collective farm in the Ukraine and his Soviet army service, right down to postwar Germany and the American army, knew how to handle a car, knew something about engines. Even on the 1948 IRO form, Demjanjuk was listed in several places as a driver.... But when he spoke before us, he tried to distance himself from anything remotely connected with mechanics, motors, and engines."

There was also, he said, the question of why write Sobibor and Pilau but hide Treblinka?

The answer, Tal read was found in the example of Federenko who testified that he "knew that their applications would be scrutinized. They would be asked to provide exact details as to how they were exiled from Poland, whether they were deported, what happened after the war, and so on. The details had to live up to the expectations of the interrogators. Therefore, they deliberately gave names of small, unknown places. Wachmanner, of course, take leaves to nearby towns, as Fedorenko testifie[d] ... so that they would have been capable of providing full descriptions of these places.... At the same time, they did deliberately conceal the main site of the crime about which there is information and there are survivors and witnesses."

Tal paused again, looking out at the hushed room. "Did the contention that Demjanjuk was at Sobibor," he asked, "suggest an alternative alibi-that he was there and not at Treblinka?

And even so, if the accused himself did not raise it, did the possibility of such an alibi place upon the court the responsibility to suggest it?"

Tal said the judges felt they were under no responsibility to consider it; but they were nonetheless convinced, he said, that the evidence "do[es] not cast any doubt as to indicate that the accused was only at Sobibor and not at Treblinka."

A short recess was held. Upon the judges' return, Judge Dorner announced she would read the section of the verdict concerning the Trawniki document.

Demjanjuk contended originally, Dorner began, that the card was a one-of-a-kind document, forged by the KGB. But this was not so, she said. There was evidence that similar service cards were drawn up routinely at the camp, and Leonhardt had seen many such passes. There was also the evidence of the three other service cards. Additional support was found, Dorner said, in the official correspondence about the loss of a Trawniki service card. Reiss's testimony, she said, was such that he would have said anything to help the accused.

Dorner said the defense had taken two positions with regard to the card: either that it was such a good forgery that it could not be detected; and/or it was forgery as proved by their experts. The first contention, she said, was based on the testimonies of witnesses Tolstoy, Shiffrin, and Flynn. But Tolstoy and Shiffrin could not provide one example of a Soviet forgery of Nazi-era documents; and the sum total of Tolstoy's opinion was that the document should be carefully checked, and this, Dorner said, had been done. Shiffrin was not an expert but an eccentric, she said. Even William Flynn had found many faults with the card. So, it was not "perfect."

Now as to proof of forgery, she said, the defense's arguments rested on the photograph on the Trawniki card and certain irregularities, in the personal details of the person on the card.

Demjanjuk was now sixty-eight. But, Dorner read, "one would say that the accused belongs to that sort of people who have not been affected with the passage of years in their features." The court had examined an entire series of authentic photographs of Demjanjuk, spanning the years 1940 to 1986, in which the judges could observe, she said, "how the accused is getting older, [but] certain outstanding features of his face, certain landmarks remained unchanged." They were able to compare this with the photograph on the Trawniki card.

"In the case of the accused before us," Judge Dorner read, her voice starting to strain, "we can, therefore, establish unequivocally that the photograph in [the Trawniki card] is that of the accused. Both Professor Patricia Smith and, also to a lesser extent, Mr. Altmann bear this out.

Smith impressed the judges, she said: "She had carried out very thorough investigations and described it in the tiniest detail to us, and her conclusions are based on very thorough research, and they are acceptable to us." But since Altmann's method was not based on measuring, there was an objective dimension missing, so the Court ruled that his conclusions could only be supportive evidence but could not be the sole basis for identification.

The defense contention that the card was not authentic, Dorner said, rested in great part on the testimony of Julius Grant. Grant's conclusion rested on two matters, the photo and the signatures. But his contentions about the photo were unexplained, she said, and his reservations about the signatures were insufficiently founded. And as for witness William Flynn, Dorner read: "Here in court the witness was subject to threats by those who had a contract with him, and he himself admitted that he did not feel at liberty to reply to questions, because of what he called a contractual agreement with the Demjanjuk Defense Fund."

Flynn's statements in court contradicted what he had said at the documents conference in the United States. "Once the witness refused to explain it in cross-examination," she said, "clearly no weight whatsoever can be attributed to his testimony in court insofar as it runs counter to what it says in the conference in the United States."

Judge Dorner paused and looked over at judge Tal. He said one word, "postings," and started to read again. The postings were the card's major fault, he said. But the question, Tal said, was not whether the testimonies of the survivors were contradicted by the fact that the Trawniki card had no posting to Treblinka. Rather, he said, the question before the court was "Did the accused serve in Treblinka?"

Tal read: "The main pieces of evidence against the accused is not the document [the Trawniki card]. His guilt is not proved on the basis of this document in itself, although in the course of the discussions and deliberations, days and even weeks were devoted to this document. Although the experts for both parties dealt in minute detail with each and every facet, starting with the staple perforations and the rust marks, it is not, after all, technical details that will seal the fate of the accused, but rather the testimony of the survivors, which is etched in their memories."

Shaked had argued, he said, that without complete knowledge of the manner in which postings were listed on the service cards, it was possible to assume that main postings, such as Treblinka, were not entered. This contention, Tal said, was unacceptable: "The fact was that the accused's posting to Treblinka should have been entered on the card, and it was not...Nonetheless, the nonentry of this information does not necessarily rule out the possibility that the accused was at Treblinka, nor does it in any way detract from the authenticity of the document."

On the contrary, he said, the omission refutes the charge that the card was part of a KGB plot. Why fake a document that runs counter to the testimonies of the survivors? Why forge a document that lists Demjanjuk as a rank-and-file guard at Sobibor rather than being Ivan of Treblinka?

The only explanation, judge Tal said, was that the card was authentic, that it was the identity card of Ivan Demjanjuk.

There was another short recess. The courtroom was crowded and had become very warm. But many stayed in their seats rather than risk losing them.

After a half-hour, the clerk called the room to attention and the judges took their seats. Levin said he would now read the sections of the verdict concerning identifications.

Sheftel had argued, Levin said, that under Israeli law a proper identification lineup was not held. But Israel case law was more variegated, and less inflexible, he said, than Sheftel would have it.

"Each and every case must be judged upon its own merits. . . ." Levin said that the judges found Sheftel's argument that the number of non-identifiers outweighed those who had identified Demjanjuk, "somewhat simplistic."

"It is not just a question of arithmetical calculation," Levin read. "It is not just a poll that was conducted-- so and so many for, so and so many against -- ...Every statement, every testimony must be examined according to its independent weight as well as the circumstances, and the factual conclusion can only be formulated on the basis of the sum total of this material, the cumulative weight from different perspectives."

Levin said that it was established that any proximity between the identifier and the suspect may do away with the need for an identification parade. This was true in drug cases, or when neighbors lived close together; there was no need here for an identification parade. It became a mere formality, he said.

"How, then," Levin read, "can we compare the extent of the forced familiarity between Ivan and the survivors, and I draw all the necessary differences here, between him and SS officer Otto Horn? How can we compare? There is no ground for comparison." But, despite the uniqueness of this case, the court must do, he said, "everything possible to avoid committing the grievous error of convicting a human being because of misidentification." Although it appeared that the identification parade was not necessary, the fact that identity parades were held could only aid the court in making the correct decision.

Levin divided the parades into three groups: the ones conducted by Radiwker in 1976 ("a preliminary step for tracking down suspects"); by Kollar ("an ordinary photospread identification procedure, because he, in fact, was dealing with someone who was already a suspect and was a candidate for denaturalization.... On the other hand, let us not forget that at that stage Kollar was acting according to the guidelines issued by the American authorities, and was fulfilling their requirements to a "T"); by the Americans, for Reichman and Horn ("a more advanced stage in the interrogation of the accused in the United States").

Contrary to the criticisms and innuendos of the defense, Levin said, Radiwker's testimony was "utterly credible." He said the judges were deeply impressed by her honesty, integrity, and remarkable memory. They categorically rejected any innuendo that Radiwker "ostensibly was working to bring about the conviction of the accused, even at the expense of the actual truth," or that she did not act in good faith or gave hints to the witnesses or coached them. Levin was emphatic: "There is absolutely no leg for this criticism to stand on."

But the court, Levin continued, did note that when Kollar re-interviewed Rosenberg and Epstein in 1979, showing them the Trawniki photo, the survivors may still have recalled the 1951 visa photo. This, he said, detracted from that identification procedure. But Kollar himself, Levin said, "acted with integrity and honesty in questioning the identification witnesses and followed all of the rules established in this regard. His reliability is beyond a shadow of a doubt."

To establish the weight of these identifying testimonies, Levin said, "both the methods and the philosophy of Professor Wagenaar is not acceptable to us." Instead, "the specific weight of each and every one will be considered, concerning also the certainty that it entered." The specific language in the statements was not, Levin said, the determining factor-each and every statement was weighed on its merits, in light of the manner in which the identification was made and the circumstances surrounding it.

The court, he said, had observed Rosenberg on the stand for many days. Levin read:

"Although there were certain inaccuracies in his testimony, we do not hesitate to establish that Rosenberg was a reliable witness who had a long-ranging memory for everything that went on at Treblinka as well as the persons involved in the wholesale massacre. Rosenberg is a hard person, a very forceful person. At the same time, he knows what he is talking about, and for us he was a reliable witness in anything to do with this case.

"What is important for us, in terms of the weight, is the immediate spontaneous reactions of the survivors when they had the photographs of the accused before them. It is the instantaneous, spontaneous reaction that shows the perception, the ability to discern, and the ability to falsify, and this is what counts in identification processes."

In the case of Rosenberg, Levin said the court had determined that Rosenberg's identification on May 11, 1976, was "an identification of a high degree of probability; and his qualifying remarks merely indicates his desire to be very, very sure of himself." Rosenberg had argued with Radiwker when she said the man was not from Treblinka. And Rosenberg was not content just to identify the picture: he gave, Levin said, a description that the court found "a very interesting, very edifying description" --and one very similar to Demjanjuk.

"Rosenberg described the ears that stand out and the beginnings of a bald patch"-features, Levin noted, not very common in a twenty-three-year-old. Demjanjuk himself had said his hair had begun to fall out in the Red Army. When Kollar put the Trawniki photo before Rosenberg in 1979, he observed "this may be a photograph from the time before Treblinka and at Treblinka he was already a little fuller. It may be that already he had better food in those days." This precision, Levin said, added to the high quality of Rosenberg's identification.

And so high was the quality of Czarny's identification, Levin now said, that the court would have been willing to convict on the basis of it alone. But it did not need to. There was the added weight of the identification by Rosenberg, which was of a high level of certainty; there was Epstein's identification of the 1951 picture and his identification of Demjanjuk's walk, which the court found of a "high standard"; Reichman's, which was of great significance; even Boraks, who, Levin said, had certain problems with dates on the stand, gave what was, in the judges' opinion, a forceful and clear identification of the accused. The cumulative weight was further enhanced, Levin said, by the recorded testimonies of the deceased survivors Turovsky, Goldfarb, and Lindvasser. Finally, as to Hellman, it was true that he should have recognized Demjanjuk, but did not. His recollection was vague, and his memory failed him.

As to Otto Horn, the court, out of extreme caution, Levin said, would not make an incriminating finding solely on the basis of his identification --but it attached great weight to it. And even Danylchenko's deposition from the Soviet Union added cumulatively to the evidence: the man Danylchenko remembered was the same Otto Horn remembered; the same as the survivors remembered.

But, Levin said, Danylchenko's testimony highlighted another problem: how to reconcile the conflicting accounts of Ivan's whereabouts after March 1943. He read: "If Ivan Grozny was stationed in Sobibor from late March until this camp was demolished, how is this reconciled with the testimony of Horn, who says that after the uprising in August 1943, he saw Ivan there?"

Levin continued to read with energy: "In fact, it can be reconciled. Danylchenko says that Ivan, who excelled in his assistance to the Germans and who was extremely efficient in performing the labor of annihilation, was sent to hunt out Jews from the ghettos in the vicinity and to supply them by vehicles to the extermination camp.

"During the uprising, something happened. There was a change in the overall situation. Several Ukrainians had been wounded or even killed. Several of them disappeared, and Treblinka was in the process of being done away with. It stands to reason that Ivan was sent to Sobibor, as Danylchenko describes it, and later back to Treblinka, to help do away with the last traces of the camp."

Could there have been two Ivans? Levin asked. "It might have been contended that perhaps there were two Ukrainian Ivans who bore a remarkable resemblance to one another," he said.

"One was Ivan Grozny, who operated at Treblinka, and the other was Ivan Demjanjuk, who operated at Sobibor. However, this would be a highly unlikely coincidence. When one speaks of an individual who has many salient features, such as being tall, balding at a relatively young age, protruding ears, a special build of nose and eyes-there has to be an extremely rare kind of coincidence in order for this to happen.

"The Ivans are indeed one and the same," Levin said conclusively. "Demjanjuk who operated at Sobibor from late March 1943 and Ivan Grozny who operated in Treblinka during the second half of 1942 and early 1943, the Ivan identified by Danylchenko and the Ivan identified by the other identification witnesses are one and the same. Otto Horn said that Ivan was there in the camp, but occasionally he would go out on leave for extensive periods in time. When there were no shipments of Jews for annihilation, Ivan was not in Camp Two. Rosenberg, too, responded to our question and said that perhaps he didn't see Ivan a few weeks before the uprising, even though, initially, he sounded like a person who was saying that he did see Ivan right up until the uprising.

"It may be remembered," Levin said, "that when it comes to the concept of time, on that different planet Treblinka, Treblinka was different from time as we know it now. One day was the same as another, day after day without change, and we read in Deuteronomy chapter twenty-eight about the fact that when one's life is in a continual state of threat and that one is continually afraid of death, in which case, one cannot know just what reality is. Under these circumstances, when the survivors said that they had seen Ivan throughout that period, it means that Ivan was there and was involved in the work of extermination.

"Be that as it may, as to the question of whether he was there until the uprising itself, we have grounds to believe that the survivors were wrong in stating this and that their testimony has nothing to rest on. Their descriptions of his evil deeds all relate to the period of the gas chambers, which in the main came to an end toward February 1943. . . ."

During the day, as afternoon gave way to evening, the room felt increasingly crowded. There were no more people than earlier --the room had been full to capacity all day-but the air became thicker. There was tremendous sadness filling the room.

As the facts piled on each other, the crimes became more and more real. There was an equation underlying the conviction: as long as Demjanjuk was not guilty, one could avoid the crimes Ivan had committed; they had been the work of a demon on that other planet, Treblinka.

But if Demjanjuk was guilty, the crimes were real. Each murder was a separate death, a corpse, a ghost that now came to life. The sadness set in because it was all true, the deaths were real. This man, Ivan, was an instrumental part of all this. It was true.

7. Crime and Punishment

Levin was now coming to what would be the climax of ten hours of reading-- the judgment --yet his voice betrayed no change of emotion when he read, that the court "having weighed and considered the evidence in its entirety, most painstakingly, cautiously, and with the utmost care, we determine unequivocally and without the slightest hesitation or doubt that the accused, Ivan John Demjanjuk, standing trial before us, is Ivan who was called Ivan Grozny."

A few persons clapped. Levin looked up from his binder, surprised. Sternly, he asked the spectators to quiet themselves, and then continued to read: "We therefore find him guilty as charged, a) of crimes against the Jewish people; b) of crimes against humanity; c) of war crimes; d)' crimes against persecuted people. . . ."

Levin suggested that the sentencing hearing be held in a week. Gill asked to argue it the next morning which was surprising because one would have imagined they needed time to study the verdict. The prosecution requested a week to prepare. The judges adjourned until then.

Many were milling outside the hall. The day had been draining. Numbing.

Among the many lost in thought was Colonel Menachem Russek. For him, this moment had been a long time in coming. He had been the one to first suggest Demjanjuk be extradited to stand trial in Israel. "It's been ten years," Russek said. "I had felt confident [about a conviction]. But to hear it pronounced is a complete satisfaction. It was revenge for all those who didn't make it."

The spectators left the hall. A little later, Demjanjuk was led from his holding cell through the courtroom. Taking small steps, he raised his arms to the reporters and said, "I feel good. I am innocent. The wrong man. This is ridiculous what has happened Ha'yom [Hebrew for today]."

A week later, on Monday, April 25, 1987, the sky was still blue, but there was a chill in the air. Seating in the courtroom was by invitation only. John Demjanjuk Jr. arrived but was asked not to sit in the first rows. The security forces didn't want him too near his father. No other Demjanjuk family members were there. Demjanjuk, who said he was in too much pain to walk, appeared in a wheelchair, and blew kisses to the spectators while he was maneuvered into his dock.

Blatman stood as he spoke: As the crimes committed showed an utter disregard of the conventions of human morality, and were done excessively, voluntarily, and zealously, he requested the death penalty. It was unimaginable, he said, that such a creature, who had physically murdered hundreds of thousands of Jewish persons, might be allowed to continue to walk the Earth.

All the while, Demjanjuk was nodding his head "no" vigorously, occasionally crossing himself, staring upward, his lips mumbling.

Gill argued that there was an irrevocable aspect to the death sentence, and in cases based on eyewitness identification, there was always a possibility of error. Gill then went further, saying: "The taking of any innocent human life is a Holocaust."

Demjanjuk then addressed the court: "Your Honors, it was very painful to hear the great tragedy that befell the Jewish people." His voice was deep and strong, "Not everyone survived, six million did not survive. They were killed in the Nazi camps, and they died a horrible death.... I hope they have all reached heaven.

"I believe the atrocities took place, and Ivan existed. It was not the prisoners who gave me the name Ivan Grozny, that human was not I, Ivan Demjanjuk."

"Last week you pointed to me. That's a mistake, a very grave mistake....I have no doubt in my head, my heart is pure. Today, I do know, you must sentence Ivan the Terrible. But your sentence will not be against him but a person not guilty. I am innocent, and it's most unfortunate. I am filled with admiration at this democratic, cultured country, Israel. But in the twentieth century, how can it be possible for such an injustice to be done? I'm referring to the conviction. I am innocent, innocent and God," he said, pointing his right index finger upward, "is my witness. Thank you."

The judges retired.

People milled about, pacing, walking. It was hot in the courtroom, smoky in the foyer. The tension was thick; the pressure exhausting.

After a three-hour recess, the judges returned. Demjanjuk was wheeled in, and shouted in Hebrew, "I am innocent." Someone else shouted back, "Atah shakran [You are a liar]."

Judge Levin, with a haggard face and a tired voice, announced that judge Tal would read the decision.

Tal's voice was equally sad, as he read: "Almost fifty years have elapsed since Treblinka. The accused has opened a new chapter in his life, far away from the scene of his crimes. He has established a new home. He has built himself a home and a family, and today when we must sentence him, we ask ourselves whether the time that has elapsed can in any way alleviate the sentence that must be imposed upon him.

Most crimes that may be committed are forgivable. Time dulls the pain. Time desensitizes to a certain extent, and they fall subject to limitations. A person who has changed his course in life need not necessarily be sentenced because of crimes committed a long time ago. This holds true for most crimes.

However, there are crimes against the Jewish people and

against persecuted human beings that must be excluded from this.

The same holds true for crimes against humanity and war crimes. These categories of crimes can never be forgiven, either within the letter of the law or forgiven in the hearts of men. The law, here and elsewhere, abrogates all prescription that would apply to such crimes.

"They can never be obliterated from memory. Any limitations, any statute of limitations on such crimes, would imply that they should be regarded as transcending time, as though Treblinka continues to exist, as though Jews are still being strangled and crying out in pain, as though the blood of the victims still cries out to us, like the blood of Zechariah the prophet. And Ivan the Terrible goes on to stab and to slaughter his victims indiscriminately, the old and the young, slashing off breasts and stabbing people, drilling in living flesh. We have not heard any arguments from the defense concerning extenuating circumstances....

The learned counsel, Mr. Gill, has cautioned us against the terrible possibility whereby sentencing the accused to death would amount to shedding an innocent man's blood in vain.... In fact, we are aware of the peril of an irrevocable sentence. This is one of the major reasons cited by those who are against the death penalty in principle. In Israel, too, this sentence may not be imposed for murder, but so long as the legislator has allowed to do so, the court, regardless of the personal views of the judges concerning capital punishment, may uphold it when it sees fit. The question is whether the present case is such a case.

"In our verdict, we established unequivocally and without the shadow of a doubt that the person before us, the accused, is Ivan the Terrible of Treblinka. Unlike the contention of the learned counsel, Mr. Gill, the fact that we did not make do merely with identification, which could, in fact, have existed in its own right, and we have seen fit to add to it cumulative evidence, which as a whole reinforces the identification, this fact in no way detracts from our certainty in determining that the accused is Ivan the Terrible.

"What punishment can be imposed on Ivan the Terrible, a person who killed tens of thousands of human beings and brutalized so many of his victims on their way to their deaths? What can he be sentenced to? A thousand deaths will not exonerate him or be weighed against his crimes....However, knowing that any punishment cannot be considered fitting or appropriate, we must nevertheless not be deterred from imposing punishment, meting out judgment against the accused.'

"True," Tal said, "the accused is not Eichmann. He was not the initiator of the annihilation. He did not organize the extermination of millions. However, he served as an arch-henchman, who with his very own hands killed tens of thousands, humiliated, degraded, victimized, and brutalized, persecuted innocent human beings zealously. It is for this reason that we sentence aforementioned crimes, to the punishment stipulated."

The room was gray. The silence thick. Levin said, "This concludes our deliberations," and informed the defense it had forty-five days to lodge an appeal. The clerk called the courtroom to order once more. The judges rose and disappeared down their exit for the final time.

The spectators rose to their feet. A few spectators broke out in spontaneous applause. The survivor witnesses who were sitting in the hall embraced. Then all turned, stunned, at the sight of teenagers near the back rows, standing on the chairs, hurling epithets at Sheftel, and singing "Am Yisroel Hai [Israel Lives]." It was a cringeworthy moment. The majority of the persons in the room were dumbfounded by this display, still too drained from hearing the day's verdict to react.

An elderly survivor, visiting from Florida, egged the

teenagers on like a coach at a soccer game. The TV cameras, which had been turned intently on the audience, now focused on the youths-and more joined in. It was as if a malevolent energy had been released.

A half-hour later, the courtroom emptied, Demjanjuk was led out again to a gaggle of reporters. Carol Rosenberg of United Press International shouted, "Are you going to hang?"

Demjanjuk shouted back: "I don't care what the judges say, I feel innocent." Reporters politely refrained from pointing out that feeling innocent is not the same as being innocent.

Tabloids around the world proclaimed Demjanjuk's guilt and his death sentence. These were followed by editorials about "Justice in Jerusalem" as well as columns that praised or condemned Demjanjuk's death penalty sentence.

The Eichmann case, Hannah Arendt wrote in Eichmann in Jerusalem, "was built on what the Jews had suffered, not on what Eichmann had done." Here the opposite was true. The crimes of Eichmann were easier to understand and believe true; it was harder to grasp the crimes of Ivan, because they were committed with such zeal by so simple, so human a criminal. But once proved, they became all the more real. Demjanjuk had given abstract evil a human face.

CHAPTER TEN:

THE APPEAL AND ITS AFTERMATH

1. Tragedy strikes the Defense Team

In March 1988, Israeli attorney Dov Eitan joined Sheftel to argue the appeal. A former district court judge, he was forced to resign in 1983 due to his being too political for a sitting judge. Eitan, while on the bench, had signed a petition to end the war in Lebanon. He was thought to be professional, smart, and knowledgeable. He believed there were grounds for appeal, and Sheftel was glad to work with him.

However, on November 29,1988, after having breakfast with his wife, and after having made an appointment to meet her at 11AM to buy a new suit, Eitan went to the Klal building, at the time one of the tallest buildings in downtown Jerusalem, and took the elevator to the fifteenth floor.

Once there, Eitan found a way to jump out a window, plunging to his death. From the police investigation of the windowsill and all other available evidence, it was clear Eitan committed suicide (there was no indication of foul play).

Though no satisfactory explanation for Eitan's death was forthcoming--there was no suicide note, and there had been no signs of depression to any friends, family, or colleagues. In hindsight, a picture of profound dissatisfaction emerged. Eitan's resignation from the judiciary had only increased his disappointment with Israeli politics. No one knew what had

375

drawn him to the Demjanjuk case, or to approach Sheftel and offer his services, but one friend reported that Eitan had found no solace in the case.

It was a tragic turn of events and yet another bizarre occurrence in the Demjanjuk process, which continued to be unpredictable.

Eitan's funeral was held on December 1. It was a somber affair. Sheftel was in attendance. So was Yisrael Yehezkeli, the same Holocaust survivor who had disrupted the trial on several occasions by shouting about the pain he still suffered because of the Holocaust.

As the funeral was underway, Yehezkeli suddenly confronted Sheftel, throwing a hydrochloric-acid solution in his face. Sheftel was rushed to the intensive-care unit of Hadassah Hospital. Although there was no scarring to his face, the vision in his left eye was blurry. Upon examination, doctors discovered that the protective cover of his cornea was seriously damaged. Sheftel underwent one operation in Israel to remove the damaged tissue and another in Boston to transplant healthy cells from his right eye to his left to help the regeneration of tissue. Sheftel regained full eyesight, but occasionally needs to wear sunglasses to protect his sensitive left eye.

Yehezkeli was immediately arrested. A Jerusalem old-age-home resident who worked part-time at the Ministry of Education, Yehezkeli had spent the war years in the Soviet Union and had lost many family members in Treblinka. Friends were quoted as saying that he was distressed by Eitan's death. He was convicted of aggravated assault and given a five-year jail sentence (two years of which were suspended), a $6,000 fine to cover the cost of surgery, and a further fine of $5,000 to compensate for Sheftel's suffering. He expressed no regret for his actions.

The Supreme Court granted a further delay of the appeal.

Ivan of the Extermination Camp

It would be easy to dismiss Yehezkeli as deranged, as the ravings of an old man, or as part of a lunatic fringe. He was an aberration that in no way represented Israeli society or 99.99% of the Israeli public.

Still, it was hard not to see Yehezkeli's disruptive and violent behavior as representing an ugly streak in Israeli society, one which had always existed, a fanatical minority, often religious, who took it upon themselves to attack those whose views or activities didn't jibe with their worldview.

It was this same fringe element, and this same type of angry and zealous individual, that murdered Rudolf Kastner on a street in Tel Aviv in 1957 and would murder Yitzhak Rabin, several years later in 1995.

They were the awful and tragic price of Israel's democratic society that also allowed zealots their freedom.

2. New Questions

The appeal was delayed a year to allow Sheftel to recover and prepare. Sheftel then received a total of another year's delay to investigate material he had received from the Demjanjuk defense FOIA suit as well as other sources. Sheftel needed time because he was now on his own. Gill and Chumak had bowed out for the appeal.

The Appeal was to begin on May 14, 1990, more than two years after Demjanjuk was found guilty and sentenced to death by the Jerusalem District Court.

Hearing the case were the president of the Supreme Court, Meir Shamgar, its vice-president, Menachem Elon, and three other senior justices, Yacov Maltz, Aharon Barak, and Eliezer Goldberg. Both Shamgar and Barak were former attorney generals.

Generally, appeals are dry matters where the rulings of the lower court are challenged; facts are not presented. But it is the task of every appellant to get the appeals court to see the case as new.

The Israel Supreme Court has great discretion both in what they can review, and in what they can decide. The Supreme Court had the power to affirm the conviction and the sentence, or only the conviction and award a different sentence, to convict on other or lesser included crimes and offense, or return the case to a lower court, or acquit Demjanjuk.

Pending the Appeal, many journalists continued to investigate the case, and raising doubts about Demjanjuk's guilt.

Gitta Sereny became particularly concerned about the Israel District Court's decision. Sereny uncovered testimony from SS man Gustav Munzberger at his trial in Dusseldorf, as well as a letter from SS man Franz Suchomel, both of which placed Ivan of the gas chambers at Treblinka, in Trieste at war's end.

Suchomel's letter referred twice to Ivan and Nikolai. Suchomel said Ivan and Nikolai served at the Riseria (the Rice Factory) di San Sabba, a concentration camp for political prisoners and Jews in Trieste, Italy. Most of the Jews present were either murdered there or deported to Auschwitz. The Riseria had cremation facilities, the only ones built inside a concentration camp in Italy, which were demolished before the camp was liberated. More than 3,000 persons were reportedly murdered there.

The second mention says, "The gas chambers fillers from Treblinka, Ivan and Nikolai were probably shot. Though it has been said they slipped over to the partisans which I don't believe."

Sereny traveled to Trieste to interview several persons who might have known Demjanjuk there. Though she found no proof positive of Demjanjuk having been in Trieste, she became convinced that Ivan of Treblinka had served in that locale.

As Sereny saw it, only one of two scenarios could be true. Ivan Demjanjuk might have been at Trieste. In that case, Demjanjuk was Ivan the Terrible, and the court had made a mistake by accepting the Danylchenko testimony which put Demjanjuk at Flossenburg, and having made a mistake, the hearing should be reopened and Demjanjuk should not be executed.

Alternatively, there could have been two Ivans: one who was the gas-chamber operator at Treblinka and served at Trieste; the other, an Ivan Demjanjuk who served at Sobibor with Danylchenko and accompanied him to Flossenburg. In this case, Demjanjuk was "Ivan the less Terrible" and his life should also be spared (Sereny was passionately against the death penalty in most instances).

379

Ivan of the Extermination Camp

Sereny even traveled to the Soviet Union to find out more about Danylchenko. She went to the Siberian city of Tobolsk and found his last-known apartment. She didn't find Danylchenko-he had passed away in 1985. But she did interview his widow, who knew little about his wartime activities.

Sereny also spoke with Madame Natalya Kolesnikova, the Soviet war-crimes procurator who confirmed that Danylchenko indeed had been tried and sentenced for his service at Sobibor and had identified Demjanjuk. But Sereny uncovered no evidence that contradicted the testimony of the survivors and that gave Demjanjuk an alibi for the crimes at Treblinka.

Sheftel was also allowed to conduct a rogatory in Germany of a seventy-year-old German woman, Josephine Dolle, to prove there were Russians at Heuberg before November 1944 as Demjanjuk had claimed. Unfortunately, her evidence was not firsthand.

Sheftel also submitted newly released material from the Demjanjuk defense: another account of Horn's 1979 OSI interview, this time from George Garand, the translator (this account varies slightly from Dougherty's 1979 account by having Horn single out the 1951 picture before the Trawniki photo).This new evidence was trumpeted in the media as exonerative.

"60 Minutes," also found a Polish witness, Mrs. Maria Dudek, who claimed she knew intimately an Ivan Marshenko from the Treblinka death camp whom she called "Ivan the Terrible." CBS did not mention how it came to her, or why she had never been called to court by prosecution or defense attorneys. It is not because she was "suddenly" uncovered. Jerome Brentar told a Columbus, Ohio, newspaper that he had spoken with the woman in question six years before.

Days before the appeal was to begin, Sheftel asked for a delay to examine her evidence. Sheftel revealed that he had traveled to Poland and that Mrs. Dudek had repeated her statement to him but refused to come to Israel or give a signed statement. Sheftel also said OSI had been withholding a document from Poland that had the name of SS auxiliaries at Treblinka including the name Marshenko.

Shaked responded that the OSI document had actually been part of the court proceedings against Demjanjuk in the U.S. The list had been compiled by Polish authorities and based on what one Polish individual said he had been told by other Ukrainian guards. As for Mrs. Dudek, Shaked said he had no objection to her statement being introduced -- as long as it was accompanied by the statement her husband, Kazimierz Dudek, who told Polish investigators in 1986that the name of Treblinka's gas chamber operator was Ivan Marshenko and then identified Demjanjuk's Trawniki photo as Ivan.

Shaked also pointed out when he had questioned on Demjanjuk as having written on officials forms that his mother's maiden name was Marshenko. "We got the impression that he instinctively felt that a connection with this name could be dangerous for him."

Demjanjuk, for his part, continued to proclaim his innocence. His family revealed that Demjanjuk's mother's maiden name was not in fact Marshenko, but Tabachuk. The defense claimed that Marshenko was as common a name in Ukraine as Smith, (it is common but not among the top ten most common names in Ukraine). Demjanjuk had chosen Marshenko, to hide his identity for fear of repatriation to the Soviet Union.

Demjanjuk's choice of the name Marshenko would be yet another puzzle, in the disturbing saga of Demjanjuk.

3. Hearing the Appeal

Eighteen months later, on May 14, 1990, Demjanjuk's appeal began.

Sheftel had submitted a 101-page notice of appeal that challenged matters factual, procedural, as well as alleging bias and unfair treatment of the defense by the District Court, as well as citing all the new and additional evidence that had recently come to light.

In ten court sessions between May 14 and May 29, Sheftel attacked the identifications, alleged the Trawniki card to be a forgery, and put forward Demjanjuk's blanket alibi of having been a POW for the entire period in question. The prosecution answered over the course of twelve sessions, lasting from May 31 to June 20 reaffirming the integrity of the identifications and the authenticity of the Trawniki Card, and Demjanjuk's lack of a credible alibi. Then the defense made its final rebuttal in three sessions between June 26-28, 1990.

The Israel Supreme Court then retired to ponder its decision.

4. How Terrible is Ivan?

In June 1992, Vanity Fair magazine published, "How Terrible is Ivan?" by investigative reporter Frederic Dannen. In its tabloid-like teaser, the magazine trumpeted that "evidence unearthed by the Demjanjuk family suggests the courts have the wrong man – evidence the U.S. government allegedly have had access to all along."

In Dannen's telling, in order to free his father awaiting a death penalty in Israel, John Demjanjuk, Jr. together with Ed Nishnic set out to "find the real Ivan the Terrible."

Notwithstanding the opinion of the Israeli District Court, Dannen deemed the photospread suggestive saying the eye was naturally drawn to the pictures of Demjanjuk and Federenko on the photospread – and, worse, that Israel Police investigator Radiwker had prejudiced the identifications by placing an ad in newspapers with Demjanjuk and Fedorenko's full names asking for survivors of Sobibor and Treblinka who knew them to contact the Israel Police.

Dannen revealed that during the late 1980s, the cleaning staff at OSI's D.C.offices had been in the habit of depositing their garbage in a dumpster outside the building. Someone had been gathering the garbage from the dumpster and sending it to Nishnic and John Jr, who went through the plastic garbage bags in search of exculpatory evidence.

In one garbage bag they found accounts of Norman Moskowitz's Otto Horn interview by historian George Garand and investigator Bernard Dougherty, Jr, that said Horn did not definitively identify Demjanjuk at first and only did so only upon remarking on the similarity between the Trawniki photo and that of Demjanjuk's visa application.

According to Dannen, in September 1990 Sheftel along with John Jr., traveled to Simferopol in Crimea where Federenko's

384

trial had taken place. They tried to get the Federenko trial protocol but were unsuccessful. However, a few months later Alexander Yemetz, a Ukrainian member of Parliament, was able to get the file transferred to Kiev where he read it and said it contained 21 confessions of Soviet former Treblinka guards, all of whom recalled Fedorenko and spoke of the gas chamber operator named Ivan. However, several said Ivan's last name was Marchenko.

"The new evidence amounts to nothing less than a political fiasco for the Jewish State," Dannen wrote.

Shaked traveled to the Soviet Union himself, Dannen reported, eventually receiving from the Soviets the complete Federenko file, and then set about having it translated which then took many months.

Among the testimonies was one by Nikolai Shalayev, the Nikolai of the gas chamber who said he worked at the gas chamber with Ivan, Ivan Marshenko. Shalayev further testified that in June 1943 several months before the uprising, he and Ivan were transferred to Trieste, Italy to guard political prisoners. He last saw Ivan in the spring of 1944 when Marshenko defected to join Yugoslav Communist partisans. Shalayev was executed in 1951.

Congressman James Traficant, Jr of Ohio, had an unconventional history prior to being elected to Congress. In 1983, as Sheriff of Ohio's Mahoning Country, Traficant was charged with accepting a bribe. He represented himself in the RICO charges and won arguing he was gathering evidence for an undercover sting.

In Congress, he was no less colorful and, at times controversial. He became a dedicated supporter of Demjanjuk, and a supporter of former Nazi rocket scientist Arthur Rudolph. In 2001, his fellow Republicans would strip him of his seniority and all his committee appointments; in 2002, he was expelled from Congress following conviction for bribery charges. Traficant served seven years in jail. He died in 2014.

It was Traficant, Dannen said, who uncovered via a FOIA request that many of these trial testimonies of Soviet Trawniki guards had been sent to the Justice department by Soviet prosecutors between 1978 and 1981 for Federenko's US trial.

Included among them was the testimony of Pavel Leleko saying the gas chamber operators were two Ukrainian guards Nikolay and Marchenko. There was also a report of five Soviet citizens who identified Demjanjuk from photos (I. N. Ivchenko on Sept. 18, 1979, in Vinnitsa; I. T. Danylchenko on November 22, 1979 in Tiumen RSFSR; P.S. Bondaruk, July 9, 1979, in Vinnitsa Ukraine; I. M. Bazeluk, Sept. 25, 1979 in Vinnitsa) and one who did not (N. P. Malagan, in Nova Pretrova). In March 1981 the Cleveland Plain Dealer reported that statements were also submitted from five Russian witnesses who served at Trawniki, one of whom, Nikolai Dorofeyev said he had heard the name Demjanjuk while at Trawniki and identified the photo of Demjanjuk as the person he knew by that name.

In December 1991 and January 1992,Nishnic traveled to Ukraine where, according to Dannen, he was able to locate Marshenko's family. Nishnic learned that Marshenko had never returned from the war and that his wife had recently passed away. However, his daughter who was only an infant when Marshenko left for the War, was able to share personal information and to provide Nishnic with Marchenko's wedding photo.

Ivan Marshenko was born in 1911 – making him some 9 years older than Demjanjuk.

In Dannen's article there was this rather chilling statement from John Jr., regarding the possibility that his father was a guard at Sobibor: "If my father were to stand up today and say,

'I lied, I was a guard someplace,' I would have to put that in the context of what happened during World War II. Knowing what P.O.W. camps were like —at Chelm, where he testified he was, people were dying of typhus, dysentery and starvation. Does a boy put in a position like that, given the opportunity to have a real meal and put meat on his bones, and faced with the choice of living and dying —is he morally wrong for choosing the option of living? Is he any more culpable than the Jew that made the decision to live and spent twelve months pulling gold out of the mouths of corpses? I don't think so."

Dannen was quick to point out the offensiveness of John, Jr.'s analogy, adding that it is in no way a defense under the law for the crimes committed by extermination camp guards. Nonetheless, Dannen saw this as "the unspoken subtext of the case" and "why Israel probably now wishes it had never heard of John Demjanjuk."

Despite this, Dannen reported, the survivors remained convinced of their identifications and the prosecutors of their case against Demjanjuk.

Pinhas Epstein said, "I don't know nothing. I won't speak, After the trial I will speak."

Eliahu Rosenberg had this to say: "My kishkes [Yiddish for guts] turn over that, four years after his death sentence, he's still alive, this mamzer [bastard]."

Josef Czarny said, "I hope the judges will reject the appeal. I hope this on behalf of all the victims of Treblinka who cannot speak. If, God forbid, the prosecution should fail, it would be terrible."

Daphna Bainvol, on behalf of the Prosecution, said, "We are going to prove to the Supreme Court that he is a Nazi war criminal who was at least in Sobibor and Flossenburg."

Dannen's overall conclusion was that although OSI's prosecutions "may not be the frameup the Demjanjuk family believes that it is ... it does make a strong case for prosecutorial misconduct."

5. The Special Master's Opinion

Dannen's Vanity Fair article had a greater impact than anyone could have predicted, particularly on one reader in Ohio, a federal Judge, Gilbert Merritt.

Merritt was the Chief Justice of the U.S. Sixth Circuit Court of Appeals, in Cincinnati.

Merritt felt that Dannen's article and its claim that OSI had withheld what could possibly be exculpatory evidence from the defense (although only exculpatory as to Treblinka), or had such knowledge and proceeded nonetheless was an indication that a possible fraud had been committed on the court, in that the Justice Department might have misled the court in the matter of Demjanjuk's extradition.

To investigate this matter and determine whether OSI needed to be prosecuted for misconduct and whether Demjanjuk's extradition should be revoked, Merritt decided to appoint a Special Master, dismissing claims by the government that Merritt lacked the jurisdiction to do so.

Although Judge Frank Battisti, who presided over the denaturalization and deportation hearings, and was familiar with the evidence in the case, would have been the obvious choice, Merritt wanted a fresh look at Demjanjuk's OSI prosecution. Merritt chose federal judge Thomas Wiseman from Nashville, Tennessee.

Wiseman was the former Tennessee State Treasurer and had been appointed as a federal judge by President Jimmy Carter. Wiseman was instructed to prepare a report after questioning government lawyers who had worked on the Demjanjuk case.

Wiseman interviewed OSI and Justice Department attorneys Allan Ryan, Norman Moskowitz, Bruce Einhorn, George Parker and John Horrigan.

Parker testified that he quit OSI after his doubts regarding Demjanjuk being Ivan the Terrible of Treblinka were ignored.

Ryan, the former OSI director, by then an attorney for Harvard University, was questioned for some four hours. Ryan was confronted by written statements made by George Parker to Ryan's predecessor Walter Rockler, saying that "we doubt that Ivan was at the gas chambers."

Ryan denied having seen the memo because if he had, "I found the things said and the assumptions made so unacceptable that, had I seen it in 1980, I would have set Parker straight." Einhorn, who by then was a federal immigration Judge, was questioned for three hours. He was asked whether he knew of any document in the Justice Department's possession that might have exonerated Demjanjuk.

"Absolutely not," Einhorn replied.

Asked if he had any doubts that Demjanjuk was the gas chamber operator at Treblinka, Einhorn replied, "None."

Moskowitz and Horrigan explained that as denaturalization was a civil trial, they were not compelled to turn over the Soviet Trawniki men testimonies. The discovery procedures were not as stringent as in a criminal proceeding. .

Wiseman's 210-page report delivered on June 30, 1993, concluded that although some mistakes were made by prosecutors, OSI engaged in no judicial misconduct and employed no fraud in its prosecution of John Demjanjuk. The defense's contention that the Justice Department had withheld critical information was, Wiseman wrote, "without merit."

Although Wiseman found there was substantial evidence that shed doubt on Demjanjuk being the Ivan the Terrible of Treblinka, the evidence against Demjanjuk fully supported the conclusion that Demjanjuk was an SS guard. Accordingly, the extradition was sound.

Wiseman also affirmed that OSI had acted in good faith. "They did not intend to violate the rules of the Ethical obligations. They were not reckless; they did not misstate the facts or the law..." Wiseman recommended that no action be taken against the government attorneys who prosecuted Demjanjuk.

Most observers assumed Merritt would adopt Wiseman's recommendations although doing so was at the Judge's discretion.

6. Ivan Marshenko of the Gas Chambers at Treblinka

After the District Court issued its judgment in March 1988, the prosecution continued to reach out to Soviet prosecutors in order to forge a direct relationship with the Procurator General's office.

Israel did not have diplomatic relations with the USSR at that time, so at first they worked through third parties. Some of those intermediaries were in the West and had high level contacts with the Soviets, and others were Soviet bloc officials who had already established good relations with the Israelis. After many months of negotiations, Israeli prosecutors succeeded in making contact with representatives from the Procurator's Office.

Contact remained limited until 1990, when the changing Soviet political situation was such that the Procurator's office agreed to allow Israeli prosecution members to visit Moscow in an official capacity and do research there.

The Israeli prosecution team, Mickey Shaked and Daphna Bainvol in particular, were given access to Federerenko's entire trial protocol, which took up some 22 volumes of material, and they were able to confer with some of the Soviet prosecutors in Federerenko's trial.

The Israelis found many statements from Soviet Wachmann who served at Treblinka or Sobibor and who themselves had been tried since World War Two, in different regions of the Soviet Union, as well as in Ukraine in particular. These statements were often from other Soviet war crimes trial which the Soviets had begun investigating as early as 1944 – before even the end of the war as they overran Nazi-occupied territory in Ukraine, Poland and Germany. The Israelis were also given access to the KGB files on these accused Nazi collaborators. Over the course of the next two years, Israeli investigators tried to go through as much as this material as possible in Moscow as well as in Kiev.

The Israeli prosecutors were able to get their Moscow counterparts to grant Demjanjuk's defense attorneys access to this same material. They arranged dates for the defense to have a week's time to examine this material but the defense decided against it.

There were many statements that spoke of the Treblinka Wachmann who was the gas chamber operator who they named as Ivan Marshenko. It soon became clear that this Marshenko was not Demjanjuk.

They found the personnel file of "Iwan Martechjenko," Personalbogen No. 496. The photo of Marshenko had very dark hair and his face looked nothing like Demjanjuk's Trawniki photo. He was nine years older than Demjanjuk and his height was listed as 184 cm. as compared to Demjanjuk's which was listed as 175cm). He did indeed have a scar on his cheek. It seemed hard to believe that the survivors had confused this person with Demjanjuk.

There was also the statement of Nikolai, who identified the picture of Ivan Marshenko, as the "operator of the motor of the gas chambers" who job was also to "help the guards put in victims who displayed resistance." Nikolai he was also gas chamber motor operator, said Marshenko had put "hundreds of thousands" of victims in the gas chambers "with the help of the Germans and the guards."

Nikolai said he last saw Marshenko in March 1945, in Fiume (an Italian City that the Nazis occupied and that, after the war, became part of Croatia). Marshenko told him that he was thinking of remaining there with a Yugoslav woman connected to the partisans that he was thinking of marrying her (despite the family he left in Ukraine).

As Sheftel said, "The unbelievable had happened."

The Israelis also found the testimonies of several Wachmann at Sobibor who had previously been posted to Treblinka. These Wachmann commented on how the two 'death factories' (their words) were operated identically, with the guards in both places serving in every capacity at the camp, including accompanying the victims to the gas chamber.

They also recovered Danylchenko's entire 1949 trial protocol, in which he named Demjanjuk as being at Sobibor when he arrived and as later being posted with him to Flossenburg, with his statement that upon arrival at Flossenburg they both received blood group tattoos under their left armpits. They also recovered Danylchenko's Trawniki card which was in all material respects identical to Demjanjuk's.

They found official Nazi records of Wachmann postings, with name, birth date, birthplace, ID number and the dates of posting. Among these was a listing that on March 26, 1943, Ivan Demjanjuk, No. 1393, – with his correct date and place of birth – was posted to Sobibor. There was also a list of Wachmann posted in October 1943 to the Flossenburg Camp that listed both Danylchenko and Demjanjuk. In addition, they found an official disciplinary complaint against Demjanjuk and three other Wachmann for leaving the area of the Majdanek concentration camp without permission. It was dated January 18, 1943 – and the posting did not appear on Demjanjuk's Trawniki card, another indication that Demjanjuk was a guard who was assigned to various camps where (and when) his talents were needed.

7. More Evidence Emerges

As each new piece of evidence emerged, Sheftel applied to the Supreme Court to immediately dismiss the case against Demjanjuk and set him free. However, the Supreme decided to keep Demjanjuk in jail while the prosecution continued its investigation in the Soviet Archives.

The Israeli prosecution returned to Germany to deepen their search, finding in the Koblenz archive three authentic German documents relating to Demjanjuk's service at Flossenburg: 1). An October 1944 list of Wachmann accompanying prisoners to forced labor at Flossenburg listing both Demjanjuk and Danylchenko with their correct Trawniki ID numbers. 2). Another list of Wachmann posted to Flossenburg with Demjanjuk's name and ID number. And 3). an Armory ledger that listed both Demjanjuk and Danylchenko as having received bayonets on October 8, 1943.

For years, Demjanjuk's defense and supporters had derided the documentary evidence against him as tainted due to having been found in Soviet archives. These documents, which confirmed Demjanjuk's Trawniki ID number, and his service at Flossenburg with Danylchenko, were found in a Western Archive. There could be no claim of a KGB forgery. And these documents supported the veracity of both the Trawniki Card as well as Danylchenko's own statements.

In June 1992, the prosecution and defense appeared before the Israel Supreme Court to address this new evidence and make final summary arguments. Sheftel argued passionately that in light of the new evidence, Demjanjuk must be set free.

Shaked made a more sober case that Demjanjuk's participation in the mass murder of the Jews was now affirmed at the Sobibor extermination camp as well as at Flossenburg and Majdanek. Shaked maintained that the identifications by the survivors remain unchallenged and there was much reason to believe that Demjanjuk, the experienced driver and death camp guard, served at Treblinka as well.

The Israel Supreme Court was scheduled to announce its decision on July 29, 1993. The survivors were adamant that Demjanjuk was Ivan and that his death sentence be carried out. Many Israelis, filled with uncertainty and malaise about Demjanjuk, wanted him acquitted and deported from Israel.

"I am persuaded that John Demjanjuk is not Ivan the Terrible of Treblinka, but most probably he is Ivan the Terrible of Sobibor," Israeli journalist Tom Segev said.

"In that sense, he is the right man convicted of the wrong crime."

8. The Israel Supreme Court's Decision

On August 18, 1993 the Supreme Court of Israel sitting as the High Court of Justice delivered its unanimous opinion. Over the next two hours, Justice Meir Shamgar read selections in summary of the Court's detailed 405-page decision.

The Court was explicit in saying that they had reviewed the testimony and identifications by the five Holocaust survivors who appeared in Court and found them persuasive. And as to the identifications administered by the Israel Police investigators, the court said that "we did not discover any technical or substantive flaw."

However, the Supreme Court also acknowledged the existence of more than 60 depositions from the Soviet Union, from former Wachmann in their own war crimes trials, many of which named Ivan Marchenko as the Ivan who operated the gas chambers at Treblinka.

These statements were of little legal value as they were unverified: The circumstances under which they were given were not fully known and the persons who gave them were dead or unavailable for cross examination.

The Court found significant that Demjanjuk had written the name Marshenko as his mother's maiden name on an official form. That his mother's correct name was Tabachuk was not important the Justices said. "The question is not what was her true name -- but why did the defendant recall that her name was Marchenko?" the Justices said.

Nonetheless, the Marshenko statements did create reasonable doubt that Demjanjuk was Ivan the Terrible of Treblinka. As the court noted of the Soviet testimonies:

"We do not know how these statements came into the

world and who gave birth to them," the court said in its verdict. "When they came before us, doubt began to gnaw away at our judicial conscience; perhaps [Demjanjuk] was not Ivan the Terrible of Treblinka. By virtue of this gnawing -- whose nature we knew, but not the meaning -- we restrained ourselves from convicting [him] of the horrors of Treblinka."

Accordingly, the Court was reversing the decision of the District Court and voiding the death penalty.

"We clear the defendant John Ivan Demjanjuk because of reasonable doubt," Chief Justice Shamgar told a crowded courtroom that included Holocaust survivors who groaned, upset.

Shamgar continued: The Court had the authority to convict Demjanjuk for lesser included offenses or other crimes uncovered during the course of the appeal. There was compelling and irrefutable evidence that Demjanjuk had served the Nazis and had been a prison guard at the Sobibor death camp where 250,000 Jews were exterminated. They also felt the evidence proved beyond a doubt that Demjanjuk served at Trawniki, as well as Flossenburg, a concentration camp where Jews were murdered.

"The facts proved the appellant's participation in the extermination process," the ruling read.

Beyond that, Shamgar noted that Demjanjuk's alibis were contradicted by historical documents, and Demjanjuk misstatements and falsehoods made his various alibis all the less credible.

Despite this, the Court found that Demjanjuk, having already spent some seven years in solitary confinement, the majority under the threat of the death penalty, and given that the center of gravity in the case had concerned Treblinka and not Sobibor or the other camps where Demjanjuk served, that he not had adequate opportunity to defend himself against those charges. The Supreme Court concluded Demjanjuk should not be further incarcerated but rather deported from Israel to a country that would accept him.

"The matter is closed, but not complete," the court wrote. "The complete truth is not the prerogative of the human judge."

The Survivors who had testified against Demjanjuk, such as Czarny, were overcome with disbelief. "I am in shock, great shock," Czarny said. "The justices made a mistake. They have done an injustice to millions, because he is the criminal, the Nazi criminal."

Czarny spoke for all the witnesses who testified against Demjanjuk that, "Not in my worst dreams did I think something like this could happen in a Jewish state. . . . The Nazis can celebrate now, this murderer will keep on living." Overwrought, Czarny went on, "They tell me I am not authentic! I am not authentic! I wonder if it was worthwhile at all to survive the camps. The six million buried in Europe will ask me, what did you do for us, Yosef Czarny, and I will say to them, I did my best."

Asher Felix Landau, writing for the Jerusalem Post's Law Reports, said of the Supreme Court's decision that "In the result, the 'Wachmann' Ivan Demjanjuk is acquitted, by reason of doubt, of the outrageous crimes attributed to Ivan the Terrible of Treblinka. Judges, who are only human, cannot reach perfection, and it is only right that they judge on the basis of what is placed before them, and on that basis alone."

Sheftel later announced that the Supreme Court's decision had brought to a close "the most needless trial in Israel's history."

John, Jr, had high praise for the Court. "We are delighted that the judges had the moral courage to stop this injustice." John, Jr. added, "He should be brought back to America and this nonsense should stop right now. His family has been through hell over the last 16 years."

Demjanjuk offered this to the press: "I miss my wife," he said. "I miss my family. I miss my grandchildren. I want to go home."

9. Supreme Court Aftermath

It bears saying that the Israel Supreme Court is held in high regard by most Israelis and by jurists, attorneys, and legal scholars the world over. Israel Supreme Court Justices are appointed by the Israeli President, chosen from a list of recommendations made by the Judicial Selection Committee and are usually eminent jurists, persons who have served as District Court Judges.

In the late 1980s and early 1990s, the Israel Supreme Court increasingly became the moral authority of the nation, sitting in ethical, moral and legal judgement over political divisions, disputes among religious authorities, and actions in which the government, the military and civil liberties clashed. As Israel found itself in the grip of the first and second intifadas, it was the Supreme Court who intervened in cases of press freedom, military censorship, civil rights, and religious rights.

The Israel Supreme Court was considered a High Court of Appeal which had great discretion in its decisions and its ability to consider new evidence. Those decisions earned the Supreme Court great respect and, at the same time, increased the Court's prestige and authority.

In deciding to overturn the District Court decision regarding Demjanjuk and set him free, the Court was widely praised and perceived as having bent over backwards to do the right thing – beyond what was legally necessary.

That Israel, whose citizens were the victims of the Final Solution, their children and grandchildren, would be compelled by its laws and its High Court to set free a Nazi murderer was seen by commentators the world over as a tribute to Israel's democracy and standing as a nation of Laws.

Today, several decades later, the politicization of Israeli society and the increasingly strident political divisions among it have caused the Supreme Court to be attacked as too political, and by former Justice Minister Ayelet Shaked (no relation to Mickey) as too activist. Recently, there have been several government attempts to limit the power of Israel's Supreme Court.

However, in the immediate aftermath of the Israel Supreme Court's decision, the U.S. Justice Department announced that as the deportation order against Demjanjuk remained in effect, they would not allow his return.

The newly independent Ukraine said Demjanjuk would be accepted there for as long as he liked – and they were not seeking to prosecute him.

Demjanjuk now fully expected he would be returned to independent Ukraine.

But Demjanjuk was not a free man yet.

Following the decision, several Holocaust survivors petitioned the Supreme Court not to release Demjanjuk but instead to bring him to trial on charges of war crimes at Sobibor and other concentration camps. Among the petitioners were Yisrael Yehezkeli, released from prison.

A Supreme Court panel consisting of Justice Shlomo Levin, Justice Gavriel Bach and Justice Mishael Cheshin reviewed their petitions. On August 18. 1993, they issued a ruling denying their petitions, saying that returning the case to the District Court could be considered double jeopardy. They left it to the Attorney General to decide whether to re-prosecute Demjanjuk but counseled that he take guidance from the Supreme Court on the matter.

10. Back to Cleveland

In September 1993, Judge Merritt ordered Demjanjuk returned to the United States to assist in his own defense at proceedings to restore his citizenship or to denaturalize him anew. This was finally the green light that allowed Demjanjuk to return home to Cleveland, accompanied by John, Jr. Nishnic and Rep. Traficant. This was the first, and as far as I know, only time someone successfully deported by OSI was returned to the United States.

Demjanjuk, spared the death penalty in the Soviet Union, and now the death penalty in Israel, was also spared returning to Ukraine. Journalist Vivian Witt would later write of "The incredible *Mazel* of John Demjanjuk."

In the U.S. Demjanjuk's defense was being handled *pro bono* by Michael E. Tigar, and his law partner and wife Jane Tigar. The Tigars are prominent defense attorneys whose sometimes controversial clients have included Terry Nichols, a co-conspirator with Timothy McVeigh in the Oklahoma City bombing, who they saved from the death penalty; and Lynne Stewart, a notorious defense attorney herself, who was convicted of providing material aid to her terrorist client, Sheikh Omar Abdel-Rahman.

However, Merritt was not done with Demjanjuk yet. On November 17, 1993, the Sixth Circuit Court of Appeals, with Merritt as Chief Judge, having considered Wiseman's findings but ignoring his conclusions, found that OSI had committed a fraud upon the Court such that Demjanjuk's extradition should be revoked and he should be allowed to remain in the United States.

The Demjanjuk family was overjoyed. "The three judges' decision in our mind proves that justice was finally done here in the United States," said Nishnic, as quoted in the

Washington Post, "The courts are the ultimate authority... and today, the courts have ruled that the Department of Justice committed fraud... You can't take that lightly. Fraud is fraud."

However, the Sixth Circuit merely had the power to rebuke the OSI attorneys. The Circuit Court held no power to mete out any punishment. Nonetheless, following the Sixth Circuit's determination of fraud the American Bar Association and the Justice Department felt compelled to conduct their own reviews.

The American Bar Association, upon review of the Sixth Circuit's opinion, overturned it clearing the OSI attorneys; as did the Justice Department's own Office of Professional Responsibility which found no prosecutorial misconduct on the part of OSI. To the contrary, the Justice Department reaffirmed their intention "to effect Demjanjuk's prompt removal from the United States," while at the same time, the Demjanjuk family went back to Court to restore Demjanjuk's citizenship.

On February 20, 1998, Federal District Court Judge Paul Matia, a Harvard Law School graduate who President George H. W. Bush appointed to the federal bench in 1991, ruled that Demjanjuk's US citizenship could be restored. However, Judge Matia specifically permitted the government to file a new denaturalization complaint against Demjanjuk, if they believed the evidence warranted it.

The OSI would have to start the case against Demjanjuk all over again. Which is exactly what they did:

11. Denaturalization Redux

On May 19, 1999, the United States Department of Justice filed a new civil complaint against Demjanjuk alleging that he had served as a guard at the Trawniki, Sobibor, Flossenburg and Majdanek concentration camps.

There was no longer any mention of Treblinka or Ivan the Terrible. Eli Rosenbaum, who had become Director of OSI in 1995, noted for the court that Sobibor where Demjanjuk was an armed guard was established for the sole purpose of murdering Jewish civilians. More than 200,000 Jewish men, women, and children were murdered at Sobibor. The OSI indictment also charged that Demjanjuk served the Nazis at Majdanek where more than 200,000 Jewish men, women and children were murdered; and, finally, that Demjanjuk also served at Flossenburg where some 30,000 Jewish victims were murdered.

It was not until May 2001 that Demjanjuk's second denaturalization trial opened in Cleveland. Although that case might have rightfully returned to Judge Battisti, he had died in 2001, at age 72, unexpectedly of typhus and Rocky Mountain spotted fever, the result of a poisonous insect bite. Instead, it fell to Chief Judge Paul R. Matia who had restored Demjanjuk's citizenship just three years earlier.

This was a much different prosecution than Demjanjuk's earlier denaturalization trial in the early 1980s. No eyewitnesses were called to testify. The Trawniki Card which in 1981 had been a one-of-a-kind contested marvel had since been tested multiple times and compared to many other Trawniki documents, all of which supported its authenticity.

Beyond that, Demjanjuk's ID number 1393, continued to turn up on document after document, which taken together irrefutably proved his Nazi service. Over the years, the OSI had been able to gather even more supporting evidence from the former Soviet Union and from German archives to further support all its contentions,

For example, Demjanjuk's arrival at Trawniki was narrowed to between June 13 and before July 11, 1942 (they had uncovered Trawniki Card 1392 which was issued on June 13).There were now also many more documents to support Danylchenko's testimony, including his Trawniki Card which indicated he arrived at Sobibor on April 4, 1943 which conformed with his testimony that Demjanjuk was already at Sobibor when he arrived (Demjanjuk having arrived there on March 27, 1943). It was these documents that now became the center of gravity in the case.

There was even more information about Okzow the labor camp to which Demjanjuk was posted on September 22, 1942 – researchers had discovered it to be part of a network of agricultural estates seized by the Nazis from the Polish gentry which were turned into small camps, or bases, where prisoners were kept, and from which raids were launched against partisans and to sweep up Jews in the surrounding area. Jewish prisoners were either murdered on the spot at Okzow or transported to one of the local death camps such as Treblinka or Sobibor.

Among the intriguing pieces of evidence OSI had gathered but chose not to use in this case was a June 25, 1990, interview with Melania Nezdymynoha, a Ukrainian woman who had worked as a laundress at Treblinka. The audio of this interview was turned over by Demjanjuk's public defender in Cleveland in 1993, while Demjanjuk was still in Israel but his defense was trying to have his original extradition thrown out.

As explained in a deposition submitted in that case, Jaroslaw Dobrowolskyj stated that in 1990 he traveled to Ukraine with Sheftel, John Jr, and others, and that they carried letters saying they were there at the behest of U.S. Representative James

Trafficant.

While in Ukraine, Dobrowolskyj interviewed Melania Nezdymynoha. Born in 1924, she explained that when the Germans occupied her town, they took young girls such as herself and put them on freight trains, first to Poland to be registered as forced laborers. From there, some girls were sent to work on farms in Germany. She was taken to Treblinka to work in the kitchen and clean the German Officer's sleeping quarters. She explained that she was there until the uprising, during which she was afraid that she, too, would be killed. Afterwards she feared that the Germans would send them to "the baths" as well to be gassed, but instead they loaded them on a transport and took them to Lublin.

At Treblinka, she was familiar with many of the officers as well as the camp's guards. When asked, she said, she knew Fedor Federenko.

Then asked about Marchenko, she said: "Ivan Marchenko, I knew." She later described him as tall and having a dark complexion.

Asked what kind of man Marchenko was, she answered: "A killer." She said that she knew this because she heard from the other "boys" that he herded the Jews to the gas chambers. She says she knew they were being murdered, not because she saw it but because of "the smell."

And that would have served the defense well. However, at some point in the conversation Dobrowolskyj asks, "Did you know Ivan Demjanjuk? A man of that name?"

"I remember," she answered.

"Do you remember it from the camp, that name?"

"Uhm-uhm"

"Did you see him; did you know him?"

"I guess I saw him," she said.

Then a few seconds later, Dobrowolskyj asks: "And you said you knew the name Demjanjuk. Do you recall what Demjanjuk did? Do you know?"

She replied, "They were all guards. What they did, where they went, these things we didn't know." She was then shown a number of photographs and said that she recognized no one.

Why this 1990 interview was not turned over to the prosecution in Israel or the United States until 1993 (and was only done so because the public defender found it among his files), remains a mystery. But the notion that Demjanjuk was identified as one of the guards at Treblinka is tantalizing.

Demjanjuk's defense attorneys were John Broadley who'd handled many of his FOIA requests and Michael Tigar. Once again, the Demjanjuk defense argued KGB forgery to no effect. In effect, they no longer challenged that the documents said Demjanjuk was at Sobibor and Flossenburg, just that they were either forgeries or that it was once again mistaken identity. However, this time Iwan Marshenko could not stand in for Demjanjuk at Sobibor, Flossenburg or Majdanek.

Instead, the defense suggested there was another Demjanjuk to blame: Ivan Andreevich Demjanjuk, a cousin who also served at Trawniki, as well as in Lublin and Lvov. Demjanjuk's defense argued that it was this person who was pictured in the Trawniki card and held ID No. 1393.

Judge Matia dismissed both arguments. The information on the Trawniki card was too specific to Demjanjuk in almost every respect, and his ID number 1393 now followed him throughout a multitude of German documents and was further supported by the Soviet trial statements of Danylchenko.

The defense did introduce one Soviet document of interest that indicated that as early as 1949 the Soviets considered Demjanjuk a war criminal, and already had his

Trawniki card with a notation of his personnel number 1393. These were probably uncovered as part of Danylchenko's trial. They indicated that Demjanjuk did indeed have reason to fear being repatriated to the Soviet Union, but not because of his claimed Vlassov Army service, but because his Nazi service was known and as a death camp guard he was identified as a murderous war criminal.

In May 2002, Judge Matia denaturalized Demjanjuk for the second time. Matia ruled that the government had proved by clear, convincing and unequivocal evidence that Demjanjuk's Nazi service during World War Two rendered his entry into the US illegal.

OSI then began deportation proceedings against Demjanjuk. The facts of Demjanjuk's Nazi service, and his having lied about them, were now even more evident, irrefutable and incontrovertible than they were in his deportation hearings twenty years before.

On December 28, 2005, the Immigration Court ordered Demjanjuk deported to Germany, Poland or Ukraine. Demjanjuk's defense appealed.

Eli Rosenbaum recalled being on the phone with one of Demjanjuk's attorneys soon after who told him, "You guys have won all the cases. But no one is going to take my client. He's going to die here." And Rosenbaum's heart sank because he feared Demjanjuk's attorney was correct.

However, in May 2007, after the Supreme Court denied Demjanjuk a hearing, the deportation order was rendered final.

Once again, John Demjanjuk was a stateless person. Once again, the Courts affirmed that there was no doubt that he had served the Nazis as a death camp guard and assisted in the murder of thousands of Jewish men, women and children. However, until a country was willing to accept Demjanjuk, he remained in the United States, a free man.

CHAPTER ELEVEN:

HELLO MUNICH!

1. Who will take Demjanjuk?

The OSI and the Justice Department were looking for a country to which they could deport Demjanjuk. The Soviet Union no longer existed. Russia was not interested. Nor was Poland. As for Ukraine, it was less than certain that Ukraine would put Demjanjuk on trial for Nazi service during World War Two.

That left Germany. Germany had conducted many post-war trials of Nazis in the 1950s, 1960s and 1970s, including trials relating to Belzec, Sobibor and Treblinka, as well as trials related to Trawniki. But in those cases, Germany was trying Germans, and the German criminal code had at times been interpreted in ways that were quite forgiving to some of the murderers, resulting in minimal sentences.

Germany had not held trials of foreign nationals who assisted the Nazis in their murderous enterprise. Beyond that, Demjanjuk had committed the majority of his crimes not in Germany but in Nazi-Occupied Poland. The victims at Sobibor, during the time period Demjanjuk served there were primarily Jews who had been expatriated from the Netherlands.

Nonetheless Eli Rosenbaum approached the German Federal authorities to accept Demjanjuk. Germany refused.

Rosenbaum wasn't one to give up. Rosenbaum knew that

Germany was a federation of many regional State authorities; and if any one prosecutor actually filed charges against Demjanjuk, then the Federal Government would have no choice but to accept Demjanjuk.

As fate would have it, an investigative Judge from Germany, Thomas Walther, was visiting OSI.

Walther, then in his early Sixties had retired as a Judge in Bavaria in 2006. Walther, who was born in 1943, was of modest height, with wings of long blonde hair circling his head. He had a broad forehead and empathetic face and wore clear rimless glasses that sat on his nose, almost invisible.

Upon Walther's retirement, much to the surprise of the German legal community, he joined Germany's Central Office for the Investigation of Nazi Crimes.

Walther had a personal reason for devoting his retirement to prosecuting Nazi War Criminals. For Walther, doing so was a tribute to his own father, Rudolf, who had saved two Jewish families on Kristallnacht, hiding them until they could escape Germany.

"We introduced him to the Demjanjuk case and he was intrigued," Rosenbaum said.

Walther told Rosenbaum that in Germany, "their position had always been that what they needed for a prosecution was a murder of an identifiable person by the subject. And we didn't have that in Demjanjuk." Walther said that their law didn't cover a situation where someone was a guard at a camp but one couldn't prove that he committed individual murders of known individuals.

They were standing in Rosenbaum's office. Rosembaum turned to Walther and said, "Thomas, you know, in my country if you conspire with another person to kill me… Imagine if you were in the office with me, and you had a colleague standing outside. And you produced a knife and started to chase me around the office to kill me, while your colleague outside held the door shut so I couldn't escape. Well, if you killed me, then you would be guilty of first-degree murder. But so would your colleague because she knew what was happening and she made it impossible for me to escape. Her participation was essential to carrying out the murder."

"That's our law," Rosenbaum said. "And I can't imagine it's any different in Germany."

Walther's response was, "Let me look into it."

Walther took on the mission of changing how German law was applied to prosecuting Nazi Collaborators such as Demjanjuk. Together with another investigating Judge, Kristin Goethe, then in her forties, they found precedent that they believed would make it possible to charge Nazi collaborators as accessories to murders committed in extermination camps.

They went to the High Court in Germany which validated their finding.

Still, Germany resisted accepting Demjanjuk for trial. One legal question was what jurisdiction in Germany could try Demjanjuk. As Demjanjuk lived in a DP camp outside Munich after the war, Munich was a choice. The Munich Attorney General denied they had jurisdiction as Demjanjuk had never lived in Munich. However, the Second Division of the Federal Criminal Court disagreed, upon finding that Demjanjuk had, in fact, stayed in 1951 at a warehouse near Munich for several months

Rosenbaum received a call from his colleagues in Ludwigsberg who suggested it would be helpful if he came to Germany and went with Walther to the Munich Prosecutors.

So that's what he did.

At the same time, in the years since the internet became ubiquitous, it had become possible to assemble data and evidence on a large scale making the undertaking of complex prosecutions possible for smaller legal teams in less time by virtue of the documents and the data compiled – that was already authenticated and did not rely on eye-witness testimony.

It was now possible with a great deal of accuracy to detail the thousands of Jewish men, women and children, sent to Sobibor during the months Demjanjuk served there. It was almost 30,000 people who, within hours of their arrival, were murdered. And as Sobibor served no other purpose than murder of its prisoners and confiscation of their belongings and valuables, anyo n e working there was complicit in the murders.

The Munich Prosecutor's office decided to charge Demjanjuk as an accessory to almost 30,000 murders at Sobibor. And so, in short order, the Federal Prosecutors in Berlin had to change their position – how could they not accept someone charged with thousands of murders?

Kurt Schrimm, the head of the Central Agency for the investigation of Nazi crimes in Ludwigsburg expressed interest in prosecuting Demjanjuk. "We believe that he can be sentenced under German criminal law," Schrimm said, adding, "There are many more who, like Demjanjuk, are not from Germany but are responsible under German law." A trial of the 88-year-old could therefore be considered as a "model case."

On December 19, 2008 Spiegel, the largest circulation German newsweekly reported that some forensic scientists at the BKA, the German Federal Criminal Police Authority, had examined the Trawniki card in 1987, and had questions as to its authenticity.

The following day, however, Eli Rosenbaum shut down those doubts in Spiegel, saying that, "The ID card is perhaps the most-reviewed documents in the history of law enforcement." Rosenbaum told Spiegel: "It's certainly real."

"We are ready to deport Demjanjuk," Rosenbaum said.

Two months later, in February 2009 Rosenbaum traveled to Germany to personally deliver the card to German authorities. After meeting with German authorities, their concerns regarding the card were addressed, and the meeting ended with a joint statement as to the card's authenticity.

2. Goodbye Cleveland

In the meantime, Demjanjuk continued to live his life as a free man, at home in Cleveland.

Demjanjuk's wife Vera, son John, Jr., and attorney John Broadley all told the press that Demjanjuk was a sick and frail old man.

Spiegel sent Cordula Meyer to report. She interviewed Demjanjuk's neighbor, Erik Keller, a young graphic designer who said, that although Demjanjuk was indeed an old man who, Spiegel reported, "Could not stand well and walk, and has problems with his knees, Demjanjuk nonetheless dug out his driveway by himself after a recent blizzard and that he has never seen Demjanjuk in a wheelchair."

In the face of these years of inaction, while Demjanjuk remained free, I felt compelled to publish an Op-Ed in the Los Angeles Times calling on Germany to accept their moral responsibility for Nazis accomplices such as Demjanjuk who were party to the murders of hundreds of thousands of innocents. Here's the Op-Ed I wrote in the Los Angeles Times on June 13, 2008, they titled "The Pariah Loophole":

John Demjanjuk's last appeal to avoid deportation was rejected by the U.S. Supreme Court on May 19. The 88-year-old accused Nazi concentration camp guard was stripped of his citizenship and ordered sent to Ukraine, his birthplace; Poland, the locus of the crimes; or Germany, the heir to the Nazi regime under which he served.

Yet, as it now stands, he is still in the United States. Why? He can't be exiled unless another country agrees to accept him. For the time being, he remains free.

In this, Demjanjuk is not alone. There are five other former Nazi criminals against whom the U.S. Justice Department

416

successfully completed deportation proceedings but whom no country has been willing to accept. Romanian-born Johann Leprich, a guard at Mauthausen camp in Austria, is one; his deportation was finalized in 2006. Another is Jakiw Palij, born in a region of Poland that is now in Ukraine. He was a guard at Poland's Trawniki labor camp (where in a single day in 1943, 6,000 prisoners were murdered), and his deportation was finalized in January 2006. Mykola Wasylyk, another Trawniki guard also found to be at the Budzyn camp, had his final appeal denied in 2004.

Theodor Szehinskyj, also born in a part of Ukraine that used to be Poland, was in the SS unit called the Death's Head Brigade and was a guard at the Gross-Rosen, Sachsenhausen and the Warsaw concentration camps. His deportation litigation was completed in March 2006.

Finally, there is Anton Tittjung. Tittjung was born in what was then Yugoslavia and is now Croatia. He was a Waffen SS member and a guard at Mauthausen.

Should any of these criminals worry that deportation is imminent, they might take comfort from the fact that the Supreme Court declined to hear Tittjung's final appeal way back in 2000. He still remains free in the United States. In addition, in recent years, four of their denaturalized Nazi peers died before they were ever deported.

In all of these cases, the countries of their birth, such as Ukraine, Romania, Poland or Croatia, and the countries where their crimes were committed, such as Austria or Poland as well as Germany, were contacted by the Justice Department, and none expressed interest in receiving these now "stateless" persons.

There is no law, domestic or international, that requires foreign countries to accept or extradite these former Nazis --or to give a reason why they don't. However, their reasons are easy to divine and include not wanting to burden the state with these aged citizens, no desire for an expensive investigation and trial, and fear that nationalist or neo-Nazi elements might be aroused by reopening Nazi-era wounds.

But that does not lift their moral responsibility to accept and/or prosecute the criminals of the Nazi era. In what society do murderers go free? What nation can forget the crimes of the Nazi era? Given that the victims of the Holocaust cannot cry out for justice, who will?

Poland, Ukraine and Romania might make the argument that they were under Nazi rule at that time. Germany has no such excuse. And although Germany has prosecuted many native-born Germans for their World War II-era crimes, they have been less eager to do so as time goes by. Germany has had even less interest in prosecuting those non-Germans, like Demjanjuk, who served the Nazis in the countries they conquered -- as though Germany could draw a border around the Holocaust crimes it is responsible for.

Regardless of any moral impetus countries might have to extradite Nazi criminals, until now there has been no legal one. That may change. On May 12, Sen. Gordon Smith (R-Ore.) introduced the World War II War Crimes Accountability Act of 2008, which would require the U.S. to evaluate foreign countries' cooperation in extraditing or prosecuting Nazi criminals the U.S. wants deported. Assistance or lack thereof would affect a nation's visa-waiver status for business travelers and tourists.

More than 50 years after the end of World War II, it is fair to ask: Why do we care? What's the point of expending our time, effort and money -- and that of other countries -- on these old men? Why not move on? What of forgiveness?

Forgiveness or mitigation as a legal, or even a moral, concept should only be available to those who are willing to fully confess their participation in the crimes of the Nazi era and express remorse. But to date, there have been no complete confessions by the guilty and no remorse.

418

Demjanjuk, for example, continues to deny any Nazi involvement whatsoever, even in the face of incontrovertible documentary evidence unearthed after the collapse of the Soviet Union that confirmed his presence at numerous concentration camps.

Still, time is passing. In the case of these criminals, there is some irony in the fact that they have lived long enough to be exposed for who they were and what they did.

If no country accepts them before they die, at least they won't pass from this Earth as innocents. It may not be final justice, but it is some comfort.

Five days later, coincidence or not, Germany announced they would take Demjanjuk and try him for the murders committed while he was at Sobibor beginning March 26, 1943 and until his transfer to Flossenburg in October 1943.

At the beginning of March 2009, Germany issued an arrest warrant for Demjanjuk. The following week, officials from Germany's Foreign Office, the Ministry of Justice and the Ministry of the Interior met to determine arrangements for bringing him to Germany. They decided that Demjanjuk should be transported to Germany on a civilian plane, not a military transport, and flown to Munich not Berlin.

A doctor and a police officer would accompany him, and the stateless Demjanjuk would need an identity document. The US issued such a document and Germany agreed they would let him enter the country with the document although he would have no visa.

The US authorities, in the interim, as they awaited Demjanjuk's eventual deportation, fitted him with an ankle bracelet. Nonetheless, Demjanjuk's family continued to insist he was too sick to stand trial. In court filings and statements to the press, Demjanjuk argued that to make him stand trial would amount to "torture."

John Jr told Spiegel that he "thinks it odd that the Germans, of all people, want to pursue his father now. The Germans against whom his father had to fight in the Red Army. The Germans, who let him vegetate under cruel conditions in captivity. The Germans, who abducted his mother from her homeland at the age of 16 and brought her to Berlin as a forced laborer," he said. "And the Germans now want to rob my father's home again?"

Nonetheless, German news reported that Demjanjuk's deportation was imminent. A German police officer and doctor had been flown to the US to accompany Demjanjuk. He was scheduled to leave that Sunday.

However, the Friday night before, Demjanjuk defense attorney John Broadley was able to get Demjanjuk a last-minute reprieve from Judge Wayne Iskra, an Immigration Court in Arlington, VA. who scheduled a health check on Demjanjuk to make sure he was fit enough to travel and stand trial.

In Germany, Dr. Ulrich Busch, took on Demjanjuk's defense. Busch, then 68, was a criminal defense attorney with more than 35 years of experience. Tall, broadly built man, with a white beard, Busch's brow was deeply furrowed and there were deep bags under his eyes, but his face nonetheless alternately went from pleased to gravely serious and indignant.

When interviewed by Scott Raab for Esquire, Busch found the German agreement to accept Demjanjuk for trial, "Sickening."

"It's a complete inhuman tragedy," Busch told Raab. "I never saw a case which touched me so much. I deal with drug dealers, murderers — everything criminal. But they are young or middle-aged, not old people, and they never have suffered so much in their life like he did."

Busch told Raab that his wife, a Ukrainian-American from Michigan, had known of Demjanjuk's case from its early days.

"I heard the first time about Demjanjuk in '86," Busch told Raab.. "I said to my wife, 'This guy I want to defend.' It took me twenty-three years of waiting to get the case."

It appeared Demjanjuk had found his German Sheftel.

Busch wasted no time in demanding of Germany's Minister of Justice that Demjanjuk's deportation be stopped immediately.

Holding Demjanjuk in isolation in a German Jail, Busch argued, would be a violation of Germany's Basic Law and of Human Rights. Further, Busch argued, Germany should not be allowed to deport Demjanjuk to Germany. If they want to try him, they should apply to extradite him and the German Courts should then hold extradition proceedings (which would have bought Demjanjuk several years of delay).

The German press noted the irony of Busch arguing about human rights in a case where a person was accused of participating in at least 29,000 murders.

The Demjanjuk case proceeded like this on two tracks: One in the United States to deport Demjanjuk; and one, in Germany, to receive and try him.

In the U.S., Demjanjuk had been served an arrest warrant and had later been taken into custody, led out of his home in a wheelchair and taken to a federal building in Cleveland, pending his deportation to Germany.

In April a US Immigration Department Appeals Committee found the deportation could proceed. However, Broadley requested an emergency stay at the US Court of Appeals in Cincinnati, claiming that Demjanjuk's medical condition was so grave that he couldn't travel to Germany.

On April 24, however, John Caniglia, a reporter for

Cleveland's Plain Dealer reported that US prosecutors had submitted video to the Court showing that Demjanjuk was in much better health than he or his attorneys were claiming.

The April 6th video shows the 89-year-old Demjanjuk walking briskly, talking animatedly and getting in and out of a car unaided – like a man twenty years younger.

This was in marked contrast to Demjanjuk's arrest that found him groaning in pain as agents carried him in a wheelchair from his home on April 14.

The prosecutors submitted this as evidence that Demjanjuk was fit to fly to Germany. An affidavit was also submitted from Aaron Roby, one of the agents who accompanied Demjanjuk from the Federal building where he was being held. "I helped him climb into the pickup truck, a Ford F-150, with a rather high seat," immigration agent Aaron Roby wrote . "He had no more difficulty than I would expect from someone his age getting into the truck, and he scooted over once he climbed in."

The Court withdrew their objection to Demjanjuk being deported.

On May 1, Busch sued the Federal Ministry of Justice to have Germany withdraw their agreement to accept Demjanjuk's deportation. The German Court rejected his motion.

In the United States, Demjanjuk turned for final mercy to the Supreme Court.

Justice John Paul Stevens, acting for the US Supreme Court, rejected Demjanjuk's application to the Court without further comment.

John Broadley, admitting that Demjanjuk's legal options were exhausted, said,, "We did everything we could."

Demjanjuk was not the first accused Nazi War Criminal to

be deported from the United States to Germany.

By 2009, the United States had denaturalized and deported to Germany more than 25 persons for lying about their Nazi past (including Hermine Braunsteiner Ryan). Over the years Germany had been accused of leniency in their prosecutions of former Nazi war Criminals (Braunsteiner, for example, was convicted of life imprisonment in 1981 but released in 1996 for "health reasons" before dying three years later).

The Demjanjuk case, many hoped, would be different.

On a clear warm spring evening in Cleveland, Demjanjuk was taken in an ambulance to Burke, a private airport. There he was loaded onto a twin engine G4 Gulfstream with the call letters N250LB, a small white jet with a blue stripe along its side and on its tail.

At 7:13 PM the plane took off, circled Cleveland and Lake Erie and headed Northeast.

It would be Demjanjuk's last glimpse of Cleveland.

3. A Historic Prison

Shortly after 9AM the following day, as morning mist hung over Munich, the plane landed at Munich airport and taxied to a Lufthansa cargo bay. Police cars and ambulances waited for Demjanjuk there.

This time Demjanjuk did not ask to kiss the ground, or even to sit in the waiting van. There were no waves to reporters, no joking with his guards.

Instead, an ambulance of the Bavarian Red Cross carried Demjanjuk who reclined on a cot inside with oxygen tubes in his nose. Shortly after 11 AM, the ambulance arrived at Munich's Stadelheim Prison.

Jochen Menzel, the deputy Prison head, said Demjanjuk was to be held with another wheelchair user in a 215 square foot community custody room with its own sink and toilet. According to the German daily Die Bild ("Bild") it was "twice the size of other cells." The shower was in the hallway. There was also a prison library with Ukrainian and Russian books that Demjanjuk could borrow.

Stadelheim is one of Bavaria's largest prison facilities, but it only holds approximately 1600 prisoners at any time.

Bild, a German tabloid news organization that is the best-selling European newspaper with the 16th largest circulation worldwide, described Demjanjuk as enjoying a "sumptuous breakfast" every day.

At noon, Bild wrote, there is a light meal at lunch from the prison such as Vegetable stew with tofu. Fridays, the paper noted, is "cream herring with tomato soup and boiled potatoes.... Salad accompanies every warm meal."

Stadelheim Prison is also historically significant. It was at Stadelheim that Adolf Hitler was imprisoned between June 24 and July 27, 1922, having been sentenced to three months for breach of the peace for assaulting Otto Ballerstedt, one of his political rivals. It was also where Hitler, once in power, would later imprison and execute both Ernest Rohm (of "the Night of the Long Knives") and Sophie Scholl (leader of the White Rose resistance movement).

Upon his arrival at Stadelheim, Demjanjuk was read his 21-page arrest warrant, first in German, then in English and Ukrainian.

Demjanjuk was next examined by a doctors who, according to Deputy Prison head Menzel, determined that Demjanjuk's health was stable and "better than you can expect in an 89-year-old."

4. Preparing for the German Trial

With Demjanjuk now in Germany, Busch sued the court again to have the charges against Demjanjuk dismissed, which they rejected.

Busch appealed to the District Court of Munich and the Munich Higher Regional Court, arguing that the evidence against Demjanjuk was not sufficient to prosecute him: There were no living eyewitnesses to Demjanjuk being at Sobibor, and second, the Trawniki card was of no evidentiary value because its chain of custody indicates it comes from the former Soviet Union. However, The Federal Constitutional Court in Karlsruhe ruled Demjanjuk's deportation from the US as legal.

Busch also argued that Germany had set a past precedent by only trying those who committed "excessive actions." Accordingly, as Demjanjuk was merely a Wachmann, a guard, with no evidence of his personal and excessive actions, they could not try him.

The Munich Regional Court disagreed saying that the established practice of German courts in cases relating to SS overseers and guards in extermination camps "does not create a precedent." The court noted that Demjanjuk's arrest warrant made clear that Demjanjuk as a guard was not compelled to participate in mass murder. "He could have deserted, as many other Trawniki men did."

Nonetheless, there was general agreement that Demjanjuk's age mandated that they act as fast as possible. Anton Winkler, spokesman for the Munich Public Prosecutor's office said they would hurry to produce an indictment.

"Demjanjuk is old. Every day counts," warned Kurt Schrimm, the German prosecutor who headed Germany's Nazi prosecution division in Ludwigsburg.

Within days after his arrival Demjanjuk had a gout attack. His blood count levels were deemed too low. Doctors determined he needed to be treated at Harlaching Hospital. The Doctors there examined him thoroughly. After treating him, it was their finding that Demjanjuk was fit to stand trial but they recommended that, given his condition and his age, court time per day and per week be limited to 90 minutes per day.

Demjanjuk was returned to Stadelheim prison to await trial. According to Spiegel,. Demjanjuk had few phone calls from home. Demjanjuk had been told not to speak about his case, Spiegel reported, because there was always an interpreter on the line. Instead, the newsweekly said, his wife Vera, then 84, only spoke about their garden at home.

Thomas Walther, together with Karin Goetze, spent four months preparing the indictment, which was submitted in final form by Munich prosecutor Dr. Hans Joachim Lutz.

Dr. Lutz, a-then-fit-40-year-old, began his career as a public prosecutor, before being transferred to the Federal Prosecutor's Criminal Division. Since June 2006, Lutz had worked as a group leader for prosecutions at the Munich prosecutor's office working on political, criminal cases, press crimes, and crimes of the Nazi era. At trial Lutz would be joined by Thomas Steinkrauch-Koch.

On July 13, 2009, the Munich Public Prosecutor's office filed its 186 page-indictment against Demjanjuk accusing him of aiding and abetting in the murders of at least 27,900 persons.

In marked contrast to defense claims that Demjanjuk was merely a prisoner of war of the Nazis who had no choice but to participate, the indictment asserted that Demjanjuk had many opportunities to flee from Trawniki, Lublin, or even Sobibor, as many other Trawniki men had done.

The indictment against Demjanjuk was novel in several respects. The German authorities argued that as Demjanjuk served the Nazis, he was in effect a member of the German civil service and therefore, the German Court had jurisdiction over him. Nazi-Occupied Poland was at that time designated "The General Gouvernment" that, as such, was a German political entity.

More importantly, this was also the first prosecution of a Nazi who was not being accused of "excessive acts" but rather of being part of the machinery of death – even at the lowest rung of participation as a death camp guard.

According to the indictment, Demjanjuk was one of the five thousand Trawniki men who served as "the foot soldiers" of the Holocaust. The Sobibor camp, it noted, had only one function: the extermination of those persons brought there, almost exclusively Jewish men, women and children, As the camp had no other purpose, the indictment said that under German Law every person working there, from the Germans in charge, to the lowliest guards, were all complicit and party to the murders committed there.

This was a remarkable statement and represented a monumental shift in German Law and prosecutions that would allow for many more cases to be made against those who participated as accomplices in the Nazi's death factories.

What this meant was that even if there were no eyewitness or documentary evidence of Demjanjuk actually murdering any individuals, his presence as a guard there meant he was part of the conspiracy to murder the Jewish unfortunates whose lives ended there. As concerned the Wachmann at Sobibor, the indictment alleged, "All herded Jews to their death."

The indictment also noted that there was historical evidence that while other Trawniki men deserted, Demjanjuk stayed of his own accord; and they referenced the testimony of

Danylchenko who stated that Demjanjuk was an "experienced guard who assisted in the gassing of Jews at Sobibor."

During the Summer of 1943 while Demjanjuk worked at Sobibor, the indictment stated, some 45,000 Jews were murdered there, most of whom came in transports from Holland. Of these, Demjanjuk was charged with the murder of almost 29,000 Jewish inmates whose names were recorded in train transport lists during the time Demjanjuk served at Sobibor

Busch denounced the indictment saying it "upends the entire postwar legal practice in Germany." Busch argued that so Germany could no longer be accused of inaction or leniency toward former Nazis, it was changing the law to make up for its past failures.

Guenther Maull was assigned as Demjanjuk's public defender in the Munich Court, joining Busch in the defense of Demjanjuk.

Demjanjuk's defense was simple, according to Busch: The Trawniki card is a forgery; and Demjanjuk was not at Sobibor. Busch also made the argument that even if Demjanjuk was at Sobibor (hypothetically speaking), it was only because he heard that Trawniki men who deserted were killed; and that he was in no way involved in gassings. Beyond that, Busch asked that the Court consider Demjanjuk's advanced age and the fact he had already spent seven years in an Israeli prison, five of which were on death row.

5. The Victims' Place in the Trial Process

Another distinctive aspect of German law was that it allowed for first-degree relatives of victims to join the lawsuit not as independent claimants but as auxiliary prosecutors or co-plaintiffs with full access to the prosecutors' files. These co-plaintiffs, called *Neborklung* in German, may call and examine witnesses, file documents, deliver statements, and make recommendations to the Court as to the appropriate judgement or sentence for the accused if convicted.

Twenty-three Dutch citizens(many of whom were hidden as children during the war and were now in their Sixties) decided to participate in the trial representing their relatives murdered at Sobibor during the period Demjanjuk served there. Another ten persons, who were contacted by the Sobibor Foundation, also agreed to take part in the trial. At a later date, nine more non-Dutch nationals (four of whom were Sobibor survivors) joined the proceedings. All in all, more than thirty persons took part in the prosecution, the most in German legal history to participate as co-plaintiffs in a Nazi war crimes trial.

"We wanted to give voice to the victims," Professor Cornelius Nestler, a criminal law professor in Cologne, who was representing the Dutch victims' relatives, told the Israeli daily Haaretz. "It is, after all, impossible to understand 27,000 murder victims from them, but it is possible to understand and identify with each case individually. We did not want the attention to be focused on the 'old man' Demjanjuk - who is on trial for the second time - but rather on the deeds for which he is responsible."

Kurt Guttmann, then 82, was one of the co-plaintiffs in the case. His parents put him on a kindertransport to England, where he spent the war years in Scotland. He never saw his mother again. He returned to Berlin in 1945 as a British solider, and in 1948 settled in Berlin. It was not until 1996 that he learned that his mother died in Sobibor. Guttman had strong feelings regarding Demjanjuk. He told Bild, "I despise the man because he debased himself by being an accomplice to [the] murders. And later denied it with excuses. I want justice for my family ... "

Rudie Cortissos, 70, was just a baby in 1943 in Amsterdam when his parents went into hiding and handed him to a gentile family for safe keeping. One day his mother, Emmy, who suffered from asthma left the hiding place to get some fresh air. A neighbor saw her and denounced her to the police who arrested her, sending her to the Westerbrook Transit camp. Before she was loaded on the transport to Westerbrook she managed to throw a letter in the street that found its way to Rudie's father.

She promised to stay strong. From Westerbrook, she managed to send a final letter which said they were being sent East to work. She believed it, writing that she would survive and return to them. Instead, she arrived at Sobibor and was murdered there.

"I have been cutting articles about Demjanjuk out of the newspapers since the 1970s," Cortissos told Haaretz. "I have researched Sobibor to the best of my ability and the moment I heard about Demjanjuk's extradition I contacted the organization for the perpetuation of the memory of Sobibor victims in Holland and within 24 hours they told me about the prosecutors' group."

Cortissos gave this reason for joining the prosecution as co-plaintiff:

"This I am doing for my mother," he said.

Before the trial started Bild reached out to Judge Dalia Dorner, then 75, about her opinions concerning Demjanjuk and his prior Israeli trial, particularly as she was part of the panel that convicted him of being "Ivan the Terrible" and sentenced him to the death penalty in 1988 (the verdict and the sentence having been overturned by the Israel Supreme Court, as described earlier).

Said Dorner: "I have no doubt that the man who stood before us was Ivan the Terrible." She added that, "The testimonies of the survivors were very credible. One testified that he sees Ivan's face every night in his nightmares, and that he will never forget it. "

Judge Dorner recalled to Bild that, "For a whole year, when the trial took place, I came home with this terrible emotional burden. It was a very difficult, terrible and horrible time. I now expect the end of this affair once and for all. "

"As the judge in the case of Ivan the Terrible," Dorner said, "I have no doubt that he was a guard in Treblinka. He was only set free because of the legal process in this country... In my court room, I heard his victims identify him and I knew that he was guilty." She found the Trawniki card authentic as well "It has always been clear to me that this person, according to all the information and testimonies I heard, was in both Sobibor and Treblinka."

In a subsequent interview, several years later in Israel for *Kan Reshet Bet* Dorner elaborated, "Eichmann was a murderer behind the writing desk, Ivan the Terrible murdered with his own hands, he would operate the gas chambers, the cruelest of the cruel. Dorner reiterated that over the years 11 persons had identified Demjanjuk as being in Treblinka. "Among the identifiers was an SS Man [Otto Horn] who identified him and could not forget him," she said, Horn "was afraid to come to Israel lest we put him on trial, so the entire court went to Berlin to interrogate him."

By contrast, Sheftel when contacted by the press would only reiterate that, "The Supreme Court unanimously decided that Demjanjuk was innocent." Sheftel continued to maintain that the German Court did not have enough evidence to convict him.

Over the years since Demjanjuk's Israeli trial, Sheftel had continued to be a very vocal and outspoken critic of the Israeli establishment and the Israeli left. So much so that he became the host of a popular radio talk show on Tel Aviv's 103FM, called "Sheftel Atzbani" [Sheftel is Cranky].

At the same time, RT, the Russian government-funded news service reported that legislators in Ukraine had passed a resolution in support of Demjanjuk. Rotislav Novozhenets, a legislator in Lviv, appeared on air to say, "Ukrainians must stand up to protect a Ukrainian who for three decades has been accused of crimes he never committed. We asked the President and the Foreign Ministry to provide legal help and stop the prosecution of Demjanjuk. We believe the case is fabricated and is a conspiracy of Zionists against Ukraine as well an evil agreement between Russia and Germany."

6. Demjanjuk's Munich Trial begins

Demjanjuk's Munich Trial had been scheduled to commence November 30, 2009 at 10AM in Room 101A of Munich's Criminal Justice Center, a courtroom regularly used for criminal matters. The German Justice Ministry and the Munich Prosecutor's office were determined to treat Demjanjuk's trial as a normal criminal matter, and avoid the optics of the Jerusalem trial, set as it was on a stage in a convention auditorium.

The trial was expected to only last 35 days. Room 101A was the largest courtroom in the building and its bright orange cloth seats would become familiar to many of the victims' families who would attend the trial.

Nonetheless, the Court was unprepared for the crowds that appeared on the first day, hoping to get a seat at the trial. The security check entrance procedures for each person ended up delaying the trial's start by almost an hour.

More than 200 journalists from all over the world had registered for press credentials for Demjanjuk's trial. The Prosecutor's Office had only allocated a certain number of seats in the courtroom for print and online journalists and some for TV and radio, but the room could not accommodate them all.

Demjanjuk was brought into the Munich courthouse in a wheelchair to a blaze of flash photos and media. Wearing a blue baseball cap and clutching a blue blanket, Demjanjuk seemed to want to be anywhere other than the courtroom.

In contrast to his Israeli trial, Demjanjuk had no shout-outs to home, no cries of "Gut Morgen! Or 'Hello Cleveland!'. Instead, Demjanjuk sat in silence with his eyes closed showing no expression. His mouth occasionally fell open. Sometimes, he moaned softly or moistened his lips. Busch said Demjanjuk was in constant pain and was "mentally absent."

Presiding Judge Ralph Alt, opened the trial by apologizing for the delay. Bald, with a fringe of close cropped-dark hair, he wore a black cloak over a shirt and white tie, Alt greeted the room in low-key fashion.

Alt was joined on the Judicial panel hearing by two associate judges, Helga Pluger and Thomas Lenz. As per German Law there were also two lay observers, called *Schoffen*, who are allowed to ask questions. A guilty verdict requires a two-thirds majority, and thus, Schoffen have the power to block a Judge's guilty verdict (it occurs rarely, if ever).

At the first opportunity, Busch called on the Judges to disqualify themselves for prejudice and because the prosecution of Demjanjuk was completely arbitrary. Busch found it improper that when Germany had tried the Germans who ran Sobibor they received lesser sentences than the time Demjanjuk had already spent in jail over the years in the US, Israel, and Germany.

"How can it be that the commanders are found innocent, while those who were following their orders are guilty?" As Busch saw it, the Court was subjecting Demjanjuk to a "moral and legal double standard."

Busch argued that even if Demjanjuk was at Sobibor as a guard, he was forced to follow the German's orders under penalty of death. To Busch, Demjanjuk was as much a victim of the Germans as the camp's prisoners. Like the camp's Jewish inmates, Busch said, Demjanjuk did what he had to, to survive -- which put him, Busch said, "on the same level" as the Jewish prisoners there. Busch said this, knowing full well how it would offend the victims' families.

Judge Alt announced a stay of the proceedings and recessed the Court hearing to consider and respond to Busch's motions.

Asked for comment on the trial by phone, John Jr. told

Spiegel that, "We know in our hearts that my father has never harmed anyone, and we know from this evidence that there is absolutely no evidence that he harmed anyone."

In a further statement released to Reuters, John, Jr., was quoted saying much as Busch had, that "We will prove that a Ukrainian prisoner of war who escaped death by starvation, was forced to be a Trawniki, who could be shot if he tried to escape and against whom there is no evidence of a specific atrocity is also a victim and comparable to the Jewish survivor who worked in death machine of Sobibor in order to avoid death."

In Germany, different news publications often reflect distinct and different political sensibilities. However, in the case of Demjanjuk, the German press was in agreement: Putting John Demjanjuk on trial in Germany was important and a landmark occurrence. Spiegel gathered the opinions across the spectrum as follows:

The Center-left Süddeutsche Zeitung wrote that: "John Demjanjuk must be prosecuted if he is fit to stand trial. That's a medical question. And he must be convicted if the charges against him can be proven. That is a legal question. He must be convicted even if other former camp guards weren't put on trial or won't be put on trial. The severity of the punishment doesn't matter. If punishing a sick old man is deemed unreasonable, he should be spared. What's important is that the truth is established.

"While the conservative Frankfurter Allgemeine Zeitung said: "Each of these trials is a signal for Germany and the world: The country -- like probably no other -- is taking its historical responsibility seriously. The determined search for the perpetrators and the trials of aged defendants are the result of the decision to remove murder from the statute of limitations. The defense attorney's insistence that a low-ranking henchman is being prosecuted while the commanders were acquitted only indicates that there are no easy answers here."

Bild, the mass-circulation tabloid daily, opined that: "The behavior of the defense attorneys of SS henchman Demjanjuk must leave all civilized people bewildered, speechless and disgusted. Saying the defendant is 'a victim of the Holocaust himself' is like killing the murdered victims a second time."

Finally, the Left-wing publication Die Tageszeitung wrote: "The trial of John Ivan Demjanjuk is a first. For the first time, a suspected foreign henchman who helped the Nazis commit the genocide of the Jews is being put on trial in Germany. The fact that that is only happening now is an embarrassment to Germany's post-war justice system. Sparing Demjanjuk the prosecution due to his advanced age would have given retroactive justification for the sleepyhead prosecutors of the Adenauer era (editor's note: Konrad Adenauer was West Germany's first chancellor, from 1949 until 1963). As long as Demjanjuk is fit to stand trial, the same applies to him as everyone else, as there is no statute of limitations on murder."

Two days later, when court resumed, Judge Alt dismissed Busch's motion to end the trial and to release Demjanjuk. Busch was offended when his co-counsel Guenther Maull did not further protest the Court's decision. "Get out of the case if you think only the judge is right!"

Maull paid this no mind, announcing that he would continue to fulfill his court-appointed mandate to represent Demjanjuk.

Demjanjuk had spent the first court sessions in a wheelchair, wearing a baseball camp and with a blanket draped over himself. On the third day, trial was suspended because Demjanjuk had an elevated temperature.

"I think he's completely unfit to stand trial," Demjanjuk's defense attorney Busch told reporters. "He's weak, he has pain, and it will be impossible for him to remember on the fifth day of the trial what was said on the third day. There is no real chance to defend himself."

Demjanjuk's Munich trial with its abbreviated and canceled sessions and many delays, moved forward at a snail's pace with Demjanjuk attending but rarely fully present. Demjanjuk often complained that he didn't feel well and didn't want to come to trial.

Most trial days began with Busch submitting a litany of motions and complaints, the overwhelming majority of which the Judges dismissed.

Judge Alt insisted that Demjanjuk be present at his trial. So, a cot was set up in court for Demjanjuk to lie on. It was near the Judge and not far from the witnesses but Demjanjuk would not look at anyone. Instead he pulled his baseball cap down, wore dark sunglasses and pulled his blanket up around him, sometimes even covering his head with it.

With Demjanjuk on his cot, a translator stood nearby whispering Ukrainian into a headset that was transmitted to Demjanjuk's ears by headphone. When Demjanjuk was in Court, his desire not to be there, his psychic battle to avoid the facts of this case, made the spectacle of Demjanjuk in the dock that much less compelling.

Demjanjuk presented himself entirely differently than he did in Jerusalem. There, he was jovial, happy, and at moments, defiant. Here, he was diminished, hobbled by the truths he had been unable to outrun.

However, just as the survivor testimony riveted the nation and the press in Jerusalem, it was the testimony of the victims and their relatives that brought the press and crowds back to Court and spurred media interest in Germany, Holland, and from press the world over.

7. The Love of his Life

Philip Jacobs's parents and his 21-year-old fiancée Ruth had been deported from Westerbork in July 1943. Jacobs, 87 at the time of Demjanjuk's German trial, told the Court that they were sent to the gas chambers immediately after their arrival in Sobibor.

"I lost the love of my life," Jacobs said weeping, the loss still keen some 65 years later. His 23-year-old sister was murdered in Auschwitz, and friends of his died in the Mauthausen concentration camp.

"I often torment myself thinking about why I survived, why I left my family alone," Jacobs said.

Robert Cohen, then 83, later testified that his life was saved because when his parents and brother were ordered to board trains to Sobibor, he had been ordered to stuff straw in mattresses at Westerbrook..

"I also wanted to be deported," Cohen said. "We were very naive at the time... I thought I would see my family again." Cohen would later himself be sent to Auschwitz.

Many of those testifying were alive because they were hidden as children, while their families were rounded up by the Nazis and their collaborators and deported, first to Westerbrook and from there to Sobibor.

Max Degen from Amsterdam recalled that he was saved because, as a six-year-old, he was put inside a suitcase and thrown over the ghetto wall. His parents and his three-year-old brother were not able to escape and so ended their lives in the gas chambers at Sobibor.

Jules Schelvis, 88, grew up Poland. After the Nazis, he and his extended family were forced by the Nazis to move to the Radom Jewish Ghetto.

At first, Schelvis thought he would be able to survive in the ghetto because he found work as a printer. However, in November 1943, the Nazis decided to liquidate the ghetto. They arrived with tanks and machine guns: "Young children and old men were shot dead in the street," Schelvis recalled. "That's what I saw," Schelvis began to sob. "I cannot talk about what I saw," he said his voice cracking.

Schelvis was then deported to Amsterdam. As the Germans had allowed him to bring a knapsack and a guitar, he thought life there might be better. However, in Amsterdam the Germans told him, "You're going to work in the East." From Amsterdam Schelvis and his extended family were taken to the Westerbork transit camp. From there they were put on freight cars to Sobibor.

They stood during the entire four-day ride, Schelvis recalled. "There was not enough room to sit." Upon first seeing Sobibor, Schelvis regained hope, briefly, thinking: "That did not look so bad, you saw wooden houses with curtains and flowers," he said.

However, in an instant, SS and Ukrainian guards surrounded the wagons. The prisoners were made to drop off their luggage immediately. Men and women were separated.

"Young children and old men were shot dead on the spot"

Because Schelvis spoke German, was 22 years old and in good health, he and his brother-in-law were immediately assigned to a work crew.

Schelvis would later learn that the women were shaved bald, and that the men were led directly into the gas chamber to be asphyxiated by the fumes from a diesel tank engine." That took about 25 minutes," Schelvis said. On that first day 2800 persons were gassed, Schelvis later learned from other inmates.

"We saw that the Ukrainian security guards were worse than the SS," Schelvis told the Munich Courtroom.

After the war, Schelvis would learn that twenty more of his relatives had been murdered in Auschwitz.

8. Demjanjuk's Roommate

Busch objected to the *Neborklung*, the family member co-prosecutors because, as he saw it, they could contribute no actual evidence regarding the charges against Demjanjuk.

Busch seemed to delight in making provocative statements or offending the victims' families. Busch called the deaths of captured Soviet soldiers in German POW camps, "the first Holocaust," equating their deaths with the mass murder of the Jews in Nazi death camps.

Referring to the deaths of Soviet soldiers, Busch said, "Unfortunately, the postwar justice in Germany shrouds the cloak of silence and oblivion about this Holocaust."

At one point, Busch tried to get Schelvis to speak of the Jewish Kapos (this is a very tired canard that revisionists delight in, claiming that the Jews in camps were the same as the guards because there were Jewish Kapos or policemen in the camps).

Busch asked Schelvis: "Was the Jewish police worse than the Nazis in your opinion?"

When Busch was asked his source for such a charge, he said he had read it somewhere. However, when pressed to name his source, he could not recall where he read it. However, Busch offered that, "If you google it, you'll find it,"

After each court session, Busch continued to rail to the Press about Demjanjuk being the victim of an "international justice conspiracy" and again demanded that the Court immediately suspend the proceedings for bias and due to the arbitrariness of the judges.

Despite Demjanjuk's German prosecution being a domestic criminal matter, it still held international ramifications, and spoke to Israel's ongoing relationship with Germany.

On the 65th Anniversary of the liberation of Auschwitz, Israeli President Shimon Peres, then 86, flew to Germany to address the German parliament, the Bundestag.

Peres, the third Israeli head of State to address the Bundestag (after Ezer Weizmann and Moshe Katzav) spoke in Hebrew saying in part, "In the state of Israel, and across the world," survivors of the Holocaust are gradually departing from the world of the living...."

"At the same time," Peres said, "Men and women who took part in the most odious activity on earth -- that of genocide -- still live on German and European soil and in other parts of the world. My request of you is: Please do everything to bring them to justice."

On February 23, 2010, 93-year-old Alex Nagorny took the stand. Thin, with grey wisps of hair, he walked into the courtroom slowly but unaided, alternating the hand in which he held his cane. He did not make eye contact with Demjanjuk, who lay on a bed next to the door through which he entered. He testified in Ukrainian.

Like Demjanjuk, Nagorny had been a Soviet soldier who became a German POW during World War Two. At the time of his capture, he said, he had no idea he would become a concentration camp guard. He agreed to serve the Germans when recruited to stave off hunger.

"I was simply asked if I wanted to work and I was hungry," the 92-year-old testified. "That was all."

Nagorny said he had been taken from the Chelm POW camp to Trawniki. At Trawniki, he testified, he was trained in weapons but he never used them. He was assigned to guard an aircraft factory in Rostock where forced laborers were used. He was then sent to Flossenburg.

"We were brought there and Ivan was already there," the 92-year-old testified, referring to Demjanjuk by his first name.

"He was a guard there. He did the same thing I did. I did not know him before Flossenburg."

Nagorny has previously told investigators he arrived at Flossenburg with Demjanjuk.

Nagorny testified he lived with Demjanjuk in a barracks in Flossenburg and then shared an apartment with him in Landshut, Germany, after the war.

A former SS Wachmann, he recognized Demjanjuk from the pictures of a younger Demjanjuk on the Trawniki card in the press and also from TV. "He did the same as me. We were security guards," he said.

Official Nazi Guard Rosters (which had been submitted to the U.S. District Court in Cleveland in 2001 and authenticated) show Demjanjuk and Nagorny as serving at Flossenburg in 1944.

A duty roster from the camp shows that on October 4, 1944, Nagorny, Guard 477, was assigned to carry a rifle and guard inmates as they worked on a water-supply system. On the same day, Guard 393, by name of Demjanjuk, carried a rifle as inmates built a bunker (In his testimony in Israel, Demjanjuk had said his activity while a POW consisted at one point of building a barracks).

In court, Nagorny was asked to identify Demjanjuk. Nagorny walked over to the bed where Demjanjuk lay and looked at him closely. When Demjanjuk removed the sunglasses that he was wearing, Nagorny said quickly: "That's definitely not him. No resemblance."

"I cannot recognize him," Nagorny said, looking at the defendant. "He was slimmer back then."

Thomas Walther thought that Nagorny's testimony was nonetheless valuable. "Here is a living witness who can say, 'I was a Trawniki man and with me was Demjanjuk who was also a Trawniki man,'" Walther told The Associated Press. "That's important here because Demjanjuk says he was not a Trawniki (man)."

At the same time, the television accounts of Demjanjuk's trial were proving a boon to finding more witnesses. In February 2010, Alexei Vaitzen, a then 87-year old Russian living in Ryazan, claimed that he was a Holocaust survivor who had escaped Sobibor during the uprising. In a radio interview, he said that he recognized Demjanjuk as part of the camp personnel at Sobibor.

Nonetheless Vaitzen was never called as a witness due to the failing nature of his memory. Time was not on the prosecution's side.

On May 14th, 2010, Bild called Demjanjuk's court behavior – lying on a cot, moaning softly, pleading seriously illness, "cheap theater." According to the paper, Demjanjuk's prison behavior was far different.

"He walks up and down the room as normal. Often goes alone out of the cell. When we saw the pictures from the courtroom, how he is there, we only laughed, "Bild reported.

"Once he had even demonstrated in prison how he marched as a soldier," the newspaper wrote. "Me now Admiral," Demjanjuk reported said in broken German and laughed.

9. Something No One Imagined Happening in Germany

Thomas Blatt, 82, who was at that time one of the few living survivors of Sobibor (he passed away in 2015 at age 88), testified at Demjanjuk's trial in early January 2010.

Blatt had long lived in the Santa Barbara area where he had a car audio business. I had interviewed him in the 1980s after Demjanjuk's Israeli District Court trial. He had told me then that although he was at Sobibor at the same time that the Trawniki Card alleged Demjanjuk was there, he did not recognize him.

About the guards, he told me, "We were more afraid of them than of the Germans."

Blatt had said that while sorting through the murdered persons' clothing he sometimes found money or gold which they would give to the Ukrainian guards to curry favor with them. The guards would then spend the money on their excursions outside of Sobibor, in the neighboring villages.

At the Munich trial, Blatt testified that he arrived at Sobibor in April 1943, and worked in Camp One sorting victims' belongings. He had no access to the death camp.

When Defense attorney Busch asked him details of certain of the camp buildings, Blatt responded angrily that the did not have time to look around.

"I was a prisoner," he said. "Every second we were threatened with death."

Busch would later tell the press that Blatt had only testified to boost sales of his memoir.

Blatt testified that there was no division of labor among the Trawniki men. The guards all did all the camp's murderous tasks from the moment the Jewish victims arrived by train to after their deaths when their bodies were incinerated. All the guards took part in herding Jews to the gas chamber.

Demjanjuk spent the entirety of Blatt's testimony lying on his cot in court with his baseball cap pulled down and his blanket pulled up high.

Philip Bialowitz, 84, who was also one of the few remaining survivors of Sobibor, also testified. Born in the Polish town of Izbica, he was deported to Sobibor where he worked for six months until the revolt. Bialowitz told the Court that the Jews arriving at Sobibor had no idea what awaited them, and he was forbidden from telling them.

"When I helped the Jewish passengers with their bags, some of them offered me a tip," Bialowitz said. "My heart was bleeding because I knew that they would be dead in less than an hour and I couldn't warn them." He often had to unload decomposed dead bodies from the trains.

Although Bialowitz, like Blatt, didn't recognize Demjanjuk, he also testified that there was no division of labor among the guards at Sobibor; they all participated in the various stages leading to the murder of Jews at Sobibor.

Still, Judge Alt, along with the prosecutors and Dr. Nestler on behalf of the *neborklung* achieved something that no one would have imagined occurring in a German courtroom: They gave dignity to the survivors. They showed them respect and allowed them to speak and be heard.

Demjanjuk's defense contention was that even if he had been a guard at Sobibor, he only did what he was ordered to do — upon penalty of death. There was no evidence, Busch argued, that Demjanjuk committed excessive actions or exceeded authority, and no evidence that he wasn't just acting on orders.

However, the Prosecution called Dr. Peter Black, formerly with the Office for Special Investigations in the U.S. Justice

Department and now with the U.S. Holocaust Memorial Museum in Washington, to present historical evidence that many Trawniki men left their ranks without permission of their superiors. He offered documentary proof that the Trawniki men were no longer prisoners (and with regard to Demjanjuk's question at his Israeli trial about uniforms Black testified that they wore Polish uniforms that were dyed black and at a later date Belgian uniforms).

Black even introduced documents showing that Wachmann at Sobibor were given pay increases for their murderous work (which conforms to Demjanjuk saying on his Visa application that during the war years he earned 40 Zlotys a week at Sobibor). They had days off and even gave some leave to go home (from which some did not return). Demjanjuk evidently stayed at Sobibor during his time there of his own accord. In other words, he was a willing participant in the death factory.

German historian Dieter Pohl was called as an expert witness. Like Dr. Yitzhak Arad at Demjanjuk's Israeli trial, Pohl gave the context of the National Socialist Regime: The Final Solution; Action Rheinhardt; the operation of the three extermination camps, Belzec, Sobibor and Treblinka; and the role of the Wachmann such as Demjanjuk. Pohl's dry historical presentation left no doubt that those who were trained at Trawniki and worked at a death camp like Sobibor were partners in the mass murders. That is what they were there to do.

What was groundbreaking in the German prosecution of Demjanjuk was the argument that to convict Demjanjuk as an accessory to the murders, they did not need witnesses who saw him commit murder, or even any evidence that he personally murdered any one individual. Every person who worked at Sobibor and served there, including Demjanjuk, was complicit in all the murders that took place there.

CHAPTER TWELVE:

DER DEUTSCHE PROZESS.

1. Revisited and Re-examined

The Trawniki Card had been tested and authenticated at Demjanjuk's American trials, as well as at his Israeli trials where both The District Court and Supreme Court panels accepted the veracity of the Card in evidence. The Card was again found authentic at Demjanjuk's second denaturalization and deportation hearings. Now it was to be revisited and re-examined in the court in Munich.

Anton Dallmayer, from the Bavarian Bureau of Criminal Investigation, confirmed that the paper, inks, lead to this conclusion that the card is authentic. He compared Demjanjuk's ID to three other Trawniki and found them all the same as to material and inks.

Busch challenged this, suggesting that all four could be fakes. Busch likened Dallmayer's conclusion to saying, "I have three counterfeit dollars and I put it with a fourth [real one], does that mean I can now they are all authentic?"

Forensic expert Larry F. Stewart, checked the typewriting and paper quality of twelve Trawniki identity cards, finding them authentic as well. In addition to roster of transfers to Sobibor that also included Demjanjuk and his correct ID number was also determined to be authentic.

The Court would also later conclude that the documents'

449

authenticity was also supported by testimony of Danylchenko who, as early as 1949, identified Demjanjuk as one of the guards at Sobibor who herded the Jews to their death. Danylchenko's account was supported not only by the various other testimonies of former Trawniki but also by the various documents that listed his correct ID number along with Demjanjuk's.

2. Demjanjuk's Statement

In November 2010 on the first anniversary of the trial's opening, Demjanjuk appeared in court and following several months of silence, his lawyer Ulrich Busch read from a statement that Demjanjuk had signed.

Demjanjuk began with a thank you to "the care personnel who help me endure the great pain that I feel during this ordeal, which I consider torture." He called the accusations against him "Wrong."

"I find it an unbearable injustice that Germany, with this trial, is trying to make me out to be a war criminal, when I was a prisoner of war, and wants to use me to distance itself from its own war crimes," defense attorney Ulrich Busch read to the court on Demjanjuk's behalf. "I am, again and again, an innocent victim of the Germans."

Demjanjuk went to place the blame on Germany for making him a "slave laborer" during his captivity. Germany was also responsible, he said, for the thousands of his Ukrainian compatriots "forced to cooperate in perverse mass exterminations by violence and death threats, and the hundreds who refused were killed." Whether Demjanjuk was referring to his own service at extermination camps he did not make clear.

Demjanjuk also pointed out that he had already served seven and a half years in an Israeli prison, five on death row, for crimes for which were rejected because of mistaken identity. He also spent ten months in detention while awaiting extradition from the United States, and he had been in custody in Germany since May 12, 2009. All told, he said that he had already been behind bars for ten years.

Finally, Busch argued that if Demjanjuk was at Sobibor, he was there "under orders" or "under command" as the Germans put it.

Demjanjuk also accused Judge Ralph Alt of conducting a political "show trial." and called the trial "a mockery of Justice."

"Nazi Germany was a terrorist state that ravaged terror and violence in every stratum of society, down to everyone under its authority," Busch said.

The prosecutor's claim that an escape had been possible without greater risk, was a historical falsehood, Busch said. Most escape attempts ended in death. Busch had put together a list of about 50 Trawniki men - mostly prisoners of war of the Nazis - who were killed during or after the escape.

Busch demanded "acquittal for the defendant, release from prison and imprisonment."

3. Final Words

In early January 2011, Spain's Supreme Court announced that an indictment had been filed against Demjanjuk for genocide and war crimes, issuing an international arrest warrant for Demjanjuk, then being held in prison in Germany. Demjanjuk was accused of the murder of 50 to 155 Spanish prisoners being held at the Flossenburg camp during the period that Demjanjuk was assigned there beginning in October 1943.

At the same time, Demjanjuk's German trial was moving inexorably to its conclusion. In February 2011, Irene Nishnic visited the trial with her now grown son, Ed Nishnic, Jr, a mixed martial arts fighter, to see Demjanjuk perhaps for the last time.

On Thursday March 17th, 2011, the prosecution and defense rested in Demjanjuk's Munich Trial, after which the victims' families as co-prosecutors were allowed to make final statements.

Martin Haas, 74,who lost his mother and two siblings in Sobibor in 1943, requested to address Demjanjuk in court.

"My family was brutally murdered in this vile murder machine," Haas said. "John Demjanjuk: We were hoping that you would apologize. You're a racist scoundrel, a coward, a willing executioner of the SS. Your baseball cap and sunglasses can't shield you from their crimes."

Mary Richheimer-Leijden van Amstel, 70, whose family died in the gas chambers at Sobibor told the press: "I hope that my parents and grandparents proudly look down on me and know that I am doing something for them."

In a trial where Demjanjuk's behavior was never less than strange, a bizarre moment occurred nonetheless in early April 2011.

Some of the survivor witnesses were testifying, when Court proceedings were paused as Demjanjuk, in his wheelchair, went to use a bathroom that had been designated for him.

When Demjanjuk emerged from the bathroom, Ulrich Busch's wife was waiting for him. She greeted Demjanjuk, shook his hand, and began to sing "Happy Birthday" to him in Ukrainian (Demjanjuk had recently turned 91). The Holocaust survivors sat there dumbstruck, shocked and appalled by the inappropriateness of this celebration.

To top it all off, she then handed Demjanjuk a chocolate Easter bunny.

4. The Verdict of the Munich Court

Demjanjuk's trial in Munich lasted a total of 93 days over 17 months and finally came to its conclusion on May 12, 2011, when Judge Alt read his verdict in the case.

That morning, once again in Room 101A of Munich's Criminal Justice Center, shortly after 10 AM, a white door recessed into the far wall opened and Demjanjuk was pushed into court in his wheelchair for the last time. He was wearing a green parka with a hood, a bright gray and blue baseball hat, a grey prison sweatshirt and dark sunglasses.

Judge Alt asked Demjanjuk if he would prefer to lie down to hear the verdict. He nodded in agreement. Two paramedics then helped him to sit down on the bed. Demjanjuk sat down on the cot, took a sip of water from a plastic cup and then leaned back, lying down on his cot.

Judge Alt dismissed the most recent motions by Busch, much as he had done throughout the proceedings. The Judge then asked the prosecution and the defense if they had any final comments. The Prosecution said 'No'. Busch said 'No' and then made a joke, saying "Should I really repeat my plea?" (It had taken five days and once was enough).

Judge Alt asked Demjanjuk if he wanted to make a final statement. Everyone in the courtroom, both plain tiffs, prosecutors and the media present had been waiting the entire trial for Demjanjuk to say something. But he did not. He just said "neh" (No) to his Ukrainian translator, without even leaving his cot.

Judge Alt then began to read his verdict. As the room became increasingly sweltering, Alt recounted the facts of Demjanjuk's life, leading up to his being recruited to be trained as a death camp guard at Trawniki.

Judge Alt affirmed the veracity and authenticity of the Trawniki card calling it the "most spectacular" piece of evidence in ascertaining Demjanjuk's Nazi service and his participation in the mass murders. The evidence submitted in Court proved, he said, that Trawniki men were not prisoners. Many who chose to escape were able to do so. Demjanjuk did not – he was a willing participant in the murders.

"An escape with a chance of survival was possible," Judge Alt said.

However, those guards who remained at Trawniki, Alt said, every one of the guards "knew he was part of an organization with no other purpose but mass murder."

Once at the death camps, Trawniki SS guards such as Demjanjuk played a key role, Judge Alt said: "The people who arrived at the camp had no time to reflect. They were told that they had been brought there to work and had first to take a shower. But then they were stripped of their clothing and all of their possessions and beaten into four-meter-square gas chambers.... Panic broke out, there was screaming and crying and those inside tried desperately but in vain to open the doors. Then the big engines were switched on. And then pumped in a poisonous mixture of gas. After 30 minutes everyone inside was dead. The Trawniki men took part in every stage of this mass murder – without them it wouldn't ever have functioned."

Judge Alt determined that as Sobibor served no other function than murder, and as every person at the camp was aware of its purpose and contributed to its functioning, and as all the guards participated in all phases of the murderous process, Demjanjuk was guilty of aiding and abetting in every murder that occurred during his tenure there. This determination was a landmark in German legal history, at once a new interpretation of German culpability in the crimes of the Holocaust, while at the same time opening the door to many more potential prosecutions of Nazi War Criminals.

In painstaking detail, Judge Alt recited the dates when the train transports filled with victims arrived in Sobibor, how many people were aboard each transport, and the names of victims whose family members were co-plaintiffs in the case. So, for example, Judge Alt noted that Rudie Cortissos's mother arrived on May 21, 1943, with 2,300 other prisoners, mostly Dutch Jews who were sent immediately to gas chambers. Another train carried mostly children, who were also gassed immediately.

As Judge Alt read about their dead relatives many of the survivors in the room held each other tightly or tried to stifle tears (they could not).

Judge Alt made the point that there were even guards who fled Sobibor after learning of the nature of the work there. Demjanjuk, he said, had a duty to do the same. But he did not. The Court rejected all arguments that Demjanjuk had no choice in working at the camps or did so while acting under threat of death or was forced to participate in the murders. He once again cited Danylchenko's characterization of Demjanjuk as already being "an experienced guard" who accompanied the victims to the gas chambers in Sobibor.

Listening to the verdict was emotionally draining, and around noon, Judge Alt called a two-hour recess.

When the Court resumed its session, the air in the room already hot and stuffy, seemed thicker still.

Demjanjuk was brought back to the courtroom and made to sit in his wheelchair.

A short while later, Alt delivered the Court's conclusion: As Alt read the crimes Demjanjuk had committed, convicting him of 16 counts of aiding and abetting the murders at Sobibor, Demjanjuk showed no emotion.

"The court is convinced that the defendant ... served as a guard at Sobibor from 27 March 1943 to mid-September 1943. As a guard, he took part in the murder of at least 28,000 people," Judge Alt said.

Judge Alt continued to read. Those in the courtroom overjoyed by the conviction were barely paying attention as Alt proceeded to discuss what sentence he was imposing.

Although the prosecution had asked for a sentence of six years, the Judge gave him five years in consideration of his age and the time he had already spent in prison in Germany, and he was to pay costs.

This was not unexpected – Demjanjuk was basically receiving the sentence the prosecutors asked for, which given his health and health problems amounted to a life sentence.

However, the courtroom was caught off-guard when Judge Alt then said that given the conviction, Demjanjuk's original arrest warrant was now lifted, and as Demjanjuk was stateless and not a flight risk, as per German law, Alt announced that Demjanjuk no longer needed to remain in prison pending his appeal.

"The defendant is to be released" Judge Alt said.

Demjanjuk's lawyer gave him the good news of his release. Demjanjuk seemed not understand at first. "You are a free man," Busch told him.

Demjanjuk was pushed out of court by his lawyer in a wheelchair - for the first time without sunglasses and baseball cap.

Margarete Nötzel, the Munich Court spokesperson told reporters that it was important to understand that "Demjanjuk is released, not acquitted." She explained that Judge Alt had acted in keeping with German law, "free of moral or political considerations," and had treated Demjanjuk the same as any person of his age convicted by a German Court.

Although Demjanjuk would be immediately returned to Stadelheim prison for the night, where he would be taken next was not immediately known.

The reaction to Demjanjuk's conviction yet simultaneous release was mixed.

Bild was unhappy with the verdict, finding it not "proportionate" to the crime. "He deserves no mercy on account of his age," Bild wrote. They argued that Demjanjuk should be imprisoned "to the end of his life."

David van Huiden, whose parents and sister were murdered in Sobibor while Demjanjuk was there, told The Guardian UK that the verdict meant that "his family's memory was finally being marked, almost 68 years after they were herded to the gas chambers."

"Did your newspaper report the death of my mother and father and sister on July 3, 1943?" Huiden asked the Guardian's reporter. "This trial means that you might do so now. Until recently most people didn't know about Sobibor. Two years ago, you probably thought it was a new kind of soap. Now you know, and it should never be forgotten."

Efraim Zuroff of the Simon Wiesenthal Center questioned the appropriateness of releasing a Nazi collaborator convicted of complicity in the murder of more than 28,000 Jewish men, women and children. Demjanjuk's conviction and release, Zuroff admitted, gave him a roller coaster ride of emotions. "At first I was thrilled, now I'm very disappointed," he said.

Rudie Cortissos told reporters that he was grateful for the opportunity to address the Court and speak of his wartime experiences. "I had an opportunity to say what I wanted to say for 50 years," Cortissos said. "I'm satisfied," He said, adding, "It doesn't mean I can forget; it doesn't mean I can forgive."

Gisela Freidrichsen wrote on May 16, 2011 in Spiegel about "The Deeper Meaning of the Demjanjuk Trial":

"The purpose of a criminal trial can also be that it takes place in the first place and ends with a convincing verdict. Were this the 1960s and 70s, John (Ivan) Demjanjuk would have either never been put in the dock, despite the more conclusive evidence that could have been presented at the time, or the proceedings would have been discontinued with the stereotypical remarks that the defendant was merely a cog in the Nazis' killing machine -- or that he never dared to refuse orders or flee out of fear for his life.

"But the German justice system has changed. Today's judges don't automatically exonerate a man like Demjanjuk....

"The importance of the Demjanjuk trial would only be inadequately described, however, if it were confined to the impact that it had on the families of the victims of Sobibor. It also has a historical dimension. Indeed, it represents a turning point...

"Unlike the tabloid media, which remains blithely ignorant of legal matters, the co-plaintiffs were not bothered by the five-year prison sentence, or the fact that the 91-year-old stateless defendant was freed despite the sentence. They know that he will have to bear the burden of his guilt for the rest of his life, whether he is behind bars or outside prison walls."

The former president of the Central Council of Jews in Germany, Charlotte Knobloch, saw the verdict as proof of how well Germany's legal system functioned. Knoblich said the unmistakable message sent from Munich was that perpetrators of the Holocaust are prosecuted for their crimes. Nazi war criminals now know, Knobloch said, "that they are held to account and that they have to answer for their actions."

Lawrence Douglas, an Amherst College professor who would write his own account of Demjanjuk's German trial,

"The Right Wrong Man," concluded that, "My own view is that in convicting Demjanjuk, the Munich Court really brilliantly grasped the essential nature of state-sponsored atrocity.... Guilt follows function and therein lies the greatness of the Demjanjuk conviction." Douglas said.

5. After the Verdict

The day after the verdict, Demjanjuk was taken to St. Lukas, a nursing home on the outskirts of Bad Feilnbach in Upper Bavaria, a quaint spa town whose main industry is tourism, with the understanding that should his appeal fail he would have to serve his five-year sentence.

Ironically, John Demjanjuk, Jr. had criticized Germany for trying his father while German "retirement homes are full of true perpetrators." There was now one more added to that list.

Busch filed an appeal of the decision. At the same time, the Prosecution filed an appeal asking for review of Demjanjuk's release pending his appeal.

Although Demjanjuk spent quiet days at the nursing home, German prosecutors were still busy with the aftermath of his successful conviction.

On July 15, 2011, German prosecutors filed new charges against Demjanjuk for his service at Flossenburg and his complicity in the murders of 4,974 people there from October 1943 to December 1944.

The new lawsuit involved two of the key figures from Demjanjuk's Munich Sobibor trial, former investigating Judge Thomas Walther and co-plaintiff's attorney Cornelius Nestler. They also charged Alex Nagorny who had testified at Demjanjuk's trial that he served with him at Flossenburg.

Nazi War Crimes prosecutor Kurt Schrimm told the media that he was confident about the new charges against Demjanjuk. Schrimm also said the recent Demjanjuk verdict had changed German case law and would allow for "far more prosecutions of Nazi war Criminals."

What came to be known as "The Demjanjuk Precedent," would allow for the filing of many new Nazi War Crimes cases in Germany, and in other countries who saw in the Demjanjuk German prosecution a new and very effective to prosecute those who participated in the mass murders of the Nazi era.

In the early hours of Saturday March 17th, 2012, almost ten months after hearing his guilty verdict, Bavarian radio reported that John Demjanjuk had died, found lifeless in his nursing home room. He was 91. A subsequent autopsy in Germany determined no foul play. However, the exact cause of death could not be determined.

Demjanjuk's defense attorney Ulrich Busch said Demjanjuk died as a "free, innocent and unjudged man." Under German law, if a person dies before their appeal is heard, the original conviction is not considered to have taken legal effect. But the fact of his conviction stands.

John Demjanjuk Jr told the press that his father died a natural death, said. "My father fell asleep with God as a victim and survivor of Soviet and German brutality since childhood," said the son. "He loved life, the family, and humanity, and history will show that Germany used it as a scapegoat to blame helpless Ukrainian prisoners of war for the actions of Nazi Germans."

Demjanjuk's corpse was flown back to Cleveland where the family buried him in a local cemetery.

Several months later, Demjanjuk's wife and son accused the doctors and nurses at the nursing home of committing "a medical execution in installments for administering to him the painkiller Novalgin" – which Demjanjuk was receiving because of his pain. Busch alleged "manslaughter" by the nursing home. Those suits were rejected.

Around the same time, Demjanjuk's estate filed an action in the 6th Circuit Court of Appeals to posthumously restore Demjanjuk's citizenship. Doing so would have enabled his widow to receive his Social Security benefits. However, the

Court ruled that Demjanjuk's death made the case moot. Despite several other motions and appeals, the Court concluded Demjanjuk's citizenship could not be restored posthumously.

Efraim Zuroff published his final thoughts on Demjanjuk's many decades of prosecution in the Times of Israel on May 19, 2012:

"...I want to begin by praising the incredible perseverance of the American prosecutors of the Office of Special Investigations (recently renamed the Human Rights and Special Prosecutions Section) of the US Justice Department, headed by Eli M. Rosenbaum, who, despite myriad obstacles and heart-wrenching setbacks, persisted in their efforts to ensure that Demjanjuk would pay for his crimes and not be allowed to enjoy his final years.

"...Demjanjuk's conviction in Germany set an incredibly important legal precedent that paves the way for the prosecution in Germany of additional Nazi war criminals whom until now could not be brought to justice. Demjanjuk was the first Holocaust perpetrator convicted without evidence being presented to the court of his committing a specific crime with a specific victim...

"In conclusion, the proverbial bottom line remains that Demjanjuk was convicted in a court of law in the country under whose aegis he served as an armed SS guard in the Sobibor death camp, where he actively assisted in the mass murder of tens of thousands of Jews. Despite all his efforts to escape punishment, and despite all his attempts to turn his latest trial into a farce, his guilt was established and justice was served, and that, in view of the complications and history of this case, is no small achievement."

Reflecting on the many years of Demjanjuk's prosecution, Eli Rosenbaum said, "To allow such a person to go unprosecuted would be to say the crimes don't matter – they were not important. The United States had a moral obligation to the survivors to see that he was brought to justice, and we accomplished that."

Rosenbaum then added, "One of the things, I'm particularly proud of is "The Demjanjuk Precedent," which has since been used for many new prosecutions of Nazi War criminals since Demjanjuk's German trial."

6. Demjanjuk's Just Epitaph

John Demjanjuk death in a nursing home in Germany at age 91, brought to a close one of the most extensive and most contested Nazi war crimes prosecution in history, a process that began in the United States in the mid 1970's and was ongoing at the time of his death forty years later.

Demjanjuk died awaiting the appeal of his conviction in Germany as an accessory to the more than 28,000 murders of Jewish men, women and children committed during the time he served as a camp guard at the Sobibor extermination camp.

In the immediate aftermath of his death there were some who argued once more that he was an innocent or at best served under duress or was at worse a mere cog in the machine. There were some who repeated the same falsehoods expressed throughout his more than 30 years of prosecution in the United States, Israel and Germany, that the damning documents which prove his Nazi service were fakes and KGB forgeries, even though every court at every stage that has examined the documents found them authentic and consistent with each other, proving that Demjanjuk was the bearer of a Nazi identification card #1393 issued at the Trawniki training camp that lists and correlates his Nazi service not only at Trawniki and Sobibor, but also subsequently at the Flossenburg and Majdanek camps.

There were those who argued against the trying of old men, against the waste of resources, time, money, and prosecutorial effort.

There were also those who, having no argument with Demjanjuk's prosecution or conviction who, in the face of Demjanjuk's long life and the thought of him spending his final days in a nursing home in Germany, asked: Was justice done?

As someone who spent many months in the Jerusalem

466

courtroom attending the trial of Demjanjuk and followed closely every stage of his American and German proceedings, I would argue that, to paraphrase a biblical phrase quoted by Justice Levin, not only was justice done, it was seen to be done.

The notion that Demjanjuk, awaiting the appeal of his German conviction, living in a nursing home was "free" is to ignore the reality of his existence during his last days, confined in a foreign country cut off from family, friends, and community, left to die with the mark of Cain upon him.

The fact that almost every article concerning his death contained the words "convicted Nazi camp guard" is only one small measure of history's judgment and of Justice being done. Although under German law, because Demjanjuk died before his appeal could be argued, the German court's guilty judgment is legally nullified, Margarete Noetzel, the court spokesman, said the conviction remains "a historical fact."

Demjanjuk's prosecutions added greatly to our knowledge of how the final solution, the unfathomable murder of millions, was carried out by the unexceptional; not only by the Germans but by their willing collaborators and henchmen.

The death camps were commanded by Germans and staffed by their auxiliary guards, such as Demjanjuk, with whom the murders could not have been accomplished.

Despite the fact that Demjanjuk denied any and all involvement in the crimes of the Holocaust, he was demonstrated to be an exceptionally bad liar whose own accounts of his whereabouts were riddled with inconsistencies, impossibilities, untruths and evasions that bordered on admissions.

The record by now is all too clear: born in Soviet Ukraine, he was a Red Army soldier captured by the Germans who volunteered to serve the Nazis. Trained at Trawniki and issued his Nazi I.D. there, he became an experienced camp guard serving at labor, concentration and extermination camps whose only function was the expeditious murder of innocent civilian Jewish men, women and children.

To those who say Demjanjuk was no Nazi, how else to explain the SS blood group tattoo he worked so hard to remove. All of which, even any of which, had Demjanjuk revealed when he applied to or entered the United States, would have been sufficient cause to deny him admission, bar him from citizenship and which were cause for his denaturalization and deportation.

Those murdered at Sobibor and the other camps where Demjanjuk served cannot cry out for justice. There are no graves to mourn them, other than the mass graves where they were murdered. It is easy to imagine that those who committed the crimes thought that no one would ever know who the perpetrators were or, worse, that no one would care.

Perhaps they imagined that they could, like Demjanjuk, deny everything. Who would prosecute them? What could they prove?

It is to the eternal credit of the United States, Israel and Germany that over the last three decades regardless of what political party was in power, they continued to prosecute the guilty, not only the planners, or the officials, not just the commandants but the guards and policemen, not just the desktop murderers but also those with blood on their hands such as Demjanjuk.

The generation that saw the Nazi horrors firsthand will soon pass from this world. Demjanjuk's trial may well have been the last major Nazi war crimes trial. If so, then Demjanjuk's epitaph is just: not that he died a free man but that he died, in the eyes of the world and for all history that follows, a convicted Nazi war camp guard.

EPILOGUE:

MY VERDICT

When I covered Demjanjuk's Israeli District Court trial and wrote my first book, *The Trial of Ivan the Terrible, State of Israel vs. John Demjanjuk* published in November 1990, I took the position that as a journalist and as the chronicler of a trial concerned with events that took place some fifty years before, what I believed to be true concerning Demjanjuk did not matter. I was not the judge and jury of Demjanjuk.

I didn't attend the trial in Jerusalem with a pre-formed opinion as to Demjanjuk's guilt or innocence. It was my contention that I would accept whatever the Israel District Court decided. It was my deeply-held belief then that the legal process was such that in trying Demjanjuk, we had all entered into a social compact by which the Court became the best vehicle to determine the facts in question, the truth of which we, who were not there, could not know personally.

What the Court found as fact I reported truthfully. I was neither judge, or prosecution or defense. I was there to tell the tale. To build "the cathedral of facts" as one writer called it.

Today, after attending the Israeli District Court trial and reading transcripts, testimonies, depositions and judgments in Demjanjuk's many hearings and trials and pondering the case for more than thirty years, I have come to my own conclusions about Demjanjuk.

There is so much today that we do know about Demjanjuk; so much about his murderous war-time activities at Trawniki, Sobibor, Flossenburg and Majdanek that is today incontrovertible.

Yet, there still remain questions, doubts and differing opinions about whether Demjanjuk served as a death camp guard at Treblinka.

At this point, after these many years, I feel it appropriate to share my own opinion about Demjanjuk's Treblinka death camp service, informed by facts that I have long pondered.

I believe that Demjanjuk was an extermination camp guard at Treblinka.

Demjanjuk was a guard there, a Wachmann, one who knew how to drive a car or a truck and who was a mechanic, one who would have known how to operate the diesel gas engine that fed the gas chambers; a guard who herded Jews to their death in the gas chambers at Treblinka.

We now know that there was an Ivan Marshenko who served at Treblinka, who worked in the death camp area at the gas chambers. This Ivan Marshenko worked together with Nikolai Shalayev. They were the Ivan and Nikolai of the gas chambers. Many of the Jewish inmates called him Ivan Grozny or Ivan the Terrible and I believe that it was Marshenko who wielded a sword or a knife and sliced at women's breasts on their way to their death.

However, this Ivan, Ivan Marshenko, was considerably older than Demjanjuk. At Treblinka he would have been 31-32 years old during the period in question. He had very dark hair (and some say a scar across his face) and his hair was plentiful with no sign of incipient baldness. He was also considerably taller than Demjanjuk.

This Ivan, Ivan Marshenko, Ivan of Ivan and Nikolai was known by several accounts (that of the Germans Munzberger, and Suchomel, and by his fellow Wachmann Shalayev) to have departed Treblinka in June 1943, several months before the uprising. This is the Ivan of the gas chambers that British journalist Gitta Sereny uncovered as having been in Trieste following his service in Treblinka. This is the Ivan who may have been killed there fighting partisans, shot, or who married a local woman there. This is the Ivan Marshenko who was never seen again after the War and never returned home to the Soviet Union.

This brings us to Ivan Demjanjuk. This Ivan, Ivan Demjanjuk, was identified by a dozen Holocaust survivors from a wide range of countries as having been at Treblinka, as well as by one former German at Treblinka. Demjanjuk was positively identified by more than half those as having been a death camp guard at Treblinka. Five survivors would do so in court in Cleveland and three others would do so in Jerusalem, testifying that he was known to have worked in the gas chambers area, as the gas chamber operator, as being the person they called "Ivan the Terrible of Treblinka."

This Ivan, Ivan Demjanjuk, was at the time of Treblinka, aged 22-23. He was already showing signs of balding. The little hair he had was light. His face had a certain architecture, his eyes, his nose and his ears sticking out a certain way.

The Survivors' identifications have been challenged again and again over the years, and every court that has reviewed them have overwhelmingly found them to be credible. The identifications conducted by Miriam Radiwker and Martin Kollar have also withstood any and all court challenges. In the press and in a variety of post-trial publications and books, these identifications have been repeatedly dismissed or called prejudiced and biased – but not in court where facts need be proven. As was made plain in the courtroom in Jerusalem -- the survivors were identifying someone they knew – they were not selecting a criminal from a police lineup.

Putting the Court verdicts aside, if you go back and re-read all of the identifications, it is possible that one or two are actually identifying Marshenko not Demjanjuk. Avraham Goldfarb, for example, recalls Ivan as not being at Treblinka in its last months. Shlomo Hellman says Ivan was 30 years old – that was surely Marshenko and not Demjanjuk whose photo Hellman did not identify.

In those identifications the survivors are speaking of someone older than Demjanjuk, with darker hair and fatter too. Someone who looks more like Demjanjuk did in 1951 in his US Visa photo, the picture that the survivors were first shown – when Demjanjuk had reached the age Marshenko was at Treblinka.

However, when you re-read the identifications of the survivors who identified Demjanjuk in Court, you see that they could only be talking about him. Some of them looking at the 1951 photo comment that he is older, more well-fed in that picture. In 1951, Demjanjuk was 31, the age of Marshenko at Treblinka. They also describe distinctive features of Demjanjuk – that he was balding, the way his ears appeared, his eyes. They say that he was there until the very last day, until the uprising. Marshenko had left Treblinka in June.

Turovsky said he remembered the name Demjanjuk. Czarny remembers him from the motor pool. Epstein recalled his gait, how he walked; and Rosenberg recalled those eyes, those murderous eyes. At a later date, a Ukrainian woman who worked as a laundress said she remembered the name Demjanjuk and that he was one of the guards at Treblinka.

As to Demjanjuk's Trawniki photo – who are the survivors identifying if not someone they knew at Treblinka? One says he looks a little thinner than he did at Treblinka, which is true: At the time he arrived at Trawniki, Demjanjuk was, to quote his own words about when he was at Chelm, "Skin and bones." This is someone they knew.

Add to these the identification of Nazi Otto Horn, whose identification of the 1951 card, "He resembles Ivan" could be talking about either Marshenko or Demjanjuk, but his identification of the Trawniki card indicates he recognizes Demjanjuk from Treblinka.

It makes no sense that the survivors would correctly identify Fedor Federenko and be wrong about recognizing Demjanjuk from Treblinka.

Over the decades, almost a dozen survivors did not choose the same wrong man as being at Treblinka. Ten survivors, some of them living in Germany (Rajgrodski) and Uruguay (Reichman) could not all choose to falsely accuse and frame the same person. It makes no sense.

The conclusions of the Bahrick study on memory remain true: When we see someone we knew from 50 years ago, whom we saw repeatedly in an intense situation, we may be wrong about certain particulars (do we know this person from high school or college? from our hometown, or from business?) but the general gestalt remains correct: That you do indeed recognize that person and know him.

So, too, with Demjanjuk. The survivors may be wrong about exactly who he was or exactly what he did when, but that they recognize him from Treblinka is not wrong. They are not mistaken.

Those who knew this Ivan did so because he was a mechanic, or from the car transport area, or even the cobbler who possibly recalled Demjanjuk's name because he fixed his shoes, they recall Demjanjuk from Treblinka.

What did Demjanjuk do at Treblinka? From the testimonies at his German trial we know that at Sobibor, there was no division of labor at the extermination camp for Wachmann. The guards did all of the tasks associated with the extermination of the Jews: From greeting them and speeding their arrival from the trains, to accompanying them to the gas chambers, to supervising workers in the death camp, to doing guard duty, to being sent on missions in the surrounding areas to roundup and capture Jews.

We also now know from the testimonies of experts at Demjanjuk's German trial that the three extermination camps, Belzec, Sobibor and Treblinka, were operated identically. That means that at Treblinka, the guards such as Demjanjuk served in all capacities in the factory of death.

Danylchenko, the Soviet Wachmann who met Demjanjuk at Sobibor in April 1943 and accompanied him afterwards to Flossenburg, says Demjanjuk was an experienced guard, one who accompanied the unfortunates to the gas chambers and who excelled in rounding up Jews in the neighboring villages. Where did Demjanjuk gain such experience? I say it was at Treblinka.

At Treblinka, the gas chambers were working all day and the crematoria all day and all night, at their height murdering some 15,000 Jewish men, women and children a day. Ivan Marshenko couldn't possibly operate the gas chambers all the time. There had to be some other Wachmann who did the task when Marshenko was on break, sleeping, was on leave or visiting the neighboring villages.

I say it was Demjanjuk, the mechanic in the death camp, the same tractor driver and operator who would one day work at the Ford plant in Ohio. It was Demjanjuk who operated the engines when Marshenko didn't during the period when the murders were at their greatest. It was Demjanjuk who continued to operate the gas chambers after Marshenko left for Trieste in June 1943. It was Demjanjuk they saw at Treblinka until the day of the uprising. It was Demjanjuk the survivors recognized from Treblinka.

As to Demjanjuk being "Ivan the Terrible," I can only surmise the following: the Jewish workers in the death camp, the sonderkommando such as Rosenberg and Epstein; and the Jews in Camp one, even Hofjuden like Czarny, lived in a state of total fear, they did not know guards' last names, and if they saw Demjanjuk at the gas chambers, when they saw him beating or murdering the Jews, they claimed him as 'Ivan the Terrible."

We know that Demjanjuk was issued a bayonet at Flossenburg – perhaps he had one at Treblinka as well and used it to prod the victims towards the gas chambers. And as Reichman said so movingly in his testimony in Jerusalem, "In Treblinka there were a great many Ivans. He was not the only one in Treblinka. There were a great many Ivans. There were many murderers."

That Demjanjuk was in Treblinka is my personal opinion. However, if I were the Israeli Supreme Court hearing Demjanjuk's appeal, I would have nonetheless agreed that the Soviet testimonies, despite being unverified and there being no ability to question or cross-examine the actual persons who made them, when read in toto, do create doubt that Demjanjuk was the Ivan the Terrible. And because of that, I, too, if I were a Judge reviewing the case would have had to acquit Demjanjuk of being Ivan the Terrible of Treblinka.

Nonetheless, if I were the Israeli Supreme Court hearing Demjanjuk's appeal, I would have convicted Demjanjuk for crimes committed as a guard serving at Trawniki, Sobibor, Flossenburg and Majdanek. If the argument was made that the defense did not fully have the opportunity to defend against those charges (as the Israel Supreme Court claimed), then I would have given them the time. But Demjanjuk's defense of the crimes he committed at Sobibor would have failed in Jerusalem much as it did in Germany. Demjanjuk would have been adjudged guilty.

As to Demjanjuk's sentence, whether he still deserved the death penalty, one could make arguments for and against. As a judge, I would certainly be open to acting with mercy to mitigate the death sentence, but that would call for Demjanjuk to admit guilt and/or express remorse, or at the very least, to finally be more honest about what he did as a Wachmann.

Being party to the death of almost 30,000 Jewish men, women and children at Sobibor, and perhaps thousands (if not tens of thousands) of others at Flossenburg or elsewhere is crime enough for life imprisonment, and if the Court so decided, crime enough to deserve the death penalty.

I may not favor the death penalty, but I would not have lost sleep about Demjanjuk being sentenced to death for the mass murders he participated in, the war crimes, the crimes against humanity and the crimes against the Jewish people, which stood so beyond the boundaries of morality as to warrant his removal from humankind. I could have lived with that.

And that is what I would have done if I were a Judge on the Israeli Supreme Court hearing the appeal.

Beyond the survivors' testimonies, as the Israeli District Court noted, there were reasons to believe Demjanjuk was at Treblinka, based on his own admissions, including his incriminating comments such as "Don't push me to Treblinka." Based on the Trawniki Card, Danylchenko's statements and the many SS transfer rosters that have surfaced over time, we know that Demjanjuk was at Okzow in September 1942, at Majdanek in January 1943, and at Sobibor at the end of March 1943.

Danylchenko only met Demjanjuk in April 1943, and he notes that Demjanjuk was often dispatched outside the camp. Demjanjuk's knowledge of the surrounding area is probably why he listed "Sobibor" on his visa application. Demjanjuk was a driver and it appears he was familiar with the roads between Sobibor and Treblinka. The uprising at Treblinka took place in August 1943 – the survivors say they saw this Ivan there until the last day – and we know that after the uprising the guards went to Sobibor. It was only in October 1943 that Demjanjuk and Danylchenko were transferred to Flossenburg.

Demjanjuk's insistent denials that he was never in Trawniki, Sobibor or Treblinka were definitively false as to Trawniki and Sobibor. So why add Treblinka to that list? Why lie about two out of three – I believe he was at all three.

However, -- and here once again I am veering into speculation and personal opinion, I'd like to make an observation about Demjanjuk's denials:

During Demjanjuk's original U.S. denaturalization and deportation trials, as well as in his Israeli trials, Demjanjuk was engaged, defiant, at times even gregarious. There were only a few occasions when he claimed he didn't feel well and didn't want to attend court. Only a few times when, despite medical staff ascertaining him as well, he remained on a cot and avoided the Court hearing.

At the time of Demjanjuk's second denaturalization and deportation hearing and for almost his entire German trial, however, Demjanjuk claimed pain or illness, arrived in a wheelchair or on a stretcher. In court in Munich, he covered himself in a blanket, and wore a hat and sunglasses as if to block out what was happening in court. All despite doctor after doctor finding no medical cause.

My theory is that Demjanjuk was confident in all those earlier trials because he claimed that they were cases of mistaken identity. Demjanjuk claimed vociferously that he was not that Ivan the Terrible of Treblinka, Ivan Grozny.

We now know that he may well have been right – that Ivan Marshenko was that Ivan Grozny and that Demjanjuk was as he put it "little," not Hitler, not Eichmann, not Grozny. And as long as Demjanjuk could cling to mistaken identity, he remained confident.

However, those few times during the Israeli trial when Demjanjuk was confronted with the truth of what he did and who he was – when the certitude of the Trawniki card weighed on him– and that, regardless of his lies and denials, Demjanjuk grasped he would have to suffer the consequences of his actions – he fell ill. You don't need to be a psychiatrist to see those as moments when the physic pain of confronting the truth became too physically painful to Demjanjuk.

Similarly, given that the entire German trial concerned Trawniki and Sobibor, and there was no Marshenko to blame, Demjanjuk tried to be anywhere but in the courtroom and even when there, to be absent.

Finally, regarding the name Marshenko, which Demjanjuk listed on one form as his mother's maiden name. As the Israeli Supreme Court noted in its insightful decision, that Demjanjuk's mother's correct name was Tabachuk was not important. "The question is not what was her true name -- but why did the defendant recall that her name was Marchenko?" the Justices said.

Over the years, I have changed my thinking about why Demjanjuk gave his mother's maiden name as Marshenko on his official visa application.

Originally, I believed that Demjanjuk wrote the name Marshenko simply because it was his matronymic, and that it was a sort of nom-de-guerre by which he was known at Treblinka. Accordingly, at first, I believed the mentions of Marshenko in Soviet protocols referred to Demjanjuk. To me, his writing of the name Marshenko was a Freudian slip by which he revealed who he was.

After the evidence surfaced that Marshenko was not his mother's maiden name, and that an Ivan Marshenko had existed, it continued to bedevil me as to why of all the possible names Demjanjuk chose Marshenko.

I do not accept or believe for a second that Demjanjuk chose this name of all possible names to conceal his identity because it is "like Smith" in Ukraine (it is not even in the top ten of family names in Ukraine).

As we saw with Demjanjuk's choice to list Sobibor, there are no real mistakes. Or rather there are reasons, conscious or unconscious, smart or not, for every choice.

Then one day, it struck me: What if Demjanjuk chose the name because he knew that Marshenko was dead. What if Demjanjuk had known Marshenko at Treblinka and had heard that Marshenko had died before war's end. If Suchomel, Munzberger and others knew Marshenko had died, why wouldn't Demjanjuk have heard those rumors as well?

Assuming the matronymic of a dead man might be a pretty shrewd idea. No one could track you to your real identity. At the same time, as that person was dead, there was no one who could complain that you had stolen their identity. Perhaps the same person advising Demjanjuk on how to fill out his forms had given him advice on how to conceal his Nazi service – chose a place where you knew the surrounding area well (Sobibor) and find a way to conceal your identity (where born, and your mother's maiden name) by choosing someone like you who was dead. This could well explain Demjanjuk's lies on his forms.

Demjanjuk chose Sobibor because he had been there and could describe the surrounding area, and he chose Marshenko because he knew Marshenko was dead and could take his name. It was a lie, that like writing Sobibor, he could live with.

However, Demjanjuk never imagined that he would be identified as Ivan Marchenko of the gas chambers at Treblinka. That he knew Marshenko and knew he was not him was why he could so vehemently claim this was a case of mistaken identity.

Demjanjuk knew that Marshenko was the Ivan who worked together with Nikolai, who stood at the entry way with a sword and sliced at women's breasts. He was not that man, but he was there.

Demjanjuk imagined that Marshenko would be his get out of jail card – and it was, dramatically so -- by the decision of the Israel Supreme Court.

But Demjanjuk would admit nothing, and so his lies continued to haunt him.

Demjanjuk was not Marshenko but Demjanjuk was a person who knew something about engines, tractor engines at first, tank engines in the Red Army, and an experienced guard at the extermination Camps such as Sobibor, where they used a diesel tank engine to murder Jews in the gas chambers. We now know from the trial in Germany that there was no separation among the guards, they all assisted in every possible capacity in the attempted genocide of the Jewish people.

Demjanjuk was not Marshenko but I believe he was at Treblinka. As do the survivors who identified him; as do the Judges of the Israel District Court such as Judge Tal and Dorner who have been vocal in saying they believe Demjanjuk was correctly identified as being at Treblinka.

Demjanjuk was not Marshenko but he was a liar, nonetheless. As much as he denied being at Treblinka, he denied being at Sobibor and Trawniki where there can no longer be any doubt that he was there. And that he arrived there already experienced as a guard.

Among all Demjanjuk's lies there is room for very little truth. Over the years, however, the truth has emerged. Demjanjuk was not Marshenko.

But he is Ivan of the Extermination Camp.

Demjanjuk was a Nazi collaborator, he was an extermination guard, he participated in the mass murder of a civilian population and was part of a conspiracy and an accomplice in the murder of tens of thousands of innocent non-combatants -- Jewish men, women and children. He was a liar which, in the end, only gave reason to further uncover his crimes at other concentration camps such as Majdanek and Flossenburg.

In the end, after almost forty years of investigations and trials, Demjanjuk's lies and evasions were reason for dedicated prosecutors, judges, researchers, historians, and experts of many kinds, in the United States, Israel, Germany, and even the former Soviet Union and Russia, to uncover vast new troves of information about the murderous actions of the Nazis and those in their service, such as Demjanjuk.

Demjanjuk was a criminal – a murderer – a party to mass murder; and when his crimes were uncovered, it is to the everlasting credit of nations such as the United States, Israel and Germany that they investigated and prosecuted Demjanjuk zealously, tirelessly, wherever the evidence led them. Regardless of politics, regardless of the government in power, regardless of the passage of time, these countries each showed themselves to be a nation of law. Justice was not just done; it was seen to be done.

Because of Demjanjuk's trials and his denials, we know so infinitely more about the Holocaust, and the crimes of the Nazis and the participation of their accomplices and collaborators at the death factories the Nazis hoped to keep secret, at Trawniki, Treblinka, Sobibor, Majdanek and Flossenburg. From this great evil, we have at least extracted some greater knowledge.

Today we can say that we know what we know. We know what we don't know. And, all in all, we know far more than we would have of the Holocaust, and the murderous actions of the Nazis and their foot soldiers because of Nazi Collaborator John "Ivan" Demjanjuk, thanks to his trials, and in spite of, and because of, his denials.

In the final analysis, in the case of John Demjanjuk, we may not know everything he did but we do know what and who he was.

Made in the USA
Middletown, DE
16 November 2021